I0043356

Foreign Bondholders
and
American State Debts

Foreign Bondholders
and
American State Debts

By
REGINALD C. MCGRANE

BeardBooks
Washington, D.C.

Copyright 1935 by The Macmillan Company

Reprinted 2000 by Beard Books, Washington, D.C.

ISBN 1-893122-94-8

Printed in the United States of America

PREFACE

WITHIN recent years there has been much discussion in the press of this country and of Europe over the difficulties encountered by creditors in the collection of debts. Creditor nations, as well as private creditors, have accused their debtors of attempting to evade their legal and moral obligations. The creditors have insisted that the debtors were able to pay and have vigorously protested against any discrimination shown by the debtors in their payments to creditors. On the other hand, the debtors have complained of the harsh treatment accorded them by the creditors and have pleaded their own inability to meet their engagements because of the world-wide depression.

The acrimonious disputes over the collection of private and intergovernmental debts has attracted universal attention. The problems confronting foreign investors in the collection of debts due them and the defalcation and repudiation by whole communities of their obligations have led to frequent references in the press to similar occurrences in the past. Among the long forgotten unpaid debts to which attention has been called are those of certain American states.

It was in the hope that a recital of the circumstances surrounding the origin of these American state debt controversies might throw some light upon the problems of lenders and borrowers that the present study was undertaken. Particular attention has been given to the political and economic background of these debts, to the inducements held out to investors to purchase the state securities, to the part paid by the press of debtor and creditor countries in aiding or obstructing the final debt settlements, and to the economic and international repercussions of these debts. It has seemed advisable to include an account of those states which ultimately made some readjustments of their debts as well as those that actually

v

repudiated, because of the light it sheds upon the methods by which some of the debtors and creditors were able, in time, to get together and devise plans to make minds and purses meet. It is hoped that the study may interest the general public as well as the specialist, because of the discussions of the evils of weak banking systems, the dangers inherent in the too rapid development of public works, the methods employed in the marketing of these states' securities, the political and economic atmosphere in which repudiation doctrines were generated, and the part played by the press and by the courts in mobilizing public opinion either for or against the payment of the debts.

In the preparation of this study I am heavily indebted to many individuals and institutions. The necessary study in Canada, England and Holland was made possible by the award of a fellowship grant by the Guggenheim Foundation. A generous grant from the Trustees of the Charles Phelps Taft Memorial Fund enabled me to complete the writing of the manuscript. I take the privilege of gratefully acknowledging the encouragement and valuable aid given me by the Honorable Charles G. Dawes; Sir Josiah Stamp; E. R. Peacock, Esq., of Baring Brothers and Company; L. E. Meinertz-hagen, Esq., of Frederick Huth and Company; Douglas Reid, Esq., of the Council of Foreign Bondholders; and Messrs. C. E. Ter Meulen and M. M. Rost van Tonningen of Hope and Company. I am under deep obligation to the staffs of the British Museum, Public Record Office, Canadian Archives, Library of Congress, Howard Memorial Library, Louisiana State University Library, Detroit Public Library, Cincinnati Law Library, Public Library of Cincinnati, the University of Cincinnati Library, and the Ohio Historical and Philosophical Library for their courtesy and assistance. To Dr. A. G. Doughty, Dominion of Canada Archivist, Miss Frances Beith, Ottawa, Canada, and Mr. Edwin Gholson of the Cincinnati Law Library I am under especial obligation for their efficient and intelligent aid. By their interest and helpful suggestions, Professors Charles S. Sydnor, University of Mississippi, R. W. Hidy, Wheaton College, and my colleagues Frederick C. Hicks, William W. Hewett, and Wilbur P. Calhoun of the Economics Department, George A. Hedger, John Oddy, and Charles Ray Wilson of the History Department, have given evidence of those ideals which should animate our profession. Without the constant encouragement and suggestive criticisms of my wife this manuscript would never have been completed.

REGINALD C. McGRANE.

CONTENTS

FOREIGN BONDHOLDERS
AND
AMERICAN STATE DEBTS

CHAPTER I

BORROWERS AND LENDERS

At certain critical periods in the history of the United States the debts of the various American states have assumed national importance. When the audacious Alexander Hamilton in his celebrated Report upon Public Credit suggested that the federal government assume, at their face value, the Revolutionary obligations of the several states, a storm of opposition arose which threatened to wreck the newly established government. Opponents of "Miss Assumption," as the measure was called, by the wits of the day, defiantly announced that they would sever the fragile bonds which loosely held the American states together before they would submit to the centralizing influences of the new measure proposed by the nationalistic Secretary of the Treasury. Party feeling ran high and the fate of the infant American republic hung in the balance as Congress sharply debated the merits and demerits of the bill. It required all the diplomatic finesse of the ingenious Hamilton to secure the passage of the act which, in his estimation, along with his other proposals, was designed to stabilize the finances of the nation and "to cement more closely this union of the states." Even Jefferson confessed to Monroe that much as he opposed the national government assuming the state debts, he realized "the necessity of yielding to the cries of the creditors . . . for the sake of the Union and to save it from the greatest calamities, the total extinction of our credit in Europe." How Hamilton bargained with Jefferson and Madison for the location of the national capital in exchange for the requisite number of votes to procure the enactment of his bill is too well known to need recounting; and how the disillusioned Jefferson in later years bemoaned the part he played in the bargain is also common knowledge. The public credit of the nation was firmly established by the adoption of the Hamiltonian scheme of finances; but in the struggle over the assumption of the state debts two rival political parties and two diametrically opposed theories of government contested for supremacy in one of the most momentous political battles in the annals of this nation.

Again in the 'forties the subject of the American state debts agitated the country. There was no longer any danger of disrupting the federal union in attempting to reach a solution; but the payment or the non-payment of these obligations did involve the good faith and honor of the American people. In the eyes of the civilized world the whole nation was disgraced because certain American states had openly repudiated their obligations and there was a danger that others might follow this example. The non-payment of the state debts united foreign bondholders; and creditor Europe poured forth its vials of sarcasm and abuse indiscriminately upon debtor America. American institutions and all Americans were held up to scorn and ridicule. State and national officials and legislative bodies were deluged with petitions and memorials from disappointed investors who saw the savings of a lifetime vanish through the non-fulfilment by some of the states of their engagements. The federal government found it impossible to borrow abroad and once more the assumption of state debts by the national government was proposed and debated in Congress. The press of England and the United States endeavored in vain to explain the rights of creditors and the economic hardships of the debtors. Timid legislators shrank from the wrath of their infuriated constituencies as revelations of mismanagement and fraud in the use of public funds were disclosed, and demagogues preached the doctrine of repudiation as a panacea for the financial embarrassments of the states. In the midst of the universal distress the efforts of the few courageous state executives, supplemented by the surreptitious aid of European capitalists, tried to awaken the American public to a moral consciousness of meeting their engagements. Never before or since has the good faith of the American people been under such a cloud of suspicion as when the list of delinquent American states steadily grew in number in the years following the panic of 1837.

The third time the debts of American states attracted universal attention was after the close of the Civil War. The financial excesses of the reconstruction governments in the southern states brought a second attack of the disease of repudiation. The Confederate war debts were outlawed by the Fourteenth Amendment; but, at the close of the reconstruction period, the southern states were overwhelmed with debts created by dishonest state officials aided and abetted by unscrupulous promoters and northern bankers. In liquidating these obligations both repudiation and scaling-down methods were drastically employed. Foreign holders of American securities again suffered serious losses, and European newspapers did not fail to call attention to previous delinquencies of certain American states.

Almost a century has elapsed since some of these state obligations have been repudiated. Yet the Council of Foreign Bondholders of London seldom fails to mention the past delinquencies of certain American states in its annual reports. Within recent years frequent references have appeared in the press of the United States and of Europe to these almost forgotten debts.

In view of the present discussion over the collection of private and intergovernmental obligations, a recital of the circumstances surrounding the state debt controversies of the 'forties and the 'seventies may be of interest for the light it throws upon the problems which confront foreign investors. It is also significant to note the part played by the press of debtor and creditor countries in aiding or obstructing the solution of financial problems; to determine to what extent debtor American states have merited the abuse which they have received; how the defaulting states finally met their obligations; and the difficulties encountered by debtors and creditors in attempting to understand each other in periods of universal distress.

In order to understand the financial difficulties of various American states in the 'forties it is necessary to recall the circumstances under which these state debts were incurred. At the close of the War of 1812 this country entered upon a period of rapid internal development. One of the most significant aspects of this economic growth was the rapid settlement of the trans-Alleghany region which, in turn, affected the economic life of the entire nation. Between 1812 and 1821 six new commonwealths—Louisiana, Indiana, Mississippi, Illinois, Alabama, and Missouri—were admitted to the Union. During the following decade the population of these states, together with that of their elder sisters, Kentucky, Tennessee, and Ohio, increased from a little over two millions to nearly four millions, the rate of increase of the individual states ranging from 22 percent in Kentucky to 185 percent in Illinois. As an ever-increasing stream of emigrants poured over the mountains into the Ohio-Mississippi basin, more acres of fertile soil were laid under cultivation and more pressing became the need for improving the transportation facilities between the interior settlements and the Atlantic seaboard. Prior to the War of 1812 the high transportation costs had rendered it impossible for western farmers to have much trade with the eastern settlements. Beyond a few cattle, hogs, and horses, which could be driven over the mountains, the west remained isolated from the east. The best market for the surplus agricultural products of the west was down the rivers to New Orleans. The introduction of the steamboat on western waters removed one obstacle to the economic growth of this section, as it supplied the western farmers with an easier means of communication, widened the scope of their markets, and opened the eastern markets to them by means of an all-water route. At the same time, the opening up of the rich cotton lands of the Gulf region and the expansion of sugar cultivation in Louisiana gave the northern farmer a larger market for his produce; and as this internal trade developed, the prosperity of the cotton planters of the south and the farmers of the north enhanced their ability to purchase the wares of eastern manufacturers. The internal trade of the country began to assume greater importance; and more insistent grew the demands of western farmers for better transportation facilities. By improving the means of transportation between the east and the west, western farmers would find an outlet for their produce along the seaboard or for shipment to Europe; while the rising manufacturers of the east would find a market for their merchandise in the newer settlements of the interior. The economic necessities of the west created a demand for internal improvements; and as the federal government was apparently willing to give only occasional aid to the advancement of transportation, the state governments undertook the task.[1]

New York State was the first to reach out to control the lucrative trade of the western country. In 1817 the Erie Canal was projected; and eight years later was completed at a cost of approxi-

[1] Callender, G. S., The Early Transportation and Banking Enterprises of the States in Relation to the Growth of Corporations, Quarterly Journal of Economics, Vol. 17, pp. 114, 130; Turner, F. J., Rise of the New West, pp. 70, 98-100.

mately $7,000,000. The success of the Erie Canal was immediate and sensational. Before the work was finished the tolls exceeded the interest charges and within ten years the bonds issued for its construction were selling at a premium. The cost of freight from Buffalo to New York dropped from $100 to $15 per ton, and the time from twenty days to eight. Villages and cities sprang up along the route; the price of farm products in western New York doubled in value, and that of the states north of the Ohio River was increased with a corresponding rise in land values. New York City became the emporium of western trade.

With envy and fear the merchants of Philadelphia and Baltimore watched their hated rival outdistancing them in the race for economic supremacy. Self-preservation as well as local pride impelled them to act. A Society for the Promotion of Internal Improvements was organized in Philadelphia; and largely due to its efforts Pennsylvania began in 1826 the construction of a vast system of internal improvements. The projection of the New York and Pennsylvania systems of public works in turn challenged the commercial prosperity of Baltimore. The Chesapeake and Ohio Canal was projected for the purpose of diverting some of the western commerce to the Potomac River, and Maryland, Virginia, the District of Columbia, and the federal government jointly agreed to finance the undertaking. On the same day that ground was broken for the Chesapeake and Ohio Canal, Baltimore began the construction of a rival enterprise, the Baltimore and Ohio Railroad.[2]

Meanwhile the enthusiasm for internal improvements had spread to the middle-western commonwealths. In 1825 Ohio began the construction of a state system of canals to connect the Ohio River with Lake Erie. The example set by her neighbors and of the older states on the seaboard caused Indiana to obtain a land grant from the federal government and commence work on the Wabash and Erie Canal. The projection of this canal created a mania for public works, and in 1836 Indiana authorized a loan of $10,000,000 for the purpose of supplying the state with a comprehensive system of

[2] Bishop, A. L., The State Works of Pennsylvania, Transactions of the Connecticut Academy of Arts and Sciences, Vol. 13, pp. 167-205; Ward, G. W., Early Development of the Chesapeake and Ohio Canal Project, Johns Hopkins University Studies, Vol. 17, pp. 1-17, 39-65; Reizenstein, M., The Economic History of the Baltimore and Ohio Railroad, Johns Hopkins University Studies, Vol. 15, pp. 9-19.

canals and railroads. Illinois also received a federal land grant for the purpose of constructing the Illinois and Michigan Canal; and in 1837 authorized the borrowing of $8,000,000 to establish a general system of internal improvements. The constitution of Michigan made it the imperative duty of the legislature to encourage the construction of public works; and with a population of less than 200,000, and the total assessed value of property within the state of less than $43,000,000, the legislature voted a loan of $5,000,000 for such undertakings.[3] By 1839 American states had issued, or authorized to be issued, state stocks amounting to $69,201,515 for canals, $42,871,084 for railroads, and $6,618,958 for turnpikes.[4]

South of the Ohio, state legislatures were urged not only to construct public works but also to create banking institutions. The failure to recharter the United States Bank gave a plausible excuse for the incorporation of numerous local banks in order to supply the people with an adequate circulating medium. In Mississippi, it was claimed, the withdrawal of the branch of the United States Bank would leave the state with a banking capital of little more than $6,000,000. This was deemed insufficient to carry on the marketing of cotton crops valued at $15,000,000.[5] To facilitate the planters in disposing of their crop, southern states began to charter land banks. The stock in these banks was subscribed by the planters and secured by mortgages on their estates. To procure the working capital for these institutions state bonds were issued or were guaranteed for those issued by the banks. Stockholders were allowed to obtain loans from these banks equal to two-thirds of their stock subscriptions. In 1824 Louisiana established the first of these planters' banks; and similar institutions were created by other southern states. By 1839 states' stocks amounting to $52,640,000 had been issued for banking purposes by various American states.

The flood of state securities for internal improvements and banking enterprises rapidly increased the public indebtedness of the American states. In 1820 the total indebtedness of American states

---

[3] Bogart, E. L., Internal Improvements and State Debt in Ohio, pp. 11-47; Esarey, L., Internal Improvements in Early Indiana, Indiana Historical Soc. Publications, Vol. 5, No. 2, pp. 47-158; Putnam, J. W., The Illinois and Michigan Canal, pp. 31-35; Jenks, W. L., Michigan's Five Million Dollar Loan, Michigan History Magazine, Vol. 15, pp. 575-581.

[4] American Almanac, 1840, p. 105, quoting report of Comptroller A. C. Flagg of New York.

[5] Mississippi Senate Journal, 1835, p. 21.

was only $12,790,728; during the next decade it rose to $26,470,417; five years later it was $66,473,186; and between 1835 and 1839 it increased nearly threefold, amounting to more than $170,000,000.[6]

In authorizing these loans, the state legislatures found it necessary to incorporate certain provisions in the laws in order to meet the requirements of the domestic and foreign money markets. The faith of the state was pledged for the payment of the interest and the redemption of the principal. In order to protect the state from possible losses, the laws in many cases specified that the bonds should not be disposed of below par. When the bonds were sold in this country and the currency received in payment was the same as that in which the interest and principal was made payable, it was not difficult to determine a par sale. Thus $1,000 must be received for every $1,000 to be repaid in order to constitute a par sale. But in negotiating for the sale of the bonds abroad, agents of the states frequently signed contracts specifying their payment in England at the rate of four shillings and sixpence to the dollar, or 225 pounds sterling to every bond of $1,000. With the rate of exchange sometimes as high as 10 to 14 percent in favor of London, state legislators often disputed the validity of these contracts on the ground that the state, in remitting the interest or in making the final payment, remitted far more than the par value of the amounts received translated into American currency. Unfortunately the state legislatures did not always point out these facts at the time of ratifying the contracts. When Michigan, however, in the original law authorizing the five million dollar loan, limited the rate of exchange to $4.44, although it permitted the state to benefit from any premium or gain in exchange, English financiers promptly objected and had the law changed.[7]

[6] American Almanac, 1840, p. 105.

[7] The difference in interpretations given to the word "par" by the English and Americans is fully discussed in Illinois General Assembly Reports, 1839-1840, pp. 123-134, 370, 389. The Americans based their arguments on the following passage from Albert Gallatin's "Considerations on the Currency and Banking System of the United States": "Being obliged to refer to the rate of exchange, it must be recollected that what is universally meant by par is the promise to pay, in another place, a quantity of pure silver or gold equal in weight to the quantity of pure silver or gold contained in the coins with which the drawer of the bill of exchange is paid." (Adams, H., editor, The Writings of Albert Gallatin, Vol. 3, p. 270.) In England the *par of exchange* was defined in Fortune's Epitome of the Stocks and Public Funds, the standard work at the London Stock Exchange, as "the equivalence of a certain amount of the *standard* currency of the one country in the *standard* currency of another"; but the *course of exchange* "is the current price between two places . . .

In negotiating the loans, authorized agents of the states first appealed to American bankers. The United States Bank, Thomas Biddle and Company, the Morris Canal and Banking Company, the Phœnix Bank of New York, and Prime, Ward and Company were some of the principal houses which handled these securities. Prime, Ward and Company were the agents of the Barings in this country; S. V. S. Wilder for the French house of Hottinguer, and August Belmont for the Rothschilds. In disposing of their stocks to these houses, American agents frequently disregarded and openly flaunted state statutes. Bonds were sold on credit and below par; and the signed contracts often specified that the interest should begin at once. Michigan bonds were given to the Morris Canal and Banking Company in advance of their payment, and negotiators of Indiana bonds received numerous favors in the way of stock and commissions from this company. Thus agents of the states violated state statutes in negotiating the loans, and American bankers aided and abetted them. These acts were unknown to foreign investors when they purchased the bonds; but they were often later the basis of the states' contention that the contracts were illegal and, therefore, the state was relieved of all obligation to meet the demands of foreign creditors.[8]

It was not a difficult task to induce European investors to purchase American bonds and stocks. There was an abundance of idle funds in the London money market. Money could be borrowed in Europe at five percent while in America the rates were seven or eight percent. Investors bought with avidity American state securities

which is always fluctuating, being sometimes above, and sometimes below par, according to the circumstances of trade, and the consequent debt due to or from one country, from or to the other." Thus what the Americans called the difference in exchange was what the English called the course of exchange and differed very widely from what was called the par of exchange. As Professor Myers says: "It is extremely difficult to follow the course of sterling exchange rates in the early years of the century. England was upon a paper standard from 1797 until 1821, and specie payments were suspended on this side from 1813 to about 1817. In addition, there was the constant legal fiction that the pound was worth only $4.44, when actually under the coinage laws before 1830 it was worth 2.73 per cent more, and after 1830, 9.45⅝ per cent more. The result of using the legal rather than the true par made exchange on London seem always to be at a high premium, even though it might actually be at a discount." Myers, M. G., The New York Money Market, Vol. *I*, p. 72.

[8] The basis for these generalizations is to be found in the later chapters on the individual debts of the separate states. Between 1821-1846 the firm of Prime, Ward and Company was known as Prime, Ward and Sands; Prime, Ward, King and Company; and Prime, Ward and King. Since the letters from the Barings were usually addressed to Prime, Ward and Company, this desigation will be followed throughout the text.

carrying higher interest rates than European stocks yielded. The British were tired of seeing their accumulated capital wasted in powder and shot, as had proved to be the case with many of the loans to foreign countries. The Americans were borrowing apparently to carry on productive enterprises; and the faith and honor of the states, as well as mortgages upon private property were pledged for the redemption of the loans. Since American stocks and bonds were not listed on the Stock Exchange, being from their very nature, and the small amount of each particular stock, unsuited for time bargains and jobbing, they were subject to less frequent fluctuations in price. This appealed to the British, for they purchased these stocks as a safe and more or less permanent investment and not for speculative purposes. The success which had rewarded English capitalists in their investments in the stock of the First and Second United States Banks, the rapid retirement by the national government of the public debt, and the apparent prosperity and enterprise displayed by Americans, enhanced the willingness of the British to place implicit faith in American securities. By 1839 it was estimated that British subjects held between 110 and 165 millions of dollars of American stocks. One-half of the capital stock of the United States Bank of Pennsylvania at that time was held in Europe; and one-fourth of all the stockholders were residents of the British Isles, 42 of them holders of titles of nobility.[9]

American state loans for canals, railroads, and banks reached the London money market through the channels of the United States Bank of Pennsylvania and various other American banking houses. In London, Baring Brothers and Company, Overend, Gurney and Company, Frederick Huth and Company, Palmer, MacKillop, Dent, and Company, the Rothschilds and others, together with Hope and Company of Amsterdam, introduced them to their clients. The Barings apparently received the most reliable information, for they were kept in close touch with American financial and political affairs by their competent representative, Thomas W. Ward, of Boston. The

---

[9] Meinertzhagen to Funes, Oct. 11, 1844; Huth to Goodhue, May 6, Sept. 14, 1836, Huth Mss.; *Circular to Bankers*, Feb. 23, March 9, 1838; March 1, May 31, 1839; Garland speech in Congress, *Niles Register*, July 21, 1838; House Reports, 27 Cong., 3 Sess., Vol. *IV*, No. 296; estimate sent Lord Palmerston by British consuls in U. S., McTavish to Palmerston, April 8, 1839, Public Record Office, F. O. 5, 337. See also McGrane, R. C., "Some Aspects of American State Debts in the Forties," American Historical Review, Vol. 38, pp. 673, 674.

data which contractors of loans were asked either to send or to bring with them were copies of the state laws, statistical information concerning the resources, wealth and total indebtedness of the state, and a statement of their authority to negotiate the loans.[10]

The Dutch as well as the English were large purchasers of American securities. The increasing importance of Holland as a market for American stocks led the Barings to propose to Hope and Company that they act in concert in introducing these loans to investors. Such an arrangement, claimed the Barings, would have many advantages. It would give general currency to good loans and check over-issues; place the borrowing system on a plan that would be profitable to both houses; and at the same time show the states the benefit of employing their firms. To accomplish this the Barings proposed the amounts of the loans be divided between London and Amsterdam, so as to give capitalists in both countries an opportunity to participate and to receive their dividends in the currency of their respective countries. It would also tend to give the public confidence in what was really good and place the loans recommended by their houses above any wild schemes which might be offered by other banking houses. There is no evidence that Hope and Company agreed to this proposal; but they did frequently consult the Barings before introducing American loans to their clients. It is also quite evident that the Dutch paid more attention to certain details in the negotiations for the sale of American securities than the English, although their minute investigations did not save them from making many serious blunders in the stocks they purchased. Dutch capitalists preferred only American bonds that carried the guaranty of the state for the payment of the interest and the redemption of the principal. They also desired the bonds to be in denominations of $200 and $400, or 500 or 1,000 guilders; and they insisted that the interest and principal should be made payable in Amsterdam at the rate of two and a half guilders to the dollar. Furthermore, the Dutch were adverse to negotiating for stock that had been offered to numerous parties. When a stock was offered or even talked about in different quarters, Dutch buyers concluded that there was a competition of sellers and held back. The experience of Colonel Gamble, president of the Union Bank of Florida, illustrates this

[10] Baring to Prime, Ward and Company, Oct., 1834. Baring Mss.

point. In attempting to dispose of the Florida bonds, Colonel Gamble spoiled his market by disregarding this caution and by negotiating with several parties at the same time. He received an offer in Holland of 95 for one million dollars of his bonds, which he declined; and then began to treat with several parties in England, with the result that the first offer was withdrawn. Before any contract was signed the Dutch were very careful about the arrangements for their commissions, the payment of the dividends, and the powers of the commissioner or party entrusted with the negotiation; and if there was any doubt as to the terms or the powers of the negotiators, the negotiations were broken off. It is not strange, therefore, that the Dutch later insisted in the debt controversies that the terms of the agreements should be carried out to the letter.[11]

New and practically unknown states found it difficult to negotiate loans either in London or in Amsterdam. There was also a reluctance upon the part of Europeans to touch stocks issued by slaveholding states. But all stocks and bonds carrying the pledge of the faith of the state were given careful consideration. As Huth wrote to one of his American agents, it was the guaranty of the state which alone made these stocks "palatable to European capitalists"; and the same statement is found constantly recurring in the correspondence of the bankers and in the columns of the press.[12]

Foreign capital supplied not only the funds for carrying on American state enterprises, but it also furnished American importers with the means of expanding their operations. Before the War of 1812 it had been the custom for American merchants to send agents to England to purchase the goods they desired. During the 'thirties this practice became more prevalent and was facilitated by the credit organization built up by the great Anglo-American houses in London and Liverpool engaged in American trade. Agents of these houses were established in the United States with authority to grant letters of credit. An American merchant desirous of purchasing goods in England through his agent applied to the English banking agent of one of these houses resident in this country. A letter of

[11] Baring to Hope, Nov., 1838, Baring Mss.; Huth to Perit, Dec. 13, 1838. Huth Mss.
[12] Hope to Baring, Aug. 16, 1833, Baring Mss.; Huth to Perit, Nov. 22, 1837, Huth Mss.; Forstall to Ward, Nov. 19, 1832; Hope to Baring, Aug. 16, 1833, Baring Mss.; *Circular to Bankers*, Nov. 8, 1839.

credit was secured which permitted the American agent in England to draw upon the London office of one of these houses for the amount of credit by a bill of exchange at four months. When the English manufacturer presented this bill at the London office it was paid, with the understanding that the American merchant would place funds in London to meet these bills at maturity.[13] When this method of conducting trade was first adopted it was customary for the English houses which had granted the credit to transmit these bills of lading and invoices to their agent in America to hold as collateral security for the ultimate payment by the American importer. But in time this conservative policy was abandoned due to overconfidence and the competition of the English houses for American trade. It seemed to be unnecessary to require any collateral security from wealthy American houses of long-established reputation for prudence in managing their affairs. American importers also resented the practice as illiberal and invidious. The bills of lading and invoices were therefore sent direct to the American merchants and the English houses were left with no tangible security to cover the amounts for which they had accepted. The consequence was that American houses of little standing or capital were able to obtain credits with the Anglo-American houses without any security whatever. Other abuses soon appeared with the establishment of this "open-credit system," as it was technically called. American importing houses obtained credits with a number of these English houses and paid off their bills when due with a bill on another.[14]

Naturally American commerce was stimulated by this liberal credit policy. Between 1830 and 1836 the total value of imports into the United States rose from $71,000,000 to about $190,000,000, or an increase of 270 percent in six years. During the same period the total value of American exports increased only from about

---

[13] Buck, N. S., The Development of the Organization of Anglo-American Trade, pp. 153-155. This method of conducting trade was employed not only with England but also with the Far East.

[14] *Edinburgh Review*, Vol. 65, No. 132, pp. 229-231. The financing of American trade was concentrated in eight houses, seven in London and one in Liverpool. They were Thomas Wilson and Company, Timothy Wiggin and Company, George Wildes and Company, Morrison and Company, Lizardi and Company, the Rothschilds, the Barings, and the Brown Brothers. Frederick Huth and Company, Palmer, MacKillop, Dent, and Company, Magniac, Jardine and Company were in time drawn into this trade. The *Edinburgh Review* claims that in certain periods of 1835 and 1836 the important houses had acceptances outstanding amounting to 15 or 16 million pounds sterling.

$74,000,000 to about $129,000,000, or 174 percent. In other words, the percentage of increase of imports over exports was not less than 96 percent. In 1836 the value of imports into the United States exceeded the value of the exports by the sum of $61,216,995.[15]

While these significant changes were taking place, other events of momentous consequence were occurring which materially affected the economic life of this country. President Jackson was carrying on his war with the United States Bank, which resulted in his vetoing the bill for its recharter; and subsequently removed the government deposits from that institution to certain selected state banks. In anticipation of the expiration of the United States Bank charter, numerous local banks were chartered all over the country. Between 1829 and 1837 the number of banks rose from 329 to 788, and the nominal capital of these banks increased from $110,000,000 to $290,-000,000. During the same period the total loans and discounts of the banks rose from $137,000,000 to $525,000,000.[16] In turn, the bank expansion stimulated the purchase of public lands; over 57,000,000 acres were sold between 1830 and 1837, the sales in 1836 and 1837 amounting to 36,000,000 acres.[17] In order to check the land speculation, President Jackson issued the Specie Circular, while to add to the general unsettling of affairs the federal government decided to distribute the surplus revenue among the states, under conditions which gave an added stimulus to inflation. Thus the stage for the panic of 1837 was set, which was to inaugurate the financial misfortunes of the American states; and the curtain was to rise in the London money market, which throughout these years of delusion had so generously contributed its credit to all American enterprises.

In England, as well as in the United States, there was every indication of prosperity during the years immediately preceding the panic of 1837. The harvests beginning with 1833 were abundant; the cotton, silk, and woollen industries were flourishing; the mining and shipping interests were expanding; money was plentiful for almost any enterprise; and, with the exception of the handloom weavers, the condition of the working classes was improved. But conditions were not so sound as they appeared. The British, like

[15] *Edinburgh Review,* Vol. 65, No. 132, p. 222.
[16] Dewey, D. R., Financial History of the United States, p. 225.
[17] MacDonald, W., Jacksonian Democracy, p. 277.

the Americans, were speculating. The success of the Liverpool and Manchester Railway inaugurated a mania for the construction of numerous other lines. Between 1825 and 1835 Parliament passed 54 railway acts and during the next two years 39 more railway bills were enacted. Five competing lines were projected to Brighton, three to Norwich. To meet the demands for credit facilities, the number of joint stock banks rose from 32 in 1833 to 79 by the end of 1836; and the practice of these new banks in discounting, rediscounting, and advancing money on questionable security gave a stimulus to the speculative fever.[18]

Meanwhile gold began to leave England. In 1834 Congress changed the ratio of silver to gold from 15 to 1 to 16 to 1. This raised the mint par of exchange between sterling and dollars from 4.44 to 4.87½ and stimulated the importation of gold. At the same time, President Jackson insisted the indemnity money due the United States from France and Naples should be paid in gold; and in 1835-1836 the United States Bank began the negotiation of a loan for 1,200,000 pounds in London "to facilitate the settlements upon the expiration of the charter." The effect of this loan upon England was further increased by the large amount of American securities for sale and the credit advanced by the Anglo-American houses. At length the Bank of England awakened to the impending danger as its own reserves declined. To check the drain of gold, the Bank raised its discount rate in July and August of 1836 to 5 percent; and announced the Bank would refuse all bills endorsed by the joint stock banks.[19]

As fall came on, the situation grew worse. In November the Agricultural and Commercial Bank of Ireland failed, and a run on other Irish banks was prevented only by the Bank of England sending two millions of gold to assist them. In the same month the Northern and Central Bank of Manchester, which had 39 branches in the industrial districts, applied to the Bank of England for help. The Bank finally consented to come to its aid and advanced 1,370,-000 pounds.[20] In March of 1837 three of the Anglo-American houses

[18] Clapham, J. H., An Economic History of Modern England, pp. 387, 511; Tooke, T., A History of Prices, Vol. II, pp. 241-243, 274-278.
[19] Tooke, op. cit., pp. 285, 286; Andreades, A., History of the Bank of England, pp. 263-268; Levi, L., History of British Commerce, pp. 219-225.
[20] Andreades, op. cit., pp. 263-268.

—Thomas Wilson and Company, Timothy Wiggin and Company, and George Wildes and Company—found themselves unable to meet their immediate engagements. The Bank of England agreed to help them providing the friends of these houses would give their personal guaranty for the sum of 750,000 pounds advanced by the Bank; and the principal other Anglo-American houses would guaranty to uphold the houses in distress. This second guaranty was to be called upon only in case the first proved insufficient. To meet the first requirement subscription lists were circulated and within a few days the necessary sums were pledged to the satisfaction of the Bank. The Bank of England undertook to obtain the second guaranty and large contributions were pledged by the leading houses engaged in the American trade. Everything would have gone well had it not been for the unusual delay in the arrival of the American packets. The consequence was that Wildes and Company was forced to make a second application to the Bank. After long deliberation, and after the bank directors, it is claimed, had obtained "a sort of sanction to their proceedings from the Chancellor of the Exchequer," the Bank determined to grant not only the required sum but to carry the house through its difficulties on condition that it liquidated its affairs and contracted no new engagements until the advances made by the Bank were fully reimbursed. The other Anglo-American houses were placed upon the same footing and a sum of six millions was advanced to carry them through their difficulties. When the three W's appealed for additional support in May, the Bank of England refused to nurse them any longer; and on June 2, 1837, these houses suspended payment.[21]

The financial crisis in England destroyed the credit bridge over which American commerce flowed. Large amounts of protested bills were returned to this country. American merchants appealed to the Atlantic seaboard banks for specie to remit to Europe; but much of their specie was already across the mountains as a result of the Specie Circular which required all payments for public lands to be made in specie. Southern merchants were unable to pay the sums owed Eastern merchants because of the sharp drop in cotton prices.

[21] The account of the early assistance rendered by the Bank of England to the 3 W's is based upon a confidential statement sent by Huth to Messrs. Goodhue in New York, Apr. 14, 1837. Huth Mss. Other accounts can be found in Tooke and Andreades already cited.

Southern banks contracted their loans and cotton firms began to fail, carrying down with them their eastern correspondents. A financial panic was temporarily averted in April by Nicholas Biddle, issuing United States Bank bonds payable to bearer in London, Paris and Amsterdam within twelve months. Four other American banks, the Manhattan Banking Company, the Girard Bank, the Bank of America, and the Morris Canal and Banking Company also issued "post notes," as the securities were called. As the post notes were of the character of bills of exchange, they enabled the merchants by extending the time of payment to continue their payments. With avidity they were purchased for shipment to London in place of specie or bills. The first day they were sold on the London Stock Exchange they advanced from 93 to 94½.[22] The spirited assistance given the mercantile community by the American banks made a deep impression upon British capitalists; and even with the general suspension of specie payments by American banks in May, 1837, there was a feeling in England that the situation in this country would soon improve.[23]

The breakdown of the financial system in the United States gave Nicholas Biddle an opportunity to demonstrate his cleverness as a financier. In issuing the post notes the United States Bank and its associates came into possession of mercantile notes representing loans made on cotton. To protect the banks from losses it was necessary to check the drop in cotton prices. If the price of cotton could be raised, not only would the banks be strengthened, and the country recover more rapidly from the crisis, but American merchants would be able to liquidate their foreign debts through the usual method of cotton shipments. Biddle, therefore, decided to advance funds to the cotton planters in order to enable them to hold their crops for a rise in price; and to set up his own establishment in Liverpool, to which the cotton could be consigned. Biddle also

[22] *Circular to Bankers*, Apr. 28, 1837; *London Times*, Apr. 24, 1837. Biddle explained his policy in detail to the Barings and Hope on Apr. 1, 1837. Biddle Letter Book. The reception of the "post notes" in England and their advance in price is discussed in Huth to Perit, Apr. 29, 1837. Huth Mss.

[23] Goodhue to Huth, Aug. 24, Sept. 1, 7, Oct. 9, 16, 1837, Huth Mss. Ward was also assuring the Barings at the same time that conditions would soon improve although he was very suspicious of Biddle's cotton transactions. Ward characterized Biddle as "clever but not sound—vain and selfish and avaricious of praise in an extraordinary degree, and bold and confident." Ward to Baring, Oct. 30, 1837; Dec. 17, 1838. Baring Mss.

determined to send abroad a representative of the United States Bank to handle all the financial operations.

The idea of a separate agency of the United States Bank in England was especially attractive to Biddle, as the relations of the bank and its London agency, the Barings, were none too cordial at this time. At the first indication of trouble the Barings had withdrawn the bank's "open credit" with their house. This irritated the haughty financier and perhaps made him more willing to listen to the plan proposed by Roswell L. Colt for sending someone to England to look after the bank's interests, with authority to issue post notes or letters of credit. In other words, Colt suggested that the United States Bank set up its own organization in England and supplant the Anglo-American houses which formerly had controlled the American trade. Such an arrangement, claimed Colt, would free the United States Bank of all obligations to the Barings, raise the value of the bank's stock, and soon bring the Bank of England to see it was for their interest to have the United States Bank account "with a running credit of one million." [24]

The plan was put into operation during the summer and fall of 1837. An agency was established in London under the management of Samuel Jaudon, the bank's cashier. Advances were made by the United States Bank to cotton planters, who consigned their goods to Humphreys and Biddle in Liverpool. When bills drawn upon this house fell due, Humphreys and Biddle drew upon Jaudon. The United States Bank began to get control of the cotton market and reap rich profits on its transactions. The movement of cotton, claimed Biddle, saved the planter interests "probably from ten to fifteen millions," while it helped to pay off the commercial debts owed by Americans to foreigners.

Unfortunately, the policy of the United States Bank started a new wave of speculation. Banks in the south, especially in Mississippi, also began to make advances upon cotton. The resumption of

[24] Colt to Biddle, March 28, 1837. Biddle Mss. The strained relations of the Barings and Biddle are discussed at length in Biddle to Barings, July 31, Aug. 5, Oct. 6, 1837. Baring Mss. As the Bank of England refused to accept the account of the U. S. Bank, Biddle refused to collect the debts of the Bank in this country. "It seems to me," wrote Biddle to Jaudon, "essential to your future success to place this Bank (the U. S. Bank) on a footing of equality at least with the Bank of England—to let it be felt, that we made no overtures and ask no favors—and above all that we shall not keep the account of any Bank which declines keeping an account with us." Biddle to Jaudon, Jan. 6, 8, 1838. Biddle President Letter Book.

specie payments in the spring of 1838 led the public to believe that conditions were sound. The states began to issue more bonds for internal improvements and banking purposes.[25]

The rapidity with which American merchants paid .off their private obligations, and the apparent recovery of the United States, enhanced the willingness of the British to purchase the new state securities. The best recommendation for an American loan was to have the indorsement of the United States Bank. The periodical statements of the bank fully justified the high esteem in which it was held abroad. With the possible exception of the Barings, few entertained any doubt of the financial stability of the United States Bank. English bankers were willing to trust it as they trusted the Bank of England; and it was upon the advice of Biddle and his London agent, Jaudon, that English capitalists accepted the Mississippi and Florida bonds.[26]

As the flood of new states' securities increased in volume, American states began to send agents direct to Europe to negotiate the loans. This increased the difficulty of the European financiers, for it deprived them of the salutary discrimination of their American correspondents, who were better judges than themselves of the security offered. Every assurance was given by these high-pressure salesmen that the loans were adequately secured. Colonel Gamble assured Hope and Company that the economic possibilities of Florida were unsurpassed; and that Congress had tacitly recognized the authority of the territorial legislature of Florida to issue the bonds. The agent of the North American Trust and Banking Company sent Huth and Company the charter of the Real Estate Bank of Arkansas, with copious statistical data and certificates from the War and Treasury Departments, showing their confidence by actual investments in these bonds. In the light of these and other statements, the lack of prudence on the part of European financiers becomes understandable. The signed contracts always specified that the principal and interest should be made payable in London and Amsterdam in pounds sterling or florins, to satisfy the investing public, and the

---

[25] McGrane, R. C., The Panic of 1837, pp. 181, 182, 193, 194. Biddle's cotton transactions are described in detail in Jenks, L. H., The Migration of British Capital, pp. 88-93.
[26] *Niles Register*, Jan. 16, 1841; Meinertzhagen to Funes, Oct. 11, 1844, Huth Mss.

commission allowed the bankers ranged up to three and a half percent.[27]

The wisdom of investing in American securities was debated in the columns of the London press. The *Circular to Bankers* and the *Morning Chronicle* urged British investors to place their surplus capital in American enterprises. "We feel convinced," announced the *Morning Chronicle*, "that persons desirous of investing money in any of the principal American securities will find on inquiry that we have never over-rated the honor and good faith which have always been shown by the United States to her creditors." Attention was also called to the investments by the United States government in state stocks as proof that the security of "even the newest and smallest states, Arkansas, for instance," was satisfactory to the government in Washington. At the same time, the *London Times* was questioning the constitutional power of individual American states to contract loans and was cautioning British investors not to purchase them. "The state loans depend upon banking projects and internal improvements, of which probably, not one in ten, for years to come," stated the sceptical *Times*, "will pay its own expenses, especially in the remoter states." The "debtor is at a great distance, compellable to good faith by no law whatever"; and investors purchasing bank bonds should realize that "there exists . . . no sort of control, no real responsibility, nothing which can protect the share holder at a distance. . . ." The advice of the *Times* was disregarded by a public who preferred to trust the word of their bankers and the prospectuses which were issued. These quoted verbatim the statements made by the authorized agents of the states.[28]

The warnings of the *Times* seemed to be verified by the publication in 1839 of Comptroller Flagg's report in New York, which pointed out the rapidity with which the indebtedness of the states was mounting. Between 1835 and 1838 the total was increased over

[27] Consult chapters on Florida and Arkansas State Debts. The data concerning the commissions is based upon numerous letters in the Baring, Huth, and Hope correspondence. The *Democratic Review*, XVI, p. 306, is incorrect as regards commissions.

[28] *Morning Chronicle*, Feb. 19, 1839; Apr. 23, 1840. The amount invested by the United States government in state stocks is given in House Doc., 26 Cong., 1 Sess., Vol. III, No. 145; House Reports, 27 Cong., 3 Sess., Vol. IV, No. 296, pp. 47-446; *London Times*, Dec. 15, 1838, Mar. 5, 1839; Prospectus of Maryland Loan in Baring Printed Material, Oct. 12, 1837.

$108,000,000. During the same period the banking capital of the Union was increased $109,000,000. In turn, the banks augmented their paper circulation $46,000,000, and their loans and discounts $160,000,000. The whole financial structure of the United States was on the verge of a collapse; and if this occurred, as it did in the fall of 1839, would the meagre resources of some of the states afford the means to meet the heavy obligations they had incurred without heavy taxation? And would the people submit to the imposition of such taxes? [29]

To avert another financial breakdown in this country, European financiers decided to suggest to Americans a possible way of relieving the financially embarrassed commonwealths. This was an unfortunate move on their part, as the subsequent reactions of the American public disclosed.

[29] American Almanac, 1840, p. 106.

CHAPTER II

WANTED: FEDERAL AID

To allay the alarm of investors and to bolster up the sagging market, the Barings determined to obtain the legal opinion of Daniel Webster on the power of American states to contract loans and the attitude of Americans upon the sanctity of contracts. Webster was in England presumably on a pleasure trip, although the journey had been undertaken at Jaudon's suggestion.[1] Webster's departure had aroused much comment both in the United States and in England. "There is an impression in Wall Street," stated the *New York Herald*, "that the appearance of Daniel Webster in London will have a beneficial effect upon the sale of stocks."[2] This was true. American financiers hoped that Webster, the close friend of Biddle, and a staunch defender of private property, would be able to quiet any fears the British might entertain regarding the safety of American loans. Before Webster sailed, a group of friends decided to present him with a gift. Ward subscribed $500 to the sum raised and charged one-half of it to the Barings. "I deem it money well spent," wrote Ward to the Barings, "and you will consider if he should require a few hundred pounds, whether you furnish it to him or make any advances—he is not likely to repay them. But he is a great man and has great power over others, and right or wrong will somehow or another always be furnished with money." There was no doubt Jaudon would take him up; and in all probability Webster would use his influence in favor of the United States Bank. It would be well, therefore, for the Barings to show Webster every attention; and Ward suggested that Joshua Bates should go to Liverpool to meet Webster. "I consider him," continued Ward in another letter, "by far the greatest man we have, and when I imagine to myself the evil he might do if he should go wrong I feel it quite important that

---

[1] Webster, F., ed., The Private Correspondence of Daniel Webster, Vol. II, p. 45.
[2] *New York Herald*, June 3, 1839.

much should be done to keep him right." There was no doubt in Ward's mind of the impression Webster would make upon the British. "His sound and comprehensive views, and great powers of mind, and his personal appearance and manner will, I think," wrote Ward, "give him an entré into the English mind which no other American and perhaps no other man could get." Of course the Barings were well acquainted with the position and influence Webster held among his countrymen; and on frequent occasions they advanced Webster funds when he was in pecuniary difficulties.[3] Nevertheless, the strong recommendations of Ward, whom the Barings trusted, undoubtedly caused them to pay more attention to the American Burke.

It is not strange, therefore, that the Barings should write to Webster on October 16, 1839, asking whether the state legislatures were empowered to contract loans at home and abroad. To this inquiry Webster replied that the legislatures did possess this authority, since each was an "independent, sovereign, political community," except in so far as certain powers had been conferred upon the general government. The security for these loans rested upon the plighted faith of the states; and in some cases the income or revenue expected to be derived from the canals and railroads, in others valuable tracts of land had been specifically set aside for their redemption. No state could rid itself of these obligations; nothing but gold or silver could be offered in discharge of these debts. Any failure to fulfill their undertakings would be an open violation of public faith, which would be followed by the penalty of dishonor and disgrace; a penalty no state would be likely to incur. Like all honest men, the citizens of the United States regarded debts, whether existing at home or abroad, "to be a *moral* as well as a *legal* obligation." If any state should so entirely lose her self-respect or forget her duty as to violate her faith, Webster was confident there was "no country upon earth, not even that of the injured creditor," where it would receive less countenance or indulgence than it would receive from the great mass of the American people. This correspondence was given to the press,[4] and there is little doubt that

[3] Ward to Baring, July 27, 1835; Apr. 29, May 4, May 13, 1839. Baring Mss.
[4] Webster's opinion can be found in *Circular to Bankers,* Dec. 13, 1839. The *Washington Globe,* Sept. 7, 1840, claimed that Webster received £1000 from the Barings for this letter. There is no evidence to prove this assertion.

the legal opinion of the American Burke carried great weight in the investing circles, for Webster later acknowledged that he was able to dispose of Massachusetts stock to the sum of £40,000 sterling while in England.[5]

Webster's opinion did not go unchallenged. The sceptical *London Times* refused to be silenced. Even though the states possessed the power to make loans, the real test would come when the sums borrowed must be paid. Would the American people, asked the *Times*, submit to taxation to satisfy the claims of the foreign creditors? Suppose the local government with all its sense of "a moral as well as a legal obligation" were outvoted? The power to make loans, the *Times* reminded its readers, did not necessarily include the power to pay them; and to reinforce their arguments copious extracts were quoted from a pamphlet written by an American who signed himself "Junius." According to "Junius," any act passed by one state legislature could be repealed by the next or any succeeding legislature. Sovereign power rested not in the legislature but in the hands of the people. To counteract the evil effects of these statements, the *Morning Chronicle* came to Webster's support. As Bates later wrote to Webster: "The only means we have found of lessening the bad effect [of the above-mentioned pamphlet] was by asserting through the *Chronicle* that the writer of the pamphlet belonged to the Fanny Wright party, who considered the obligation to pay debts of marriage vows and all the fixed forms of religion as tyranny and therefore to be resisted." [6]

It was realized, however, that more than Webster's word was needed to uphold America's credit. Two days after Webster's letter was received, the Barings issued a circular upon American stocks, in which they pointed out that if the whole scheme of internal improvements were carried into effect by means of foreign capital, a more comprehensive guaranty than that of the individual states would be required. "A national pledge would undoubtedly collect capital together from all parts of Europe." [7]

[5] Speech of Webster in New York quoted in *London Times*, Nov. 6, 1840. For reference to Webster's transactions regarding Massachusetts stock see Kenyon to Webster, July 30, 1839; Baring Mss.

[6] *London Times*, Nov. 21, 1839; Apr. 21, 22, 24, 27, 1840; *Morning Chronicle*, Apr. 27, 1840; Bates to Webster, Apr., 1840, Baring Mss.; "A Reply to Webster" by Junius. Bates wrote Webster it was believed that this pamphlet was written by C. J. Ingersoll of Philadelphia.

[7] The Baring Circular can be found in *Circular to Bankers*, Jan. 10, 1840.

The Baring Circular attracted considerable attention in the United States. Leading Whig journals throughout the country sponsored the proposition of federal assumption of the state debts. The *National Intelligencer* called attention to the fact that most of the bonds had been issued for the purpose of aiding internal improvements and asked whether it would not be a wise move for Congress "to set aside certain amounts of the public land for their ultimate redemption?" The *New York Herald* declared that it was the only way to make money "easy" in the United States. By issuing federal stocks, Americans could go to Europe and raise enough money to complete their projected public works. The *New York American* pointed out the advantages which would be gained and suggested a plan of operation. The ends to be attained by issuing federal in lieu of state stocks were twofold: (1) The immediate benefit which would accrue to the states and to the community; (2) the permanent objects to be accomplished by the substitution of the credit of one great nation "for the separate and oftentimes conflicting pretensions of twenty-six isolated states." It was estimated that state stocks to the amount of $200,000,000 had already been created, bearing an average interest of 5½ percent, the annual interest charges of which were about $11,000,000. A United States stock, bearing 4 percent, "which would be one percent more than that of the British consols," could be readily exchanged "at a premium in most cases of 25 percent for the state stocks." This would mean a saving of $50,000,000 of the principal to the states and a reduction of the annual interest charges to about $6,000,000. With Indiana and Illinois stocks down 50 percent, Maryland sterling bonds selling at 58, and even New York stock as low as 82, it was imperative to act promptly. By the conversion of state stock into United States stock, the western states would be relieved from all apprehension of taxation; and they would be able to complete the internal improvements which would develop their resources. In order not to penalize the more prudent states while assisting the debtors, $200,000,000 of the United States stock might be issued, based upon the proceeds of the public lands, and this could be distributed among the states according to the provisions of Clay's Land Distribution Bill. This proposal was heartily supported by other New York Whig journals; while their views were echoed west of the Alleghanies by the able Whig *Cincinnati Gazette*.

The only objections, declared the editor of this paper, which could be advanced against the scheme were: (1) that the federal government had no constitutional right to assume the debts of the states; and (2) that it could not be done without enacting another national debt. The first difficulty would be obviated by passing Clay's Land Bill; while the idea of creating a new public debt did not frighten the editor of the *Cincinnati Gazette.*[8]

Democratic papers stigmatized the scheme as a Baring and Webster plot to foist upon the national government the debts of the states. They erred, however, in ascribing its origin to foreigners. The plan owed its inception to the necessities of the United States Bank. On October 1, 1839, a close friend of Biddle wrote Joshua Bates, the Yankee member of the Barings, of the need of procuring foreign capital to complete the public works. "I would suggest," wrote Davis, "that some intimation be given from a source that would command attention—that a *reasonable* amount of capital can be relied on from England on the United States government security, but little if anything on *State Security* alone. The same interest that controlled the State in issuing State Bonds will prevail in Congress, and Congress will be compelled to assume all State Bonds." By uniting the interests of the state bondholders at home and abroad with those of the canal and railroad groups in the United States, both would be saved. But if the English creditors refused to coöperate with the canal and railroad men, the latter might throw up their hands and say: "Well, look out for yourselves. John Bull has ruined us and now collect your bonds. They are unconstitutional and we can't help you."[9] In other words, the foreign creditor could be saved only by uniting the banking, canal, and railroad interests. By much the same means the United States Bank had secured its recharter from the State of Pennsylvania;[10] and now it hoped to save itself again by bringing the same pressure to bear upon Congress.

With the failure of the United States Bank on October 10, 1839, the foreign investors realized the importance of pushing federal

---

[8] *National Intelligencer* quoted in *Globe*, Sept. 7, 1840; *New York Herald*, Nov. 15, 1839; *New York American*, Nov. 20, 1839. Extracts from Whig Journals are given in Congressional Globe, 26 Cong., 1 Sess., App. pp. 127-128.

[9] Davis to Bates, Oct. 1, 1839; Bates to Davis, Oct. 18, 1839. Baring Mss.

[10] McGrane, R. C., The Panic of 1837, pp. 70-91.

assumption. As Huth was informed, the stocks of the western states were practically worthless in the United States and many people could not see how the governments of these new states could raise the funds necessary to pay the interest on their debts; and it was ridiculous to think of laying "taxes upon their thin and semi-barbarous population." Prudent and reflecting people agree that "some day or other the interest from the western and southern states" would not be forthcoming, and "the whole kite-flying concern," as these state loans, trust companies, etc., were called, would fall to the ground with a crash, "unless some unforeseen circumstance should happen to save them." "Really these people," continued the writer, "have a character of so much elasticity that there is no saying what may turn up." Assumption would please the eastern people, who had no debt that they were not able and willing to pay, as it would oblige the government to raise the tariff, while the southern people, although opposed to the tariff, would be satisfied, as it would "save the honor of their states." [11]

At the same time Huth was receiving this information, Ward was writing to the Barings that there were too many objections to federal assumption for it to be accepted. In the first place, it was "inexpedient," as it was better for the "states to get out of their own difficulties"; assumption in the end would lead to greater evils and corruption. Furthermore, it was "unconstitutional," for the United States could not do indirectly what they could not do directly; and besides, it was contrary to the "whole doctrine of the Democratic party." Moreover, the apportionment on the basis of Clay's Land Bill "would not meet the necessities of the new and borrowing states," whose debts were out of proportion to the shares they would receive; while it would also be opposed as a foreign scheme. Yet on the eve of the assembling of Congress another correspondent wrote the Barings that a plan would be brought forward to consolidate the state stocks and, although the President and his Cabinet were opposed to the scheme, it would be carried through the House, as many members from the older states thought that this was the only way they would ever receive anything from the sales of the public lands. [12] The "internal improvement interest" was

---

[11] Kindermann to Huth, Oct. 31, 1839. Huth Mss.
[12] Ward to Baring, Nov. 29, 1839; Dec. 12, 1839 with enclosure. Baring Mss.

"the most powerful interest that ever existed in the United States," wrote Davis to Bates, and they would treat all such abstractions as states rights and constitutionality as a railroad treated cows on a railroad track—"blow the alarm whistle first and then" proceed to run them down. The "railroad interest" would advocate an increase in tariff rates and a distribution of the land sales; and Bates was told to explain the plan of operation to "state commissioners" abroad who were negotiating loans in order that they might "take care to give it a local adaptation." [18]

Whatever expectation the bankers had that their plan might succeed was destroyed by the prejudices aroused over its supposedly foreign origin. The country was on the eve of a Presidential election. Both the Whigs and the Democrats were desirous of gaining the favor of the rapidly growing West, which held the balance of power. The Whigs hoped to obtain this by sponsoring the need of the indebted states which, with the exception of Pennsylvania and Maryland, were confined to the south and west. But assumption either direct or indirect through the distribution of the land sales did not appeal to the settlers of the newer communities, as it would endanger the passage of graduation or preëmption acts, which would make it easier for the newcomers to secure lands. Assumption did appeal, however, to the moneyed element in the west and south who held state stocks, as the value of these securities would be enhanced by federal guaranty. The Whigs preferred, therefore, to wait until after the campaign before they disclosed their full plans, for fear they might lose votes in these regions, and so they had disguised their scheme in the form of the distribution of the land sales. On the other hand, the Democrats were anxious to create the impression that the Whigs were openly for federal assumption of the state debts. This, it was hoped, would arouse the antagonism of the older states, whose debts were small and resources large as compared with the newer states. By alarming some and exciting the prejudices of others, by insinuating that assumption would benefit only the foreign creditors, the Democrats hoped to strengthen the cause of Van Buren in the Presidential campaign. It was evident that whatever merit the scheme might have possessed was to be lost sight of in the scramble for votes.

[18] Davis to Bates, Nov. 16, 1839. Baring Mss.

When Congress assembled in the fall, Senator Benton of Missouri endeavored to force the Whigs to reveal their intentions by introducing a series of resolutions denouncing assumption as unconstitutional, inexpedient, and unjust. Benton claimed assumption would compel the non-indebted states to incur burdens for others; it would establish a dangerous precedent for later assumptions; it would lay the foundation for new and excessive duties on foreign imports, which would fall unequally upon different sections of the Union and most heavily upon the planting and grain-growing states; it would tend to the consolidation of the Union; and it would enhance the value of state stocks to the advantage of foreign capitalists, jobbers, and gamblers, thereby holding out inducements to foreigners to interfere in our affairs.

Benton's resolutions were referred to a select committee composed of five Democrats and two Whigs. On January 30, 1840, Grundy presented the report of the committee endorsing the views set forth in Benton's resolutions. The committee disclaimed all responsibility upon the part of the federal government for the state debts. Assumption was condemned as a gross and flagrant violation of the United States Constitution. By the Constitution, Congress was authorized to pay the debts of the United States; but nothing was said about the state debts. As the federal government was one of delegated powers, Congress had no power, therefore, to pay these debts. If the federal government assumed these obligations, Congress would be giving money to the states; and if it could give money to the states to enable them to complete their internal improvements, what was to prevent the federal government from taking upon its broad shoulders the burden of every unsuccessful speculation of this kind? The Constitution provided that "all duties, imposts, and excises shall be equal throughout the United States." Of what value were these restrictions if money could be constitutionally taken from one state and given to another, through the instrumentality of the general government? The proceeds of the land sales could not be applied to such objects, as the lands belonged to the federal government and they had been ceded for the common benefit of all. Moreover, to use the money from the public land sales would retard the settlement of the new states and delay the passage of graduation and preëmption measures. The Whigs immediately condemned the report as an aspersion upon the honor of the states. Since no state had asked the federal government for relief, the Whigs declared that it was indelicate and unjustifiable to intimate that any state in the Union would not pay its debts. To cater to the injured feelings of the indebted states, Crittenden introduced resolutions to substitute for the Grundy report, declaring there was "no ground to warrant any doubt of the ability or disposition of those states to fulfill their contracts," although it would "be just and proper to distribute the proceeds of the sales of the public lands among the states, in fair and rateable proportions." The Crittenden resolutions, however, were defeated and the Grundy report was passed.[14] Benton's resolutions had given the champions of the debtors a theme and an opportunity to attack the gigantic schemes of internal improvements and the manner in which the banks had marketed their securities. To offset this advantage the Whigs nominated, not Clay, the champion of distribution, but Harrison, a western man, whose views on the land question were not so well known, and issued no platform.

In the ensuing Presidential campaign Democratic leaders fanned the flames of national prejudices and appealed to the masses on the ground that assumption was a move on the part of foreigners to dictate to the United States, and designed to aid the rich to the detriment of the poor. Some basis for these charges was given a semblance of plausibility by the publication after the campaign of letters written by the wealthy English-German banker, Huth and Company, to the president of the State Bank of Missouri. Commenting on the inability of marketing Missouri bonds in London, the English banker remarked in a letter of June 3, 1840, that the "attention of our capitalists and others engaged in American affairs is now turned to your internal politics, and if the prospects for your new Presidential election held out by the latest accounts should be realized, this circumstance will contribute more than any other to restore the general confidence." Elaborating upon this theme in a later letter, the writer suggested that "if, however, your elections for the presidentship should have the result now anticipated, it is

[14] Cong. Globe, 26 Cong., 1 Sess., Vol. 8, App. pp. 85-93; Sen. Doc., No. 18, 26 Cong., 1 Sess., Vol. 2, pp. 1, 2; Sen. Doc., No. 153, 26 Cong., 1 Sess., Vol. 4, p. 15; *London Times* March 19, Apr. 6, 1840; Davis to Bates Feb. 3, 1840, Baring Mss.; Wellington, R. G., The Political and Sectional Influence of the Public Lands, 1828-1842, pp. 78-82.

very probable that an impulse will be given to all state stocks," and advised against the recalling of the Missouri bonds "without seeing what effect a change of your executive will produce." [15]

Such statements were immediately pounced upon by the Democrats as a direct suggestion that Harrison was the choice of the English financiers. The Missouri legislature ordered the publication of the correspondence; demanded the recall of their state bonds from Huth and Company; and passed resolutions to the effect that the letters disclosed "evidence of a direct interference on the part of British capitalists in the internal politics of the United States." [16] That British bankers did not place more confidence in the conservative Whig leaders than in the anti-bank, anti-English Democrats, was true; but in the maelstrom of party politics a mercantile letter had been given a sinister note. What was more natural than that Huth, writing to an American banker, should say that the ascendancy of conservatives in office would promote the sale of American stocks? Instead of stabilizing the market for American securities, the inadvertent moves of international bankers assisted in discrediting state stock. Assumption had given the Senate an opportunity of undermining American credit; and the Huth letters helped to destroy any possibility of securing a federal guaranty. After the fall of 1839 no considerable amount of state securities was sold abroad, and the credit of the states steadily declined.

Although the Whigs carried the election of 1840, foreign investors had cause to be alarmed by the state of affairs existing in the United States. In the fall of 1839 the United States Bank had failed. This had precipitated the panic of 1839, the full force of which fell upon the western and southern states. Every section of the country was now in the grip of the depression which had begun in 1837.[17] In February, 1840, Pennsylvania delayed in paying her semi-annual dividend. Pennsylvania was one of the wealthiest states in the Union, and if this state was finding it difficult to meet her payments, it was an indication of what was likely to occur elsewhere.

By the beginning of 1841 the possibility of some of the states repudiating their debts was being debated in the columns of the

[15] Huth to Smith, June 3, Sept. 11, 1840. Huth Mss.
[16] Reprinted in *London Times*, Jan. 21, 1841.
[17] The West did not feel the full effects of the panic of 1837 until 1839. Cf. McGrane, R. C., *Panic of 1837*, pp. 123-130.

American press. The *Globe* acknowledged that the doctrine of repudiation was sweeping over the country. *Niles Register* denied the accusation and affirmed that no state would violate its plighted word. Nevertheless meetings were being held in Illinois and Mississippi advocating repudiation, and Governor McNutt of Mississippi in his message of 1841 defiantly declared in favor of repudiation.[18] Meanwhile the death of President Harrison and the internecine strife within the Whig party was adding to the confusion. In the spring of 1841 the Rothschilds, Hope and Company, and Joshua Bates of Baring Brothers and Company addressed letters to President Tyler and Webster, Secretary of State, calling their attention to the non-payment by Indiana, Florida, and Mississippi of their obligations. Webster deemed it advisable not to reply to these communications;[19] and President Tyler in his message of 1841 declared that the states alone were responsible for their indebtedness, although he expressed the belief that each state would "feel itself bound by every consideration of honor, as well as of interest, to meet its engagements with punctuality."[20]

The desire upon the part of the United States government about this time to float a loan in Europe seemed to afford an opportunity to European capitalists to impress the national government with the disastrous effects of state repudiation. Webster, Secretary of State, was informed by Edward Everett, United States Minister to England, that it would be difficult to obtain subscriptions to the proposed plan.[21]

That certain European capitalists were contemplating a refusal of the federal loan is disclosed in the correspondence of Hope and Company with the Barings. On May 23, 1842, Hope wrote to the Barings proposing that all the influential financiers of Europe should unite not to touch the loan of the United States government until the states resumed their payments, or at least until the doctrine of repudiation was done away with. This would compel the national government to take energetic measures toward those states which had failed to meet their payments, perhaps even give them pecuniary

---

[18] *Globe*, Jan. 3, 1841; *Niles*, Jan. 16, 1841; Kendall's Expositor, Apr. 7, 21, 1841; Miss. Senate Journal, 1841, pp. 17-21.

[19] *New York Herald*, July 14, 1841.

[20] *Niles*, Dec. 11, 1841.

[21] Everett to Webster, May 6, 1842. State Department Mss., Vol. 49

assistance. "The Americans cannot go on without European capital," wrote Hope, "and we ought to withhold it, until we see proper measures taken to replace their credit by conducting themselves like honest debtors ought to do." This was imperative, as the Democratic party, which had originated the repudiation doctrine, was gaining ground in several of the states and there was no saying how far these ideas might spread "if not checked in time."

Replying to this communication, the Barings agreed that it was the duty of financiers to refuse further loans to a government which had failed to comply with its engagements. Such principles should guide capitalists in regard to those American states which were defaulters; but the Barings doubted the wisdom of enforcing that principle "towards the United States government and towards those states that had always punctually met their engagements." The Barings reminded their fellow financiers that the twenty-six states which formed the United States were "all sovereign and independent, and although circumstances might in time enable the general government to aid the states, that government has no power or *right* to interfere." Of the twenty-six states, ten had no debts; ten others might be considered perfectly good. Maryland and Pennsylvania were in difficulty, but they would ultimately work themselves into a right position. The only case of positive repudiation at that time was Mississippi. Almost all the other states through their legislatures had expressed themselves strongly against repudiation. "Is it wise," asked the Barings, "for this single instance of dishonesty, in a remote and unimportant state to endeavor to brand the whole United States as wanting in good faith? We think not." A contrary course would be more likely to achieve the purpose in view. Lord Ashburton, former senior partner of the house, had been sent on a diplomatic mission to the United States to settle outstanding differences between England and this country; and if he succeeded it "would be very desirable both for England and the United States that $10,000,000 should be borrowed here. The drafts against such a loan would protect the specie in the banks; enable them to increase their issues a little; trade would revive with the revival of confidence and the revenue would exceed the disbursements of the general government." It was calculated that Sir Robert Peel's tariff would benefit the western states and, "with the general improvement, the other states would find less difficulty in collecting their revenue." All would be able to meet their obligations, except possibly Mississippi, Indiana, Illinois, and Michigan. There was no doubt the general government would be able to borrow at home if unable to obtain it abroad. Thus an attempt to enforce principles which should apply only to the delinquent states to the case of the United States would fail in its effect. It was a mistake to suppose that the United States could not get along "without borrowing from Europe." The Americans had been encouraged to borrow in Europe because of the low interest rates which prevailed abroad. They had secured large loans in order to carry on their works of internal improvement. In some of the states the money had been injudiciously spent, but it had not been thrown away. No new undertakings were contemplated. Instead of employing coercion, capitalists should "treat every state on its own merit" and give confidence where it was deserved. As for the defaulters, there was no doubt that the doctrine of repudiation even in Mississippi would be soon out of fashion, and these states could be brought "amicably around to honest principles much better than by taking the hostile course." "With regard to the dangers of democracy," continued the Barings, "they have always been put forth since the days of Jefferson. In the meantime the progress of things has been unexampled in that country; and the people seem generally quiet and orderly." [22]

Nevertheless, the views of the Barings were overruled by the opposition of the other bankers and the hostility of a disillusioned investing public. Hope agreed with the Barings that the best course to adopt was the one they had suggested; but the Dutch investors did not entertain such views. No one in Holland would touch any more American securities unless the federal government did something to restore state credit. For this reason Hope believed that the best way to induce the federal government to come to the assistance of the honest but embarrassed states was to withhold European capital until this was accomplished. The Barings quickly pointed out to the Dutch capitalists that "the buyers of American state stocks never contemplated until lately that the general government was in

[22] Hope to Baring, May 23, 1842; Baring to Hope, May 27, 1842. Baring Mss.

any way accountable or that it would or could interfere with them." [23] But their arguments apparently failed to convince their fellow financiers. Overend, Gurney and Company of London notified the United States commissioners that they could expect no assistance unless the federal government assumed the debts of the states. [24] Baron Rothschild told Duff Green in Paris that he could tell his government he had seen the man who was the head of the finances of Europe and that he had told him "you cannot borrow a dollar, not a dollar." [25] When American newspapers expressed surprise at the lack of interest in Europe for the United States loan, the *London Times* cynically commented: "It is this kind of astonishment that shows that the nation is not sensible of the very delicate nature of public credit, and that even in the face of ample security a moral blemish in a people is fatal." [26]

The failure to float the United States loan revived the hopes of foreign creditors that the federal government would come to the relief of the states. A representative of Huth and Company was told in Washington by President Tyler and many members of Congress that everyone was anxious to advocate any measure which might help restore the credit of the states. Henry Clay assured him that some such plan as W. Cost Johnson of Maryland was then proposing would be adopted, no matter whether the Whigs or the Democrats carried the election of 1844. Johnson was urged by English bankers to send copies of his letters explaining his plans to persons in the west in order to combat the doctrines of repudiation. But Huth and Company was warned by their representative in America not to be too sanguine about the immediate success of federal assumption of state debts. The majority of politicians in Washington were still opposed to the scheme, as they feared they might endanger their own popularity with their constituents. Nothing could be accomplished until the people were convinced of the merits of the plan, and to do this "would be the work of years." [27]

[23] Hope to Baring, June 5, 1842; Baring to Hope, June 10, 1842. Baring Mss.
[24] This correspondence was published in *London Times*, Apr. 21, 1843.
[25] Green to Calhoun, Jan. 24, 1842, American Historical Association Report, 1899, Vol. *II*, pp. 842, 843. Duff Green claimed that Colonel Robinson, one of the American commissioners, told Green that he was the only man in Europe "who could carry through the loan." Duff Green to Lucretia M. Green, Sept. 17, 1842. Duff Green Mss.
[26] *London Times*, June 24, 1842.
[27] Meinertzhagen to Huth, Jan. 5, 21, Feb. 1, 12, 1843. Huth Mss.

Meanwhile the debates in Congress clearly revealed the opposition to federal relief for the states. John Quincy Adams believed that there would be war with Great Britain if the state debts were not assumed. Gwin of Mississippi defiantly announced the fear of such war did not frighten him. If the alternatives were war or assumption, Gwin "was for war as were his constituents." He would prefer "slapping John Bull in the face than to quail before his power." [28] On December 29, 1842, a select committee of the House was appointed to report on the advisability of employing the credit of the United States for the relief of the states; and on March 2, 1843, William Cost Johnson, chairman of this committee, presented a voluminous report covering all aspects of the subject.

Johnson pointed out in the report that the total indebtedness of the states on January 1, 1843, amounted to $231,642,111. To this amount must be added the liabilities of the cities, amounting to $27,536,422 and the United States debt which was $20,210,226. The grand total stock debt of the country was, therefore, $279,388,-760, bearing an annual interest of $14,894,232, payable by 17,063,-353 people. This was equivalent to a per capita debt of $16. The debts of the southern and southwestern states alone amounted to $75,127,113, bearing interest of $4,441,410, while the value of the exports of these states in 1841 was $68,917,151. Since a large portion of the whole amount borrowed was owed abroad, it must be paid in specie or its equivalent. It was evident, however, that so large an amount could not be remitted yearly "without impoverishing the country." The whole export of domestic produce from the United States in 1841 was $106,000,000. Of this amount, one speaker said, about $15,000,000, or 14 percent, must be paid to meet the annual interest charges. This was more than the profits on the exports. It amounted "to 85 cents on every barrel of flour and $4.25 on every bale of cotton." To liquidate this enormous indebtedness, Johnson proposed that $200,000,000 of the United States stock should be issued and credited or distributed among the states, territories, and District of Columbia. The proceeds of the sales of the public lands were to be pledged for the redemption of the interest and principal of this stock. The proportion which each state and territory would receive was as follows:

[28] Cong. Globe, 27 Cong., 3 Sess., Vol. 12, p. 273.

States	Amount	States	Amount
Maine	$ 6,563,876.66	Kentucky	$ 8,519,823.80
New Hampshire	4,607,929.52	Tennessee	9,171,806.18
Massachusetts	8,519,823.80	Ohio	15,691,629.98
Connecticut	4,607,929.52	Louisiana	4,607,929.52
Vermont	4,607,929.52	Indiana	8,519,823.80
Rhode Island	3,303,964.76	Mississippi	4,607,929.52
New York	24,167,400.26	Illinois	6,563,876.66
New Jersey	5,259,911.90	Alabama	6,563,876.66
Pennsylvania	17,647,577.52	Missouri	5,259,911.90
Delaware	2,651,982.38	Arkansas	2,651,982.38
Maryland	5,911,894.28	Michigan	3,955,947.14
Virginia	11,779,735.70	Florida	651,982.38
North Carolina	7,867,841.42	Wisconsin	651,982.38
South Carolina	6,563,876.66	Iowa	651,982.38
Georgia	7,215,859.04	Dist. of Columbia	651,982.38

Total $200,000,000.00

According to Johnson, there were many advantages to be derived by adopting his plan. Excluding the debts of the cities, the states had to meet annual interest payments of about $12,000,000, the greater portion of which had to be paid abroad either in specie or its equivalent. This was a heavy drain upon the metallic currency of the country and a heavy burden upon the states which they could only meet by increasing their taxes. Already some of the states had not been able to comply with their engagements. They admitted their obligations but expressed their inability to pay. All attempts to disown or disclaim their debts had met with disfavor by the people. The federal constitution emphatically declared that "no state shall pass any law impairing the obligations of contracts." The debts were binding; there was no power either in the states or in Congress to extinguish them, except by payment upon the conditions of their engagement or by modifying and postponing them with the full consent of the contracting parties. The inability, however, of some of the states to meet their obligations had led to a want of confidence in their good faith. This loss of confidence affected not only the defaulting states but all the states. Missouri had passed a stay law not because its people were heavily in debt, but "from the consequences of the embarrassments of a neighboring state." The stocks of Maryland were below par because it was delinquent. South Carolina had punctually met its payments, yet its stocks were selling in London below par. Even the credit of the federal government had been impaired by the actions of the delinquent states. It should also be realized that the fear of increased taxes would retard emigration to the indebted states, thereby lessening the sales of the public lands. Furthermore, all classes would be benefited: the manufacturer would sell more of his products as the farmer would be enabled to purchase domestic fabrics; while the farmer, relieved of his burdens, would spend his money for many of the comforts and luxuries which he at present denied himself. Since it was believed that foreign bondholders were willing, for the most part, to exchange their state bonds for national stock bearing 3 percent interest, there would be a saving of $6,000,000 a year on the interest, which set aside as a sinking fund, at 6 percent, would liquidate the principle of $200,000,000 in about nineteen years.

Some objected to the plan because they claimed that it aided the indebted states without extending any benefits to the non-indebted states, who were not responsible for the debts of the former. Others declared that the states could not be trusted to apply the stock or bonds of the federal government to the payment of their debts; while still others held that if the states were relieved from their present difficulties they would in all probability incur more debts. Since all the states, as shown above, equally benefited by the distribution of the stock, there was no valid basis for the first objection. As for the second, the plan proposed that the states should be credited on the books of the Treasury with their respective shares, and the transfer was to be made, not to the indebted states, but to the holders of their bonds. In answer to the third objection, Johnson maintained that the evils which then oppressed these states would teach them a lesson of prudence which they were not apt quickly to forget.

In conclusion, Johnson pointed out that the scheme he was proposing had already been tried out at various times in the history of the country. In 1790 the United States government had assumed the debts of the states. In 1802 the National Government had assumed debts amounting to £600,000, due by American merchants to merchants in Great Britain; and in 1836 the general government had assumed the debts of the cities of the District of Columbia amounting to $1,500,000.[29]

Johnson probably hoped that assumption would be carried for

[29] Johnson's report can be found in House Reports No. 296, 27 Cong., 3 Sess., Vol. 4, pp. 1-15 *et seq.; Cong. Globe,* 27 Cong., 3 Sess., Vol. 12, App. 178.

two reasons. In the first place, there was a precedent for such measures, as the federal government had assumed the debts of states, cities, and private individuals. In the second place, since there were so many indebted states in 1843 it was hoped that their combined interests would insure the adoption of such a plan. But Johnson erred in diagnosing the public sentiment upon the subject. Pennsylvania and Maryland might be in favor of assumption; but elsewhere it was not popular.[30] It was true that the Whig party was more favorable to such a policy than the Democratic party; yet the Whigs were no more willing than the Democrats to sponsor assumption. The real differences between the parties were the divergent views they held in regard to the public lands. Clay and those who followed him considered the public domain the property of the states and therefore believed the proceeds of the land sales should be divided among the states on the basis of their population. The Democrats held that the proceeds of the land sales were a part of the revenue of the general government and, therefore, ought not to be divided but appropriated toward paying off the contingent expenses of the government.[31]

The leaders of both parties carefully refrained from publicly advocating direct assumption. Webster, the confidant of American and English bankers, might privately bemoan the fact that Congress would not assist the states and might intimate publicly the desirability of utilizing the land sales to rehabilitate state credit but in his public addresses he merely stressed the moral obligation of the states to meet their engagements. Clay might tell representatives of English bankers that some such scheme as Johnson proposed would be carried out by either party after 1844 but he never came out publicly in favor of direct assumption. Van Buren cautiously avoided committing himself; and Calhoun could not sponsor such measures without abandoning his doctrine of states rights.[32]

[30] The memorials in favor of assumption came largely from Pennsylvania and Maryland and a few scattered counties in Virginia and Ohio. Cf. House Reports No. 296, 27 Cong., 3 Sess., Vol. 4, pp. 17-47. For opposing views consult *Globe*, Jan. 17, 1840; Mississippi Laws, 1840, p. 269.

[31] For a clear analysis of party views on the land question, see *London Times*, March 19, 1840.

[32] For a statement of the views of Calhoun and Webster, consult Cong. Globe, 26 Cong., 1 Sess., Vol. 8, App., p. 177; *London Times*, Oct. 17, 1842. There is a good analysis of the views of the party leaders in Anderson to Dillon, Oct. 7, 1843, Huth Mss.

In the south and the west the great mass of the people were not interested in the subject. In these regions the people had given little thought to monied and commercial transactions. The moral force of sustaining the public faith weighed lightly with those who were overwhelmed by their own personal indebtedness and in the legislatures there were few who had the moral courage or political honesty to urge the maintenance of state credit. "In Arkansas," wrote a correspondent to Huth and Company, "not more than 20,000 of her 90,000 of population" had "any property to tax"; and "more than one-half of this 20,000" were indebted "to the banks that were founded with the money borrowed on the faith of the state." In addition to what the people owed the banks there were "other and more urgent debts owing amongst each other and to the citizens of other states. In this depressed condition, it is not to be believed that the people of the state will regard that as relief, which only extinguishes the debt of the state without releasing them from these accumulated burdens." Relief to the state was not relief to them. "Its honor weighs lightly with men whose personal concerns claim a paramount regard; they have neither time nor inclination to avert public calamities whilst harassed by those that press around their fireside. The event will show that they will seek relief in a way better suited to their circumstances. They will repeal the law requiring suits to be brought against the debtors to the State Bank. They will openly resolve that the state was not liable to her guaranty until it can be ascertained how much of the debt can be paid by the mortgages of the bank; and, having done this, they will rest better pleased with their condition than they would be were the general government to step in and release the state by satisfying the bondholders."[33] In Mississippi the people were moving to Texas to evade their debts; and when repudiation came the report of the state treasurer showed a balance in the Treasury of thirty-four cents and receipts for claims upon broken banks and notes of insolvent railroad companies.[34] Florida with a population of less than 50,000 had a per capita debt of $200.[35] Suppose foreign capitalists did not lend any more to the states? "Well who cares if they

---

[33] Anderson to Dillon, Oct. 7, 1843; Davies to Beers, Dec. 6, 1842. Huth Mss.
[34] Governor's message quoting State Treasurer's report, Miss. Senate Journal, 1843, p. 26. See also unsigned memorandum on state debts, Dec. 12, 1839. Baring Mss.
[35] House Doc. No. 111, 26 Cong., 2 Sess., Vol. 4, pp. 257-259.

don't," thundered the *Floridian.* "We are now as a community heels over head in debt and can scarcely pay the interest." [36]

There was no chance for assumption being adopted. The manner in which Congress dealt with Johnson's report showed this. As soon as the report was presented John Quincy Adams introduced a series of resolutions as a substitute for those offered by Johnson. Adams, probably alarmed by the wild threats of the extremists, proposed that any state which violated its faith by repudiating its debts and involved "herself in war with any foreign power" should receive no aid from the United States government in such a conflict and should cease "to be a state of the Union." The Adams' resolutions were defeated and the House tabled the Johnson report. [37] The election of Polk in 1844 destroyed all hope of distributing the land sales as a means of aiding the states. Long before this foreign creditors had realized the futility of inducing the federal government to come to the relief of the states. Their only hope lay in arousing the public consciousness of the American people to the serious effects of repudiation or continued defalcation.

[36] *Floridian,* March 14, 1840.
[37] House Reports, No. 296, 27 Cong., 3 Sess., Vol. 4, p. 559.

CHAPTER III

CHARGE AND COUNTERCHARGE OF DEBTOR AND CREDITOR

A CREDITOR always hopes to recover what is due him; but the collection of a debt depends, in part, upon the ability of the debtor to meet his engagement and also his willingness to acknowledge his obligation. Where the citizens of one country owe those of another, the resources of the debtors and the attitude of the people on the sanctity of contracts determine to a large degree whether the creditors will ever receive their payment. For these reasons the reactions of the American public to the defalcation and repudiation of state debts are significant for they help to explain not only why certain actions were taken by the debtors but also the methods employed by the foreign creditors to safeguard their investments beyond attempting to induce the federal government to assume the state debts.

The first severe shock to American credit came in February, 1840, when Pennsylvania delayed in meeting her semi-annual dividends. Pennsylvania was one of the wealthiest states in the Union and over $20,000,000 of its $34,000,000 of debt was held by British subjects. The stock of Pennsylvania had been considered so sound that many persons of moderate means had invested a large part of their savings in its securities. They were dependent for their support upon the punctual payment of their stock dividends.[1] A feeling of uneasiness regarding all American securities spread through the investing circles of Europe when Pennsylvania announced its inability to meet its payments when they fell due. Although the delinquency was of short duration, foreign creditors grew alarmed. If Pennsylvania found it difficult to pay how could the newer communities in the south and west meet their obligations? The caustic

[1] In 1842 the public debt of Pennsylvania was $34,454,356.47; $23,738,206.00 was held by subjects of foreign countries (*Niles*, July 23, 1842). In 1843 it was estimated that over $21,000,000 was held in Great Britain; two millions in Holland and Germany (Allison to Bates, May 13, 1843, Baring Mss.). The above figures on the distribution of the Pennsylvania debt are based on this data. That Pennsylvania stock was held by persons of small property, cf. Baring to Ward, July 4, 1842. Baring Mss.

London Times reminded Pennsylvania that foreign creditors expected their dividends when they were due and denounced the state legislature for hesitating to impose heavier taxes.[2]

The strong language employed by the British press gave Nicholas Biddle an opportunity to assume the rôle of defender of American integrity. Ignoring the havoc wrought by the failure of the United States Bank, which had helped create the present financial embarrassments of Pennsylvania, the former autocrat of Chestnut Street called upon his fellow citizens at the Tidewater Canal celebration to uphold the plighted faith of the American states. "Whatever shades of distinction we may find among ourselves," declared the financier, "to foreign nations we are essentially one single people. The stain which falls on the youngest member of the Confederacy spreads over the whole. The states are firmly linked, hand in hand with each, and the elective shock which touches one instantly thrills through the whole. The first state then which shall be false to its engagements should be tabooed—stricken from the rolls."[3] These were noble sentiments but they would have been more appropriate if they had been uttered by some one else who had not been so instrumental in creating this unfortunate state of affairs. A month later Biddle wrote to Daniel Webster declaring it was his intention "to defend our people from the arrogance of the Europeans who affect to disparage free institutions by showing how much more faithfully our commonwealths have been than the European monarchies. This I should incline to do," continued the financier, "in a letter to you. If then you will drop me a line stating that you have seen with pleasure the conduct of Pennsylvania, allude to the Tidewater Celebration, and ask how the people" are disposed to new taxes, "I will write an answer which may be published, if you please."[4]

Accordingly, on August 3, 1840, Webster addressed a letter to Biddle as requested. After complimenting the latter for "his manly and just defense" of American credit, Webster referred to his own indignation "at the injustice and arrogance of certain European journals" in slandering "the integrity of the governments of the American states." To Webster it seemed that lurking at the bottom

[2] *London Times,* March 10, May 23, 1840.
[3] *New York American,* June 5, 1840.
[4] Biddle to Webster, July 30, 1840. Biddle Mss.

of these aspersions was "a strong desire to disparage free institutions, by representing them as unworthy of reliance on the part of foreigners and unsteady in the sacred obligations of public faith."

In reply to this inspired letter, Biddle launched forth upon a detailed history of the previous lapses of credit by English, French, and other European governments. The British were reminded that before they started to deliver lectures upon the infidelity of republics, they should not forget that they had been the first and greatest violator of faith to public creditors. "The very foundation of their national debt was an enormous wrong." Had not the government borrowed, partly for the use of the navy, a sum of 1,328,526 pounds sterling at 8 percent; and then stopped for a year and then indefinitely the payments? In vain the creditors had applied to Parliament for redress; and when after a lapse of twelve years the courts had rendered a judgment in their favor, the Chancellor had reversed the decision of the courts. When the House of Lords reversed the decision of the Chancellor, and the creditors hoped at last to receive what was due them, Parliament had intervened by passing an act which said "that they should receive only 3 percent on the principal and that even this principal might be redeemed on the payment of one-half of it." Thus a debt of about $17,000,000 at 8 percent was reduced to $3,000,000 at 3 percent. Well might Hume say of this transaction that it was "a forfeiture of public credit and an open violation of the most solemn engagements, both foreign and domestic." Well might Bishop Burnet call it "a dishonourable and perfidious action." Furthermore, had not the House of Commons in 1811 when the currency of England was greatly depreciated passed an "ever memorable" resolution stating that the notes of the Bank of England should be accepted in all transactions at their par value: and when the notes continued to depreciate until they were at one time at a discount of 41 percent did not the government of England announce that public creditors were to be paid in depreciated paper currency and "in nothing else." By this action the government saved and the fund holders lost not less than 47,000,000 pounds sterling or $137,000,000 which was the difference between the value of the paper currency and specie. France also had defrauded her creditors when she issued assignats as the French historian Thiers acknowledged.

In marked contrast to these actions the conduct of Americans to public creditors should be examined. Had not the whole debt of the United States, "more especially the foreign debt contracted during the Revolutionary War, that incurred during the last war, and that for the purchase of Louisiana and Florida, amounting to about $184,000,000, all been paid, principal and interest, to the last cent; the very 3 percent being paid off at par." Why then did the Americans, in the light of these past omissions of honesty upon the part of Europeans, take to heart all this abuse? The Americans were accused of having a great deal of national vanity. "I wish," wrote Biddle, "they had a little more national pride. It would wean them from their childish sensitiveness to small jests about trifling peculiarities of manner, and raise their thoughts to the great interests in which superiority is worth contending for; it would teach them to estimate the true value of their institutions and dispose them while never wounding other countries always to defend their own. Here, for instance, is a great outcry about American credit, and the danger to public faith from popular governments, both of which are denounced in a strain of financial virtue quite ferocious; and yet after all it appears that these reproaches are made by people who do not pay against the people who do pay; and that those who have been most faithful to their engagements are precisely these abused republicans."

It could not be denied that the United States was financially embarrassed. It was equally true that here as elsewhere there were some who hoped to profit by the public troubles, and "finding the country dispirited, sought to make it dishonest." But these had made no impression upon the great body of the people of the nation. All these embarrassments would soon disappear; but in the meantime "our great purpose should be to preserve and to vindicate the good of the country, as the safest element of its future prosperity."[5]

The reactions in the United States and abroad to the publication of this correspondence were quite different from those which Biddle anticipated. The *London Times* did not fail to point out that Webster and Biddle had both carefully refrained from referring to the United States Bank, "an institution which Mr. Biddle first raised,

[5] The Webster-Biddle correspondence can be found in *Circular to Bankers,* Sept. 18, 1840.

then deserted, and left to flounder on as it could in a state of bankruptcy." To have done so might have been embarrassing to Biddle in his new rôle of champion of American integrity. As the *New York Journal of Commerce* remarked, Americans had no cause to complain if they were treated with less confidence by Europeans. In fact one source of the present distress of the states and of individual American merchants was that Europeans had been too careless in trusting Americans.[6] If Biddle, therefore, hoped to rally American public sentiment to the payment of debts by declaring that republican institutions were on trial; or if he hoped to divert criticism from his own institution and the defaulting states by citing the lapses of other countries, he failed to achieve either purpose. The Webster-Biddle correspondence did not assure Europeans that American credit was sound; nor did it check the spread of repudiation doctrines in the United States. All Biddle had actually accomplished was to furnish the repudiators with historical precedents for defaulting public creditors.

American states could not be excused, however, for the nonpayment of their debts because parallel examples could be found in the actions of other countries. Whig newspapers quickly pointed out that inability to pay was no justification for refusal to pay. If a man was unable to pay all his debts, he should try to pay all he could; no reasonable creditor could ask or expect more; and the same was true of the states. The *New York Journal of Commerce* denounced the repudiation of indebtedness, either by states or by individuals as downright "knavery." A discerning public would not be hoodwinked by flimsy arguments based upon technicalities of the law or constitutional scruples. It was well known that the individual states could not be sued, for they were protected by the Eleventh Amendment to the federal Constitution; but this only made their villainy less excusable. For this very reason "friends of good morals, or good order, and of common honesty" should speak out and act promptly to check dishonest practices. Persons and acts should be called by their appropriate names. If a sovereign state deliberately forfeited its plighted faith and under the cover of specious pleading violated the confidence reposed in it, the public should

---

[6] *London Times* comment and statement of *New York Journal of Commerce* can be found in *London Times*, Sept. 16, 1840.

not call it "repudiation" but "swindling." If a trusted officer abstracted or withheld public funds, he should not be called "by the soft and dulcet name of defaulter, but openly and boldly robber"; and those who had filled "their own pockets with spoil from the vaults of institutions" they had been appointed to guard and protect should be called "plunderers." While those who, in order to avoid payment of a just debt sneakingly availed themselves "of some flaw or some legal technicality" should be denounced as "scoundrels." "Let the world see," demanded the *New York American*, "that there are men who dare assault vice, even though it have the sanction of a 'sovereign state' as a protection." If the reasons given by Governor McNutt of Mississippi for the repudiation of the Union Bank Bonds were admitted in mercantile transactions, every note or other obligation would be under suspicion. The Union Bank commissioners may have exceeded their powers in some particulars but essentially the purpose of the legislature had been fulfilled. The bonds had been sold for the benefit of the Union Bank; and whether it had turned out "to be a bad operation for the state or a good one," had nothing to do with the case. If the State of Mississippi had been wronged either by the Union Bank or its commissioners, or the United States Bank or Nicholas Biddle, her remedy lay in prosecuting the offender or offenders not in injuring the innocent holders of her bonds. Until the Mississippians "can rail the seal from off the bonds" and until they could show cause why the signature of Governor McNutt on the bonds did not bind the state, "they not only offend their own lungs, but the public sense, by mouthing about repudiation," thundered the *New York American*.[7]

The public needed these lectures on the subject of public faith; but they were delivered by the organs of the bankers, many of whom had already forfeited the trust of the people. In many instances the same persons and newspapers who a few years previously had vindicated the banks for suspending specie payments were now clamoring that the states should scrupulously fulfill their obligations.[8] As the *New York Evening Post* remarked "a bank may

---

[7] *New York American*, Nov. 30, Dec. 2, 7, 1841; *New York Journal of Commerce*, Nov. 25, Dec. 22, 1841.
[8] See Biddle's justification for bank suspensions in 1837 in McGrane, R. C., The Panic of 1837, pp. 94-96.

violate its engagements fairly made, and justly binding, and its bad faith 'was trumpeted' as an act of virtue." Let a state decline to fulfill a promise made in its name, "not only without its assent, but contrary to its express injunction," and those who applauded the banks were quick "to decry its conduct as an act of the foulest dishonesty." [9] It is needless to remark that the arguments advanced by the *New York Evening Post* were not sound; but they help to explain why the clarion calls of financial journals for honesty seemed somewhat incongruous to thousands of debtors overwhelmed with their own personal misfortunes. The American people were individually moral and anxious to pay their obligations. As the Barings said: "people will try to be honest when they feel more at ease." [10] But the universal indebtedness had created throughout the country loose morals; and the fact that men in legislative bodies and in corporations would do "what individually they would shrink from with indignation and shame" worked against the adoption of right views.[11]

Even among men of character and purpose Ward found an apathetic and indifferent attitude upon the subject of state debts. This he accounted for, in part, because many had not reflected upon the matter and partly from the fallacy that it was a state "and not an *individual* concern." [12] It is true that many of the state legislatures passed resolutions loudly proclaiming their intention of upholding state honor; but having done so, the legislators rested contented. "It would be more fortunate," cynically reminded the state auditor of Indiana, "for the reputation of the state as well as gratifying to the creditors should this evidence consist hereafter of some definite action rather than general expressions of legislative opinions." [13] The legislators realized, however, that everywhere there was sullen resentment against taxation and determination upon the part of the masses to hold the banks responsible for their difficulties. Few had the moral courage or political honesty to urge the maintenance of state credit by imposing heavier burdens upon their

[9] *New York Evening Post*, Nov. 29, 1841.
[10] Ward to Baring, May 14, 15, 1843. Baring Mss.
[11] Ward to Baring, Apr. 8, 1841. Baring Mss.
[12] Ward to Carey, March 21, 1844. Cf. also unsigned memorandum on state debts, Dec. 12, 1839, Baring Mss.
[13] Esarey, L., Internal Improvements in Early Indiana, Indiana Historical Society Publications, Vol. *V*, p. 132.

constituents even when the resources of the communities permitted such drastic measures. Let the bondholders look to the United States Bank and to the other banks for their payment declared the people. Why should the poor be taxed to support the opulent classes in foreign lands who, it was believed, held the bulk of these securities. On the other hand, the banks were unable to meet their obligations due to the insolvency of their debtors; while state repudiation freed the stockholders of their liabilities.[14]

European capitalists and holders of American securities watched with interest the reactions of the American public to the payment of the state debts. Reports upon the banking situation in the United States and the measures proposed in the various state legislatures to meet these obligations were published in lengthy articles in the London press. The Barings instructed their agents to collect and send to them the messages of the governors of the different states. "We wish you so to act" in Maryland and Pennsylvania, wrote the Barings to Ward, that when these states "cease to pay their dividends, which you seem fully to expect, we may be able to answer the question, what efforts our agent has made to prevent such a calamity, we may reply that he has done everything in his power." For this reason the Barings desired Ward to use "all gentle means" to get the people in power in these states to adopt the right course. He was told to go to Baltimore to see what could be done about the Maryland debt; and to get in touch with Governor Porter of Pennsylvania.[15] No time must be lost in inducing these and other states to meet their interest charges. English holders of American securities did not want their invested capital returned to them; but they did want to be certain of their dividends.[16] The Barings and other European banking houses were well aware that their clients would hold them in part responsible for any losses they might incur. The investors had purchased these securities upon the advice of their bankers; and if any of the states failed to meet their engagements, the bankers knew their own reputations would suffer.

This touched the pride of old-established houses such as the Barings. They had relied upon the integrity of the American states

[14] Pike to Huth, Nov. 28, 1843, Huth Mss. Cf. also chapter on Mississippi debt.
[15] Prime, Ward and King to Baring, March 9, 1840; Baring to Ward, Oct. 16, Nov. 18, 27, 1841; Ward to Baring, Dec. 8, 1841. Baring Mss.
[16] Baring to Ward, Nov. 27, 1841. Baring Mss.

and their future development to meet the loans when they fell due. The Barings had recommended American state stocks and bonds as safe and profitable investments to their customers who had taken their recommendation as turning the thing recommended into gold. Should the states suspend payments on these loans, their customers would naturally recollect that the Barings had recommended these investments. The Barings would willingly have sacrificed their own pecuniary interest, if in doing so, they could have relieved the distress of any of their customers. The high standing which the firm enjoyed in the investing circles of England was justly deserved for the partners in that house could truthfully say they had made it their "invariable practice" not to offer any stock to the public which they themselves did not deem good.[17] But, like the over-enthusiastic agents of the American states who painted rosy pictures of the future development of their states' resources, the Barings had counted too much upon the rapid uninterrupted development of the United States. Therefore, if the citizens of the American states were to blame, in part, for their financial difficulties, the English capitalists were also partly responsible for the collapse of American credit. The latter had poured their superfluous wealth into the United States with a freedom and a generosity that had led to improvident schemes of improvement which had ended in profligacy and ruin. The Barings could not explain away their own mistakes in judgment by claiming, as they did at times in their letters to their correspondents, that the buyers had had the same means of judging of these loans as they had.[18]

The fears of the European capitalists that their clients would hold them in part responsible for their losses soon became apparent. Articles began to appear in the London press sharply criticizing the old banking firms for ever sponsoring the flotation of these loans in England. One correspondent of the *London Times,* evidently the holder of some American securities, wrote to that paper suggesting the expediency of some inquiry into the manner in which American state bonds and other securities of the United States had first ob-

---

[17] This statement is based upon a careful examination of the Baring Mss. There is an illuminating letter of Latrobe to Ward, Jan. 29, 1849, in the Baring Mss. on why the Barings wanted the Maryland debt settled which stresses these points. See also Baring to Ward, Nov. 27, 1841.

[18] Baring to Ward, Nov. 27, 1841; *Morning Chronicle,* Aug. 27, 1842.

tained circulation in London; "into the conduct of the mercantile or banking firms who first introduced them, more especially as regards the preliminary investigation by which they satisfied themselves of the resources and the means of credit of the borrowing states"; and "above all into the rate of commission paid to them for giving currency and lending their names to such securities."

The *London Times* confessed that there might be much difficulty in following out these lines of inquiry but the propriety of such an investigation was heartily approved of. Was it not customary for merchants to correspond one with another respecting the credit of prospective purchasers; and if the references given did not turn out as expected, did not some taint attach to the parties who had given misleading information? Certainly the same principle ought to hold good in the case of those who had recommended American state securities to their customers. Of course, in both cases there might have been instances of innocent deception; but the parties involved, if called upon, ought certainly to be willing to explain in what manner they themselves had been deceived. The bankers ought to welcome the suggestion of a rigid inquiry into the way in which American stocks and bonds had reached the London money market. Furthermore, it was certainly desirable that English banking houses that had handled these loans should take a prominent part in protecting the rights of the creditors. It was generally believed by the public that the contractors, almost uniformly had derived great advantages from these transactions; frequently they were the only persons who ever did; and yet in times of danger when it was necessary for the creditors to fight for their rights, the contractors usually kept aloof instead of occupying a prominent position which their character and standing as capitalists enabled them with great benefit to do. If bankers would only feel their moral obligations to their clients, contracts might not be entered into so loosely as they often were and when broken the unfortunate victims would enjoy much better protection.

An appeal was actually drafted by holders of American state stocks to the bankers and capitalists and press of London. Pointing out that many who held these securities had been reduced from affluence to indigence "by the dishonesty and bad faith of the American people," the creditors demanded that "any loan for the federal government of America collectively, or for any state government individually" should be discouraged and prevented as far as was dependent on English bankers and capitalists. Furthermore, the British Parliament was urged to pass a law that would render "contractors of a loan for a foreign state *legally* responsible in their persons and fortunes" as they were *"morally* for the due and regular payment of the interest and the ultimate disbursement of the capital." [19]

Thus a disillusionized public in England, as well as in America, turned against the bankers who had handled the American loans. The *London Times* went so far as to declare that the eminent firms in London who had introduced these securities into the London money market had proved alike a "curse" to America and to England. They had induced the poorer states to "go-ahead" in their mad career of supposed interminable prosperity which had resulted in throwing "them back half a century in the natural progress they would otherwise have made." At the same time the English bankers had tempted the small capitalist to invest his savings in these holdings because they carried a higher rate of interest, thereby destroying the comforts of innumerable families; while by building upon an excited state of trade between England and the United States upon these worthless securities, the reaction which followed the collapse of American credit had deranged the manufacturing life of England.[20]

In order to retain, if possible, the good will of some of their customers, the banking houses of Europe realized that they must do something to protect their clients' interests. Memorials were drafted by these firms setting forth the claims of the creditors and sent to the various state governments. An unsuccessful attempt was made by the Rothschilds to induce the British government to present the case of the Mississippi bondholders through official channels.[21] Letters were addressed by the Rothschilds, Joshua Bates, the Yankee member of the Barings, and Hope and Company of Amster-

---

[19] *London Times*, Apr. 14, Oct. 20, 1842; Appeal on behalf of the holders of American State Stocks to the Bankers and Capitalists and to the Press of London, Dec. 26, 1842, Newspaper clipping in Baring Mss. The *London Times*, Apr. 14, 1842, insinuated that the commissions of the bankers were from 5 to 10%. This was inaccurate.

[20] *London Times*, Nov. 18, 1842.

[21] See chapter on Mississippi debt.

dam, to President Tyler and Webster, the Secretary of State, calling the attention of the Federal government to the nonpayment by some of the states of their debts.[22] European financiers refused to touch a loan of the federal government and encouragement was given to the movement for the assumption of the state debts.[23] Rumors of the proposed organization of the holders of foreign securities into a foreign loan association for the purpose of collecting information respecting the resources of the indebted American states and to enable the bondholders to coöperate with the state governments in working out plans for the restoration of their credit appeared at times in the London newspapers;[24] but no such association of the foreign bondholders was formed, although a number of the banking houses did get together, as we shall see, in 1843 for other reasons.

A memorial was addressed to the United States Minister in England, Edward Everett, by the principal holders of American securities in which the suffering caused both by the states which professedly repudiated and those which simply abstained from paying was earnestly set forth. "In becoming holders of the public securities of your states," declared the petitioners, "we trusted—as the whole of the past history of your country and the universal opinion of mankind then seemed to warrant us in doing—to the untarnished honor of the people of America. . . . We hold that to whatever extent a contract is binding on an individual, to the same extent it is binding on a sovereign state; . . . we can never admit the doctrine . . . that a state which had once pledged its faith, and its resources is at liberty, on the mere plea, that its engagements are irksome and inconvenient, or even oppressive, to relieve itself from them by making a sacrifice of its creditors. In such a proceeding we can see —and at one time, we are sure your countrymen would have seen— nothing but a crying injustice; might trampling on right; public faith reduced to a mockery; and the most solemn obligations treated as so much wastepaper. . . . We protest, too, earnestly against the doctrine that the innocent holders of the genuine public securities of a country can be justly made to suffer for the fraud or negligence

[22] *New York Herald,* July 14, 1841.
[23] See chapter II.
[24] *London Times,* Oct. 15, 1842, Jan. 12, 1843.

of the officers, whom the government, in its uncontrolled discretion, may have employed in the transaction of its business; a doctrine, we must add, so utterly at variance with the simplest elements of jurisprudence that . . . we are quite sure . . . no court of justice in your country would tolerate it for a moment, in any private suit between man and man." Particular care was also taken by the creditors in their petition to remove the erroneous impression that the bondholders "in great measure" were "men of large fortunes to whom a failure in their securities" could "occasion but little inconvenience. Even if such were the case, it would . . . furnish no grounds for any departure from the ordinary obligations of good faith. In fact, however, though there may be a few amongst us in more affluent circumstances," stated the petitioners, "yet by far the larger portion of us are persons in the middle ranks of life—officers on half-pay, superannuated clerks, retired tradesmen living on small means, aged spinsters, widows, and orphans, many of whom have invested their all in the purchases of your securities, at high prices, and now depend for their subsistence, some even for their daily bread, on the good faith of your people." [25]

At the same time this memorial was presented to Everett with a request that it be forwarded to the President of the United States and laid before both houses of Congress and the governors of the various states, a similar petition was sent to Lord Aberdeen, the British Foreign Secretary. His Lordship was asked to lay this statement before President Tyler through the medium of His Majesty's Minister; and Lord Aberdeen was further requested to intimate to the bondholders whether he would lend his support to a petition of the bondholders to both houses of Congress at the ensuing session. [26]

The replies to these memorials were not encouraging. Lord Aberdeen declared that since the bonds were those of the separate states and not those of the federal government, the government of Great Britain had "no concern with the securities in question and no power to compel payment of the sums required; therefore, . . . any good offices which His Majesty's Government might be disposed to em-

[25] *Ibid.*, Feb. 28, 1843.
[26] Memorial to Lord Aberdeen on American Securities, Feb. 27, 1843. F. O. 5, 399, Public Record Office.

ploy with that of the United States . . . would, under the circumstances, be ineffectual." [27]

The courteous refusal of the British government to act in behalf of the bondholders was in marked contrast to the stinging rebuke administered the creditors by the *London Spectator*. Referring to the advisibility of Great Britain employing vigorous measures against the debtors, the *London Spectator* reminded the holders of American securities that when they "parted with their money they were satisfied with a mere promise to pay of the respective governments to whom it was lent. They acted upon their own estimate of the value of such promises, and, if that estimate was erroneous, they must abide by the consequent loss, as they would contentedly have taken the profit if it had turned out to be correct." For the British government "to assume the task of collecting the debts due to its subjects" it should have been asked before those debts had been contracted. "Had it been consulted as to the propriety of staking the peace of the world upon the good faith of the state of Arkansas or the territory of Florida," it was "probable that some of the present claims would never have existed. Money-lenders would find little difficulty in disposing of their capital, and little need for circumspection, if they could recklessly part with it to foreign states under the assurance that Great Britain" would "at all times step in to enforce the punctual payment of their dividends." [28]

The foreign bondholders were treated with more consideration by Everett than they had been by their own government or their own press. In his reply Everett pointed out "that in as much as the general government" was "not a party to the contracts of the separate states," the subject of the memorial did "not fall directly within the President's province." Nevertheless, Everett agreed, acting in his unofficial capacity, to forward the petition to the President. He concurred with the bondholders in protesting against the doctrine that a state "which had pledged its faith and resources" could "release itself from the obligation, however burdensome, in any way but that of honorable payment"; and he expressed the belief that those states which unhappily had failed to make provision for the interest due on their bonds had done so because "of the

[27] Reply of Lord Aberdeen to memorial on American securities, March 6, 1843. F. O. 5, 399, Public Record Office.
[28] *London Spectator* quoted in *Niles*, March 4, 1843.

pressure of adverse circumstances and not with the purpose of giving legislative action to a doctrine so pernicious, unworthy, and immoral." [29]

The assurances and the support given the bondholders' cause by Everett may have been some consolation to them; but what puzzled the British were the views set forth by President Tyler that the defalcation of some of the states ought not to injure the credit of those who punctually met their obligations. To English bondholders this line of reasoning was totally foreign to their way of thinking. They could not understand why a citizen of New York did not consider it a reflection upon his state if some other state in the Union defaulted or repudiated its debts. The lack of a national consciousness upon the part of the American public of such a disgrace was beyond the comprehension of the British. [30]

The American public soon became aware, however, that no explanations on their part could remove the moral blemish cast upon all the states by the delinquencies of some. They could not convince the foreign creditors that the states were legally unconnected as debtors one with another and with the federal government. President Tyler was soon cognizant of this when the federal government encountered difficulties in floating a loan abroad. [31] Not only did the credit of the federal and state governments suffer but private American citizens traveling in Europe likewise found themselves exposed to humiliating indignities. The *London Times* declared "an American gentleman of the most unblemished character was refused admission to one of the largest clubs in London on the sole grounds that he belonged to a republic that did not fulfil its engagements." In all probability the example set by this club would be followed by others. No distinction would be made as to the state to which an individual might belong for in the eyes of Europeans the whole of the United States was looked upon as equally tarnished. [32] Instead of American citizenship being a passport of individual honor and honesty, it marked the holder for suspicion and one to be avoided.

No matter how much Americans protested and tried to explain

---

[29] *London Times*, Apr. 3, 1843.
[30] *London Times*, Dec. 31, 1841, Dec. 2, 1842; Baring to Ward, Jan. 1, 1842. Baring Mss.
[31] *London Times*, Apr. 22, 1842.   [32] *London Times*, Oct. 31, 1844.

the federal character of their government, they were regarded as a "nation of swindlers." Foreigners did not or would not distinguish between the individual states in the Union. Perhaps, they should not have done so. The Americans were always boasting "of being many in one"; and Englishmen could not forget how the whole nation had rallied to the defense of the State of Maine in sustaining her claims to soil in which the other states had no direct interest. If the other American states were willing to stand by Maine even to the extent of going to war, why, asked the irate creditors, did some of them seek to separate themselves from Mississippi in her dishonor? The holders of American securities did not expect all the states to pay their debts immediately. They knew this was impossible. They would have been satisfied if such of the states as were in default would say in plain language "we cannot pay now" but "we will do so when we are able" and would "accompany this declaration by the adoption of some system for the ultimate redemption of their bonds." In order to remove the obloquy which was attached to all Americans, a citizen of New Orleans, traveling in Europe, suggested to his fellow countrymen that a convention composed of the business men residing in the indebted states be held where a thorough investigation should be made of the debts and the resources of the various states in order to find the best means of restoring their credit.[33]

The insults to which American travelers were subjected were a source of mortification to all Americans; but it was feared by some that even these irritating incidents were not the only results which would follow the nonpayment of the state debts. Suppose some of the European countries should resort to retaliation, even to war, to protect their citizens' interests? The American people did not know the attitude of Lord Palmerston and Lord Aberdeen on the debt question although they welcomed the statements of the *London Spectator* in opposing the employment of force to collect the amounts due the foreign bondholders. Americans were reminded, however, by the *Boston Atlas* of the refusal of Great Britain to give up certain forts on the northern frontier at the close of the American Revolution because of the nonpayment of debts due

---

[33] *Niles,* Jan. 14, 1843. See also *Circular to Bankers,* March 31, 1843, for a somewhat similar suggestion originating in England.

to British subjects. Had not President Jackson threatened war with Mexico because that government had refused to indemnify American claimants? Had not President Jackson also recommended reprisals on French property because of claims held by American citizens against the French government? Who could say some of the European countries would not likewise resort to similar measures to protect their nationals' rights?[34] Even if repudiation did not involve the United States in international complications, it would certainly have a most injurious influence upon the domestic affairs of America. The nonpayment of the state debts would engender a laxity of morals and a general disregard of private as well as public obligations. The American character might survive the gibes of princes and the subjects of princes but it would not outlive the leprosy that would spread over the whole body politic unless resisted by some active and efficient remedies.[35] Already the states were encountering great difficulty in collecting their taxes and debtors were being protected by stay laws. Private as well as public faith was being undermined.

The serious consequences which might result from the nonpayment of the state debts led to a few feeble efforts in the United States to check the spread of repudiation. Numerous state legislatures passed pious resolutions denouncing the doctrine of repudiation as "unconstitutional, immoral, and subversive of the fundamental principles" of republicanism.[36] General Hamilton addressed an open letter to Calhoun pointing out the failure and ruin of American financial credit in Europe which had followed the indisposition upon the part of some of the states to pay their debts.[37] Clay declared Mississippi's repudiation of her debts had placed "a foul stain upon American character" which it would take years to efface.[38] Webster upbraided his countrymen for their breaches of

---

[34] *Boston Atlas* quoted in *Indiana Journal*, Apr. 27, 1842.

[35] *Niles*, Jan. 14, 1843.

[36] Some of the states that passed resolutions were Vermont, Pennsylvania, Kentucky, Ohio, Louisiana, New York, Illinois, and Indiana. Copies of these resolutions can be found in Vermont Senate Journal, 1842, App., p. 97; Pennsylvania Senate Journal, 1842, Vol. I, pp. 85, 86; Mississippi Senate Journal, 1842, p. 213; *National Intelligencer*, Jan. 14, Feb. 24, 1842; *London Times*, Jan. 18, 19, Feb. 8, March 22, 1842; *Arkansas Shield*, March 26, 1842; *Niles*, Jan. 21, 1843; Kendall Expositor, Vol. 3, Jan. 24, 1843.

[37] *Baltimore American*, Oct. 5, 1842, quoted in full in Fox to Aberdeen, Oct. 13, 1842. F. O. 5,377, despatch 29, Public Record Office.

[38] *Circular to Bankers*, Aug. 5, 1842.

faith;[39] while Biddle suggested that foreign holders of American securities assign their holdings to the sovereigns of their countries and let these sovereigns commence a prosecution of the defaulting states in the federal courts.[40]

No amount of persuasion or threats by any American, however, aroused such intense excitement in the United States as did the pungent and pithy letters written in 1843 by the Reverend Sydney Smith upon the pecuniary delinquency of Pennsylvania. In language that never will be forgotten for its sarcasm and witticism, the caustic former editor of the *Edinburgh Review* poured forth his feelings in words that revealed his pocket and his heart were beating in unison. In his Humble Petition to the House of Congress at Washington, the anger and disillusionment of innumerable holders of American securities were portrayed:

> ... Your petitioner lent to the State of Pennsylvania a sum of money, for the purpose of some public improvements. The amount, though small, is to him important, and is a saving from a life income, made with difficulty and privation. If their refusal to pay (from which a very large number of English families are suffering) had been the result of war, produced by the unjust aggression of powerful enemies; if it had arisen from civil discord; if it had proceeded from an improvident application of means in the first years of self-government; if it were the act of a poor State struggling against the barrenness of nature—every friend of America would have been contented to wait for better times; but the fraud is committed in profound peace, by Pennsylvania, the richest state in the Union, after the wise investment of the borrowed money in roads and canals, of which the repudiators are every day reaping the advantage. It is an act of bad faith which (all its circumstances considered) has no parallel, and no excuse.
>
> Nor is it only the loss of property which your petitioner laments; he laments still more that immense power which the bad faith of America has given to aristocratical opinions, and to the enemies of free institutions in the old world. It is in vain any longer to appeal to history, and to point out the wrong which many have received from the few. The Americans who boast to have improved the institutions of the old world have at least equalled its crimes. A great nation, after a tramping under foot all earthly tyranny, has been guilty of a fraud as enormous as ever disgraced the worst king of the most degraded nation of Europe.

[39] *Annual Register,* 1843, pp. 323-325; *Circular to Bankers,* Oct. 21, 1842; *London Times,* Oct. 17, 19, 1842.
[40] *Niles,* Aug. 12, Sept. 23, 1843; *London Times,* Sept. 18, 1843.

. . . Little did the friends of America expect it, and sad is the spectacle, to see you rejected by every State in Europe, as a nation with whom no contract can be made, because none will be kept; unstable in the very foundations of the social life, deficient in the elements of good faith, men who prefer any load of infamy, however great, to any pressure of taxation, however light.[41]

In a letter to the *London Morning Chronicle* the Reverend Sydney Smith explained the motives which prompted him to undertake the task of rebuking the Americans for not paying their debts:

. . . No conduct was ever more profligate than that of the State of Pennsylvania. History cannot pattern it: and let no deluded being imagine that they will ever repay a single farthing—their people have tasted the dangerous luxury of dishonesty, and they will never be brought back to the homely rule of right. The moneyed transactions of the Americans are become a by-word among the nations of Europe. In every grammar school of the world *ad Graecas calendas* is translated—the American dividends.

I am no enemy to America. I loved and admired honest America when she respected the laws of pounds, shillings, and pence; and I thought the United States the most magnificent picture of human happiness. I meddle now in these matters because I hate fraud—because I pity the misery it has occasioned—because I mourn over the hatred it has excited against free institutions. [Then the Dean of St. Paul's indulged in a piece of exquisite bitterness.] . . . I never meet a Pennsylvanian at a London dinner without feeling a disposition to seize and divide him; to allot his beaver to one sufferer and his coat to another; to appropriate his pocket handkerchief to the orphan and to comfort the widow with his silver watch, Broadway rings and the London guide which he always carries in his pocket. How such a man can set himself down at an English table without feeling that he owes two or three pounds to every man in the company, I am at a loss to concede; he has no more right to eat with honest men than a leper has to eat with clean men. . . .

Figure to yourself a Pennsylvanian receiving foreigners in his own country, walking over the public works with them, and showing them Larcenous Lake, Swindling Swamp, Crafty Canal, and Rogues Railway, and other dishonest works. This swamp we gained (says the patriotic borrower) by the repudiated loans of 1828. Our canal robbery was in 1830; we pocketed your good people's money for the railroad only last year. All this may seem very smart to the Americans; but if I had the misfortune to be born among such a people, the land of my fathers should not retain me a single moment after the act of repudiation. I would

[41] The petition can be found in *London Times*, May 19, 1843.

appeal from my fathers to my forefathers. I would fly to Newgate for greater purity of thought, and seek in the prisons of England for better rules of life.

The conclusion of this clever letter had a twofold aspect which might be made to cut both ways.

And now, drab-coloured men of Pennsylvania, there is yet a moment left: the eyes of all Europe are anchored upon you. . . . Start up from that trance of dishonesty into which you are plunged: don't think of the flesh which walls about your life, but of that sin which has hurled you from the heaven of character, which hangs over you like a devouring pestilence, and makes good men sad, and ruffians dance and sing. It is not by Gin Sling alone and Sherry Cobbler that man is to live; but for those great principles against which no argument can be listened to—principles which give to every power a double power above their functions and their offices, which are the books, the arts, the academies that teach, lift up, and nourish the world—principles (I am quite serious in what I say) above cash, superior to cotton, higher than currency—principles, without which it is better to die than to live, which every servant of God, over every sea and in all lands, should cherish. . . . [42]

The witty, sharp, insulting letters of the Reverend Sydney Smith created a hubbub on both sides of the Atlantic. It is true they set everybody into fits of laughter except American creditors and American citizens. They excited no little discussion of the whole topic of the state debts as their author intended they should. But whatever good might have accrued from such a discussion was marred by the unwarranted coarse language of a host of poor British imitators who poured forth their unmeasured and indiscriminate abuse upon the whole American name.[43] Certain portions of the American press burst forth in indignation at what they termed the meddling interference of the reverend gentleman in American affairs. The *Boston Courier* characterized his petition as a piece of "impudence, bombast, and impertinence." The *New York Evening Post* stigmatized it as the ravings of one who had been disappointed in reaping that "profit from his speculations which he expected

---

[42] Quoted in *London Times*, Nov. 4, 1843. Cf. *London Times*, Nov. 11, 16, 1843, for Duff Green's reply to Sydney Smith. For other comments on these letters, consult A Memoir of the Reverend Sydney Smith by his daughter Lady Holland, 2 Vols., London, 1855; Reid, S. J., A Sketch of the Life and Times of the Reverend Sydney Smith (London, 1884); and a review of Lady Holland's book in *Edinburgh Review*, Vol. 102, pp. 236-274.

[43] *Morning Chronicle*, Nov. 15, 1843.

and desired." The *United States Gazette* referred to "that Xantippe, in small clothes, the Reverend Sydney Smith." He was upbraided for departing from the meek and lowly spirit of his Christian profession and twitted about the personal loss which it was known he had suffered.[44] A few Americans vainly cautioned their fellow citizens not to indulge in extravagant language in replying to his letters. They reminded their countrymen that he asked only to be paid that which he was justly entitled to. No doubt he had used strong phrases—stronger than was respectful—but after all in the bitterness of his words lay the truth.[45]

Thus debtor and creditor hurled charge and countercharge at each other in a fog of bewildering misunderstanding. Each strove to justify his position by citing extenuating circumstances; but both agreed, though in obviously different ways and for different reasons, that the doctrine of repudiation was odious in the eyes of the civilized world.

[44] *Boston Courier* and *New York Evening Post* quoted in *London Times,* Aug. 8, 1843; *United States Gazette* quoted in *Niles,* Dec. 2, 1843; *London Times,* Dec. 14, 1843.

[45] A defense of Smith's letter can be found in the *Boston Daily Advertiser and Patriot* quoted in *London Times,* Aug. 8, 1843.

CHAPTER IV

THE KEYSTONE STATE DEFAULTS AND RESUMES

A DETAILED account of the debts of various American states before the Civil War can well begin with a recital of the financial difficulties of Pennsylvania in the 'forties. There are many reasons for selecting Pennsylvania from the list of insolvent states for particular consideration. Pennsylvania was the last of the states to suspend payment upon her obligations and the first to correct the evils that flowed from an unsound credit system. The origin of the Pennsylvania state debt and the efforts made by her citizens to rehabilitate the state credit throw much light upon the manner in which even conservative communities were induced to indulge in unwise financial practices in the boom period of the 'thirties and the obstacles which had to be surmounted in restoring the credit of the state. Furthermore, the magnitude of the Pennsylvania debt, the large amount of the state stock held by foreigners, and the financial prominence of the state caused foreign creditors to regard the delinquency of Pennsylvania as unpardonable. To what extent the citizens of Pennsylvania deserved this harsh abuse is made clear by reciting the causes of Pennsylvania's financial embarrassments and the way in which the state ultimately resumed payment upon its stock.

Pennsylvania was brought to the verge of bankruptcy because the state planned unwisely to construct an extensive system of public works, unsound financial legislation was enacted, and the public had an aversion to taxation. The desire upon the part of the eastern seaboard states at the close of the War of 1812 to capture the lucrative trade of the rapidly developing west inaugurated a mania for internal improvements. In 1803 Ohio was admitted to the Union, Indiana in 1816, and Illinois in 1818. As the center of population was steadily pushed westward, more acres of fertile soil were placed under cultivation, and an ever-increasing stream of agricultural products moved from these newer communities towards eastern and European markets. The commercial cities along the Atlantic coast awakened to the importance of securing control of this western trade; and since the federal government was willing to give only occasional support towards improving communication between the east and the west, state legislatures were urged to undertake the task. In response to public pressure, New York State projected in 1817 a canal to connect the waters of the Great Lakes with the Hudson River. The success of the Erie Canal aroused the fears of merchants of Philadelphia and Baltimore as they witnessed their hated rival outdistancing them in the race for economic supremacy. Self-preservation as well as local pride stimulated a demand among the citizens of Pennsylvania and Maryland for better transportation facilities.

The Pennsylvania legislature soon felt the pressure of the public clamor for internal improvements. In 1824 a Society for the Promotion of Internal Improvements was organized in Philadelphia for the purpose of agitating the urgent need of improving transportation. The efforts of this society were largely responsible for the legislature in 1826 authorizing the construction of a canal and horse-power railway by way of Pittsburgh and Johnstown to Philadelphia. The state should have directed all its energies towards the completion of this work; but local interests and sectional jealousies made this impossible. Representatives of remote counties refused to vote funds for this enterprise unless the desires of their constituencies were gratified by similar works. To conciliate these interests the state undertook the onerous task of constructing supplementary lines of public works in addition to the Pennsylvania canal. By 1834 all the lines of canal and railway authorized by law had been completed and were open to traffic; but the works had been conceived without judgment and had been executed without skill. They had been laid out "less with a view to their ultimate success than to benefit private lands. The contracts were political jobs, shamefully performed" at great expense to the state.[1]

Not only were the state works unwisely planned but no adequate

[1] Pennsylvania House Journal, 1840, Vol. 2, Pt. 2, pp. 254, 255; Hunt's Merchants' Magazine, Vol. 20, pp. 256-269; Bishop, A. L., The State Works of Pennsylvania, Transactions of the Connecticut Academy of Arts and Sciences, Vol. 13, pp. 167-205.

provision was made for financing their completion. The funds which were placed at the disposal of the canal commissioners as early as 1830 were found insufficient to meet the interest on the state loans. The governor strongly advised the adoption of a system of taxation in order to provide the necessary amounts to meet the interest charges; but the taxes which the legislature passed were designed more to raise the credit of the state than to furnish the required revenue.[2]

Notwithstanding the unwillingness of the legislature to resort to taxation in order to pay for the public works, all the state loans floated to 1834 bore a substantial premium. Governor Wolf pointed out in his annual message of 1835-1836 that the state had expended since 1826 over $22,000,000 in the construction of canals and railroads; and that the whole of this amount had been borrowed at 5 percent and had yielded to the treasury, in premiums, a sum in excess of $1,000,000. This was due to the confidence which money-lenders had in the determination of the people of Pennsylvania to preserve the credit of the state and to the abundance of money both at home and in Europe for investment.[3]

Unfortunately two events occurred in 1836 which gave an added impetus to the spirit of speculation then sweeping over the country. These were the distribution of the surplus revenue and the rechartering by Pennsylvania of the United States Bank. By these two transactions between five and six million dollars were thrown into the public treasury. By the act incorporating the United States Bank as a state institution, the state tax on real and personal property was repealed, while the United States Bank "obligated itself to pay as a bonus for its charter, $4,500,000; to purchase Pennsylvania stocks, at a high rate, to the amount of $6,000,000; to loan the state, at 4 percent interest, for a period not exceeding one year, $1,000,000; and to subscribe to railroad and turnpike stocks,

[2] Bishop, State Works of Pennsylvania, pp. 205-212.

[3] Pennsylvania House Journal, 1840, Vol. 2, Pt. 2, pp. 254, 255; Bishop, State Works of Pennsylvania, p. 212. "By 1835 the state had borrowed and expended for public improvements the sum of $19,332,967.64. Up to this year the tolls taken on the various branches amounted to $1,261,730.28, an average of $210,288.38 per annum; a very inadequate return for the money invested, as is evident. Nevertheless it was thought that in fifteen or twenty years the revenue from the public works would pay off the entire debt contracted for their construction and afford a fund for the support of government and the public schools." Worthington, T. K., Historical Sketch of the Finances of Pennsylvania, Publications of the American Economic Association, Vol. 2, p. 26.

$675,000. . . . The burdens thus imposed upon the bank were equal in the aggregate to at least $6,000,000 in cash." [4]

Henceforth the credit of the state was intimately associated with the financial fortunes of the United States Bank of Pennsylvania. The bank was made the depository of the state funds, the agent of the state in disposing of its stocks, and the medium through which the semi-annual interest payments were made. As the state pushed forward its scheme of internal improvements, the drain upon the resources of the bank increased. Soon after the United States Bank of Pennsylvania undertook to make these heavy payments, a stringency occurred in the money markets of England and the United States. This was followed by the suspension of specie payments by all the banks of this country. The failure of the United States Bank of Pennsylvania forced the state to postpone the interest due on its stock in August until December 1837. This frightened foreign creditors who held a large portion of the state stocks and the credit of the state was lowered. It was customary for the foreign stockholders to receive their remittances in the form of bills of exchange transmitted by the United States Bank of Pennsylvania to Baring Brothers and Company of London who credited these sums to their accounts; but the general derangement of the currency made it impossible to obtain satisfactory bills of exchange.

Meanwhile the progress of the Pennsylvania public works was marked by a steady decline of the credit of the state. In 1838 the state treasurer pointed out in his report that there would be a deficit in the treasury of over $3,000,000 by the end of the following year; and he recommended the adoption of an adequate system of taxation to carry out the internal improvement plan. Governor Ritner, however, did not endorse the proposal in his annual message; and the legislature decided to borrow more money.[5] European capitalists were assured by their American correspondents that the wealth and resources of the commonwealth were amply sufficient to secure the new loans. It was also expected that the revenues from the public works would soon restore entire confidence in the state stocks. As no bids, however, were received for the new loans, the United

---

[4] Hunt's Merchants' Magazine, Vol. 20, pp. 256-269; Pennsylvania House Journal, 1840, Vol. 2, Pt. 2, pp. 254, 255. An account of the rechartering of the United States Bank can be found in McGrane, R. C., The Panic of 1837, Ch. 3.

[5] Bishop, State Works of Pennsylvania, pp. 215-217.

States Bank of Pennsylvania by its charter was compelled to take them.[6]

At the same time the bank was pursuing a policy which was to wreck the credit both of the state and that institution. The United States Bank of Pennsylvania had entered the cotton market and was loaning its notes to American planters and cotton factors in order to enable them to hold their crops for a rise in prices. This cotton was shipped to the agency of the bank in England; and upon these cotton shipments and the stocks of Pennsylvania and other American states, the United States Bank of Pennsylvania obtained credits abroad. But in 1839 the bank found it impossible to dispose of the 5 percent stock of Pennsylvania which had sold in 1833 at 115.[7] At the same time the bank had a surplus of cotton on hand which it could not market. The failure of the crops in England in 1838 necessitated a drain of $40,000,000 from the vaults of the Bank of England to purchase grain from neighboring countries. Rumors of revolutionary movements in France, together with rumblings of the Chartists in England and unsettled political conditions on the Continent contributed to the general unsettling of European money markets. Unable to sell its surplus cotton in a declining market and without ready funds to meet its pressing obligations, the United States Bank of Pennsylvania on October 10, 1839, was forced a second time to close its doors. The failure of the bank left the State of Pennsylvania practically without resources owing to the repeal of the tax laws.[8]

In his message of 1840 Governor Porter explained the financial embarrassment of the state. The indebtedness of the state amounted to the enormous sum of $34,141,663.80. The ordinary expenditures of the commonwealth during the past year had exceeded the revenue obtained from all sources to the amount of $1,087,743.63. With such a deficit in the treasury, and with the large sums owing by the state, Pennsylvania was on the verge of bankruptcy. The people were reminded that the public debt had been lawfully contracted and that the faith and honor of the state was pledged for the payment of the interest annually accruing and for the final payment of the principal. But for many years they had deceived themselves

---

[6] Prime, Ward and King to Baring, Jan. 2, 15, 1839. Baring Mss.
[7] Hunt's Merchants' Magazine, Vol. 20, pp. 256-269.
[8] McGrane, R. C., The Panic of 1837, pp. 205-207.

into believing the internal improvements would in the near future not only pay the interest on the whole state debt but yield in addition a surplus which could be applied to the extinguishment of the principal.

Governor Porter was the first man in public office to reveal to the citizens that the public works had not been so productive as had been anticipated. Hitherto it had been customary to state the gross amount of tolls derived from the canals and railroads in such a manner as to convey the impression that they yielded this sum clear of all expenses. The constantly yearly increase of tolls had acted as a powerful stimulant to prosecute and extend the system. But it was the net revenue, not the gross, which must be taken into consideration in determining the productiveness of the public works. When these figures were examined they disclosed an entirely different state of affairs. During the past five years the average annual net revenue from the public works had only been $139,697.43; while the average annual interest on the sums borrowed to carry on the works had exceeded $1,200,000. To meet this drain on the state's finances, the people could either submit to taxation, sell the public works, or resort to more loans. Since the public works could not be sold except at a ruinous sacrifice and it was doubtful whether more loans could be procured, the governor urged the legislature to adopt an adequate system of taxation.[9]

The candid, courageous message of the governor was referred to the Committee of Ways and Means in the House and a bill was introduced to carry out his recommendations. But the legislature was not yet convinced of the necessity of imposing heavy taxes upon the people. The legislature adjourned without passing any measure; and the state was compelled to default temporarily in the payment of its February interest. The shock to the credit of the state and to the nation at large by the delinquency of Pennsylvania, although of short duration, revealed the need of taking some action. The legislature was called in extra session and on June 11, 1840, a tax bill was passed.[10]

[9] Pennsylvania Senate Journal, 1840, Vol. *I*, pp. 16-20.

[10] Pennsylvania House Journal, 1840, Vol. *II*, pp. 1017-1019; *New York American*, May 7, 1840. Some of the Philadelphia banks agreed to advance the state funds to meet the interest on its stocks which was proof, declared the *United States Gazette*, of the sincere desire of the state to maintain her faith untarnished. *United States Gazette* quoted in *London Times*, March 10, 1840.

The tax law of 1840 failed to provide the desired revenue. It was drafted primarily for the purpose of raising the credit of the state rather than to procure the necessary funds. The act was to continue in force for five years and provided for the assessment of taxes which would weigh less heavily upon those unable to bear additional burdens. The articles taxed were those in the category of luxury, such as gold watches, pleasure carriages, household furniture exceeding in value $300, together with the stocks of banks and other corporations yielding dividends of at least 1 percent, salaries of public officials and real estate. It was estimated that the new taxes would yield an income of about $6,000,000 which sum, with the other resources of the commonwealth, it was supposed would be sufficient to liquidate the interest account without resorting to additional loans. In designing this law, however, the legislature either had no conception of the seriousness of the situation or had deliberately neglected to perform its duty. They introduced a system of taxation which at the most would yield only $600,000 a year when in 1839 the expenditures of the state amounted to $6,971,490 in view of the permanent loans contracted in that year, while the revenue, exclusive of the loans, was only $1,899,551. Furthermore, it was found extremely difficult to collect the new taxes as the people were averse to all taxation and availed themselves of every technicality to avoid payment. Instead of yielding $600,000, only $33,292.77 was obtained in 1841; and by the close of the year the deficit in the treasury had increased to $1,773,519.42.[11]

The inadequacy of the tax law of 1840 led to the adoption of a new plan the following year. An address signed by more than two hundred of the wealthiest citizens of the state was sent to the governor urging the increase of taxes in order to provide for the payment of the state debt and preserve the faith of Pennsylvania. The act of May 4, 1841, passed over the governor's veto, instead of relieving the financial embarrassment of the state made conditions worse. A tax of twenty cents was levied upon every $100 of property, besides duties on licenses for all kinds of traders and taxes on some articles of luxury. It was expected that the new taxes would produce an annual income of nearly $1,000,000; but this sum was never realized. Unhappily the same act authorized the banks to sub-

[11] Hunt's Merchants' Magazine, Vol. 20, pp. 256-269; Pennsylvania Senate Journal, 1841, Vol. I, pp. 16, 17, Vol. II, p. 32; Worthington Historical Sketch of the Finances of Pennsylvania, p. 54; Bishop, State Works of Pennsylvania, p. 320.

scribe for a new loan of not more than $3,100,000 to the commonwealth and to issue notes in denominations of one, two, and five dollars equal to the amount of their subscriptions. Holders of these notes, in amounts not less than one hundred dollars were entitled at any time to demand state stock at par in liquidation of them. As there was no other provision for the redemption of these "relief notes," as they were called, and the notes were issued by the authority and upon the credit of the state, they were in reality state "bills of credit." This was a palpable violation of the Federal Constitution which prohibits the issuance of "bills of credit" in the states; and Pennsylvania, like the colonies in the Revolutionary period, suffered severely from the consequences of issuing this worthless paper. It was believed, however, that the new notes would enable the government to pay the domestic creditors of the state as well as increase the limited circulation of currency. Since only $2,220,265 of these notes were originally issued the amount was not large enough to pay a large portion of the domestic creditors to whom the state owed about $3,000,000; and as the notes rapidly depreciated in value, the credit of the state was lowered and industry was disrupted.[12]

Then it was that some in Pennsylvania began to advocate the repudiation of the state debt as a means of alleviating the distress. At a tumultuous meeting held in Philadelphia on December 30, 1841, resolutions were passed declaring "that in the contracting of the so-called state debt, the faith of the commonwealth has been unconstitutionally and illegally pledged; and the people are under no moral, legal, or political obligation to bear any burden of taxation or make any sacrifice of personal comfort to keep it unbroken." The advocates of repudiation denied the authority of the legislature "to construct works of internal improvement or to contract loans"; and asserted their intention "unitedly and determinedly" to resist "by all constitutional and legitimate means, the collection of the present, or any future tax, levied for the purpose of paying either the interest or principal of the so-called state debt." Copies of these resolutions were sent to the legislature when it assembled in the following month.

To the lasting credit of Pennsylvania the legislature dealt with

[12] Hunt's Merchants' Magazine, Vol. 20, pp. 256-269; *Circular to Bankers*, Nov. 24, 1843.

these petitions in a manner to leave no cause for uncertainty in the minds of the creditors that repudiation would never be countenanced by the Keystone State. The doctrine of repudiation was condemned in two able reports of select committees appointed in the House and Senate. The disposition to create a want of confidence in the public faith was denounced as being the work either of a few unprincipled stock jobbers who hoped to profit by playing upon the timidity and fears of holders of the state loans or of those animated by a spirit of agrarianism intent upon destroying the industry and enterprise of the citizens of the state. If those who participated in the meeting were influenced by good motives, the committee declared that they were to be pitied; if they were motivated by evil intentions their course could not be too severely condemned. What were their arguments in favor of repudiation, asked the committee? There could be no question as to the authority of the legislature to borrow money and to construct public works. To sanction resistance to a tax law imposed to pay the state debt to-day was to prepare the way for open rebellion to-morrow. If one law could be violated, all others became weak, futile and inoperative. It was the duty of every citizen to give strict observance to all laws. To nullify any law was the end of government. The stock of Pennsylvania was mostly held by foreigners. To pay it was a point of national honor. Resolutions were accordingly passed by unanimous vote in both houses of the legislature affirming the determination of Pennsylvania to meet its obligations and denouncing the doctrine of repudiation as obnoxious and calculated to destroy the free principles on which the government was based.[18]

Pennsylvania would not repudiate its debt; but the state was soon forced to default in the payment of its interest. Relief notes soon became the only medium in which the state received its revenue. To make matters worse, the United States Bank of Pennsylvania failed. Some of the banks in Philadelphia losing confidence in the bank refused to accept its notes. This started a run on the United States Bank of Pennsylvania. The governor, convinced that the bank had been paying out state funds on deposit in that institution to meet other demands, instructed the attorney general to apply for

[18] Pennsylvania House Journal, 1842, Vol. 2, pp. 44-48; *National Intelligencer*, Jan. 10, 14, 1842; *Baltimore American*, Jan. 12, 13, 1842.

an injunction and on the last day of January 1842 the bank closed its doors. The state authorities seized the most valuable assets, thereby recovering $500,000 of the state's money, although it lost $280,000 which had been deposited in the bank. By the middle of February the state was able to meet the interest due on the first of the month. When the August interest fell due the treasury had no funds on hand except relief notes. Under these circumstances the legislature passed a law authorizing the issuance of 6 percent scrip to the creditors instead of money; and this practice was continued until the improved means of assessment and revision of the tax laws restored the finances of the state to a sound basis.[14]

Many American and European families suffered by the defalcation of Pennsylvania. Ten million of the thirty-four million dollars of Pennsylvania stock were held by citizens of the United States; the remainder was owned by foreigners, principally by the English, Dutch, and French. Twenty million dollars of stock was held in England, about two million dollars in Holland and nearly six hundred thousand dollars in France. In England the stock was held principally by persons who were dependent upon their dividends for support.[15] Some of the injured creditors, like Sydney Smith, gave vent to their feelings of rage and despair in scathing attacks upon the integrity of all Pennsylvanians. Others, like the poet Words-

[14] Hunt's Merchants' Magazine, Vol. 20, pp. 256-269; *Circular to Bankers*, Nov. 24, 1843.
[15] Baring to Ward, Aug. 3, 1842. Baring Mss. According to *Niles Register*, Dec. 10, 1842, the official statement of the debt of Pennsylvania in July 1842, was $34,454,356.47. The distribution was as follows:

Amount held in the United States		*Amount held in foreign countries*	
Pennsylvania	$ 9,635,613.47	England	$20,026,458.00
New York	417,856.00	Holland	1,822,266.00
Massachusetts	129,000.00	France	570,000.00
Dist. of Columbia	86,220.00	West Indies	563,161.00
Virginia	84,700.00	Switzerland	239,677.00
Delaware	76,180.00	Portugal	250,803.00
Indiana	67,500.00	East India and China...	147,968.00
South Carolina	59,987.00	Mexico	40,700.00
Maryland	24,900.00	Canada	30,588.00
New Jersey	13,994.00	Italy	30,525.00
Ohio	10,000.00	Denmark	6,000,00
Illinois	7,700.00	Spain	5,000.00
North Carolina	2,500.00	Halifax, N. S.	3,000.00
Sec. of War of the U. S. for sundry Indian tribes	100,000.00		$23,736,206.00
	$10,716,150.47		

worth, found expression for their emotions in lamenting the misfortune suffered by members of their families caused by the nonpayment of Pennsylvania and the repudiation by Mississippi of their obligations. In Amsterdam a member of the firm of Hope and Company was threatened with personal violence by a mob of enraged holders of Pennsylvania stock. To the outside world Pennsylvania became a synonym for American discredit.[16]

In his message of 1843 Governor Porter attempted to quiet the fears of the creditors. The abundance and nature of the resources of Pennsylvania were amply sufficient to enable the state to meet all her engagements. The state would not prove faithless or unwilling to discharge her obligations. "To do what she agrees to do and to pay what she promises to pay," declared the governor, "are two of her distinguishing characteristics. . . . She may be temporarily obliged to postpone the discharge of her engagements until a more convenient season; but to deny the obligation itself, or to refuse to comply with it, would be a reproach upon her integrity which no public man dare advise or sanction." These were comforting words to the creditors of Pennsylvania; but they would have preferred some tangible evidence of the noble intentions of the state instead of mere words. It is true the legislature passed a law to sell certain stocks the commonwealth held in banks and other incorporated companies. But from this sale the state realized only $1,395,411.84 on stocks which had cost the treasury $4,192,383.[17]

In an effort to stimulate among the citizens of Pennsylvania and those in other insolvent states a moral consciousness of the importance of paying the state debts, a group of European financiers determined to secure writers and speakers in America to set before the public the claims of the foreign creditors. For months T. W. Ward, the American agent of the Barings, had been urging the London house to procure able writers to set the Americans right on the debt question. To this the Barings had always replied "people will try to be honest when they feel more at ease." While Ward

[16] For the reactions of Sydney Smith consult Chapter III. Two sonnets of Wordsworth entitled "Men of the Western World" and "To the Pennsylvanians" had relation to the American state debts. A letter written by Wordsworth to the mother of S. S. Prentiss on the repudiation of Mississippi of the Union Bank bonds was republished in the *London Times*, March 17, 1930.

[17] Pennsylvania House Journal, 1843, Vol. 2, pp. 4, 5; Worthington, Historical Sketch of the Finances of Pennsylvania, p. 57; Bishop, State Works of Pennsylvania, p. 221.

agreed this might be true, he was in favor of the foreign bondholders adopting more energetic measures to safeguard their interests. "Very great matters," wrote the realistic Ward, "are often left to chance in the conduct of this world." If the foreign creditors had upon the first indication of financial disorders in America raised a sum of money among the holders of American securities and had placed this sum at the disposal of some judicious person in this country, Ward was convinced much good might have been accomplished in formulating correct views upon the subject of the state debts. Evidently the views of Ward were shared by others for in June, 1843, the Barings notified him that they had agreed to join five other banking houses in subscribing to a fund of £2,000 for the purpose of appointing one or more agents in Pennsylvania to represent the foreign creditors.

Ward was selected to direct the campaign. He was to choose as agents persons of tact and discretion who were to receive "a liberal but not extravagant compensation, not more than five thousand dollars besides a reasonable allowance for contingent expenses." These agents were to write for the newspapers; organize meetings of the domestic stockholders for the purpose of explaining the importance to the state of keeping good faith with its creditors at home and abroad and the ease with which this could be achieved. The agents were also "to endeavor to enlist the clergy to point out from the pulpit" the "moral wrong and danger to the people of not acting honorably." The English holders of American stocks were determined to hold their state stocks in preference to exchanging them for shares in corporations organized to take over the canals or other public works. The states must be induced to pay either in part or in full their obligations according to their ability; and it was hoped that the resumption of payments by Pennsylvania would have a salutary effect upon other states.[18]

Under the competent leadership of Ward a nation-wide campaign was inaugurated to rehabilitate state credit. As the Barings were particularly interested in reëstablishing the credit of Pennsylvania and Maryland because they had disposed of large quantities of these stocks to their clients, Ward centered his attention upon these states; but in time he extended his field operations to include other states.

[18] Ward to Baring, May 14, 15, 1843; Baring to Ward, June 19, July 3, 1843. Baring Mss.

His most difficult task was to find suitable persons in these various states to represent the foreign creditors. The Barings would have liked Albert Gallatin to take charge of the operations in Pennsylvania; but his advanced age precluded this choice. Walter Forward, Horace Binney, and George M. Dallas were also considered; but Ward selected Nathan Hale, editor of the *Boston Advertiser,* as his chief lieutenant and Hale directed the campaign in Pennsylvania. In order to stimulate public opinion articles appearing in Hale's paper were republished in other newspapers. The columns of the *New York Journal of Commerce, New York Evening Post, New York American, New York Courier and Enquirer,* and other leading newspapers inserted articles either written or inspired by the adroit hand of the indefatigable Ward. The editors were generally paid ten dollars for such insertions; in the case of the *New York Evening Post* and the *New York American* and for an editorial notice in one or two papers, twenty dollars; while occasional articles were published without pay. Gales and Seaton of the *National Intelligencer* were offered two hundred dollars to republish two articles. They declined to do so but expressed their willingness to coöperate. Not much assistance, however, was rendered by this paper. Ward could not explain "the backwardness of editors" to espouse the cause of the creditors and wondered whether it was due to the unpopularity of the subject or merely to their apathetic attitude.[19]

The religious press and church organizations cordially coöperated with Ward. Individual members of the American and Baptist boards, and particularly Dr. Francis Wayland of Brown University, assisted in distributing material, writing to clergymen, and lending their counsel. No evidence has been found that the religious press was subsidized. Articles did appear in the *New York Observer* at Ward's suggestion and a former member of the staff of that paper was sent to interview the Lutheran clergymen in Pennsylvania, for it was claimed that the Germans in that state opposed heavier taxes. Lutheran leaders indignantly denied these charges although they acknowledged that the Germans "were more indignant than others

[19] Baring to Ward, July 3, 1843; Ward to Gales and Seaton, Nov. 23, 1843; Ward to Baring, Dec. 27, 1843; Ward to T. W. Ward, Jan. 9, 1844; Ward to Latrobe, Jan. 11, 1844; Ward to Perit, Jan. 13, 1844; Latrobe to Ward, Jan. 15, 1844. Baring Mss. Ward's activities in the other states will be discussed in later chapters in connection with the debts of these states.

at the dishonesty of politicians and therefore less disposed to trust them with money for any purpose." [20]

The most effective articles published were those written by Alexander Everett and Benjamin R. Curtis, later a Justice of the United States Supreme Court, which appeared respectively in the *Democratic Review* and the *North American Review* for January, 1844. Both were prepared under Ward's personal supervision. The comprehensive account by Judge Curtis, which has been quoted by every writer on this subject, was based upon an outline furnished by Ward; and upon its publication the latter arranged for its wide distribution in the United States and England.[21] When Curtis was later offered $350 for his services he declined the remuneration. A friend of his had questioned "whether it would be best" for him "to be paid by your friends." "I cannot now state any very strong reason why I should not treat it as a matter of business," wrote Curtis to Ward, "except the feeling which constantly recurs that I had rather not; and it is a rule which I have endeavored to follow that when I have any scruples respecting any pecuniary matter it is safest and best to be governed by them without attempting to find much logic for their support." [22]

The services of political leaders were also solicited. Webster was most anxious to help and delivered a number of speeches. "The state of his (Webster's) private concerns," wrote Ward to the Barings, "appear to be always such as to require all the money he can get; and this seems to be to him a national necessity." Ward felt the time was opportune to awaken public sentiment and set it strongly in the right direction. This could "be done best by Webster and through the press." Webster wanted "to have the profits on the rise of a given quantity of stock"; but Ward told him it was not the rise in stock but the payment by the states the creditors wanted. Webster, therefore, agreed as a matter of principle to do all he could to bring about the resumption of payments by the delinquent states. For a time Ward thought it might be useful to invite Webster to appear as counsel for the domestic and foreign

[20] Wayland to Ward, Nov. 28, 1843, Jan 9, 1844; Ward to Perit, Jan. 4, 1844; Ward to Wayland, Jan. 4, 10, 1844; Tracey to Latrobe, Jan. 25, 1844. Baring Mss.
[21] Ward to Baring, Aug. 29, 30, Nov. 14, 29 (with enclosure), Dec. 8, 1843. Baring Mss.
[22] Ward to Curtis, Jan. 11, May 13, 1844; Curtis to Ward, May 15, 1844. Baring Mss.

creditors before the Pennsylvania legislature; but this plan was abandoned.

The Barings doubted the wisdom of employing Webster. As a public man he should see the necessity of acting while "the fact of his being paid would lessen his influence." When Ward on his own initiative gave Webster $200 the Barings objected. "We should have liked," they wrote Ward, "when we are sometimes made the objects of attacks to be able to say that as a business and foreign house we remain neutral in all political struggles." Ward recognized their point of view and paid Webster himself. "It is a humiliating fact," wrote Ward on one occasion, "that the first talents in the country even must be bought and paid for in the highest of causes." It is quite evident from a careful examination of the Baring manuscripts that they were sincere when they acknowledged to Ward some years later that they were never able to reconcile themselves to the propriety "of taking American papers into pay for the purpose even of advocating principles of honesty. It ought to be done without English money." [23]

Ignorance, apathy, and party politics made Ward's task a difficult one in Pennsylvania. In Philadelphia he found many doubted whether the state would ever pay; but Ward cynically remarked to the Barings that he was "accustomed to the obtuseness and wrongheadedness of very many respectable Philadelphia gentlemen." Dallas told him that neither party would do anything pending the Presidential election for fear of losing popularity by proposing to tax the people. Ward believed that Elihu Chauncey, who later rendered valuable service in restoring the credit of the state, wished to keep Pennsylvania in confusion until a Whig administration headed by Clay came into power in the national government. Gallatin confessed that he was sceptical about a democracy ever consenting to tax itself to pay debts. Fox, the British minister in Washington, entertained the same misgivings. The only way the debts could ever be paid was by direct taxation; but "I do not expect," wrote Fox to Lord Aberdeen, the British Foreign Secretary, "that either the State legislators or the people at large will have enough common honesty to consent to that sacrifice. . . .

[23] Ward to Baring, Sept. 15, Oct. 31, Nov. 1, 15, 18, 1843; Jan. 30, Sept. 27, Oct. 16, Nov. 2, Nov. 22, 1844. Baring Mss.

Wherever the state works, for the construction of which in almost every case the state debts have been contracted, are found to return a sufficient income, that income will be applied to pay the interest of the debt. Wherever these means fail, the interest of the debt will not be paid. Direct taxation will not be resorted to. There seems to be a settled resolution to this effect in the minds of the whole people. I believe that after all the volumes which have been written upon the subject the above will be found to contain in a few words the true history of the American state debts and finances." [24]

Among the defenders of the foreign creditors was Nicholas Biddle, former autocrat of Chestnut Street. Since the Pennsylvania legislature was unwilling to levy sufficient taxes to pay the debt, Biddle resolved to point out to the creditors a legal method of compelling Pennsylvania to meet its engagements.

In a public letter on the debt of Pennsylvania, Biddle called attention to the fact that three distinct classes of political persons were capable of suing the state in the federal courts—the United States, any sister state, or any foreign state which had a controversy with Pennsylvania. The government of the United States in buying lands from the Indians had invested a large part of the purchase money in funds from which they expected to derive annual dividends, and by a special act of Congress about $4,500,000 had been invested in state stocks. Among the list of Pennsylvania stockholders published in 1842 was the Secretary of War who had purchased $100,000 of the Pennsylvania state bonds for sundry Indian tribes. Since the United States government must, of course, continue to pay the Indian annuities, Biddle declared that it was in the power of the federal government by suing out the bonds in the United States Supreme Court to compel Pennsylvania to pay them. Another way to force Pennsylvania to meet her obligations was for one of her sister states to become the possessor of these bonds and to institute suit in the federal courts; but the most dangerous plaintiff would be a foreign state. What would happen, asked Biddle, if, for instance, the paternal governments of Switzerland—Berne, or Zurich or Lucerne, should take up the cause of their honest moun-

---

[24] Ward to Baring, July 10, Sept. 11, Oct. 31, Dec. 27, 1843. Baring Mss. Fox to Aberdeen, Jan. 31, 1844. F. O. 5, 410 (number 10), Public Record Office.

taineers whom Pennsylvania had wronged out of $300,000 and received their bonds into their own hands and demand payment of them? They would not have to go to war with the United States. They could go to law with us and they could go to law exactly after our fashion and before a tribunal of our own making. Pennsylvania could raise no objection to the jurisdiction of the United States Supreme Court for upon entering the Union Pennsylvania had agreed that if ever she had a controversy with a foreign state it should be settled by the United States Supreme Court. The foreign state could produce the bonds. The plaintiff could point out that they bore the seal of the state; the signature of the proper officials; the promise of the state to pay so much money with interest at stipulated periods. Before the United States Supreme Court, Pennsylvania might plead against the payment of the bonds anything which any private man might plead against the payment of his bond, to show its invalidity, and if any such could be proved the state would be relieved from payment. But no plea which would not release a private citizen would be of the slightest avail to Pennsylvania. It would be absurd to plead that a State had too much dignity to be honest and as a sovereign had the right to cheat its neighbors.

Suppose a judgment were given in favor of the foreign state. Execution would follow. The marshal of the United States would seize and sell all the property of Pennsylvania; all the canals and railroads belonging to her would be sold first; and all the public lands of Pennsylvania, the eastern and western penitentiaries, the state house. Then as the taxes were paid into the state treasury they would of course be attached to pay the debt; and Pennsylvania would be divested of its property and deprived of its future means of support.

There was not the least danger, according to Biddle, that the decree would not be enforced. There would be big words—long speeches in the legislature—high-sounding resolutions; but when the question was raised whether the people of Pennsylvania would stand by the legislature in its attempt to cheat foreign creditors there would be no fear of the results. Upon three occasions popular opposition had tried to check the federal marshal in executing writs. In the insurrection of 1794 the marshal was resisted by large popular meetings; whereupon an army of Pennsylvania joined by the forces of New Jersey, Maryland, and Virginia took the marshal with them to the scene and saw that he executed his writs. In 1798 the marshal was again resisted in Northampton and an armed force of Pennsylvania alone enforced the law; and the ringleader of the resisters was condemned to death. More recently a federal marshal had executed his writ and arrested and imprisoned a Major General, of the Pennsylvania militia, who was under orders from the governor to resist the marshal. This proved, thundered Biddle, that the plan was practical.[25]

Biddle's proposal enraged the Americans; while Europeans doubted its effectiveness. Before the hopes of the foreign bondholders were raised too high, the sceptical *London Times* cautioned them to look at the arguments advanced on the other side. The *London Times* quoted an article published in the *New York Commercial Advertiser* which claimed that Biddle had overlooked the legal technicalities involved in bringing suit by assigning the bonds to a foreign state. One of the clauses of the eleventh section of the Judiciary Act of 1789 provided: "Nor shall any district or circuit court have cognizance of any suit to recover the contents of any promissory note, or other chose of action, in favor of an assignee, unless a suit might have been prosecuted in such court to recover the said contents if no assignment had been made, except in cases of foreign bills of exchange." According to the *New York Commercial Advertiser* the Pennsylvania bonds were what was termed in law "choses in action"; and as such, it was manifest that no suit could be commenced by any assignee, whether such assignee was a foreign state or one of its citizens, unless a suit had been prosecuted in the United States courts by the assignors. "How then," asked the *New York Commercial Advertiser*, "can a foreign state, deriving its ownership through a transfer executed by a party confessedly not competent to sue, sustain an action in the federal courts." The United States Supreme Court on several occasions had given consideration to this clause of the Judiciary Act of 1789; and in no instance had the court failed to give it the fullest operation. "Indeed, in one case, even where the subject of the suit was not a chose in action, and, consequently, not within the letter of the law, but a

[25] *Niles*, Aug. 12, 1843. It is interesting to note the change in Biddle's position regarding the debts.

party had, by an assignment made for the purpose, endeavored to acquire the privilege of suing in the circuit court, the court extended the spirit of the law to that case, and held that they had no jurisdiction." [26]

Western newspapers were not so technical in their criticism. The *Cincinnati Gazette* ridiculed the idea that if a judgment were rendered in favor of a foreign country that all the states in the Union, as Biddle claimed, were bound to carry it into execution—by arms if necessary! How was this to be done? No execution could go against the *body* of the state, it issued against the property of the state; and under it the property might be taken and sold. But how far would the proceeds go to discharge the indebtedness? Not far. The debt would remain unpaid and no property would remain to be taken into execution. The scheme was impractical. It was worse than useless because it was calculated to deaden all honorable obligation in the State to pay. [27]

Meanwhile Ward strove valiantly to bring about the resumption of payments by Pennsylvania. He realized, however, that more than articles published in the daily press or sermons and addresses were needed to accomplish this. The State must be shown how the debt could be paid; and the friends of sound credit must help the legislature in drafting proper measures. But the members of the legislature must be given to understand that they were to receive no pecuniary remuneration for any services they rendered in restoring the credit of the state. Hale was sent to Harrisburg where in communication with the committee on ways and means a tax bill was drafted. When the bill was introduced in the legislature, Elihu Chauncey, deeming it important to bring every influence to bear upon some doubtful votes in both houses, sent two men to the state capital to assist Hale. As Ward said the final settlement of the Pennsylvania debt was due to the "ability, sagacity, force of mind, and long experience" of Hale and Chauncey. Ward estimated that the campaign in Pennsylvania had cost the foreign bondholders between £1,300 and £1,500. [28]

On April 29, 1844, the Pennsylvania legislature enacted a tax

[26] *London Times*, Sept. 18, 1843.
[27] *Cincinnati Gazette* quoted in *Niles*, Sept. 23, 1843.
[28] Ward to Baring, Dec. 13, 1843, Jan. 22, 30, 31, Feb. 3. Apr. 14, May 1, 1844. Baring Mss.

law which prepared the way for the payment of the state debt."[20] A tax was levied on all real estate not exempt by law; all personal estates; all shares or stock in banks and incorporated companies; all salaries from professions, trades, and occupations, excepting farming. The proceeds of these taxes were appropriated exclusively to the payment of the interest on the public debt. The act also provided for equalizing the assessment and taxes in the different counties and for the establishment of a board of revenue commissioners. On February 1, 1845, Pennsylvania, the first of the insolvent states to place her finances on a sound basis, resumed the interest payments on her debt.

[20] Pennsylvania Laws, 1844, p. 497.

CHAPTER V

THE FINANCIAL TROUBLES OF MARYLAND

THE history of the public debt of Maryland in the 'forties is, in many respects, similar to that of Pennsylvania. Both states piled up enormous debts in the construction of public works. Both were forced to default upon their interest payments—Pennsylvania for three years, Maryland for six years. Neither state was able to resume its payments until the people were made fully aware of the urgent need of their respective state keeping its engagements. There was some repudiation sentiment in both states although it received even less popular support in Maryland than in Pennsylvania. The citizens of Maryland as well as those of Pennsylvania ultimately realized the necessity of revising their taxation systems and providing for the prompt collection of the taxes. On account of the wealth and resources of Pennsylvania and Maryland, and the large amount of their securities held by foreigners, the efforts to restore the credit of the states attracted considerable attention abroad. The Barings were particularly interested in restoring the financial standing of Maryland since their house, in its capacity of fiscal agent of Maryland, had been largely instrumental in introducing Maryland bonds to English investors. Ward and his associates employed the same methods in Maryland that they used in Pennsylvania in order to stimulate public sentiment in favor of paying the public debt; but they found their task more difficult in Maryland due to the rival ambitions of the Chesapeake and Ohio Canal and the Baltimore and Ohio Railroad.

Maryland contracted its public debt by lending the credit of the state to various internal improvement enterprises.[1] The most

[1] Various aspects of the internal improvement projects of Maryland and the financial problems of the state are discussed in the following works: Meyer, H. B., History of Transportation in the United States before 1860; Reizenstein, M., The Economic History of the Baltimore and Ohio Railroad, Johns Hopkins University Studies, Vol. 15, pp. 281-371; Bryan, A. C., History of State Banking in Maryland, Johns Hopkins University Studies, Vol. 17, pp. 1-145; Ward, G. W., Early Develop-

important of these were the Chesapeake and Ohio Canal and the Baltimore and Ohio Railroad. The projection of the New York and Pennsylvania canals and turnpikes challenged the commercial prosperity of Baltimore. The citizens of Maryland had long been aware of the advantages to be derived from improving their transportation facilities; but the economic differences within the state militated against the formulation of a definite policy. The southern and eastern counties of Maryland were closely allied in soil and economic pursuits with the southern states. To them the improvement of the navigation of the Potomac was a matter of deep concern. On the other hand, as the economic center of the state gradually shifted in the first quarter of the nineteenth century from the southern to the northern counties, the ambitions of Baltimore clashed sharply with those of the tidewater counties. The merchants of Baltimore realized the improvement of the Potomac would tend to divert the western commerce which reached their city over the turnpike connecting Baltimore with the Cumberland Road towards the City of Washington. For this reason the citizens of Baltimore were more interested in developing the navigation of the Susquehanna River since the products carried down this river from the great valley of Pennsylvania and the agricultural sections of south-central New York, found their natural outlet in the Chesapeake Bay near enough to Baltimore to make it the principal port. Thus economic differences in Maryland bred sectional animosities.

Of all the schemes of internal improvement undertaken by Maryland, the Chesapeake and Ohio Canal was the one which involved the state in the greatest difficulties and absorbed most of its means. As early as 1784 a company was chartered in Virginia and incorporated the following year by Maryland for the purpose of "opening and extending the navigation of the Potomac." The Potomac Company, as it was called, under the presidency of George Washington, planned to open the channel of the Potomac as far as Cumberland; and then build a road connecting Cumberland with the headwaters of the Ohio River. The engineering problems encountered in attempting to make the Potomac navigable, as well

ment of the Chesapeake and Ohio Canal, Johns Hopkins University Studies, Vol. 17, pp. 425-539; Hanna, H. S., A Financial History of Maryland, Johns Hopkins University Studies, Vol. 25, pp. 349-483. There is a brief discussion of the Maryland state debt in Hunt's Merchants' Magazine, Vol. 20, pp. 481-494.

as the opposition of Baltimore, exhausted in time the funds and energies of this company. Nevertheless, Virginia and Maryland did not lose their interest in the plan. In 1823 a convention composed of delegates from Virginia, Maryland, and the District of Columbia meeting in Washington enthusiastically passed resolutions advocating the construction of a canal alongside the Potomac to its upper waters and its extension to the Monongahela or Youghiogheny in order to connect with the Ohio. The reluctant acquiescence of Baltimore was secured by agreeing to build a lateral canal between the Potomac and that city so as not to divert its western trade to the Potomac cities.[2]

By 1826 the Chesapeake and Ohio Canal Company had been chartered by Virginia and Maryland and the consent of Pennsylvania had been obtained. To finance the enterprise, Virginia, Maryland, the District of Columbia, and the national government jointly agreed to subscribe to the stock of the company. In March of that year Maryland subscribed $500,000 for stock in the Chesapeake and Ohio Canal Company, "in addition to the stock and debts owned by the state in the Potomac Company, amounting to $163,-724.44," with the proviso that Congress should first subscribe $1,000,000 to the Chesapeake Canal Company. In May, 1828, Congress directed the Secretary of the Treasury to subscribe this sum; and on July 4, with elaborate ceremony, President Adams broke ground for the commencement of the canal.[3]

In the meantime Baltimore had lost whatever interest it may have possessed in the undertaking; and forward-looking merchants of that city were planning to reach the western country by other means. In 1826 a board of federal engineers reported the estimated costs of constructing the Chesapeake Canal would in all probability be over $22,000,000. This figure staggered the promoters of the enterprise as the capital stock of the Chesapeake and Ohio Canal Company was only $6,000,000. Henceforth Baltimore was no longer interested in the canal even though lower estimates were procured by the company from more flexible engineers. But her merchants realized whatever advantages Baltimore possessed from her geographical position and her former internal improvements were

---

[2] Ward, Early Development of the Chesapeake and Ohio Canal, pp. 1-17, 39-65.
[3] Hunt's Merchants' Magazine, Vol. 20, p. 482.

threatened by the ambitious plans of New York and Pennsylvania. Baltimore was nearer geographically to the Ohio Valley than any other Atlantic seaport; and by building turnpikes connecting the city with the Cumberland Road her merchants had hoped to retain their share of the valuable western commerce. In desperation, the citizens of Baltimore determined to build a railroad across the mountains to the Ohio in the hope that this new means of transportation would in the future demonstrate its superiority to waterway communication as the latter had already shown its advantages over turnpikes. Therefore, charters were obtained in 1827 from Virginia and Maryland, and subsequently from Pennsylvania by the Baltimore and Ohio Railroad Company. Maryland and the City of Baltimore each agreed to subscribe $500,000 to the stock of the company. Thus Maryland gave its blessing both to the canal and the railroad; and on the same day, July 4, at Baltimore, another pageant was enacted as work began on the construction of the Baltimore and Ohio Railroad.[4] Within the next few years the state legislature gave additional subsidies to both of these companies.

From the beginning of their operations, the canal and the railroad were rivals. They followed almost parallel routes and their purposes were almost identical. The railroad soon demonstrated its economic value as it opened up the country through which it passed. It soon had more freight than it could handle. In 1832 the progress of the road was arrested by a judicial decision which gave the canal priority of right of way up the valley of the Potomac. Although the companies adjusted their difficulties by compromising, the dispute delayed construction. This proved especially injurious to the canal company as there was no longer any hope of the federal government granting financial assistance in view of President Jackson's well-known opposition to such a policy. The success of the railroad made it still more difficult for the canal to obtain private aid. The only resource left the canal company was to solicit the aid of the state. Accordingly in 1834 the Maryland Legislature made a loan of $2,000,000 to the canal company and $100,000 to the Baltimore and Susquehanna Railroad. In the meantime the Baltimore and Ohio Railroad had received a further subsidy of $500,000 from the state in order to construct the Washington and Baltimore branch. In

[4] Reizenstein, The Economic History of the Baltimore and Ohio Railroad, pp. 9-19.

order to meet the loans to the Chesapeake and Ohio Canal and the Baltimore and Susquehanna Railroad, when demanded, the state treasurer was authorized to issue and sell 6 percent bonds redeemable in 1870 provided they were not sold for less than 15 percent premium. Ward notified the Barings this was a good investment for he claimed that slavery was wearing out in Maryland and that the state was rich. As the money market was active at this time the state was able to dispose of these bonds at an average premium of 17 percent.[5]

By 1836 the mania for internal improvements was at its height in Maryland. The canal company had exhausted the additional funds granted it and new estimates showed that $3,000,000 more was needed to complete the work to Cumberland. In order to assist the canal and at the same time placate the desires of other sections for similar enterprises, the legislature on June 4, 1836, appropriated $8,000,000 for the purpose of developing a well-rounded scheme of internal improvements. In order to raise the money, the state issued 6 percent 50-year bonds with the understanding that these bonds were not to be sold for less than 20 percent premium. The $8,000,000 loan was to be subscribed to the stock of various internal improvement companies in the following proportions: $3,000,000 to the Chesapeake and Ohio Canal Company; $3,000,000 to the Baltimore and Ohio Railroad; $1,000,000 to the Eastern Shore Railroad Company as soon as a company was organized to build this railroad; $500,000 to the Annapolis and Potomac Canal Company; and $500,000 to the Maryland Canal Company to construct a canal from Baltimore to the Potomac. Thus the small state of Maryland, with an area of 10,000 square miles, and a white population of a little over 300,000 assumed a burden that would have taxed the financial resources "of the whole kingdom of Great Britain." At one and the same time the state was projecting or constructing "a railroad to Annapolis, a railroad from Baltimore to the Susquehanna, a railroad on the Eastern Shore, a railroad from Baltimore to the Ohio, and a magnificent canal from tidewater on the Potomac to the Ohio River."

In assuming this debt the public gave little attention to its ulti-

[5] Hunt's Merchants' Magazine, Vol. 20, p. 483; Ward to Baring, Apr. 13, 23, 1835, Baring Mss.; Hanna, Financial History of Maryland, pp. 80-85.

mate payment. As Governor Thomas later declared: "They depended for the payment of the interest upon contracts entered into with the various companies to which bonds had been issued, and those companies relied upon the remote and very contingent possibility that the works projected would, when completed, afford an income to pay interest on the cost of their construction." [6]

When the legislature passed this act, the state anticipated no difficulty in negotiating the loan. Money was abundant in Europe seeking investment and American securities were in demand. The public debt of Maryland was under $5,000,000 and the credit of the state was unimpaired. The commissioners appointed to sell the Maryland loan determined to proceed first to England and, if they were unable to dispose of the bonds there, to go on to France and Holland. [7]

Before they reached Europe, however, a great change had taken place in the money markets of the world. The panic of 1837 was sweeping over the United States and foreign investors were unwilling to purchase the bonds at the price stipulated in the law. Upon their return home the commissioners concluded an agreement with the Chesapeake and Ohio Canal Company and the Baltimore and Ohio Railroad Company for the sale of $6,000,000 of the bonds. The legislature, however, refused to sanction this contract because they were afraid the companies might be compelled to sacrifice the credit of the state in order to meet their own private obligations. But the legislature did agree to a modification of the agreement by which the commissioners should deliver the bonds to the canal and railroad companies as soon as they had paid into the treasury in cash the premium of 20 percent required by law. At the same time the legislature directed the delivery of $2,500,000 of stock to the Chesapeake and Ohio Canal Company. The following year the legislature, in order to make the bonds more acceptable to foreign investors, converted the 6 percent currency bonds into 5 percent

[6] Maryland Documents, 1842, pp. 7-9. "The project of a canal from Annapolis to the Potomac River was speedily abandoned; and in 1837 there was substituted a plan for a railroad from Annapolis to Elkbridge to connect with the Washington Branch of the Baltimore and Ohio Railroad. To this undertaking the state subscribed $300,000." Hanna, Financial History of Maryland, pp. 93, 94.
[7] McTavish to Palmerston, June 3, 1837. Board of Trade, 333, No. 51 (enclosure), Public Record Office, London. The commissioners were Buchanan, Emory, and Peabody.

fifty-year sterling bonds and relinquished entirely their demand
for a 20 percent premium but stipulated that each company should
guarantee, for three years, the interest on the $3,000,000 loaned to
them. Whatever advantage the state might have gained by this
requirement was weakened, however, by the further provision, "that,
in the exchange, $3,200 worth of the new sterling stock should be
given for each $3,000 worth of the old currency," without a corre-
sponding increase in the state's interest as a shareholder in the
respective companies.[8]

It could hardly be expected that the canal and railroad companies would be able to dispose of the bonds on better terms than the
commissioners could obtain or be as anxious to maintain the credit
of the state. Furthermore as soon as the bonds were transferred to
the companies the state had no more control over their disposal than
it had over the management of the companies. Each company, accordingly, proceeded to dispose of the bonds as best it could upon
terms which ultimately discredited the state and diminished its own
resources, thereby defeating the purpose of the loans. The Chesapeake and Ohio Canal Company either sold or hypothecated its
bonds with banks and brokers on both sides of the Atlantic. Two
hundred and forty-three thousand pounds sterling of bonds were disposed of in the United States; £175,000 of sterling bonds were sold
to various parties in New York and to banks in Baltimore and
Washington; while the remainder was pledged for temporary loans
to cover contracts the company had made when wages and prices
were exorbitantly high.

George Peabody, as agent of the company, succeeded in disposing of the rest of the loan in Europe. In November, 1839, the Barings purchased £300,000 sterling bonds and agreed to pay 70 percent for them which amounted to £210,000. This sum was credited
to the Chesapeake and Ohio Canal Company and they were allowed
to draw upon it to meet their engagements. It was also agreed that
the Barings should have an option on similar bonds at the same
price to the amount of not less than £200,000 and not more than
£300,000. Should the Barings decide not to avail themselves of
this option they were to be given the choice of making advances on

---

[8] Maryland Senate Journal, 1839, pp. 4, 5; Hanna, Financial History of Maryland, pp. 89, 90.

the Maryland bonds at 65, at the current bank rate of interest; and such advances made to the company were to be repaid by sales of the stock, at their discretion, including their commissions of 2 percent and usual brokerage fees; but on sales where no advances were made their commission was to be reduced to 1 percent. It was distinctly understood, however, that the Barings were to have the sole and entire control of the sale of these bonds, as well as the sale of the remainder of the state bonds of Maryland issued for the Chesapeake and Ohio Canal Company; and Peabody agreed to use his influence with the canal company to obtain for the Barings the agency of the State of Maryland for the payment of its dividends in London. The Barings later confessed to Ward that they had profited considerably by this contract for they were able to sell the bonds which they had bought at 68 or 70 for 75 up to 82½.[9]

The Baltimore and Ohio Railroad Company also made an agreement with the Barings. In the fall of 1839 Louis McLane, president of the road, at the suggestion of the Barings visited England. McLane was authorized by his board of directors to sell or pledge the bonds as he might deem most advantageous. In the execution of this trust, McLane deposited the bonds with the Barings who agreed to become the agent of the company on the following terms. They were to sell the bonds at certain prices and charge their customary commissions and were to allow the company, after February, 1840, to draw upon them for £10,000 sterling a month, under the limitation, that their advances were never to exceed £40,000 sterling at any time. They were at liberty to sell as much stock as might be required to cover their advances without any restriction as to price or time. After thus reimbursing themselves, they were to permit the company to draw in like manner for similar sums; and this operation might be repeated until the bonds were all forced into the market for the payment of the temporary loans. "For some time before the bonds were sent to England, the scarcity of money and the abundance of American securities, and their rapid fall in value, made it impossible to effect a sale or negotiate a loan on reasonable terms; and the introduction of so large an amount of Maryland stock into foreign markets, under such circumstances, and for so

[9] Peabody to Baring, Nov. 27, 1839, Apr. 21, 1840; Peabody to President of Chesapeake and Ohio Canal Company, Nov. 30, 1839. Baring Mss. Baring to Ward, Dec. 31, 1839. Baring Letter Book.

slight an inducement, was calculated to sink more deeply, if possible, the credit of the bonds which had been unfortunately pledged by the Chesapeake and Ohio Canal Company." [10]

British investors were given every assurance in the prospectus written by McLane and issued by the Barings that the Maryland state loans were adequately secured. The agricultural region of Maryland was described as unsurpassed "in fertility by any other portion of the Union." The state, it was claimed, possessed "some of the richest and most extensive deposits of iron and coal yet discovered"; while independently of these mineral resources, the real and personal property in the state was of great value—that in the City of Baltimore alone was assessed at upwards of $60,000,000. Although Maryland had abolished direct taxation in 1824 the investing public was assured that such was "the sense of public credit and the familiarity of the citizens of the state with the system of direct taxation," that the City of Baltimore annually raised $60,000 by this means to pay the interest on its subscription to the Baltimore and Ohio Railroad. While it was acknowledged that the public debt of Maryland was large investors were assured that there was no cause for alarm as the stock subscriptions of the state were either "investments in the shares of works of intercommunication which" were "reasonably expected to be profitable . . . or loans upon the bonds of the companies engaged in the construction of those works." There was also a sinking fund provided for out of the state's share of the surplus revenue distributed by the federal government; and while this fund was not sufficient to absorb the aggregate indebtedness when redeemable, there was provision "for augmenting it from certain branches of the domestic revenue." In his eagerness that the Maryland bonds should be given "a preference over all others," McLane urged the Barings to persuade the *London Times* to refer to the "important arrangement" that he had made with their house as an additional proof of the safety of the Maryland loans. [11]

Foreign investors were not told, however, of the follies committed by Maryland in planning its internal improvement schemes. While the Baltimore and Ohio Railroad Company conducted its

[10] Maryland Senate Journal, 1839, p. 78; Bates to McLane, May 24, 1839; McLane to Bates, July 30, 1839. Baring Mss.
[11] McLane to Bates, Oct. 12, 15, 1839. Baring Mss. The Prospectus of the Maryland state loans accompanied the first letter of McLane to Bates.

affairs better than the Chesapeake and Ohio Canal Company, there was no doubt that Maryland had undertaken a task beyond its resources. The canal was a constant drain upon the state treasury; while the demand of other sections for similar works of internal improvement increased the burdens upon the state. The legislature had tried to safeguard the state's investments by making them in the form of common and preferred stock and bonds, but the care thus displayed had little immediate effect. "At first most of the companies did make an effort to pay the interest on their bonds; and, from this source and occasional dividends, the state for some five years derived a considerable revenue. But, with the exception of the Baltimore and Ohio Railroad, none of the companies were actually earning net profit sufficient for this purpose; and, therefore, the payments to the state could not continue." Furthermore, there was no adequate provision for the augmentation of the sinking funds in the case of the improvement loans, contrary to the statement in the prospectus, beyond trusting to its increase through the accumulation of interest and "to Providence for its ultimate and sufficient enlargement." By 1840 the public debt of Maryland was more than $15,000,000, bearing an annual interest of nearly $600,000. With Maryland bonds selling at a discount of 35 percent, and the state no longer able to borrow, the treasury found itself without funds to meet the interest payments falling due in October, 1841.[12] From that time until January, 1848, Maryland paid no interest upon its public debt.

[12] Hanna, Financial History of Maryland, pp. 94-104. The following table taken from Hanna, op. cit., p. 94, itemizes the Maryland debt and "the form and amount of the state's investment in each of the improvement companies aided."

	Amount of State Bonds Issued	FORM OF INVESTMENT		
		Common Stock	Bonds	Preferred Stock
Chesapeake and Ohio Canal	$ 7,194,667	$ 625,000	$2,000,000	$4,375,000
Baltimore and Ohio Railroad	3,697,000	500,000		3,000,000
Baltimore and Washington Branch	500,000	550,000		
Baltimore and Susquehanna Railroad	2,232,045	100,000	1,879,000	
Tidewater Canal	1,000,000		1,000,000	
Annapolis and Elkbridge Railroad	219,378			299,378
Eastern Short Railroad.....	151,744			86,862
Chesapeake and Delaware Canal		50,000		
	$14,994,834	$1,825,000	$4,879,152	$7,761,240

During these years the people of Maryland had to decide whether they would repudiate their debts or submit to taxation. These were the only alternatives. Like their neighbors in Pennsylvania, they were shocked to discover the public works were unproductive. They had never expected to be called upon to pay the sums borrowed to construct the canals and railroads. The internal improvements were supposed not only to pay for themselves but in addition to furnish the state with funds for other purposes. Now the public was informed that the ordinary revenues of the state were barely sufficient to meet the current expenditures while the annual interest charges on the public debt amounted to nearly $600,000. It was a rude awakening for the people. The legislature, however, had no intention of repudiating the state's obligations.

In March of 1841 the legislature set to work devising means whereby the state could meet its engagements. As no system of taxation existed in the state, and not more than $60,818 had ever been levied in any one year in direct taxes,[18] there was grave apprehension in the minds of the legislators whether the state would be able to meet the interest payments by means of direct taxes. Nevertheless in March of that year an act was passed authorizing the levy of a direct annual tax of 20 cents in the $100 on the assessed value of the real and personal property of the state. When this law was enacted and a supplementary law was passed at the December session of that year, imposing a tax for the first year of 20 cents, and for the next three years 25 cents in the $100, it was assumed that these taxes would bring into the treasury during the next four years $1,818,256.57. To aid these estimated incomes other acts were passed which it was expected would yield each fiscal year $200,000; and at the December session of 1841 several revenue laws were enacted imposing taxes on incomes, brokers, silver plate, watches, and ground rents which, it was confidently asserted, with the addition of the interest expected from the Baltimore and Susquehanna Railroad and the Susquehanna and Tidewater Canal Companies, would add to the resources of the year $145,000.

All of these estimates proved fallacious for they were based upon insufficient data. When the direct tax was levied it was esti-

---

[18] Hunt's Merchants' Magazine, Vol. 20, p. 487.

mated that the value of the real and personal property of the state was $300,000,000. When, however, the property was actually assessed, it was found to be valued at only $190,723,788; and this figure was subsequently reduced to $177,139,645 by the action of the appeal tax courts. In view of this discrepancy, the legislature should have increased the levy from 20 to 30 cents in the $100 if they hoped to secure an income from this source sufficient to pay the interest on the public debt by direct taxation. Instead of doing so, the legislature decided to rely upon other sources of revenue with the result that the incomes actually received fell far below the anticipated returns. In December 1844 the governor reported that the whole amount received from the direct tax laws of March and December 1841 was only $985,155.17, instead of $1,818,256.57; while the income expected from the acts which it was hoped would yield $200,000 each fiscal year had added only $15,297.95 to the revenues of the state; and the total income from the taxes imposed on incomes, etc., was $32,732.95, instead of $145,000.[14]

The second fatal error committed by the legislature was the failure to set up adequate machinery for the collection of the taxes. The county commissioners and the mayor and council of Baltimore were intrusted with the duty of enforcing the law. But the people resented the property tax and in some counties the timid local authorities never levied the unpopular tax. In other counties the levy was made but either no collectors were appointed or those appointed refused to serve. In a few of the counties the tax was collected; but no returns were received for three years from the counties of Somerset, Worcester, and Calvert. Aware that some amendment to the law was absolutely necessary in order to ensure its execution the legislature in 1842 combined for purposes of collection the local and state taxes in the hope that the local authorities would be forced to levy the state taxes. The only effect of this amendment was to stop the collection of all taxes in the delinquent counties. The forbearance and indulgence shown the delinquents by the legislature engendered in the public mind a doubt as to their determination to maintain inviolate the public faith. In this state of

[14] Maryland Public Documents, 1844, pp. 3-6; Hunt's Merchants' Magazine, Vol. 20, p. 487.

affairs, other counties were encouraged to follow the example of the delinquents; and by 1844 there were seven instead of three counties within whose boundaries the tax laws were not enforced.[15]

In such an atmosphere some began to advocate the repudiation of the public debt. Resolutions were passed at a meeting held at Bel-Air on May 13, 1843, declaring that the people were unable to pay the direct tax. Even if this tax were punctually paid, it was claimed, the credit and honor of the state would not be saved because the yearly interest on the public debt was twice as much as the direct tax. The people of Maryland were urged at their next election to express their disapprobation of this oppressive system of taxation and to demand the repeal of the obnoxious law.[16]

The newspapers and those in favor of sustaining the credit of the state promptly and indignantly repelled all such arguments. To counteract these sentiments both the Whigs and the Democrats held meetings in Baltimore denouncing the doctrine of repudiation. The people were reminded that the public debt had been contracted to pay for public works undertaken by the state upon the petition and recommendation of a large portion of the electorate. The public had sanctioned the borrowing of the money from their own citizens and from foreigners who had a good opinion of the sagacity of the Marylanders in projecting their public works and a "still better opinion" of their integrity in fulfilling their engagements. Ridicule was poured upon the repudiators who claimed to be benefactors of the people because they taught the public how to pick flaws in the state contracts and by quibbling over the wording of the contracts shuffle off their obligations.[17]

The legislature also denounced the repudiators. Mississippi might disavow her debts upon the ground that her public debt had not been contracted as prescribed by her constitution, stated the committee of ways and means in their report, but no invention of man could devise an excuse for Maryland departing from the plain path of honor and honesty. No ingenuity or sophistry could raise a doubt "of the direct and palpable obligation of the state to pay to the last dollar" all she had borrowed, principal and interest. It was

---

[15] Maryland Public Documents, 1843, pp. 3-5; 1844, pp. 3-6.
[16] Baltimore American quoted in London Times, June 16, 1843.
[17] Baltimore Sun, June 10, 1843; Boston Advertiser, July 11, 1843. Baring Printed Documents. McTavish to Aberdeen, Aug. 5, 1843. F. O. 5, 395, Public Record Office.

claimed by those favoring repudiation that the legislature had no authority to levy taxes to pay for debts incurred for purposes of internal improvement because the Bill of Rights stated that every person, except paupers, "ought to contribute his proportion of public taxes for the support of the government." The repudiators held that the laying of taxes to pay for debts contracted for purposes of internal improvement was not for the support of the government. "It would be strange," stated the committee, "if the improvement of the internal condition of the country were not the legitimate exercise of the powers of the government. Those who assert the doctrine must maintain, not only, that the State has no power to do this, but that she cannot communicate the power to others, for it could hardly be insisted, that she can impart faculties to others, which are denied to herself; and yet from the adoption of the constitution to the present time, the legislature has been in the unquestioned exercise of the power of incorporating companies to make roads and canals." In the opinion of the committee there did not exist "a government in the world without this power" for it was "indispensable to the welfare and prosperity of the people."[18]

Maryland would not openly repudiate its public debt; but the anxiety to avoid an increase of taxation induced the legislature to attempt to distribute the state's interest in the public works among the holders of the state bonds in settlement of their claims. In March 1843 an act was passed authorizing the sale of the state's investments in the Chesapeake and Ohio Canal, Baltimore and Ohio Railroad, Susquehanna Railroad, and the Tidewater Canal. The treasurer was authorized to accept not less than $5,000,000 for the state's interest in the Chesapeake and Ohio Canal; Baltimore and Ohio Railroad, $4,200,000; Susquehanna and Tidewater Canal, $1,000,000; and the Baltimore and Susquehanna Railroad, $1,500,-000. The payments were to be made in 5 percent state bonds. As no offers were received which the treasurer deemed acceptable, the attempt to disguise repudiation proved a failure.[19]

The financial difficulties of Maryland were a source of embarrassment to the Barings. This house was the financial agent abroad of the state and through the efforts of the Barings the Maryland

<hr />

[18] Maryland Public Documents, 1843-1844, pp. 1-10.
[19] Hunt's Merchants' Magazine, Vol. 20, p. 488.

bonds had been introduced to English investors. For this reason the Barings were vitally concerned in the Maryland debt. When the state first defaulted upon its interest payments, the Barings advanced the funds to pay the dividends abroad rather than have their clients accuse them of having sold worthless securities. They felt their reputation as sound and conservative bankers whose judgment could be trusted in the choice of American investments was intimately associated with the financial fortunes of Maryland. From the beginning of the financial difficulties of Maryland the Barings kept in close communication with the leaders in the state. McLane was urged to impress upon the proper authorities the importance of maintaining the credit of the state. Ward was directed to pay particular attention to the actions of the legislature in regard to the public debt. When the Barings finally agreed to associate themselves with other banking houses in a movement to arouse the moral consciousness of the American people to meet their obligations the Barings stressed the importance of bringing about a restoration of payments by Pennsylvania and Maryland. They hoped that the resumption of payments by these states would set a good example for the other delinquent states.[20]

The same methods were employed in Maryland as were used in Pennsylvania. Ward selected John H. B. Latrobe, counsel of the Baltimore and Ohio Railroad, to direct operations in Maryland. Latrobe's patience, good nature, social qualities, gift of speech, and residence in the state well qualified him for the position.[21] He had a high regard of Ward's sound judgment and Hale's journalistic ability on practical subjects. As Latrobe later confessed: "We wrote Maryland right; and Mr. Hale's articles were among the best that passed through my hands."[22] Articles were inserted in the local

[20] Baring to McLane, Jan. 18, 1841, Jan. 3, 1842; Ward to Baring, Feb. 15, 1841; Baring to Ward, March 11, 1842. Baring Mss. On inception of creditors' moves in Pennsylvania and Maryland consult chapter *V*.

[21] This statement is based upon Ward's characterization of Latrobe when the former suggested that Latrobe be employed in connection with the Mississippi debt. Ward to Baring, Dec. 5, 1850, Baring Mss.

[22] According to Latrobe, Nathan Hale was "a tall, square-shouldered New England looking man, but the very impersonation of common sense and one of the cleverest writers I ever met with on practical subjects." Latrobe declared Ward on one occasion said: "It is the time for me to go off the stage; the world is moving too fast for me. The telegraph confuses me. This having to act on the instant is not what I have been accustomed to. I used to think I could anticipate months ago commercial possibilities. Now I have to make up my mind at a moment's notice. What is to be the end of it, who can tell? Can you?" And yet, according to Latrobe "there probably never was

newspapers either written by Hale or Latrobe to set the people right on the debt question.[23] The Barings, at the request of George Peabody, agreed to contribute between $3,000 and $4,000 to secure the election of Whig candidates to the legislature who were known to be in favor of paying the debt. But the Barings insisted that the money should be used "for proper purposes"; and for that reason they requested that Peabody and Latrobe should handle the funds. The Barings did not wish it to be known that they had contributed money for campaign purposes in Maryland. "You will use your discretion in all this," wrote the Barings to Ward. "It is a delicate matter and of course we do not wish to do any thing that is improper."[42] Through the influence of Latrobe, John P. Kennedy was made Speaker of the House of Delegates with the understanding that he was to appoint Thomas Donaldson chairman of the Ways and Means Committee; and the date for the resumption of interest payments was finally determined upon by the deciding vote of Latrobe at a conference held in Baltimore.[25] George Peabody, J. J. Speed, and the state treasurer, D. Claude, ably assisted Latrobe in all of his efforts.[26]

a man who was more accurate in his judgment than Mr. Ward. He may be said to have been never wrong. Cool and determined action with him was intuition, and while he really believed all that he said of himself, he never fell short of the occasion. It was only necessary to look into his twinkling hazel eye to see determination. He was not misled by false and glittering statements. He never lost sight of the true point. That much for one whom history will make no mention—one who did his duty only, and who has passed away." Semmes, J. E., John H. B. Latrobe and his Times, pp. 460, 461.

[23] Ward to Latrobe, Jan. 13, 1844; Ward to Baring, March 14, 1844. Baring Mss.

[24] Baring to Ward, July 18, 1845. Baring Letter Books.

[25] Semmes, *op. cit.*, p. 463.

[26] Maryland passed a resolution on March 8, 1848 thanking Peabody for his work in bringing about resumption (Bankers Magazine, Vol. *III*, p. 394). On one occasion, J. J. Speed of Baltimore in discussing the repudiation of public debts said: "Let us not disguise matters. Historians and posterity are to come after us, and they will speak of our actions with the praise or censure, the pride or the scorn that they may deserve. I affirm that repudiation of the public debt is an act which embodies all the turpitude of the above enumerated felonies. It is the result of a purely dishonest emotion in the public breast. It is the open expression of a determination to withhold from another what rightfully belongs to him. It is the deliberate, undisguised, and base avowal of a dishonest purpose. The offence is not in the slightest degree mitigated by an argument drawn from the inconvenience of paying the debt or the burthens of taxation that may be necessary to remove it. This should have been inquired into before the debt was contracted; at any rate it is a question with which the creditor has no concern; it has nothing to do with the validity of his claim, or the obligation of the state to meet it. Complaints of heavy taxation should be addressed to the government that may have made the burthen necessary, by unwise or profligate legislation; and not to the honest creditor who has shown his respect for the state by relying upon the faith and honor of its rulers." *Ibid.*, Vol. *I*, p. 309. On the work of D. Claude, the State Treasurer, consult Hunt's Merchant's Magazine, Vol. 20, p. 493.

All attempts to profit by the misfortune of Maryland by those on the inside were frowned upon by Ward and Latrobe. While Maryland was behind in her interest payments an opportunity presented itself by which the Barings, as agents of the state, could have made large profits by purchasing the state's securities at the market price. When the advantages of such a speculation were suggested to Ward, both he and Latrobe promptly vetoed the proposition. As Ward said the question was not what profit the Barings might make but what it became "the House of Baring to do." [27]

The efforts of Latrobe were aided by the gradual improvement of business conditions throughout the country as the nation gradually recovered from the effects of the panic of 1837, the curtailing of expenditures by the legislature, and the strengthening of the machinery for the collection of the taxes. This was in line with the views held by the Barings. They had always maintained that good management and economy on the part of the state and a little patience on the part of its creditors were all that were required to enable Maryland to resume. [28]

When it became evident that the federal government would never assume the state debts, the legislature set to work reducing the expenditures of the state government. Minor offices were abolished; salaries of officials were reduced; and a considerable amount was saved by substituting biennial for annual sessions of the legislature. [29] To accelerate the collection of taxes, the state agreed to accept the interest coupons on the state bonds, thereby diminishing the accumulation of the arrears of interest. [30]

Measures were also taken to enforce the collection of the taxes. In 1844 the governor was given the authority of appointing collectors in those counties where none were selected by the local authorities; and if neither the governor nor the local authorities acted, the treasurer was empowered to appoint special agents to receive the taxes. The odium attached to the office of collector rendered it almost impossible for the governor to find individuals residing in the delinquent counties willing to accept such appointments. To remedy

---

[27] Semmes, *op. cit.*, p. 460.
[28] *Ibid.*, p. 458.
[29] At this time the governor's salary was reduced to $2,000, the secretary of the state's to $1,000, and the chancellor's to $3,000. Hanna, Financial History of Maryland, p. 122.
[30] Hunt's Merchants' Magazine, Vol. 20, p. 489.

this defect in the law, the governor was authorized to appoint collectors, irrespective of residence, wherever the county authorities either neglected or refused to discharge their duties. Unfortunately, however, he was given no power to compensate these persons for their services. The treasurer, therefore, appointed special agents to receive the taxes; and after the election of Governor Pratt in the fall of 1844 conditions began to improve.[31]

Governor Pratt was a courageous, forceful executive. In his inaugural Governor Pratt called upon all classes and all parties to relieve the state from its humiliating position; and during his administration he devoted all his energies to the payment of the public debt. At his suggestion the legislature passed a number of coercive measures to enforce the collection of taxes and several additional revenue laws were enacted. Taxes were imposed on collateral inheritances and for the first time in the history of the state a stamp tax was imposed.[32] The determination of the executive to restore the credit of the state rallied to his support all those in favor of payment. The result was the prompt and successful execution of the laws. Some of the most influential citizens in the state consented to become collectors in the delinquent counties and the levies in these counties were collected without further trouble.[33]

But there was one law passed by the legislature which for a time obstructed all progress to the speedy resumption of interest payments. This was the measure postponing the state's liens on the property and revenues of the canal and giving the company the power to issue preferred bonds to the amount of $1,700,000.[34] The people of Maryland looked to the completion of the canal to Cumberland as their only relief from most of the direct and indirect taxation. The completion of the canal, it was hoped, would supply the state with sufficient funds to lessen the burdens of taxation. The extension of the canal, however, encountered the strong opposition of its competitor, the Baltimore and Ohio Railroad. Webster was employed by the contractors of the canal to watch after their interests; and W. Cost Johnson was sent to England to induce the

[31] Maryland Public Documents, 1845, pp. 3-28.
[32] There is a copy of Gov. Pratt's inaugural address, Jan. 4, 1845, in the Baring Printed Documents.
[33] Johnson to Baring, Aug. 1, 1845. Baring Mss.
[34] Ward, G. W., The Early Development of the Chesapeake and Ohio Canal Project, p. 110.

Barings to take the canal bonds. The Barings informed both Webster and Johnson that there was no chance of disposing of these bonds until Maryland resumed its interest payments. At the same time McLane was told by the Barings that the Baltimore and Ohio Railroad would not be granted a loan of $1,000,000 as long as Maryland was in default. By bringing pressure to bear upon the canal and the railroad, the Barings induced both of these companies to exert their influence upon the legislature to fix a day for the resumption of interest payments and the funding of the arrears oi interest.[35]

The result was the passage on March 8, 1847 of the Maryland Resumption Law. The state treasurer was directed to resume the payment of the current interest on the public debt on January 1, 1848. All outstanding arrears of interest were to be funded after October 1, 1847 in bonds redeemable at the pleasure of the commonwealth bearing an annual interest of 6 percent. If the funds in the treasury were found inadequate to pay the interest, the treasurer was authorized to pay pro-rata on the arrears of bonds and to issue a certificate for the balance to be paid thereafter out of any future surplus. All taxes and state dues after October 1, 1847, were to be paid in current money; and in case of a temporary deficiency in the treasury, the treasurer was given the power to borrow on the hypothecation of bank stock belonging to the state, the amount required to meet the deficiency. The sums borrowed were to be immediately repaid out of the first receipts in the treasury. Any surplus in the treasury after paying the current expenses of the state and the interest on the principal debt and on the funded arrears, was to be appropriated, either to the purchase or redemption of the arreared bonds until the surplus was entirely extinguished; after which it was annually to be devoted to the increase of the sinking fund. Thus Maryland capitalized her arrears of interest due to the bondholders by issuing new securities at par, bearing 6 percent interest, and redeemable at the pleasure of the state.[36]

[35] Latrobe to Ward, March 20, 1845; Ward to Latrobe, July 31, 1845; Ward to Webster, July 30, 1845; Johnson to Baring, Aug. 1, 1845; Ward to Baring, Aug. 1, Sept. 29, 1845; Ward to Latrobe, Sept. 20, 1845; Ward to Webster, Jan. 2, 1846. Baring Mss. Baring to Webster, Aug. 22, 1845; Baring to Johnson, Sept. 3, 1845; Baring to McLane, Aug., 1846; Baring to Ward, Nov. 3, 1846. Baring Letter Book.
[36] The law is quoted in full in Hunt's Merchants' Magazine, Vol. 20, p. 489. There is a good abstract of the bill and a discussion of its passage in McTavish to Aberdeen, March 24, 1847. F. O. 5, 474. Public Record Office.

Within two years about 25 percent of the entire amount of bonds were paid off; in the next year not less than 56¼ percent were cancelled; and in 1851 the remaining 18¾ percent were discharged.[37] Upon the resumption of payments Latrobe was paid $1,000 by the Barings for his services and given a credit of £500 on the house to cover his expenses for a trip to Europe.[38] In 1849 the Barings purchased $1,000,000 of Baltimore and Ohio Railroad bonds.[39]

[37] *London Times,* July 28, 1851.
[38] The account given in Semmes, *op. cit.,* p. 459, on this point is misleading. Latrobe declares the credit of £500 was given him by the Barings because they considered that he had underrated his services. As a matter of fact Latrobe had complained when he received the $1,000, and had definitely said he wanted his traveling expenses for a trip to Europe paid. Latrobe to Ward, Apr. 27, 1847.
[39] Ward to Baring, Apr. 10, 1849. Baring Mss.

CHAPTER VI

THE SETTLEMENT OF THE ILLINOIS STATE DEBT

ILLINOIS was one of the defaulting western states in the 'forties. For five years the state paid no interest on its public debt; and for a time there was grave doubt whether Illinois would ever resume its payments. A few extremists favored repudiation as a solution of Illinois' financial troubles; but a courageous executive, a willingness upon the part of the poverty-stricken citizens of Illinois to bear increased taxation, and the additional financial aid given to the state by her creditors to complete the Illinois and Michigan Canal, saved the reputation and credit of Illinois. The history of the final settlement of the Illinois state debt reveals what could be done even under the most adverse conditions when these three factors were present and worked in harmony.

In common with her sister states in the Mississippi Valley, Illinois projected numerous canals and railroads far beyond the limited resources of her people and out of all proportion to the needs of a pioneer community. The success of the Erie Canal stimulated a desire upon the part of other American states to undertake similar enterprises. Illinois fronted on Lake Michigan as New York did on Lake Erie and the Illinois River held the same relation to the internal navigation of the state as the Hudson River did to New York.[1] As early as 1823 the feasibility of joining the waters of Lake Michigan and the Illinois River were discussed in Illinois; but no progress was made because of the lack of capital in the new state. In 1827, however, Congress donated to Illinois 290,914 acres of public land for the purpose of constructing such a canal. The work was delayed because the people of Illinois were undecided whether a canal or a railroad should be constructed. Finally in 1835 the legislature gave its sanction to the Illinois and Michigan Canal by authorizing the negotiation of a loan not to exceed $500,000 giving

---

[1] Hunt's Merchants' Magazine, Vol. 27, p. 661.

as a pledge for the security of the loan the canal lands and tolls as well as any other means the federal government might thereafter grant for its construction. Certificates of stock, bearing 5 percent, redeemable after 1860, were issued by the state; and ex-Governor Coles was appointed special agent of the state to negotiate the loan.[2]

Since the state had made no provision for paying the interest beyond what might accrue from the sale of the canal lands and lots, eastern capitalists were reluctant to take the Illinois loan. As the interest rates in this country were higher than 5 percent it would be necessary to dispose of the bonds in Europe; but European capitalists hesitated about advancing funds to a comparatively unknown state. To meet the demands of the domestic and foreign money markets, the legislature, at the suggestion of ex-Governor Coles, passed an act January 9, 1836 authorizing the governor to negotiate such a loan "on the credit and faith of the state"; and the interest rate on the bonds was raised to 6 percent. All the revenues arising from the canal and from the sale of the canal lands were pledged for the payment of the interest.[3]

About the same time the people of Illinois began to clamor for the establishment of banks. The constitution adopted upon the admission of Illinois into the federal union specified that there should be no other banks in the state except a state bank and the two territorial banks, the Bank of Illinois at Shawneetown, and the Bank of Cairo, already provided by law. The Bank of Cairo never accepted its territorial charter and no organization was attempted until much later. The Bank of Illinois ceased to do business in 1821; and ten years later the first State Bank of Illinois ceased to exist.[4] With the increase in population and the consequent enlargement in the volume of trade the public began to demand that a bank should be established to supply the community with sufficient currency to carry on ordinary business transactions. There was also a fear that Illinois would be inundated with the notes of neighboring banks upon the expiration of the charter of the United States Bank unless a local bank was established; while land speculators were anxious to see such an institution created in order to facilitate their

[2] *Ibid.*, Putnam, J. W., The Illinois and Michigan Canal, p. 31.
[3] Acts Illinois, 1835-1836, pp. 145-154.
[4] Greene, E. B., and Thompson, C. M., Governor's Letter Books, Vol. *II*, pp. 59, 60, Illinois Historical Society Collections, Vol. 7.

purchases. To meet these demands the legislature on February 12, 1835 chartered a second State Bank of Illinois and at the same time extended the life of the Bank of Illinois twenty years. By the act of incorporation the state reserved for herself $100,000 of the authorized capital of $1,500,000 of the State Bank and one-third of the $300,000 capital of the Bank of Illinois. The charter of the State Bank prohibited the institution from owning real estate; and the directors were forbidden "to deal directly or indirectly in the purchase or sale of any goods or wares." [5]

Meanwhile the mania for internal improvements was growing in Illinois. Not satisfied with undertaking the herculean task of constructing the Illinois and Michigan Canal the legislature on February 27, 1837 passed an act to establish a general system of internal improvements. The construction of seven railroads was authorized as well as "the improvement of the navigation of the Kaskaskia, Illinois, Great and Little Wabash and Rock Rivers." Besides this $200,000 was appropriated for distribution "amongst those counties through which no roads or improvements were to be made." As a crowning act of folly the bill provided that the work should commence simultaneously on all the roads at their intersections and connection with the navigable streams and should progress in both directions in order that the roads might become productive of revenue as soon as possible. To carry out this stupendous scheme, the state was authorized to issue $8,000,000 of 6 percent bonds, redeemable in 1870. The faith of the state was pledged for the payment of the interest and principal of these bonds; but the law specifically prohibited their sale below par. [6]

In order to carry out the provisions of this act it was decided to make the banks an integral part of the general improvement plans. Both the State Bank and the reorganized Bank of Illinois were at that time in a prosperous condition; and it was hoped that by the state subscribing for bank stock a profitable income would be obtained which would lessen the burden of the heavy internal

[5] Dowrie, G. W., The Development of Banking in Illinois, pp. 60-64, University of Illinois Studies in the Social Sciences, Vol. *II*, No. 4.
[6] Acts Illinois, 1836-1837, pp. 121-152; Illinois Senate Journal, 1839, p. 136; Ford, Thomas, History of Illinois, pp. 183, 184. There is a detailed discussion of the internal improvement system in Pease, T. C., The Frontier State, Chs. *X, XI,* and *XVII.*

improvement load. As the *Sangamon Journal* said: "In connection with our internal improvement system it is impossible not to associate the banks of the state—the interests of both are alike and rest alike upon enlightened public opinion. One is the handmaid of the other, and since the internal improvement system is based upon credit it cannot be carried on without the aid of the banks." [7] The capital stock of the State Bank was therefore increased to $3,500,000 and that of the Bank of Illinois to $1,700,000. The state reserved for herself the entire subscription of the increased capital stock of the State Bank and $1,000,000 of that of the Bank of Illinois. To secure the necessary funds to purchase the bank stock, the Fund Commissioners were authorized to negotiate a loan of $3,000,000 and to issue stock known as the "Illinois Bank and Internal Improvement Stock," bearing 6 percent, redeemable after 1860. The faith of the state was pledged for the payment of the principal and interest of this stock. The banks were made public depositories and the fiscal agents of the canal and the railroads. [8]

Two months after the passage of this act the panic of 1837 swept over the country. In June of that year the Illinois banks were forced to suspend specie payments. Since the banks were the depositories of the public funds and the fiscal agents of the canal and the railroads, their suspension threatened to wreck the whole scheme of internal improvements. When the State Bank suspended there was on deposit nearly $400,000 of the canal funds; and by its act of incorporation the bank forfeited its charter if it did not resume within sixty days.

To avert this calamity the governor called the legislature in special session. In his message the governor explained the situation without making any recommendations that the legislature legalize the bank suspensions; but he did suggest a repeal or classification of the internal improvements. The legislature sanctioned the bank suspensions; but it was unwilling to acknowledge at that time that the state had undertaken too elaborate a scheme of internal improvements. Instead of curtailing their expenditures for such projects, the legislature at its next session authorized the construction of

[7] *Sangamon Journal*, Jan. 27, 1837 quoted in Dowrie, *op. cit.*, p. 78.
[8] Acts Illinois, 1836-1837, pp. 19-22.

additional works; and on February 23, 1839 authorized a loan of
$4,000,000, bearing 6 percent interest, for the Illinois and Michigan
Canal.[9]

In negotiating these loans, the fund commissioners and the
agents of the canal encountered many obstacles. They were ham-
pered in their operations by the wording of the laws authorizing the
loans and the stringency existing in the money markets of America
and of Europe. The state statutes prohibited them from disposing of
the bonds for less than their par value. The condition of the
money markets made it impossible to sell the bonds on these terms.
By 1839 Illinois stocks could not be sold in the New York money
market at 75 cents on the dollar. The prospects for sales abroad
were not much better. There were nearly $100,000,000 of American
stocks and bonds for sale in the London money market in the summer of 1839.[10] With so many American securities for sale in London, and with money not so plentiful for investment purposes, it
was extremely difficult to negotiate the Illinois loans on terms that
were in strict accord with the letter of the state statutes. Yet if the
representatives of the state and of the canal followed the spirit of
the laws rather than a literal interpretation of their provisions, their
actions were liable to be sharply criticized by the members of the
legislature who were unacquainted with the conditions existing in
the money centers but were most desirous of winning popular
approval by posing as the champions of the people. This does not
excuse, however, the representatives of the state for violating the
state statutes in negotiating the loans. They were the authorized
agents of the state; they were definitely instructed to dispose of the
bonds on certain terms. On the other hand it must be remembered
that the people of Illinois as well as the agents were anxious to negotiate the loans in order to carry out the internal improvement
plans.[11]

Furthermore, European bankers were sceptical of the Illinois
loans. Even though Huth and Company were informed by one of
their American correspondents that Illinois was "one of the most

[9] Ford, History of Illinois, pp. 191, 192; Putnam, *op. cit.*, pp. 42-46; Dowrie,
op. cit., pp. 83-85.
[10] Reports General Assembly, 1839-1840, Senate, p. 373; *ibid.*, 1840-1841, Senate,
p. 352.
[11] The difficulties encountered by one agent are discussed in R. M. Young's
report to Gov. Carlin. Reports General Assembly, 1840-1841, Senate, pp. 356, 357.

prosperous of the new states," the firm hesitated about taking the Illinois stock. With a favorable report on the economic condition of the state, Huth believed that the Illinois bonds might be equal to those of Indiana and might be disposed of at 83 or 85; but he felt that it would be difficult to sell the Illinois securities to English investors unless the interest and principal were made payable in London at the rate of 4 shillings 6 pence on the dollar "so as to render the stock available and desirable" to the great mass of English capitalists who did not want "to have their investments connected with a speculation on the exchange." Besides, as Huth wrote his agent, the State of Illinois was "quite in embryo, hardly known in this country," and its "cash resources must necessarily be very limited at present, however good its prospects for the future may be." [12]

The resources of the American money markets were tapped first by the fund commissioners and the canal agents. The contracts signed with the American bankers reveals the expedients resorted to by the state representatives to procure funds; and the advantages taken by the American bankers of the eagerness of the agents to dispose of their securities. On April 23, 1839, Rawlings and Reynolds, agents of the Illinois and Michigan Canal, signed a contract with John Delafield, president of the Phoenix Bank of New York. By the terms of the contract the agents sold to Delafield $300,000 of canal bonds, the interest commencing on June 10. Delafield agreed to pay $50,000 within fifteen days after the delivery of the bonds; another $50,000 on August 1; and the same amount on the first of each month from October to January inclusive. Six days later the canal agents sold 1,000 bonds of £225 each to Thomas Dunlap, president of the United States Bank of Pennsylvania, the interest on the bonds commencing July 1. This contract specified that the principal and interest were made payable in London at the rate of 4 shillings 6 pence on the dollar; and the United States Bank agreed to pay for the bonds in ten equal installments of $100,000 monthly in the notes of the bank.[13]

After considerable discussion the legislature approved these contracts. Governor Carlin justly protested that the contract with

[12] Huth to Goodhue, Oct. 14, 1837; Goodhue to Huth, Oct. 19, 1837; Huth to Perit, Nov. 29, Dec. 14, 1837. Huth Mss.

[13] Reports General Assembly, 1839-1840, House, pp. 149-152.

the United States Bank did not come within the purview of the law authorizing the loan. "Although the sale may not be a literal violation of the law," wrote the governor to Reynolds, "yet I am fully persuaded it never contemplated the authorizing of a loan by which the state should realize a less sum than par value for the bonds or incur a loss over and above 6 percent interest." The contract bound the state to pay the principal and interest in London; but as the rate of exchange was at that time 10 percent in favor of London, the governor estimated that the state incurred a loss of $285,000. The governor acknowledged to Reynolds that no doubt he had acted "upon the principle that any sacrifice must be incurred rather than permit the work on the canal to stop." But Reynolds was admonished "to use the utmost circumspection and economy" in his future operations and "to make no sale by which the state" could possibly "incur additional loss." "Now is the time," wrote the governor, "to escape the curses of posterity." A joint judiciary committee of both houses of the legislature considered the contract a glaring "departure from the letter and spirit of the law." In their opinion the Delafield contract also violated the law for it was preposterous to say the sale had been made at par when the state was required to pay interest from June 10 while she did not receive "the consideration money, except in instalments, payable at such distant days as to involve a loss (interest paid on the bonds) of near $5,000." [14]

In the meantime the fund commissioners had signed a contract with Delafield which caused even more trouble for the state. On May 7, 1839 the fund commissioners delivered to Delafield $283,000 of state bonds, the interest commencing from the date of the sale. Delafield agreed to pay for the bonds in five installments of $50,000 each on the first of December, February, March, April and May, and the last installment of $33,000 on June 1, 1840. In commenting on this contract, a hostile committee of the Senate under the chairmanship of O. H. Browning pointed out that by the terms of the agreement the state paid 9 months interest (less 7 days) upon the whole sum of $283,000 before she received any payment at all and before the last installment was received the state would have paid interest for one year and one month (minus 7 days) upon the whole

---

[14] Reports General Assembly, 1839-1840, Senate, pp. 370, 371; *ibid.*, House, p. 150.

amount. Since the commissioners had no authority to dispose of the bonds on a long credit, the committee held that the contract was a palpable violation of the law. If the commissioners could not have sold the bonds on better terms, the committee declared that they should not have sold them at all. "Why pay Mr. Delafield upon money which he retained in his hands and continued to use? Why make him a gratuity of $14,000 without any corresponding advantage to the state?" The committee therefore, recommended the adoption of a joint resolution repudiating the contract. A resolution to this effect was passed by the Senate in consequence of the protests of the drafts for the December and January installments; but later the Senate rescinded its action. The proposal was never entertained in the House.[15]

It appears that Delafield only paid the first two installments on his debt. The fund commissioners, therefore, brought suit against him in the Federal Circuit Court for the Southern District of New York for breach of contract. Delafield pleaded in his defense the bad faith of the State of Illinois and cited the repudiation resolution which he claimed seriously depreciated the value of the Illinois stocks. Webster, one of the state's attorneys, maintained that Illinois had instituted the suit in order to prevent Delafield from disposing of the bonds in his possession to innocent purchasers. In his argument before the Court, Webster declared that Illinois did not intend to repudiate the bonds or to question her liability for their payment. In rendering the decision the Chancellor said: "if these securities (the state bonds), therefore, pass into the hands of bona-fide holders who have no notice of any irregularity or want of authority on the part of the officers or agents of the State who put them into circulation, the complainant (Illinois) is both legally and equitably bound to pay them to such holders."

Notwithstanding the fact that the state did not dispute her liability for the bonds in the hands of bona-fide holders and the Court had decided that these parties were entitled to full payment, the Delafield case caused much anxiety in London among holders of Illinois bonds. There was fear that the controversy between the State and Delafield foreshadowed an intention on the part of Illinois to repudiate her bonds. Besides contributing to the lowering

---

[15] Illinois Senate Journal, special session, 1839-1840, pp. 136-146, 161, 165.

of the credit of the State, the dispute undoubtedly made foreign creditors more cautious in their later dealings with Illinois when proposals were made to them looking toward a resumption of interest payments on the public debt.[16]

When the resources of the American money market were exhausted, the fund commissioners and the canal agents turned to the London money market. On August 22, 1839, the fund commissioners agreed to deposit with John Wright and Company state bonds to the amount of $1,500,000 in denominations of $1,000 or £225 each. Upon the delivery of the bonds Wright and Company agreed to advance £20,000; and on the fifteenth day of February, March, and April further sums of £10,000, making in all the sum of £50,000. Wright and Company were constituted the fiscal agent of the State of Illinois and were allowed a commission of not more than 5 percent. On October 30, 1839, the canal agents delivered to the same firm 1,000 bonds of £225 each, the principal and interest payable in London. Wright and Company were authorized to sell the deposited bonds at not less than 91. The surplus on all sales between 91 and 95 were to be retained by Wright and Company; and the excess on all sales over 95 were to be divided equally between Wright and Company and the State of Illinois. Wright and Company were allowed a commission of 1 percent for their services in paying the interest; and were to advance £30,000 on the deposited bonds.[17]

There was much discussion in the legislature over the Wright contracts. A Senate committee recommended the repudiation of the contract made by the fund commissioners on the ground that it was not in conformity with the state statutes. The committee pointed out that for every £225 bond sold in London the state received $1,000. As the rate of exchange between London and Illinois was 14 percent, the committee held that the bonds had not been sold at par because in remitting the interest at the current rate of exchange the state would pay $1,140 in American currency for every $1,000 received. Since the bonds were reimbursable after 1870, the committee estimated that the state would lose in thirty years the sum

<hr />

[16] For the decision and British reactions consult *London Morning Chronicle*, Jan. 7, 12, Apr. 3, Dec. 31, 1841.
[17] Reports General Assembly, 1839-1840, Senate, pp. 393-409; *ibid.*, House, pp. 391-397.

of $378,000 in interest alone. Furthermore, the law forbade the commissioners to contract for the payment of a greater interest than 6 percent per annum. The interest on $1,500,000 of bonds at 6 percent would amount to $90,000 per year; but at the present rate of exchange, the state, according to the committee, would pay in interest every year the sum of $102,600, which was more than the law permitted. "Well may we say of London," declared Browning the chairman, " 'the shark is there, and the shark's prey—the spendthrift and the leech that sucks him.' " [18] The Senate committee on internal improvements ridiculed the argument that the cost of remitting the interest would raise the rate above 6 percent. "It is doubtful if the state bonds could ever be sold at par," declared the chairman of this committee, "if a condition should be added that the cost of paying the interest should be deducted from the amount of interest to be paid; an idea so preposterous could only find a resting place in the minds of those who were predetermined to find fault." [19] A joint judiciary committee of the legislature held that the sale of $1,000,000 of the canal bonds to Wright and Company was illegal; but the House Finance Committee were unable to decide on the legality of the sale and presented majority and minority reports.[20] The Senate adopted and then rescinded a resolution repudiating the fund commissioners' contract with Wright and Company.[21] On May 1, 1840 Governor Carlin reluctantly confirmed the canal contract with Wright and Company. The discussions in the legislature over the legality of these contracts unquestionably weakened the credit of the state abroad; and to make matters worse Wright and Company failed in November, 1840.[22]

The increasing financial difficulty of the state at last awakened the people to a realization of the heavy burden they had assumed. In August 1838 the Illinois banks resumed specie payments only to suspend a second time the following October. By that time the total indebtedness of the state amounted to more than $11,000,000 and carried an annual interest charge of $637,800. If the funds needed to carry out the authorized public works program were procured the

[18] Illinois Senate Journal, 1839-1840, pp. 136-146.
[19] Reports General Assembly, 1839-1840, Senate, pp. 209-220.
[20] Reports General Assembly, 1839-1840, House, pp. 123-134.
[21] Illinois Senate Journal, 1839-1840, special session, pp. 161, 165.
[22] Reports General Assembly, 1840-1841, Senate, pp. 352, 374, 393.

total liabilities of the state would be increased to a sum over $21,000,000.

In view of the alarming condition of the state's finances, Governor Carlin summoned the legislature in session early in December 1839. In his message the governor recommended the suspension of work on the general system of internal improvements and the concentration of all future labor and expenditures on a few important projects. The legislature carried out the governor's recommendations and ordered a cessation of all work on internal improvements. "Thus terminated," stated the governor in 1842, "our unfortunate and short-lived scheme of improvements, leaving the state with less than thirty miles of a single railroad completed, out of the multitude that had been projected, with an immense debt overwhelming her, and without any permanent means whatever provided to meet the interest that was so rapidly accruing upon it." [23]

In his message of 1839 Governor Carlin also recommended that no laws should be passed legalizing the suspension of specie payments by the State Bank and suggested that the legislature institute a rigid investigation of its condition. Governor Carlin was a thoroughgoing partisan Democrat and as an adherent of the Jackson-Benton school was hostile to all banks. Throughout these years the Whig party endeavored to defend the banks but even the staunchest defenders of these institutions were forced to admit that the public had good grounds to complain of the actions of the banks. The result of the legislative investigation of the State Bank intensified the popular hatred of the banks. The investigation revealed that the State Bank had abused the public confidence by assisting speculators dealing in Illinois produce and had granted loans to its directors and to certain members of the legislature. Some of its assets were found to be of questionable value. The legislature, however, decided to legalize the State Bank's suspension of specie payments while at the same time placing restrictions on its loan policies because there was a feeling that the financial embarrassment and distress would be increased by a sudden withdrawal of the bank's notes from circulation. [24]

[23] *Ibid.*, pp. 3-13; Reports General Assembly, 1842-1843, pp. 3-19.
[24] Reports General Assembly, 1839-1840, Senate, pp. 12, 13, 241-359; *ibid.*, 1842-1843, Senate, p. 12; Dowrie, *op. cit.*, pp. 85-95.

Meanwhile the state was finding it increasingly difficult to pay the interest on the public debt. The legislative session of 1839-1840 provided for the interest due on the canal bonds from the proceeds of the sales of the canal lands. The interest on the state bonds due in July 1840 was paid in London by Wright and Company advancing £20,000; and $45,000 was borrowed in New York to meet the payments in the United States. As the canal contractors were anxious to continue the work on the canal which had not been abandoned they agreed after the legislative session of 1839-1840 to take $1,000,000 of state bonds at par in payment of their estimates. W. F. Thornton, president of the Board of Canal Commissioners was sent to Europe with instructions to sell these bonds at not less than 75 percent of their par value, the contractors agreeing to stand the loss. To their surprise and gratification Thornton succeeded in disposing of the bonds at 85 to Magniac, Smiths and Company of London. This enabled the contractors to continue their work several months longer.[25]

How to pay the interest on the public debt due in January 1841 still remained unsolved. Various plans were proposed in the legislature but the one which met with the most favor was a "new issue of bonds to be hypothecated for whatever they would bring in the market." Ford in his History of Illinois acknowledges that "this was a desperate remedy"; but claims it "showed the zeal of the legislature in sustaining the public honor." There was no doubt that such a policy pursued for any length of time would bring the state to bankruptcy. But the plan was only feebly opposed on this ground. The principal objection was "to paying interest at all; and particularly to paying interest upon bonds for which the state had received nothing, or less than par." On the other hand, there was a strong feeling in the legislature that the state should do everything in its power to meet its engagements.[26] After considerable debate and some shrewd political maneuvering on the part of those desirous of sustaining the credit of the state, the legislature decided to levy

[25] Reports General Assembly 1840-1841, Senate, pp. 26, 27, 50. Ford in his History of Illinois, p. 208, claims that the canal contractors could afford to make this agreement because they had signed their contracts "when all prices were high. By the fall of prices, they could make a large profit on their work, and lose twenty-five per cent."
[26] Ford, op. cit., pp. 209, 210.

an additional tax of 10 cents on the $100 worth of property, establish a rate of valuation on land at not less than $3 per acre for taxation purposes, and, in case the revenues from these and other sources did not provide the necessary funds, the fund commissioners were authorized to sell bonds at the market price to any amount to make up the deficiency. "Now we ask," said the *Illinois State Register,* "what more the legislature could have done to sustain the credit of the state. We say they have amply sustained it and we hope the croakings in New York against Illinois will cease in the future." [27]

By these measures the state was able to meet the interest payments due in January and July 1841. The fund commissioners hypothecated internal improvement bonds for the January interest; and $804,000 of the interest bonds were hypothecated with Macalister and Stebbins of Philadelphia as security for a loan of $321,000 to meet the July interest.[28] This was the last interest payment made by Illinois until 1846.

The hard times, the enormous public debt and the heavy taxes, caused some in Illinois to advocate repudiation as a solution of their troubles. In Bond County, a meeting of the taxpayers, protested against the revenue laws and the payment of the public debt. It was claimed that the state debt had been contracted in violation of the federal and state constitutions; "that the system of internal improvements out of which it grew was a fraud upon the people"; and that the people were neither able to pay nor legally or morally bound to do so.[29] At a meeting in Montgomery County it was announced that the people were not morally obliged to meet their obligations when taxes were excessive or when the state had received no return upon the sale of its bonds. In Scott County it was claimed that the bonds were bills of credit and therefore unconstitutional and "not binding on the state." [30] How could the people of Illinois be expected to pay their debts, it was asked, when the population of the state was less than half a million? The great bulk of the people lived in rude log cabins. They had everything to buy; and

---

[27] *Niles,* May 8, 1841.
[28] Ford, *op. cit.,* pp. 210-211. Ford claims that the state never received more than $261,500 from Macalister and Stebbins.
[29] Kendall's Expositor, Apr. 7, 1841.
[30] *London Times,* May 22, 1841; Pease, The Frontier State, p. 232.

but little to sell. All the money they had brought with them was expended in purchasing land and in making such improvements as were indispensable to the sustenance of their families. It was unjust to sneer at Illinois and compare her with the wealthy state of New York which regularly met its engagements. The men who composed the legislative body of Illinois were the agents of the people; their powers were defined by a written constitution which was published and was accessible to every intelligent man, whether in Europe or America. These agents had never possessed the power to impose upon the people such an enormous debt.[31]

So argued the extremists; but the more sober elements in Illinois refused to countenance such doctrines. What Illinois, as many of the other insolvent states needed, was someone to show the people how imperative it was for the state to meet its engagements and how this could be done. The gubernatorial election of 1842 placed in the executive chair a man who had both the courage and the imagination to grapple successfully with this problem.

The inauguration of Governor Ford ushered in a new era in the financial history of Illinois. The new executive inspired confidence by his candid exposition of the state's finances and his determination to sustain the honor of the state. The total amount of the state debt, excluding the unpaid interest, in December 1842 was $15,178,348. The governor was convinced that this could not be paid by raising the taxes at that particular moment. By the assessment of 1841 the value of the taxable property in the state was $69,831,419. To pay the public debt by taxation it would be necessary to levy a tax of 1½ cents on the dollar. The governor frankly declared that the people could not bear this burden in addition to the county taxes. They were scarcely able to pay the present tax of 30 cents on the $100. There were not more than 85,000 taxpayers in the state. Both the State Bank and the Bank of Illinois had become insolvent since the last session of the legislature. The notes of these banks had greatly depreciated and what specie they had was locked up in their vaults. Consequently the people were left without money; the value of property had fallen; and the products of the farmers were almost unsaleable. There was only one way to provide the community with a sound currency. The

[31] *Niles,* Dec. 18, 1841.

banks should be compelled to resume specie payments, and if they were unable to do so, the legislature should provide for their liquidation and the withdrawal of their notes from circulation.

Creditors were assured, however, by the governor, that Illinois had no intention of repudiating its debts. The measures passed by the last legislature, even though they had proved unfruitful, should have demonstrated this to the creditors. If additional proof were needed, it could be found in the results of the recent election, for those who had sponsored repudiation had been defeated at the polls. The governor acknowledged that the people of Illinois were largely responsible for their own misfortunes. They had indulged in every form of speculation and had planned extravagant works of internal improvement far beyond their limited resources. But those who criticized Illinois should remember the whole world had been speculative mad a few years ago. "The main thing which the world can justly reproach us," truthfully said the governor, "is that we were visionary and reckless; that without sober deliberation, we jumped headlong into ambitious schemes of public aggrandizement, which were not justifiable by our resources." The original creditors were open to the same reproach. "They, as men of intelligence, sufficient for the proper management of large capital, ought as well as ourselves, to have foreseen our future want of ability, and the consequent catastrophe which our common error has produced."

There was, of course, the bare possibility that a rigorous system of taxation might yield a sum sufficient to pay interest for a single year. The governor warned the creditors, however, that "such a tax could not be repeated. The apprehension of it would spread consternation and alarm throughout the breadth of the land. Our citizens would sell their property at any sacrifice and leave us for some happier home. The whole world would avoid our shores, as they would avoid certain destruction. We would depopulate the state of its present inhabitants, and prevent any future accession by alarming strangers abroad."

Under these circumstances it was neither to the interest of the debtors nor to the creditors to make a violent change in the taxation system. "If our creditors are ever to be paid," frankly stated the governor, "it will not be by the mere territory composing the State, nor by the abstract thing called State sovereignty, but by the people, who may be here, the inhabitants of the land; and how are they to be paid if we depopulate our country?" Therefore, to quiet the fears of the debtors and the creditors the governor recommended that the legislature let it be known in a decisive manner there would be "no oppressive and exterminating taxation"; and at the same time convince the creditors and the world that Illinois would not countenance "the disgrace of repudiation." The practical backwoods statesman knew how to make himself popular with his constituents while he assured the creditors of the good faith of the state.

In the meantime the governor felt that Illinois should make "every exertion and sacrifice consistent with self-preservation" to keep its engagements. The governor, therefore, suggested that the legislature offer the creditors all the property of the state at fair and reasonable prices. This would include the 42,000 acres of land purchased by the state under the internal improvement system; the 210,000 acres of land given to Illinois by the federal government, together with the finished and unfinished railroads. But the canal lands and lots and other property belonging to the canal stood on a different footing. This property had originally been given to the state in trust to make the canal. It had afterwards been appropriated by the General Assembly for the specific purpose of constructing a canal and had been solemnly pledged to the creditors for the payment of the money borrowed. Of course, the creditors had a right to demand that the debtors surrender it to them in payment of the debt; and the debtors were in honor and duty bound, if so requested, to hand it over. The creditors must realize, however, that if this property were surrendered to them, the state would have "no means of payment for a long time to come"; whereas, if the canal were pushed to completion, "the lands and lots and waterpower" would be "quadrupled in value, and the tolls alone would in a short time pay interest on all the debt contracted for its construction." The canal was already five-eighths finished; and by changing it to a lock canal, the work could be completed at an estimated cost not exceeding $1,500,000. For these reasons the governor urged the legislature to provide for the completion of the canal.

Governor Ford also had some practical suggestions to make regarding the banking situation. In his estimation the state had erred in becoming a partner in the banks. Nevertheless, the governor was not in favor of a sudden divorce of the state from the banks, because it would leave the people without an adequate medium of exchange and might lead to litigation on the part of the banks. Moreover, he considered it a breach of faith on the part of the state to throw its stock into the open market, thereby forcing down the market value of the stock held by the private stockholders. Such a move would not help the state secure any additional aid from the creditors in completing the canal. It would be much wiser to compromise with the banks by inducing them to exchange the state bonds they held for the state's stock, dollar for dollar.[32]

The legislature proceeded to carry out the governor's recommendations. A resolution was passed authorizing the governor, auditor, and fund commissioners to ascertain upon what terms an amicable separation could be effected between the banks and the state. A report of these negotiations was submitted to the legislature to guide them in reaching a final decision. The books of the State Bank show that the bank was indebted to the state as a stockholder to the amount of $2,100,000 while the liability of the state to the bank as the owner of state bonds, state scrip, and money advanced by the bank to the state, aggregated $2,152,404.09. The State Bank signified its willingness to surrender the state's securities and claims of the bank, dollar for dollar, in exchange for the stock of the bank owned by the state, provided the legislature allowed the bank to use its present charter during the period of liquidation. To meet all constitutional objections, the state was requested to retain a nominal amount of the stock of the bank. A bill along these lines was drafted by the governor. It passed the House of Representatives by a vote of 107 to 4. In the Senate it encountered some opposition, under the leadership of Lyman Trumbull, whom the governor was compelled to remove from his office of Secretary of State. The State Bank accepted the terms of the act; and on February 9, 1843, state bonds, and auditor's warrants amounting to $2,073,501.51 were burned in front of the State House. The Bank of Illinois also agreed to deliver immediately to the state $500,000 of state bonds and other evidences of indebtedness, and the remaining $500,000

[32] Reports General Assembly, 1842-1843, Senate, pp. 21-32.

within a year with 6 percent interest. By these various laws, the amount of the state debt was reduced over $3,000,000.[33]

In his inaugural address Governor Ford had also urged the completion of the canal. This was a sound suggestion for a finished canal would materially aid the state finances. The revenue obtained from the canal would help pay the interest charges; the interest in land values would yield a large return from taxes; while the sale of the canal lands would help diminish the burden of the public debt. But more money was needed to complete the work even though the original plans were changed; and the only hope of securing these funds was from the present holders of the canal bonds. Accordingly on February 21, 1843, an act was passed authorizing the governor to negotiate a loan of $1,600,000 solely on the credit of the canal, canal lands, tolls, and revenue. Holders of canal bonds were given preference in subscribing to this loan. The canal and its property were handed over to three trustees, two of whom were to be chosen by the subscribers and the third appointed by the governor. The trustees were to hold and manage the canal for the benefit of the bondholders under certain restrictions which safeguarded the interests of the state.[34]

Charles Oakley and Michael Ryan were appointed by the governor to negotiate the new loan. The commissioners proceeded to New York where for a time their negotiations were delayed on account of malicious reports circulated in eastern financial circles by opponents of the canal measure. It was rumored that another Illinois legislature would take away from the creditors whatever protection they had under the present law as soon as they had advanced their money to finish the work. The commissioners succeeded in refuting these calumnies and with the assistance of David Leavitt, an influential New York banker, induced the American creditors to agree to subscribe their portion of the loan.

With this assurance the commissioners departed for England carrying with them letters of introduction to Magniac, Jardine, and Company, Baring Brothers and Company, of London, and Hope and Company of Amsterdam who represented the interests of the foreign creditors. Oakley and Ryan found the bankers willing to

[33] Reports General Assembly, 1842-1843, Senate, pp. 93-96; *ibid.*, House, pp. 201-206; Greene and Thompson, Governor's Letter Books, Vol. *II*, p. 54.
[34] Acts Illinois, 1843, pp. 54-61.

consider the proposition provided the security for the loan was satisfactory.[85] The sceptical *London Times,* however, cautioned the foreign creditors not to trust the people of Illinois as long as they showed an unwillingness to endure taxation.[86] This was a typical reception given to many of the agents of insolvent American states who visited England requesting additional financial assistance. The bankers who had sold the original bonds in Europe realized the need of aiding the defaulting states if their clients ever hoped to recover their funds; but they exercised more care in examining the new loans than those first offered to them. On the other hand, the London press stressed the legal rights of the bondholders without taking into due consideration the economic and political conditions in the newer states.

The bondholders agreed to examine for themselves the situation in Illinois. A committee, consisting of Abbott Lawrence, Thomas W. Ward, and William Sturgis, all of Boston, was appointed to represent the foreign bondholders in America. This committee was requested to select two competent persons who should visit Illinois, examine the canal and the property, estimate its value and debts, and report their findings to the creditors. Ex-Governor John Davis of Massachusetts and Captain William H. Swift of the engineering corps of the United States Army were chosen to make the investigation. Davis and Swift proceeded to Illinois in the fall of 1843; and after a thorough examination confirmed the statements of the state commissioners.[87]

Notwithstanding this report, the European bondholders were unwilling to subscribe to the loan. They were not convinced that it was wise to advance more money until more definite assurance was given that conditions in Illinois were sound. They pointed to the nonfulfillment by the American creditors of their subscription pledges as an indication of a lack of confidence upon the part of American investors. Governor Davis was summoned to England by the foreign creditors to give them a more detailed account of the situation in Illinois.[88] The Barings and Magniac, Jardine and Company proposed to the canal bondholders that they accept the propo-

[85] Ford, *op. cit.,* pp. 370-372.
[86] *London Times,* June 23, 1843.
[87] These negotiations are discussed in detail in Circular of Illinois Commissioners to Holders of Illinois Stock, May 25, 1843; Proposal to Holders of Illinois and Michigan Canal Bonds, June 25, 1844. Baring Printed Documents.
[88] Ford, *op. cit.,* pp. 373-374.

sition provided the next session of the legislature reënacted the interest tax.[39]

At this juncture of affairs Governor Ford acted in a decisive manner. In an open letter to William S. Wait, the governor declared that the state must give the creditors some tangible evidence of their intentions. The state must either provide for the payment of the interest or repudiate its obligations. As the governor said, the question could not be postponed; putting off the evil day would not settle it. It would do no good for the men of today to throw it upon the future; and if the people of Illinois decided against the honest claims of their creditors, the moral sense of the world would be against them.[40]

The publication of this letter clarified the atmosphere. Leavitt and Oakley hurried to England to press the case of the canal. The news of Governor Ford's letter had preceded them and they found the creditors willing to agree provided the legislature reimpose the interest tax. "There is no doubt in our minds," wrote the Barings to Oakley, "that had those states which possessed the undoubted ability to pay, kept their respective engagements with their creditors, those states who must look forward for the necessary means would have obtained additional facilities which might be required, and Illinois would have got her money; but it is the conduct of Pennsylvania, Maryland, and Louisiana which has created a general distrust and mainly militated against the success of your project." There was no foundation for the rumor that European disinclination to invest in the United States was the result of a combination of bankers and capitalists. "In reality it originated in a prejudice created by individual losses spread over the whole community; and that is a distrust and prejudice which no influence or combination of bankers can counteract, and which can only be removed by the gradual experience that good faith will be strictly preserved in the States."[41]

In this candid letter the Barings voiced the feelings of foreign

[39] Proposal to Holders of Illinois and Michigan Canal Bonds, June 25, 1844. Baring Printed Documents.
[40] Ford, op. cit., pp. 378-384.
[41] Baring letter quoted in *London Morning Post*, Nov. 27, 1844. At the critical moment when the Davis and Swift Report reached England, the disastrous news reached London of the adjournment of the Maryland legislature without having made any movement towards redeeming its faith. This destroyed all confidence in American securities; but the action in Pennsylvania revived confidence. Democratic Review, Vol. 14, pp. 653-655.

investors toward the United States. Some of the Democrats, including Ryan, declared that the delay in the negotiations was due to the Whig advisers of the English bankers who counseled postponement of the subscription until after the election of 1844 in the hope that the return of the Whigs to power in the national government would bring about federal assumption of the state debts. While there is an abundance of evidence to prove that the Whig politicians in many of the states hoped to profit by the chaotic conditions in the state's finances in the campaign of 1844 and that foreign creditors would have been pleased if Clay instead of Polk had been elected, it is also true that the individual settlements of the debts in the various states reacted upon one another. To foreigners the United States was a unit. The credit of the federal government and of the separate states were interwoven; all were affected by what each state individually did.[2]

When the legislature assembled Governor Ford urged the passage of some form of taxation. Colonel Oakley, David Leavitt, and Governor Davis visited Springfield to place the proposition of the creditors before the legislature. To many of the members of the General Assembly the representatives of the creditors were emissaries of the bloated aristocrats of Europe come to coerce the poverty-stricken farmers of Illinois. Therefore, their proposals should be rejected. By carefully abstaining from all factional quarrels in the legislature, and by frankly stating the demands of the creditors, the representatives of the foreign bondholders gradually changed this attitude of hostility to one of friendliness;[3] and on March 1, 1845, the legislature passed an act providing for a permanent interest tax of one mill in 1845 on each dollar of property and thereafter one and one-half mills. While this was not entirely sufficient to pay the interest, it was a good beginning; and this was increased by the constitution of 1848 which provided for a permanent tax of two mills to be applied to all state indebtedness, except canal and school bonds. At the same time, a canal bill was passed incorporating the provisions of the act of February 21, 1843. The canal was deeded in trust to the subscribers of the loan which practically gave them a first mortgage on the property; and the subscribers were permitted

---

[2] On the political aspects of the debt question in Illinois consult Ford, *op. cit.*, pp. 374-377; Pease, *op. cit.*, p. 323; Greene and Thompson, *op. cit.*, Vols. *II, LXXI.*
[3] Ford, *op. cit.*, pp. 391, 392.

to register their old bonds when they made their subscriptions on the basis of 32 percent of their holdings. Thus the interest charges on the old bonds were paid out of the receipts of the canal "as soon as the new loan and its interest had been provided for." [44]

In a confidential report to Magniac, Jardine and Company and Baring Brothers and Company, Leavitt and Davis gave their private opinions on the Illinois settlement. In view of the light which this letter sheds on Illinois politics and the character of the advice which European bankers had to rely upon in making their final decisions, this illuminating document is quoted at length.

It has seemed to us [wrote Davis and Leavitt], both expedient and necessary to make you acquainted with many things which cannot be fully and freely communicated in any way which shall give a just and fair understanding of them (Illinois legislators) without exposing our motives to misrepresentation, ourselves to unwonted abuse, and your interests to injury, unless we draw over the facts exposed, a veil which shall secure them from the public eye. We have seen enough to satisfy us that the truth may not be told with impunity but if it could we are not aware that our exposure of it could in any way prove serviceable to your best interests.

We begin then by stating that our visit to Illinois has not strength-ened our confidence in the integrity, ability, or disposition of the people to pay their public debt. . . . The canal is a northern measure and being considered by the south local fails to secure many friends in that region and there is an evident reluctance among that population to assess any tax. . . . All parties denounce repudiation but while they do this many take refuge under the plea of inability and refuse to make any grants whatever to liquidate the public debt. . . .

The north avows different and more favorable sentiments. . . . How far all this springs from a regard to obtain the money is a question which we cannot decide. Many no doubt are influenced by just and honorable sentiments and sincerely desire to maintain the faith of the state; but we cannot shut our eyes to the fact that no party was bold enough to stand up and advocate a law which should bind the honor and faith of the state for its continuance till the debt was satisfied. On the contrary they had expressly saved the right to future legislatures to annul or modify the law at pleasure. We were constantly assured, that a stronger law could not be carried, and if it could, that popular resentment would at the next election sacrifice the advocates of it.

We saw much of this demagogical timidity and became rather satisfied, that the people are more disposed to fulfil their duty, as honest men, than

[44] Acts Illinois, 1845, pp. 31, 32, 44; Ford, *op. cit.*, pp. 394, 395; Greene and Thompson, *op. cit.*, Vols. *II, LXI, LXXIII.*

their representatives who seemed to be haunted with the fear of losing popular favor. . . . Even in the halls of the legislature the advocates of taxes were denounced as cruel and unworthy of public confidence as they extorted from the poor to add to the abundance of the rich. . . .

It seemed to us too apparent through all the varied occurrences at Springfield, that the question was with many to say the least, what is the smallest amount of taxation that will bring the money to complete the canal? We were severely pressed on this point under various plausible pretences. . . . We gave more or less of them to understand that we comprehended their views and that it would not be very likely to produce a favorable impression. We thought there was much reason for believing that no tax would be levied after two years for the interest on the canal debts. The friends of the canal have given such strong assurances that its resources are adequate to provide for the debt, that a tax in aid of those resources is viewed as an unnecessary and oppressive burden and we fear will be discontinued when the legislature shall meet two years hence. In the meantime, however, a new apportionment of the representation is to take place which we are told will give a much more decided preponderance to northern feeling. . . . This fact is greatly relied upon to keep public opinion and public faith upon a steadfast basis and we are inclined to believe not without some reason for the population of the north is undoubtedly more to be relied upon in this particular. But it is to be remembered that the moral obligation to pay a public debt which the newcomers had no share in contracting may hang rather loosely upon their consciences and they, too, may fall into the doctrine of compromise under the seductive argument that such would be a facile mode of disposing of the debt. We do not therefore feel the greatest confidence in the assurance that the councils of the north should they prevail will be wise and patriotic. It is necessarily a heterogeneous (population) coming as it does from most of the free states and from Europe, and it would be a hazardous assumption to take it for granted that its disposition and future policy will be characterized by the wisdom and integrity which high minded men hope to realize.

Most of the emigrants who settle in the state are poor. . . . We entertain no doubt that they might well enough bear much heavier taxation than they subject themselves to and still be less burdened in this way than the population in most parts of the old states. The habit does much to reconcile the people to such exactions and probably what now is viewed in Illinois as a mountain may in a few years dwindle into a mole hill.

· · · · · · ·

The demagogues of whom the government speaks are numerous; and like the carrion crow set watching for a dead carcass. You must expect from them every species of intrigue, falsehood, and baseness. If you yield to them you will not escape pollution and if you resist you must carry on the war by the best means in your power. Conciliation is idle unless you deliver yourselves up soul and body to be employed after their fashion. . . . You are little aware of the corrupt morals of the law, stealthy, base intriguing politician of the west, and it is difficult to decide which is most to be shunned, his friendship or his enmity. It is enough when we suggest these considerations to show that the duties of trustee will necessarily be both arduous and difficult. The obstacles thrown in the way of his progress may be numerous and difficult to surmount—base men will employ base means. They will slander you and your agents by misrepresenting your conduct, impugning your motives, and charging you with the very crimes they intend to perpetrate.[45]

To the Eastern capitalists, the people of the West were little better than the dregs of society. Fortunately, foreigners had more faith in the people of Illinois than their own countrymen; and the subscriptions were made.

[45] Davis and Leavitt to Magniac, Jardine and Company and Baring Brothers and Company, March 20, 1845. This theme was elaborated in a private letter of Davis to Barings, March 29, 1845: "The citizens are from all parts of Europe as well as all parts of the United States, thinly scattered over a wide wild region where the possession of many acres is no certain proof of a comfortable or independent condition. Among public men the great art seems to be to learn what means may be most effectually employed to sway the public mind and gain over it the ascendancy which will produce favorable results at the polls. Falsehood, misrepresentation, erroneous reasoning and all such appliances designed to rule public opinion have in such a country a greater chance of success than in most places because of the thousand obstacles in the way of pursuing and correcting what is false and erroneous. A seven by nine paper published in some obscure place is probably the only periodical read for 50 to 100 miles around it. . . . We heard it often said that this man or that could be secured upon such and such considerations—which sometimes seemed to us to imply that his own interest was to say the least paramount to all other considerations. Many will attempt to ride into power as the friends par excellence of the people because they are opposed to the payments of the debts and having by such base means obtained power they will turn round and refuse to levy revenue on the ground that they are instructed to oppose it." Baring Mss.

CHAPTER VII

THE INDIANA STATE DEBT

An account of the public debt of Indiana reads very much like that of Illinois. The public indebtedness of both of these states originated in much the same way. Both states planned extensive systems of public works without adequately providing for their financing. In Illinois the banks were closely associated with the internal improvement plans. For this reason it was impossible for Illinois to solve her financial difficulties until the state severed its connection with the banks. This was not the case in Indiana where the affairs of the State Bank were well managed and were kept as far as possible separate from those of the internal improvements. Beyond this difference the financial experiences of Indiana and Illinois were similar. Both states found it impossible to carry out their original plans; but both were anxious to complete certain canals. Illinois wanted to finish the Illinois and Michigan Canal; Indiana was interested primarily in the Wabash and Erie Canal. Each state offered to deed its canal in trust to the creditors provided they would advance more money for its completion. In both instances the creditors accepted the terms proffered them. But in Illinois the proposal originated with the people themselves whereas in Indiana the suggestion came from the bondholders; and the terms of the Indiana settlement, together with the subsequent fate of the Wabash and Erie Canal, lends an added significance to the history of the state debt of Indiana.

The first important work undertaken by Indiana was the construction of the Wabash and Erie Canal. In May 1824 Congress authorized the state to open a canal through the public lands to connect the Wabash River with the "Miami of the Lake." Governor Ray urged the legislature to accept this gift and suggested that Congress be further petitioned to add a land grant. The attention of the legislature was called to the advantages the citizens would derive by improving the means of transportation. The construction of canals would not only give an impetus to agriculture and manufacturing but also improve the finances of the state. For these reasons the governor stressed the importance of internal improvements and intimated that the necessary funds to complete such works might be raised by means of loans. But the legislature was cautioned not to enter too hastily upon such schemes. All expenditures for internal improvements should be based upon the assured utility of the works. Under such circumstances the interest of the community would not be jeopardized by borrowing the money for public works of permanent value which would ultimately pay for themselves.[1]

The governor did not need to press the legislature to accept his views. A bushel of corn worth ten or twenty cents at Indianapolis could be sold on the river board for fifty cents. It was estimated that the annual loss on 100 acres of farm land due to inadequate transportation facilities was $1800. There was a legitimate economic basis for the popular demand for internal improvements; but the proposed canal was too far north to benefit more than one-tenth of the people of the state. It was only on the tacit understanding that it would be the first of a general system of internal improvements which would benefit all sections of the state that the Wabash and Erie Canal was undertaken. Furthermore, Ohio had already begun the construction of two canals to connect the Ohio River with Lake Erie. The desire to emulate what other states were doing, as well as to derive the economic advantages of such enterprises, gave an added stimulus to the popular clamor.[2]

On March 2, 1827, Congress granted the request of Indiana. A tract of 5 miles wide and 160 miles in length was given to the state for the purpose of constructing the Wabash and Erie Canal. A portion of this land was later surrendered to Ohio on condition that the state would construct the canal from the Indiana boundary to Lake Erie. The acceptance of the federal grant of land inaugurated the canal era in Indiana. A board of three commissioners was elected to locate the canal, select the donated lands, and ascertain upon what terms funds could be obtained upon the pledge of the canal

[1] Indiana Senate Journal, 1825, pp. 18-26.
[2] Ibid.; Esarey, L., Internal Improvements in Early Indiana, Indiana Historical Society Publications, Vol. 2, No. 2, pp. 91, 92.

lands. Little progress was made until 1832 when the legislature passed a supplementary act providing for a board of three fund commissioners to administer the canal fund and authorized a loan of $200,000 bearing 6 percent interest. The faith of the state, the tolls, and the canal lands were pledged for the payment of the interest and the redemption of the principal of the loan. Agents were appointed to negotiate the loan; and on Washington's birthday work commenced on the middle section of the canal. By 1835 the canal was opened for traffic between Fort Wayne and Huntington; but it had been found necessary to authorize another loan of $400,000 to carry on the work.[3]

Meanwhile the popular demand for a comprehensive system of public works to embrace all portions of the state grew in volume. A bill was introduced in the lower house of the legislature in the session of 1834-1835 providing such a plan; but it met with little approval. The main objection to the measure was "not that it contained too much but that it did not contain enough." Amendment after amendment was passed until the whole state was literally checkered with imaginary canals and railroads. The bill became so ponderous that even its sponsors decided to table the measure. But they did not give up all hope of carrying out their plan of a general system of internal improvements for the state. To accomplish this, they counted on the support of the friends of the Wabash and Erie Canal who were anxious to extend the canal to Lafayette. What was their consternation when word was received that the Senate had passed such a bill. The internal improvement forces were thrown into confusion. They fully realized that the passage of this bill would take away from them many votes upon which they had confidently counted. Quickly rallying their forces each one pledged his support to the other's favorite proposal. By adopting such tactics the representatives of the "system" killed the Wabash and Erie bill; and substituted in its place a measure calling for a general survey of all possible routes for internal improvements.

These surveys awakened a lively interest in internal improvements throughout the state. As the engineers, chain gangs, and their

[3] Indiana Senate Journal, 1827, pp. 9-27; Laws of Indiana, 1828, pp. 10-12; 1832, pp. 3-8; 1834, pp. 49-54; Benton, E. J., The Wabash Trade Route in the Development of the Old Northwest, Johns Hopkins University Studies, Vol. 21, p. 49.

workers passed through the country making their surveys, the people lost their "mental balance"; every neighborhood became so intoxicated with the idea that a railroad or a canal was to pass near it "that the public was unable to judge of the propriety of any proposed measure" or "of the amount of taxation that they should safely impose upon themselves." Leading politicians openly told the farmers that the extra burden of taxation could be borne from the profits of the sale of an "additional hen and chickens!" At the next session of the legislature, nine-tenths of the members took their seats instructed to adopt a general plan of internal improvements. Every representative was there to urge the claims of his favorite work.[4]

Under these circumstances the Mammoth Bill of 1836, as it was called, providing for a general system of public works passed the legislature with the support of all parties. The act authorized the governor to appoint a board of internal improvements who were to locate and supervise the construction of the several works of internal improvement. Appropriations were made for the construction of a number of canals, railroads, and turnpikes, with the Wabash and Erie Canal as the main trunk line of the system. The canal fund commissioners were authorized to make loans not exceeding $10,000,000, redeemable in twenty-five years, at the rate of 5 percent. For the payment of the interest and the final redemption of the principal all the sums borrowed, the canals, railroads, turnpikes, rents, profits of waterpower, and the faith of the state were pledged. The canal fund commissioners were also authorized to negotiate a loan of $500,000, for the Wabash and Erie Canal in order to extend the canal from the mouth of the Tippecanoe River to Terre Haute and from there by means of the Cross Cut Canal to the Central Canal on the White River.[5]

The passage of the internal improvement bill was the signal for universal rejoicing. The newspapers heralded the event as the dawn of a new era in the history of Indiana; villages were illuminated; and an almost unbroken voice of approbation pervaded the state.

[4] The origin and passage of the Mammoth Bill is based upon Judge David Kilgore's speech in the Constitutional Convention of 1850, found in Const. Conv. Debates, 1850, Vol. I, pp. 676-680; Consult also the Report of the Board of Internal Improvements, 1839, in Indiana Senate Doc., 1840, pp. 26-29.
[5] Laws of Indiana, 1836, pp. 6-21.

The press of other states announced the measure was an example of Indiana's enterprise and was worthy of imitation elsewhere. Instead of viewing the plan and its consequent expenditures as too large and costly, the public demanded more, even though the engineers confessed at the next session of the legislature that they had underestimated the cost by $2,600,000. Localities which had not been provided for in the bill began to urge their claims; and for two years these representatives brought forward bills proposing other works costing several millions more. In an endeavor to appease the popular impatience the board of internal improvements ordered work to commence upon every line; and, at a later period, at several points on the same line. When objectors questioned the wisdom of the simultaneous construction of all the works and suggested that it would be more economical, and lighten the burden of taxation by finishing one portion of the system at a time, their objections were overruled by the people and the policy of the board was sustained.[6]

The prosecution of the public works program brought the state to bankruptcy. The mismanagement and dishonesty of some of the state officials made this inevitable. State statutes were violated; public funds were squandered and embezzled. The public paid little attention to the actions of the commissioners until the state funds were exhausted. Then the people were stunned by the revelations of the manner in which the loans had been negotiated and the way in which the contracts for the public works had been made.

The board of internal improvements was composed of nine men appointed by the governor, three of whom retired each year. As soon as the board was organized, each commissioner was assigned the duty of supervising the construction of the public works in his district. This was a fatal blunder as each member determined to complete the work in his locality as soon as possible in order to win popular approval. The result was a scramble for funds. Friends and relatives of the board were given contracts with little regard to the usefulness of the works projected or the cost to the state; appropriations were exceeded and state money was used by some of the members of the board for their own private purposes.[7]

[6] Indiana Senate Doc., 1840, pp. 26-29.
[7] Report of the Investigating Committee, 1842, pp. 6-10.

The state suffered serious losses in the negotiation of its loans. One hundred thousand dollars of the loan issued for the Wabash and Erie Canal was sold in August 1832 on credit and on an unfair bid to J. D. Beers and Company. The Morris Canal and Banking Company was the largest and best customer for Indiana bonds. The manner in which this company obtained some of the state bonds was later disclosed by a committee of the legislature appointed to investigate the transactions of the different agents of the state. The Morris Canal and Banking Company was chartered in New Jersey in 1824 for the purpose of constructing a canal; and was authorized to do a banking business. In 1836 the paid-in-capital of the company was $4,000,000, of which $3,100,000 was invested in the canal and the remainder used for banking purposes. Louis McLane, ex-United States Senator, Minister to England, Secretary of the Treasury and Secretary of State, and later president of the Baltimore and Ohio Railroad, was president of the company; and the board of directors was composed of some of the most prominent business men in the country. In the spring of 1837 the company was reorganized and large quantities of its stock were issued to certain men at fifty cents on the dollar. The United States Bank of Pennsylvania became a large stockholder in the new corporation; and among the new directors elected were E. R. Biddle, a cousin of Nicholas Biddle, and Thomas Cadwalader, a trusted adviser of the president of the United States Bank of Pennsylvania. Dr. Coe, one of the fund commissioners of Indiana, was one of the largest stockholders in the Morris Canal and Banking Company, the New York Staten Island and Whaling Company, and also a director of the Staten Island Bank. In 1836 the Morris Canal and Banking Company received $898,824 of Indiana bonds from Dr. Coe. By February 1837 the company owed the state $584,890; and in February 1838 this amount was increased to $733,138. During this period it appears that Dr. Coe received 338 shares of stock at fifty cents on the dollar. The investigating committee "obtained an account of the numerous benefactions received by Dr. Coe from the Morris Canal and Banking Company," which, in the words of the report, "upon their face evince anything but a just regard to his duties as fund commissioner, as a mere expression of the facts alone will make evident:

"He is credited with a commission of 5% upon a sale of $400,000 (supposed
   stocks) $20,000
"His half of profits on a sale of 280 bonds............................ 11,200
"All his stock, 398 shares in the Morris Canal Bank at par, which at the time
   were not worth more than 15 cents on the dollar, making a difference
   of about 33,680
"Also his note for about.. 39,000

                                          Total $103,880

"Here we have it evident that Dr. Coe received commissions and profits and benefits from the Morris Canal and Banking Company alone of more than $100,000. It needs no comment."

Concerning the transactions of one of the other fund commissioners the committee reported: "You can deem it impracticable to test the conduct of this gentleman by the rigid rules of right and wrong. The task would be interminable, for the enquiry would not be, what has he done wrong, but what is there in his whole business correctly done? His complicated negotiations with Sherwood, Danforth, Dodge, Robinson and others (bankers of New York and Ohio), his loans of state property to sustain tottering swindling shops, his ante-dated letters and receipts, his negligence and confusion in business, his improper connections with brokers, shavers, and swindlers, are facts, too glaring to be denied, too grossly wrong to admit of palliation, and too palpably indefensible to invite attack." [8]

It is estimated that the state lost $3,559,791.34 in the negotiation of its bonds; of this amount the Morris Canal and Banking Company owed $2,195,769.34. Of the total amount of $15,000,000 of bonds issued by Indiana it is claimed that the state realized $8,593,000 in cash, $4,000,000 represented by worthless securities, and lost over $2,000,000 through the embezzlement by various state officials. [9]

It was through the agency of the Morris Canal and Banking Company that some of the Indiana bonds reached the European markets although Prime, Ward, and Company handled some of the loans for the Wabash and Erie Canal. The sales were negotiated abroad by the Rothschilds, Palmer, MacKillop, Dent, and Company,

---

[8] *Ibid.*, pp. 34, 37, 65, 77, 87, 89, 107, 115; Hunt's Merchants' Magazine, Vol. 21, pp. 150-153.

[9] Hunt's Merchants' Magazine, Vol. 21, pp. 154, 155; Esarey, Internal Improvements in Indiana, p. 123.

Jaudon, the London agent of the United States Bank of Pennsylvania, Baring Brothers and Company, and Hope and Company. In 1834 Louis McLane, then Secretary of State, assured the United States chargé d'affaires at London that entire confidence could be placed "in the good faith of the State of Indiana and the ample security offered for the redemption of their obligations." [10]

Indiana soon found herself in financial difficulties. The canal commissioners depended upon the punctual payment of the monthly installments on the bonds held by the Morris Canal and Banking Company and the other companies to meet their engagements with the contractors. In the summer of 1839 these companies were unable to fulfill their contracts because of the stringency in the money markets on the eve of the second suspension of the United States Bank. The result was the cessation of all work on the public improvements with the exception of the Madison and Indianapolis Railroad. Much private indebtedness had been created during the progress of the public works; and when operations ceased and prices fell at the same time, the people were left in a great measure without the means of paying their debts. The contractors began to clamor for payment and the people demanded a reduction of the taxes. The legislature decided to take care of the domestic creditors; and treasury notes were issued to settle the claims of the contractors. In order to lighten the burdens of taxation the tax levy was reduced from 30 cents to 15 cents; and the treasury notes were made receivable for the taxes. As no provision was made to pay the interest due on the public debt, Indiana was unable to meet the interest due in 1841. [11]

When the legislature assembled in December 1840 the condition of the state's finances was the paramount question before the people. Governor Bigger informed the legislature that it would require the expenditure of an additional sum of $14,000,000 to carry out the original program of internal improvements. Since this was impossible, the legislature divided the public works into two classes. Appropriations were made to carry on the work of those in the first class; while the unfinished portions of those in the second class

[10] McLane to Vail, Apr. 17, 1834; Hope to Barings, Dec. 14, 1841. Baring Mss.
[11] Indiana House Doc., 1840, No. 9, pp. 119-124; Indiana Senate Journal, 1841, pp. 12-28.

were handed over to private individuals and corporations for completion. The more delicate question of providing for the state debt remained unsolved.

The governor called upon the legislature to sustain the credit of the state; but he intimated that it would be unwise to increase the rate of taxation beyond the reasonable ability of the people to pay. "Our citizens should be favored as much as possible," stated the governor, "until the pressure of their own debts shall be removed." He therefore suggested that the legislature make some provision for supplying any deficiencies which might occur in the revenue; but he offered no definite recommendations beyond calling their attention to the possibility of receiving aid from the federal government through the distribution of the proceeds of the land sales. In other words the governor held that Indiana could not do much to help herself.

The legislature accordingly did little to relieve the financial stringency of the state. They did increase the tax levy to 40 cents; and they did pass an act to classify the public works. But in order to provide for the payment of the interest on the public debt they resorted again to borrowing by authorizing the issuance of 7 percent state bonds.[12]

The futility of these measures soon became apparent. The fund commissioners were unable to dispose of the state bonds; and not enough was received from the taxes to meet the July installment of interest.[13] Yet Indiana was unwilling to acknowledge the nonpayment of the interest had seriously injured the credit of the state. It was claimed that if the legislature had authorized the hypothecation of these bonds when it was found they could not be sold at par that such was "the confidence of capitalists in the integrity and resources of the people that the requisite amount" would have been obtained. "This is all very well," cynically remarked the *London Morning Chronicle,* "but the people of Indiana must set their shoulders to the wheel and looking their financial difficulties fairly in the face make up by direct local taxation, if they wish to maintain their character in the commercial world." [14]

[12] Indiana House Doc., 1840, No. 9, pp. 119-124; Laws of Indiana, 1841, pp. 47, 48, 200, 207, 208.
[13] Indiana Senate Journal, 1841, pp. 12-28.
[14] *London Morning Chronicle,* Aug. 17, 1841.

Indiana resented these aspersions cast upon her integrity. Governor Bigger confessed the inability of the state to discharge her liabilities; but he strenuously asserted that Indiana did not deserve this censure. "It is true," remarked the governor, "that the heartless usurer is incapable of distinguishing between the blameless inability to pay and that fraud which avoids an honest debt." Indiana was not a repudiating state and it was unjust to classify her with those who were repudiators. It was, to say the least, unwise for the foreign creditors to exact impossibilities and then attach the brand of infamy upon Indiana. No man's honesty was quickened by reproaches which he felt were unmerited. Moreover, some of those who were so quick to censure Indiana in unmeasured terms should not forget that they were not guiltless, if there was any guilt. Indiana had resorted to no false pretences; she had not entrapped the unwary and incautious. All parties relying on their own sagacity had had equal opportunities of estimating the probable consequences of the profit and loss of every transaction. As for the past neither party should complain of the other. It was the future that would determine whether Indiana could be trusted; and as for himself, the governor was confident that the integrity and enterprise of the people of Indiana would be found beyond reproach.[15]

The same sentiments were reiterated by his successor, Governor Whitcomb. The governor declared that the great mass of the citizens were willing—"nay anxious—to meet their just obligations"; but it was beyond their power to do so at present. Even though a select committee of the legislature cited statistics presenting conclusive evidence of the increasing wealth of the state and suggested the funding of the debt by converting the 5 percent state bonds into stock bearing 3 percent, Governor Whitcomb rejected the proposal and announced that there was no way in which the state could meet its obligations. Yet the legislature on January 13, 1845, passed a joint resolution denouncing repudiation in strong language and directed the governor to transmit copies of this resolution to all other states.[16] "It would be more fortunate for the reputation of

[15] Indiana House Journal, 1842, pp. 19-21.
[16] Indiana Documents, 1844, pp. 30, 100, 101. The joint resolution of the legislature on Jan. 13, 1845 declared "that we regard the slightest breach of plighted faith, public or private, as an evidence of the want of that moral principle upon which all obligations depend: that where any state in this Union shall refuse to recognize her great seal, as the sufficient evidence of her obligation, she will have forfeited her

the state as well as gratifying to her creditors," caustically remarked the state auditor, "should this evidence consist hereafter of some definite action rather than general expressions of legislative opinions." [17] While the Indiana legislature and the governor were bemoaning their inability to pay their obligations, yet vigorously asserting their opposition to open repudiation, Illinois under the leadership of a courageous executive was adopting a system of taxation to satisfy the demands of its creditors; and in Ohio the people were submitting to a tax of 75 cents on the $100 for the specific purpose of paying the interest on its public debt. [18]

It was at this time that Charles Butler, the negotiator of the Michigan settlement, arrived in Indiana to represent the claims of the foreign bondholders. He found conditions in Indiana worse than he had met with in Michigan. Everything was merged in local politics; leaders in both the Whig and Democratic parties were afraid to suggest payment or taxation for fear of losing popularity with the masses. Governor Whitcomb impressed Butler as a most cautious, timid executive; honest and willing to do what was right providing it did not injure his political fortunes. Butler quickly realized that two things were necessary to save the state from repudiation. In the first place the moral consciousness of the people must be awakened; and then a definite plan must be placed before the legislature showing them how the state debts could be liquidated without placing extra burdens upon the people. [19]

The campaign called for skillful tactics and diplomacy. The experience Butler had gained in Michigan proved a valuable asset in the new field of operations. In May 1845 Butler outlined his plan in an address at Terre Haute. He proposed the interest on the public debt should be divided into two parts, one-half of which chargeable to the state and the remainder to the canal. Such a scheme was attractive to the friends of the Wabash and Erie Canal who were anxious to complete the work; while the possibilities of the plan appealed strongly to all those in favor of sustaining the public credit.

station in the sisterhood of States and will be no longer worthy of their confidence and respect." Laws of Indiana, 1844, p. 28.

[17] Quoted in Esarey, Internal Improvements in Early Indiana, p. 132.

[18] See chapter VI; also referred to by Butler in later statement of his proposed plan for adjustment of the debt quoted in Prentiss, G. L., The Union Theological Seminary, p. 459.

[19] Butler described his negotiations in Indiana in his letters to his wife. These are found in Prentiss, G. L., The Union Theological Seminary, pp. 452-498.

As in other states articles began to appear in the country papers on the state debt; and a convention at Evansville endorsed the plan.

When the legislature assembled in December Butler was in Indianapolis to lay his proposal before the Assembly. The governor's message prepared the way for Butler's mission; but the whole responsibility of reaching an agreement was thrown upon the latter's shoulders.[20] Butler was requested to submit a written statement of his proposition for submission to the legislature.

Butler spent much labor and reflection in drafting this letter. Every word was carefully weighed. Particular stress was laid upon the moral aspects of the debt question and the example of other states was cited as proof of what Indiana could do. No allusion was made to any topic that might irritate local sentiment on the subject. Attention was called to the increasing internal prosperity of Indiana as well as that of all the other states in the Mississippi Valley. These states were rapidly becoming the granary of the world and their prosperity was interlocked with that of Indiana. Then very adroitly Butler referred "to the brilliant example of Ohio" in levying taxes to maintain its credit. Certainly the citizens of Indiana would not claim that their soil was less fertile than that of Ohio or that their people were not equally as industrious and enterprising. The progress made by Pennsylvania, Maryland, Michigan, and Illinois in restoring their credit only revealed the recuperative energies of the American character and their sense of justice in prevailing over every obstacle. A movement to restore state credit enlisted the sympathies of every American wherever his residence might be and was a challenge to the admiration of the world. Why should not, asked Butler, the Indiana legislature take immediate steps to relieve the foreign creditors? For a long period they had received no payment although they did not ask for the immediate redemption of their securities. All they requested was the payment in full of the arrears of interest and the assurance of a continuance of these payments. The bonds of Indiana like those of Pennsylvania and New York were held by trustees, guardians, retired and aged persons, widows and orphans whose whole reliance for support depended upon their income. But Indiana was a sovereign state and could not be constrained to make payment; she was the sole judge

[20] Prentiss, G. L., The Union Theological Seminary, p. 456.

of her ability and it would be presumptuous for a creditor to question her integrity and disinterestedness in deciding this question. The statements of her executive and representatives and especially the emphatic language of the joint resolution of January 1845 was proof that the people of Indiana could be relied upon to maintain the honor and good faith of the state. Yet there was a danger of a tacit or passive repudiation by the continued nonpayment of the interest which with the passage of time and the changing character of the population might dull the public consciousness. For these reasons, concluded Butler, he had prepared this statement, trusting that his language had not failed to convey his respect for the executive, for the legislature, and for the people of Indiana.

This was a masterful statement. Butler was permitted to read it before the legislature and a thousand copies were printed for distribution. Yet his Western listeners were not swept off their feet by his subtle presentation of the case of the foreign bondholders. As one plain country member of the legislature remarked, Butler's letter "was first a little sugar, then a little soap, then sugar and then soap, and it was sugar and soap all the way through." Another shrewdly commented that Butler had "mollassoed" it well.[21]

A joint committee of twenty-four, composed of farmers, lawyers, and doctors, was appointed by the legislature to draft a bill. Every step in the progress of this measure was contested; every possible device was employed to defeat it. To secure its passage it was necessary for Butler, in his own words, to be "all things to all men." He gave counsel and advice to both the Whigs and the Democrats; he gained votes by paying particular attention to the wives of recalcitrant senators; he encouraged and restrained his impetuous supporters as occasion demanded. The Presbyterians rallied to his aid. Henry Ward Beecher delivered a sermon on the debt question in Indianapolis while the legislature was discussing the bill. Governor Whitcomb now declared that he was willing to risk his political career upon the issue and rendered invaluable assistance; so also did Michael G. Bright and many others. After much discussion both parties endorsed the measure at their party conventions and the bill passed the lower house by a vote of two to one. A more bitter fight was waged in the Senate where Butler was denounced as a Wall

[21] *Ibid.*, pp. 458-464.

Street broker and the representative of British bondholders. At the last moment an attempt was made to insert an amendment providing that all bonds must be surrendered before the act should go into effect. This was defeated and on January 19, the governor, sick in bed, signed the bill.[22]

The act of January 19, 1846, made the payment of the debt as easy as could reasonably be expected by the people of Indiana; but the creditors suffered a considerable loss of interest. The bill provided for the funding of the debt and for the completion of the Wabash and Erie Canal. The state agreed to pay one-half the principal and interest of the debt out of taxation and for the remainder the bondholders were to look to the revenues of the canal. The canal was deeded to three trustees and the bondholders were asked to advance $2,250,000 for the completion of the work to the Ohio River. The arrears of interest from January 1, 1841, to January 1, 1847, were funded; but no interest was paid on the $3,327,000 due the bondholders January 1, 1847, up to 1853. This amounted to $998,100, "without reckoning the back interest due on each coupon from the time it was dishonored." Special stock was issued for the principal and arrears of interest chargeable to the state and to the canal. The canal and its lands were pledged for the loan of $2,250,000 for its completion, and the canal stock amounting to $1,663,500. The canal also had to pay annually 6 percent on the loan for its completion which amounted to $135,000 a year, and 2½ percent on the state debt, or $327,155, which made a total of $462,155 over and above its current expenses. On the other hand, Indiana assumed the payment on $3,000,000 of bonds for which nothing had been realized by the state.[23]

Upon the passage of the bill, Butler departed for England to explain the terms to the foreign bondholders. Here he encountered opposition. The creditors were unwilling to advance $2,250,000 to complete the canal as they felt enough money had already been lost. Furthermore the law presupposed joint assent on the part of all the bondholders. This concurrence could not be accomplished since large portions of the bonds were held under public and private

[22] *Ibid.*, pp. 465-498.
[23] Laws of Indiana, 1846, pp. 3-18. There is an excellent analysis of this law in Hunt's Merchants' Magazine, Vol. 14, pp. 177-178. Consult also Bankers Magazine, Vol. I, pp. 262-264.

trusts, by persons and corporations who could not make any change in the securities without involving themselves. For instance the Rothschilds and Hope and Company of Amsterdam held $600,000 of Indiana bonds as collateral security for loans made to the United States Bank. They could not surrender this stock without the consent of the holders of the debentures of the bankrupt bank. As the bondholders were willing to accept the principle of the law Butler informed them that he believed the legislature could be induced to modify the act to the extent of allowing them to subscribe 20 percent on not less than $4,000,000 of their holdings. In other words that the law should go into operation when the bondholders had advanced $800,000 instead of $2,250,000 to complete the canal. The bondholders, therefore, instructed Butler to return to Indiana and secure certain modifications in the law.[24]

After another long struggle a supplementary act was passed on January 27, 1847. By the provisions of this law the state debt was divided into two parts. For one-half of the principal, the state issued 5 percent state stock, payable half yearly, commencing July 1847; 4 percent to be paid in cash, and 1 percent funded to 1853; after that date the whole amount was payable in cash. For one-half of the unpaid interest, the state issued deferred state stock, bearing interest at the rate of 2½ percent after 1853. For the other half of the principal, canal stock, bearing 5 percent interest after January 1847 was issued; and for the other half of the arrears of interest, canal stock bearing 5 percent interest after January 1853 was issued. The bondholders were to advance $800,000 to complete the canal which was deeded to three trustees.

Whereas the act of January 1846 had allowed the state the option of calling in all the outstanding stock and again funding it, the new law compelled the bondholders to accept this settlement. This is clearly indicated in the second proviso of section 8 of the law which stated: "that the state will make no provision whatever hereafter to pay either principal or interest on any internal improvement bond or bonds, until the holder or holders thereof shall have first surrendered said bonds to the agent of the state and shall have first received in lieu thereof, certificates of stock as provided in the

[24] For these negotiations consult Bankers Magazine, Vol. I, pp. 262-264; also Hunt's Merchants' Magazine, Vol. 21, pp. 157, 158.

first section of this act; anything in this act to the contrary notwithstanding."[25]

The London press and the bondholders vigorously protested against the terms of the new law. As might be expected the *London Times* told the bondholders not to accept the proposed settlement. It pointed out that by converting the bonds from sterling bonds to dollar bonds the creditor suffered a loss of 9 percent. It ridiculed Indiana's plea of inability to meet its obligations and called attention to the boast of the Western states that no poverty was known there. Such contradictions suggested "a stiff prevalent smartness" on the part of Indiana. Referring to the threat of coercion embodied in the law the *London Times* said: "And these are the people whom it is deemed advisable to make a fresh advance to the extent of $800,000." The creditors were, therefore, urged by the *London Times* "to disregard the threat and recognizing the axiom that in a treaty between an honest man and a rogue the latter is always the winner, to refuse to make terms with a state by whom an announcement so shameless is promulgated. Sooner or later the people of Indiana will find themselves rich enough to buy a character and wise enough to know that it is worth the price." On the other hand, the "impudent declaration" was recommended by the Rothschilds, Palmer, MacKillop, Dent and Company, Baring Brothers and Company, Frederick Huth and Company, Morrisons and Sons, and Magniac, Jardine, and Company. These firms, as well as Butler, probably realized a sharp bargain had been driven by Indiana; but they undoubtedly thought that it was the best that could be obtained and would save at least a portion of their client's investments. Nevertheless, some of the creditors filed protests when they surrendered their bonds in which they clearly acknowledged their subscriptions were only made under compulsion and for fear of losing more if they did not acquiesce.[26]

The subsequent history of the Wabash and Erie Canal made the lot of the creditors even harder. The canal failed to produce the revenue expected; and the later construction of railroads in Indiana cut more deeply into its income. No human foresight could have predicted at the time of the settlement the rapidity with which the

[25] Laws of Indiana, 1847, pp. 3-33; Hunt's Merchants' Magazine, Vol. 21, pp. 158-160 has a good analysis of the working of this law.
[26] *London Times*, Apr. 29, 1847; Indiana Senate Journal, 1848, pp. 445, 446.

railroads would supplant canals within the next decade. It was only natural that Indiana should avail herself of the new means of transportation even though it might prove disastrous to her creditors. In 1857 the legislature refused a request of the bondholders to purchase the Wabash and Erie Canal on the ground that it was unconstitutional and impolitic; and in 1873 an amendment to the state constitution was approved at a special election disavowing the liability of the state to pay or redeem any stock issued under the acts of 1846 and 1847.[27]

Thus Indiana, like Illinois, settled her debt by deeding her canal to her creditors on terms, however, which they themselves had proposed. But the manner in which the settlement was forced upon the bondholders does not reflect honor upon Indiana although the state should not be held accountable for the subsequent outcome of the arrangement. Modern invention made inevitable the later misfortunes of the creditors.

[27] Laws of Indiana, 1857, p. 130; *ibid.*, 1873, pp. 83-86. For the later difficulties of the Wabash and Erie Canal consult Benton, The Wabash Trade Route, pp. 74-88; Esarey, Internal Improvements in Early Indiana, pp. 143-155.

CHAPTER VIII

THE FIVE MILLION DOLLAR LOAN OF MICHIGAN

In 1837 the legislature of Michigan authorized a loan of five millions for internal improvements. The manner in which this loan was negotiated subsequently involved the state in difficulties with the bondholders. Michigan refused to recognize the validity of those bonds for which the state claimed it had received no payment. In liquidating the portion of the debt which the state recognized Michigan agreed to sell certain railroads and to accept in payment for these roads full-paid bonds and part-paid bonds after scaling the latter at a rate determined upon by the legislature and forced the creditors to accept her terms. Although Michigan was always classified as a repudiating state by foreign investors there were certain differences between the repudiation by Michigan and that of other repudiating states. Michigan did not repudiate all of her obligations as Mississippi did; nor was repudiation adopted in Michigan in the same way as in the latter state. Furthermore, the state debts of Mississippi and Florida were created by the establishment of banks; that of Michigan for the construction of public works. Mississippi and Florida realized little, if anything at all, on their investments; Michigan was able to dispose of her railroads for nearly what they cost the state. These facts are made clearer by recalling the events connected with the origin and liquidation of the public debt of Michigan.

The first constitution adopted by Michigan provided for the encouragement of internal improvements. The governor called the attention of the legislature to this injunction of the constitution at the sessions of 1836 and 1837; and after considerable discussion and the harmonizing of local interests, an act was passed on March 23, 1837, making provision for a general system of public works to meet the popular demand for adequate transportation facilities. The governor was authorized to negotiate a loan or loans not exceeding $5,000,000, redeemable after twenty-five years, at an interest rate of not more than 5 percent, on the best and most favorable terms which in his judgment could be obtained. For this purpose the governor was instructed to issue certificates of stock or bonds in denominations of $1,000 each. The law specifically provided that the state bonds should not be sold for less than their par value and the proceeds of the sales should be expended for purposes of internal improvement. The faith of the state was pledged for the payment of the loans contracted and the governor was authorized to negotiate the loans in the United States or in Europe as he might deem advantageous for the public interest. Provision was made for a sinking fund consisting of the proceeds of all railroads and canals constructed, the interest from certain loans and the dividends from bank stock owned by the state. When this law was passed, four-fifths of Michigan was a wilderness and the total assessed value of property within the state was less than $43,000,000. Nevertheless, the legislature of Michigan, confident in the future rapid development of their infant commonwealth, and led astray by the example set by older and more populous states, boldly assumed the task of supplying their constituents with an extensive system of public works out of all proportion to their local wants and utterly beyond their limited means.[1]

In the spring of 1837 Governor Mason proceeded to New York for the purpose of negotiating the loan. He held interviews with John Delafield, president of the Phoenix Bank, who had successfully negotiated a previous loan for the state, and other capitalists of that city. The embarrassed state of the money market soon convinced the governor that it would be impossible to dispose of the bonds at that time. He, therefore, returned home, leaving a copy of the loan law with Delafield with instructions to correspond with other capitalists in this country and abroad. In the fall of the year Delafield informed Governor Mason that no portion of the loan could be negotiated unless the interest rate was raised to 6 percent and both the interest and principal were made payable in Europe. In the event the law was amended, Delafield declared Mr. James King of Prime, Ward and Company of New York, who was planning to visit

---

[1] Fuller, G. N., Messages of the Governors of Michigan, Vol. I, pp. 158-176, 194; Michigan Laws, 1837, pp. 152, 153.

Europe, had signified his willingness to take charge of the loan and give it his personal attention. To meet these requirements the original law was amended in November. The interest rate was raised to 6 percent and was made payable in New York and Europe; but in case the loan was negotiated abroad, it was made redeemable at the rate of $4.44 for every pound sterling or at the rate of 40 cents for the guilder of Holland. The amended law and $300,000 of the bonds were sent to King in London.[2]

King found the European financiers unwilling to take the Michigan bonds. He reported they objected to the terms of the amended law since it specified only for the payment of the interest in Europe but made no provision for the payment abroad of the principal. Furthermore, the law limited the rate at which payment of either or both should be made in London to $4.44 per pound sterling although it permitted the state to benefit from any premium or gain of exchange. Such an arrangement would allow the state at the current rate of exchange to receive $4.88 per pound sterling while it remitted only $4.44.[3] This illustrates the care with which European financiers accustomed to the fluctuations in the rates of exchange tried to protect their clients' interests. On the other hand, it was this very lack of caution upon the part of many of the agents of American states in negotiating loans which gave state executives and legislatures an opportunity to declare the contracts made with foreign capitalists were unfair since the state in remitting payments at the current rate of exchange transferred more than they received in the currency of this country.

There were, however, other reasons besides those given by King to the governor which helped to explain his failure in disposing of the Michigan stock. Thomas W. Ward, whose advice the Barings frequently followed, warned the London house not to take the Michigan loan as it was for "a poor and new state (although free)."[4] A few days later the Barings received another letter from Prime, Ward, and Company, cautioning them to have nothing to do with the Michigan bonds as their American correspondents were not pleased with the course pursued by Governor Mason, who had disposed of some of his bonds to other parties in America in viola-

---

[2] Fuller, *op. cit.*, Vol. I, pp. 263, 264; Michigan Laws, 1838, p. 3.
[3] Fuller, *op. cit.*, Vol. I, pp. 245-248.
[4] Ward to Baring, Jan. 12, 1838. Baring Mss.

tion of the agency confided to King.[5] This probably referred to Governor Mason's transactions with Oliver Newberry, to whom the governor sold $500,000 of bonds. Newberry paid $200,000 on this contract but was forced to return the remainder of the bonds because of his inability to meet the payments or to negotiate the stock either in American or European markets.[6] Prime, Ward and Company finally agreed that the Barings take the bonds and sell them charging 1 percent commission for their services.[7] In the meantime, however, Governor Mason had signed a contract with E. R. Biddle to take the entire loan at par. Biddle was at that time vice president of the Morris Canal and Banking Company but apparently he took the bonds for himself. Eighty thousand dollars was paid upon the execution of the contract but owing to the inability of Biddle to meet the payments, this contract was canceled and the money was later returned.[8]

It is claimed that Thomas Romeyn, a lawyer of Detroit, who was with Governor Mason in New York, called the attention of the Morris Canal and Banking Company to the Michigan loan. It will be recalled that this company was reorganized in the spring of 1837; and that E. R. Biddle, a cousin of Nicholas Biddle, was a director in this corporation.[9] The Morris Canal and Banking Company began to negotiate with Governor Mason for the entire Michigan loan. The company offered 97½ for the bonds; but the law prohibited their sale below par. To overcome this obstacle, the attorneys of the company, it is claimed, suggested that the contract should be in the form of an agency instead of a bill of sale. The governor agreed to this; and on June 1, 1838 the contract was signed.[10]

The provisions of this contract are important because of the later controversies between Michigan and the bondholders. By the terms of the agreement Michigan employed the Morris Canal and Banking Company as agents to sell $5,000,000 of state bonds, that is, the balance of the $5,000,000 loan, amounting to $4,800,000, to-

[5] Prime, Ward and Company to Baring, Jan. 20, 1838. Baring Mss.
[6] Fuller, op. cit., Vol. I, p. 264.
[7] Prime, Ward and Company, March 17, 1838. Baring Mss. The Barings had already proposed this plan to King on Jan. 3, 1838. Ibid.
[8] Fuller, op. cit., Vol. I, pp. 264, 265.
[9] Consult Chapter VII.
[10] Hunt's Merchants' Magazine, Vol. 22, pp. 131-145.

gether with $200,000 of state stock issued for the benefit of the Allegan and Marshall, and the Tecumseh and Ypsilanti Railroads. For its services the company was allowed a commission of 2½ percent on the proceeds of the sales. The Morris Canal and Banking Company guaranteed in case the proceeds of sales did not equal the par value of the aggregate amount of the bonds sold to make up any deficiency. The company also agreed to advance and pay for the bonds on the following terms: $250,000 upon the execution of the contract; $1,050,000 as might be required by the state; and the remainder in quarterly installments of $250,000 beginning July 1839 until the whole amount was paid whether the company should be in funds from such sales to meet the installments or otherwise. If the sums realized on the sale of the bonds were over and above the par value, the excess, to the amount of 5 percent, was to be equally divided between the two parties to the contract. $1,300,000 of the bonds were to be delivered to the company on the execution of the contract and the company was always to be in possession of $1,000,000 of the bonds in advance of the installments paid to the state. By the terms of the contract the agency was irrevocable; and by a supplementary agreement signed three days later the governor agreed to receive the sum of $1,300,000 in notes of the Morris Canal and Banking Company. On July 14 the parties mutually agreed that drafts at ninety days should be substituted for the first year's installment instead of disbursing the notes of the company. Under the terms of the contract the governor delivered to the Morris Canal and Banking Company $1,300,000 of bonds and prior to November 10, 1838 the further sum of $500,000. Of this amount the company sold prior to November 15, 1838 to various individuals $1,187,000 for cash, all of which was duly accounted for to the state.[11]

In the fall of 1838 Governor Mason again visited New York. In view of the approaching session of the legislature the governor wrote to E. R. Biddle requesting a complete statement of the sales of the bonds up to date. Instead of furnishing this information Biddle suggested the advisability of closing the sale of the balance

[11] Michigan Senate Doc., 1839, pp. 551-555; Michigan House Doc., No. 15, 1843, pp. 71-75; Michigan Laws, 1838, pp. 259-262.

of the bonds and passing the whole amount to the credit of the state at par less their commission. Biddle approved such a move because of the unfavorable reports from London of the prospects of American securities. In order to accomplish this, Biddle proposed that the governor deliver immediately the residue of the bonds—amounting to $3,700,000—and take the obligation of the United States Bank of Pennsylvania to pay three-fourths of the amount due and that of the Morris Canal and Banking Company for the remaining one-fourth. Michigan was to be credited with interest at 6 percent by both the company and the bank from January 1, 1839, up to the maturity of the respective installments to become due. Although such an arrangement did not alter the terms of the original contract Governor Mason should have realized the full significance of handing over $3,700,000 of bonds in advance of payment and taking the obligation of the United States Bank to pay three-fourths of the amount due upon them. The governor replied that he had no objection to the proposed plan but insisted the Morris Canal and Banking Company, as the agent of the state, should assume all responsibility of determining whether this was in the best interests of the state. No suggestion was made by the governor that either the company or the bank should furnish collateral security to cover their obligations. It is quite apparent that Governor Mason was convinced he was performing a thankless task and was anxious to bring to an end his negotiations for the loan. The governor knew that Michigan needed the funds to carry out her internal improvement plans; and he was willing to be guided by the advice of New York capitalists as to the best course to pursue. On the other hand, it is evident that E. R. Biddle wanted to purchase $5,000,000 of Texas bonds and had offered to sell the Michigan bonds to his cousin Nicholas Biddle in order to carry out his plans. For this reason E. R. Biddle assured the governor that the proposed transaction was the best that could be made under the present circumstances; and to support his argument quoted from a letter written by Charles Butler, a prominent New York financier then in London, of the discouraging prospects of disposing of the Michigan stock abroad. In his reply of November 15, therefore, E. R. Biddle informed the governor that the Morris Canal and Banking Company had closed their agency by an absolute sale of the balance of the bonds to the United States Bank on the terms already mentioned.[12]

Governor Mason reported these negotiations to the legislature in his message of 1839. In his estimation the contract with the Morris Canal and Banking Company would ultimately prove beneficial to Michigan; and he declared that it was the best the state could hope for at that time. A joint committee of the legislature was appointed to investigate the governor's negotiations and reported favorably.[13] Apparently the legislature was as anxious to procure funds on any terms as the governor for they likewise raised no objection to the delivery of the bonds in advance of payment. Nor did they call attention to the fact that the original contract with the company made no provision for the payment of interest either by the state on the bonds delivered to the company or by the company on its installments. Furthermore, the legislature made no reference to the advisability of obtaining collateral security to cover the obligations of the company and the bank; and the authority of the governor to enter into this contract was never questioned by the legislature. Accordingly on March 13, 1839, in order to consummate the agreement with the Morris Canal and Banking Company and the United States Bank, the Morris Canal and Banking Company gave the state two separate obligations, one for $1,048,562.50, the other for $3,145,687.50, making in the aggregate $4,194,250. The United States Bank guaranteed the payment of the second obligation and agreed to pay the sums due in case of default on the part of the Morris Canal and Banking Company. The following June it was agreed that the state should pay the interest on the $1,300,000 credited to Governor Mason by the company from May 1, 1838 to January 1, 1839, and on the $5,000,000 from the latter date while the payments due the state from the company and the bank were to be made in fifteen installments.[14]

In the fall of 1839 Alexander Trotter, a member of the London Stock Exchange, published his illuminating treatise on American state debts. In this work Trotter attempted to supply the general public with the information they sought respecting the relative

[12] Michigan Senate Doc., 1839, pp. 555-559; Jenks, W. L., Michigan's Five Million Dollar Loan, Michigan History Magazine, Vol. 15, p. 584.

[13] Fuller, *op. cit.*, Vol. I, pp. 245-251.

[14] Michigan House Doc., 1840, p. 125; *ibid.*, No. 15, 1843, p. 78.

merits of American state stocks. Trotter warned British investors that in the case of loans for internal improvements considerable time must elapse before these works would make any profitable returns; and in all probability many of them would fail altogether "to produce a revenue sufficient to keep them in repair and to pay the interest on the cost of their construction." He also cautioned English creditors to be prepared for a conflict of opinion among the various state legislative bodies as to the propriety of levying taxes for the purpose of paying these obligations. In his estimation there was grave danger that universal suffrage had given too much power to those who were "little fit to judge of the true interests of the state and most open to the influence of uncontrolled feelings." In commenting on Michigan Trotter wrote: "This state may be destined to hold a high position among the United States; but in the meantime the works undertaken have involved it in a debt which is disproportioned to the number and resources of the inhabitants." [15] Unfortunately by the time this valuable work was in the hands of the English investing public, the Morris Canal and Banking Company and the United States Bank had disposed of large quantities of Michigan bonds in European markets; and in October 1839 the United States Bank was forced a second time to suspend specie payments.

One month later Governor Mason attempted to safeguard the state from any possible losses that might occur on account of the possible inability of the company or the bank to meet their installments. The governor was becoming nervous regarding the solvency of the Morris Canal and Banking Company and the United States Bank and E. R. Biddle had suggested to him that it might "become an object of the Bank as well as of Michigan, to cancel the existing contract and obligations." In November, therefore, the governor instructed his personal friend, the bank commissioner of Michigan, Kintzing Pritchette, to go east and secure an abrogation of the contract. [16]

Pritchette carried on a lengthy correspondence with the Morris

[15] Trotter, Alexander, Observations on the Financial Position and Credit of such of the States of the North American Union as have contracted Public Debts, pp. 74, 343, 352, 353; see *London Times*, Jan. 7, 1840, comment on importance of Trotter's work.
[16] Michigan Senate Doc., Vol. *II*, 1840, pp. 503, 504.

Canal and Banking Company and the United States Bank. The bank informed Pritchette that all of the stock of which it had guaranteed the payment had been transmitted to Europe and either sold or disposed of in such a manner as to prevent an immediate action.[17] This was quite true; for between October 1829 and January 1840 the bank hypothecated $900,000 of Michigan bonds with Denison and Company; $1,431,000 with the Rothschilds; and $952,000 with Hope and Company of Amsterdam, making in the aggregate $3,283,000. For subsequent loans made to the bank by Hope and Company, the amount held by the Dutch was raised to $1,220,000, and an additional $272,000 was hypothecated with Morrison and Sons, making a grand total of all the bonds hypothecated abroad by the bank, $3,855,000.[18] "It is therefore obvious," as one writer says, "that the bank had acquired the entire amount of $3,700,000 turned over by the state at the time of the new arrangement, and had also purchased $155,000 of the $1,300,000 bonds which had been fairly paid for by the Morris Canal and Banking Company." [19] Pritchette finally succeeded in inducing the Morris Canal and Banking Company to surrender a total amount of $624,500 of Michigan bonds and to deliver two mortgages, aggregating $375,000, the company to retain out of payments to be made to the United States Bank, $250,000. The company required these terms to be accepted within thirty days. In turn the United States Bank proposed to surrender $2,275,000 of Michigan bonds by January 1, 1841.[20]

When the legislature met in the fall of 1839 to consider these transactions Michigan was already in financial difficulties. The auditor general's report revealed a deficit of $16,098.59. In his last message to the legislature Governor Mason reviewed the progress of the public works and urged the need for careful and prudent legislation, economy in governmental expenditures, and a revision of the taxation system. His successor, Governor Woodbridge, suggested a classification of the internal improvement projects and the completion of only those works which were nearly finished and

---

[17] *Ibid.*, 1840, Vol. *II*, App., p. 56.
[18] Memorandum of stocks pledged by United States Bank. Baring Mss. The United States Bank also hypothecated $1,045,000 of Michigan bonds with the Barings but later covered the advances made by them to the Bank.
[19] Jenks, *op. cit.*, p. 595.
[20] Michigan Senate Doc., 1840, Vol. *II*, pp. 510, 514, 523, 524.

would pay a fair return upon their cost. On January 29, 1840 the legislature therefore passed a joint resolution directing the internal improvement commissioners to suspend all operations on the public works.[21]

In view of the alarming condition of the state's finances, the legislature should have given careful attention to the propositions submitted by Pritchette. Instead of doing so, the legislature proceeded to exploit the situation for political purposes. It is quite evident that the Whig legislature wanted to get the credit for saving the state. Therefore the majority report of a select committee in the House opposed the cancellation of the contract and sharply criticized Governor Mason for attempting on his own authority to change the terms. They recommended that "some competent person should proceed to New York and take such steps, under the direction and advice of the governor and auditor general, as the exigencies of the case 'might' seem to require." The minority asserted the majority report had been drafted for political purposes and that "these constant and clamorous assertions of the absolute desperate condition of Michigan was everywhere producing the most disastrous effects." In their estimation the terms offered were probably the best the contractors were able to make and it would be a useless expense to send another agent to deal with the company and the bank. While the legislature fruitlessly debated the matter, the Morris Canal and Banking Company defaulted upon its April installment.[22]

The financial needs of the state forced the legislature to take some action. The state treasurer, Robert Stuart, was authorized to ascertain whether any portion of the balance due upon the $5,000,000 loan was not well secured and to take such measures as he deemed advisable in order to protect the state.[23] Stuart found upon his arrival in New York that the bond of the Morris Canal and Banking Company upon which there was due to Michigan about $823,000 had been protested for the nonpayment of the April installment and that the company was unable to meet its engagements to other creditors. The state treasurer therefore directed his efforts toward obtaining adequate security for the ultimate payment of the

[21] Fuller, *op. cit.*, Vol. *I*, pp. 274-285, 313; Michigan Laws, 1840, p. 237.
[22] Michigan House Doc., 1840, Vol. *II*, pp. 514-524, 531-534.
[23] Michigan Laws, 1840, p. 148.

whole debt. Since the company requested additional time, Stuart returned to Detroit but in November he revisited New York. A month later he signed an agreement with the Morris Canal and Banking Company whereby the company agreed to deliver various securities valued at $621,000 as collateral security for the payment of $823,295.83 due the state with interest thereon and to pay Michigan the sum of $100,000 on or before January 1, 1844. The State of Michigan, on its part, agreed not to bring suit against the company before the latter date. In reporting his results to the governor, Stuart declared that the hypothecated securities obtained from the company at the most reduced calculation would be worth $500,000. The portion of the loan guaranteed by the bank was, in his estimation, safe and would doubtless be paid. As a matter of fact the bank defaulted on its payment in October 1841 and Michigan never did recover the balance of the principal, amounting to $1,087,000 due to the state while it only realized $23,835.50 on the securities which Stuart claimed would ultimately be good for at least half-a-million. Stuart reported that the bonds retained by the Morris Canal and Banking Company had long since been disposed of and were in the hands of third parties beyond the control of the company.[24]

In a special message to the legislature Governor Woodbridge reported the result of these negotiations and declared they gave him "great satisfaction." Apparently neither the governor nor the legislature apprehended any danger to the state by the increasing financial difficulties of the company and the bank. Upon the governor's recommendation Stuart was authorized to proceed to New York and Philadelphia in order to procure upon the best terms he could obtain the April and July installments due from the bank; and to pay the interest due on the state bonds in May and July 1841. To accomplish these objects the state treasurer was authorized, if necessary, to hypothecate any of the securities received from the Morris Canal and Banking Company.[25]

Stuart carried out these instructions in a peculiar manner. He obtained from the bank payment of the April installment; but apparently he made no effort to secure the payment of future installments

[24] Michigan House Doc., 1841, Vol. I, pp. 266-311; Jenks, *op. cit.*, pp. 593, 614.
[25] Michigan Laws, 1841, pp. 154-156.

although the newspapers were filled with accounts of the embarrassed financial condition of that institution. The Morris Canal and Banking Company was then in default upon five of its payments and yet Stuart took no measures against the company, probably due to the fact that his agreement with the company prohibited any suit before 1844. In view of the disquieting rumors regarding the solvency of the company and the bank, the actions of the State Treasurer are inexcusable. The incompetence of Stuart, together with the dilatory policy pursued by the governor and legislature in taking effective measures to protect the state's interests were increasing the financial difficulties of Michigan.

The public debt of Michigan demanded the immediate action of the legislature when it assembled in January 1842. The failure of the United States Bank to meet its payments in October 1841 and January 1842 rendered it impossible for Michigan to pay the interest on the state bonds due January 1. In his message to the legislature the new Democratic governor, John S. Barry, discussed in detail the internal improvement plans and the indebtedness of the state. He pointed out that the whole system of public works planned by Michigan embraced 596 miles of railroads, 233 miles of canals, and the improvement of five rivers. In projecting these works the state resorted to a prodigal use of its credit and lavishly expended the money borrowed upon the pledge of the good faith of Michigan. The total indebtedness of Michigan by 1842 amounted to more than $6,000,000. The annual interest on this sum at 6 percent was over $375,000. There was at that time due to Michigan on the $5,000,000 loan from the Morris Canal and Banking Company the sum of $852,625, and from the United States Bank, $1,306,312.50. To pay the accruing interest on the public debt Michigan possessed no other revenue than that "arising from the net earnings of the Central and Southern Railroads." Notwithstanding these obstacles, the governor urged the legislature to sustain the public credit. "If those who make and administer the laws," declared the governor, "are found in their official capacity to disregard the obligations of good faith, little respect will be felt or observed by the citizens to their most solemn enactments or to the highest tribunals of public justice." He therefore recommended that the legislature should authorize someone to obtain from these defaulting institutions the bonds for which

Michigan had received no consideration and to make a settlement with them; and in case no settlement could be made, to ascertain who were the holders of the outstanding bonds.[26]

The governor's suggestions precipitated a debate over the payment of the public debt. A resolution was introduced in the House calling attention to the fact that some of the newspapers in the state had suggested repudiation. Since this might cause the holders of the bonds to believe the people of Michigan entertained such views the legislature desired to announce that although Michigan was then unable to meet the interest due on the state bonds the Senate and the House denied "the doctrine of repudiation as being the sentiments of the people of Michigan"; and they would do all in their power "to keep inviolate the public faith of this state." [27] This resolution was defeated by a vote of 40 to 6; and in its place the legislature passed a resolution announcing "that for themselves and their successors they pledge the good faith and resources of the state, for the payment at as early a day as possible, of all outstanding warrants and just demands against the treasury," and that Michigan felt bound to redeem the warrants, issued by the auditor general in anticipation of the payments by the bank and the company with interest on them,[28] looking for her remedy to those who have, without any fault on her part, brought the state into her present condition.[29]

Having thus provided for the claims of the contractors, the legislature proceeded to deal with the bondholders. On February 17, 1842 an act was passed requiring the auditor general and the state treasurer to make out a full statement of all the moneys received by the state on the $5,200,000 of bonds issued for internal improvement purposes with interest thereon at 6 percent to July 1, 1841. The auditor general and the state treasurer were also required to make an estimate of the damages accruing to the state from the failure of the contracting parties to meet their engagements and to deduct these damages from the amount of moneys received with interest thereon. This statement and estimate was to be submitted to the governor who should issue a proclamation to be published in the

[26] Fuller, op. cit., Vol. I, pp. 432-456.
[27] Michigan House Journal, 1842, pp. 261-263.
[28] Michigan Laws, 1841, pp. 154-156.
[29] Michigan House Journal, 1842, pp. 163, 265.

Detroit, New York and Philadelphia papers "that the holders of the bonds for the $5,000,000 loan and for the additional stocks negotiated in connection therein will be required to deliver to the state treasurer, that the same may be cancelled [being] the amount of said bonds for which no equivalent shall be ascertained to have been received by the state; or that the whole amount of said bonds may be so returned and that thereupon new bonds will be issued for the amount due by the state to holders of the original bonds." Upon the return of the unsatisfied portion of the original bonds or upon the issue of new bonds, the auditor general, state treasurer and secretary of state were authorized to sell to the holders of all outstanding bonds the railroads and other public works at cost or at a fair valuation and also a portion of the public lands granted to Michigan by the federal government. Evidently fearing the auditor general and the state treasurer had been given too much power the legislature, on February 17, passed a joint resolution fixing the damages sustained by the state at 25 percent of the unpaid installments.[30]

In accordance with the authority vested in him by the legislature, Governor Barry on April 27, 1842 issued a proclamation calling upon the holders of the five million dollar loan to return $2,857,039.76 of bonds to be cancelled, being the amount outstanding for which the state had received no consideration; or to deliver the whole amount of bonds to the state treasurer and receive new bonds to the amount of $2,342,960.20 which was the sum due from the state to the holders of bonds. Upon the return of the unsatisfied portion of the original bonds or upon the issue of new bonds the auditor general, state treasurer and secretary of state, under the sanction of the governor, were authorized to sell or convey to the bondholders the railroads or other public works belonging to the state at cost or at a fair valuation; and also a portion of the public lands granted to Michigan by the federal government.[31]

The repudiation by Michigan of a portion of her bonds attracted considerable attention in this country and abroad. The *New York American* denounced the Governor's Proclamation; but reminded foreign holders of Michigan bonds that the United States was a

[30] Michigan Laws, 1842, pp. 102-104.
[31] The Governor's Proclamation is quoted in *National Intelligencer*, May 21, 1842.

country of laws and of tribunals for the administration of laws. Although governors and legislatures might forget the obligations of honesty and proclaim to the world that just debts would not be paid, foreigners should remember there was always an appeal from their decision to the courts; and until these, in all their forms, up to last and highest judicial authority—the Supreme Court of the United States—should confirm such dishonest repudiation, the obligation still remained, and "the original bond with all its accumulations of interest and damages must be paid. The inability to pay," thundered the *New York American*, "if frankly avowed would at least not forfeit the character, though it might bring into question the prudence of a state; but to borrow money and then refuse to acknowledge the debt is sheer robbery; and for that the laws of the State and of the United States will furnish redress." Because the agents chosen, employed and contracted with by Michigan, had cheated and defrauded the state, Michigan pretended it had an excuse to turn round "and cheat and defraud innocent third parties holding its bonds upon the faith and credit of the official seal of the state and the signatures of its appointed officers." [32]

The comment of the *London Times* upon the policy adopted by Michigan was particularly interesting. The *Times* cited the case of a British holder of Michigan bonds who had written to the Secretary of State of Michigan for the interest on his securities and had received in reply a very concise letter enclosing a neatly printed copy of the Governor's Proclamation. "According to the letter," stated the paper, "there appears this difference between the creditors of Michigan and those of Mississippi, that the former are in the most hopeless condition of the two; for while in Mississippi the legislature went in favour of the bondholders at the time of the Governor's repudiation, and consequently it was the act of the State Executive alone, it appears by the Secretary of Michigan's letter that Governor Barry cannot act otherwise than expressed in the proclamation. Any fortunate chance might remove a dishonest Governor but this letter which seems to refer the repudiation to the legislative body makes the case of the bondholders as bad as possible." [33]

This was a keen analysis of the difference between the way in

[32] *New York American*, May 14, 1842.   [33] *London Times*, June 1, 1842.

which Michigan and Mississippi moved toward repudiation. Governor McNutt in Mississippi was undoubtedly in large part responsible for Mississippi's repudiating her bonds. On the other hand, the repudiation sentiment was spreading in Michigan when Governor Barry entered office; and the governor was unable to control or guide public opinion. No one dreamed of increasing the taxes at that time and the executive was convinced the state of public opinion would not warrant suggesting it. Governor Barry, like many other state officials, therefore refrained from proposing an increase in taxation and allowed the legislature to take the lead in dealing with the question of payment of the public debt. He did urge the legislature to sustain the credit of the state but he offered no concrete plan whereby this could be accomplished. Moreover Governor Barry failed to call attention to the fact that the state must have realized that the Morris Canal and Banking Company and the United States Bank would dispose of the bonds in their possession to third parties and that these purchasers bought the bonds relying upon the good faith of Michigan to pay the interest and ultimately redeem the principal. Nor did the governor point out the injustice of the state deducting damages of 25 percent because of the non-fulfillment of the contracts. In other words Governor Barry was so cautious and so fearful that his own popularity and that of the Democratic party might suffer by proposing unpopular measures that he permitted an unrestrained legislature to sweep Michigan into repudiation.[84]

In his message of 1843 Governor Barry evidently considered it necessary to justify Michigan's action. "While our relations to our constituents," declared the Governor, "makes it our duty to protect their interests, we are equally bound to do justice to the public creditor of the state." Michigan would recognize every just claim and would provide means of payment with the least possible delay. "That state," announced the Governor, "which resorts to its sovereignty to avoid pecuniary obligations, of which the justice is not denied, while it does not cancel its indebtedness, sets an example that tends to subvert all government." The same rules that bound individuals to meet their engagements should regulate the conduct

[84] This analysis is based upon the correspondence of Charles Butler to his wife in connection with the passage of the Butler Act and especially the letter of C. J. Hammond, the Auditor General to George Griswold on the Butler negotiations. Prentiss, G. L., Union Theological Seminary, pp. 435-452.

of states. The same moral obligations which required individuals to observe their pledges should be observed by sovereign states. Circumstances rendered it impossible for Michigan to meet promptly all just claims upon her treasury; but the governor assured the creditors there was no disposition upon the part of state officials to do injustice. "Present inability and consequent temporary delay should not be construed into refusal or wilful neglect." Michigan was willing to offer without reserve her works of internal improvement in order to liquidate her indebtedness. They were the only means the state possessed with which Michigan could satisfy the insistent claims of her creditors. The governor regretted that he was unable to lay before the legislature "some just and equitable proposition from the holders of the bonds of the state for which no consideration" had been received and "which every principle of justice" required should be surrendered.[35]

It was at this time that Charles Butler arrived in Detroit as the representative of the bondholders. Butler was a prominent New York business man who, it will be remembered, was indirectly associated with the transfer of the Michigan stock to the United States Bank. It was Butler's report upon the unfavorable prospects of disposing of Michigan bonds in European markets which E. R. Biddle quoted to Governor Mason in order to convince the latter of the advisability of making the new agreement. Butler came to Michigan for the purpose of inducing the legislature to make some provision for the payment of those bonds which the state presumably was willing to recognize but had not made clear in the Act of 1842 or in the Governor's Proclamation. Neither the act nor the proclamation had made a clear distinction between the bonds for which the purchasers had paid and Michigan had received payment and those which had not been paid for but had been hypothecated abroad by the United States Bank. The holders of none of these bonds had received any interest since July 1841.

The task which Butler had undertaken required a great deal of tact and resourcefulness. The sentiment in favor of repudiation was spreading and there was the danger that Michigan might disavow all of her obligations. As Butler later wrote his wife: "Ninety-nine persons out of one hundred did not feel that there was any *obliga-*

[35] Michigan House Journal, 1843, pp. 29, 30.

tion resting upon them to recognize or pay any of the bonds; and though they said that the state would acknowledge and pay what she received, still that even was considered a matter of grace rather than of legal and equitable liability." To many members of the legislature it was *"monstrous"* for anyone to presume to suggest that Michigan should fulfill her engagements. Such audacity was an affront "to the honor and dignity of a sovereign state!" The mere fact, however, that Butler had come all the way "from New York through the mud" on such a mission made it possible for him to say and do things which no one else dared to do and say "without being charged with treason." [36]

Butler cautiously set to work to change public opinion in favor of payment. He carried on an active campaign of lobbying. He held personal interviews with the governor and individual members of the legislature in which he stressed the importance of a democracy demonstrating to the world that it would faithfully carry out its pledges. He adroitly pointed out that the bonds he represented were those held by the Farmers Loan and Trust Company and certain New York banks and private individuals, amounting to $1,362,000. The Farmers Loan and Trust Company had purchased $907,000 of the bonds from the Morris Canal and Banking Company and had paid for them and Michigan had received the money. [37] It was therefore unfair to the holders of these bonds, claimed Butler, that they should be made to suffer on account of the failure of the United States Bank to complete its contract. When the bonds were issued Michigan had pledged the faith of the state for their payment and had set aside the proceeds of the railroads and certain other funds for this purpose. Nevertheless the bondholders had received no interest for a year and a half. Butler proposed the interest on these bonds up to January 1, 1844 should be funded into new bonds.

A bill designed to carry out these provisions passed the Senate on February 24; but when it reached the House the real contest began. The Committee on Ways and Means to whom the Senate bill was referred presented a report in which a clear distinction was made between the bonds sold by the Morris Canal and Banking Company, while acting as the agent of Michigan, and those which

[36] Prentiss, G. L., Union Theological Seminary, pp. 439-443.
[37] Michigan House Doc., No. 15, 1843, p. 75.

that institution and the United States Bank, by the agreement of November 15, 1838, purchased and agreed to pay for; but which they had failed to do. "The former," declared the committee, "is a transaction not between the state and the bondholders but between other contracting parties whose agreements are to be judged of by the circumstances attending them."[38] In other words the committee recognized as valid obligations of the state those bonds sold prior to November 15, 1838; those sold after this date were questionable. The committee overlooked the fact, however, that the Morris Canal and Banking Company had actually paid for the first $1,300,000 of the bonds and that Newberry had paid for $200,000 of the bonds in his possession. Moreover the committee held that the state had only received $998,000 by the sale of the bonds to these institutions and therefore Michigan would acknowledge only this amount of the $3,813,000 part paid bonds.

After an animated debate over the question of repudiation or no repudiation, the House passed an amended bill, the most significant change being the funding of the interest up to July 1, 1845 instead of January 1, 1844. The measure was then returned to the Senate where it again passed, every member but one voting in the affirmative although many leading senators violently attacked the bill on the ground that no tax should be levied to pay the debt. Opponents of the measure held the bondholders should be given no other security beyond a lien upon the income of the railroads; if that proved insufficient, they should bear the loss as it had never been contemplated when the loan was issued that the people should be taxed and the pledge of the faith of the state did not involve any such consequences. Thus open repudiation was definitely advocated; and even after the bill had passed both Houses the struggle was not over. For a time Governor Barry thought of vetoing the bill unless the tax clause was stricken out. The governor claimed that he and the Democratic party would be ruined politically if the measure became a law. Butler refused to agree to this elimination and not until great pressure was brought upon the governor did the bill receive his signature.[39]

The Act of 1843, popularly known as the Butler Act, provided for the liquidation of the public debt and for the payment of the

[38] *Ibid.*, pp. 78-80.   [39] Prentiss, *op. cit.*, pp. 443-450.

interest. The governor was authorized to issue new bonds upon the surrender of the coupons attached to certain bonds, specified by numbers, of the original $5,000,000 loan, amounting in all to the principal sum of $1,387,000. The coupons included those falling due since July 1, 1841 up to July 1, 1845, with interest on all the coupons after the same became due up to the latter date. The new certificates of stock were to bear 6 percent interest from and after July 1, 1845, payable semi-annually, and for the payment of these bonds the faith of the state was pledged. For the payment of the interest accruing on these bonds after July 1, 1845 the net proceeds of all public works of the state was pledged; and the bonds were receivable in payment for certain public works of the state. In case of any deficiency arising from the proceeds of the public works to pay the interest on these bonds, the same was to be made up of any moneys in the treasury not otherwise appropriated and if there were no funds available a tax was to be levied and collected for this purpose. The law also called attention to the large amount of state bonds delivered to the United States Bank and the Morris Canal and Banking Company in accordance with the contract made in November 1838 which these institutions had neglected to fulfill and the state had received only a small portion of the contract price; and as it was understood the bank had hypothecated these bonds as security for loans, and the bank was bound to surrender the whole of these bonds, the law authorized the governor upon the surrender of the bonds held or hypothecated by the bank to issue new bonds, similar in character to those first provided for to the amount which the state had actually received from the United States Bank, subject, however, to the deductions specified in the Act of February 17, 1842 and the proclamation of the governor, with interest calculated to July 1, 1845.[40]

The passage of this act aroused considerable comment abroad. The *London Times* ridiculed the claim that this law should be regarded as a "wonderful display of good faith" upon the part of Michigan. In fact it raised the state to a position of "inglorious celebrity." The *Times* pointed out that of the $5,200,000 of bonds issued, $200,000 had been paid for by Newberry and $1,300,000 by the Morris Canal and Banking Company, making in the aggregate

[40] Michigan Laws, 1843, pp. 150-153.

$1,500,000 of bonds unquestioned. When the remaining $3,700,000 of bonds were sold on credit to the Morris Canal and Banking Company and the United States Bank and the state accepted the obligations of these companies a title for sale was as fully completed as if ready money had passed. "The mercantile principle is," stated the *Times*, "that if a purchaser gives a bill of exchange for goods he has a perfect right to sell, the vendor cannot cancel this right, and make the ultimate purchasers the sufferers, because the bill happens to be dishonored. In the same manner, if Michigan has parted with her bonds for obligations which turn out valueless, that is no affair of the *bona-fide* purchasers who bought under a legitimate title, but the state, according to commercial principle, must abide the consequences." [41]

The views set forth by the *Times* were also advanced by B. R. Curtis in his article on State Debts in the January 1844 number of the *North American Review*. Even though it has been shown in another connection that this article was written at the suggestion of Thomas W. Ward, the representative in this counry of the Barings, [42] the high standard of Curtis as a lawyer lend particular significance to his comments on the legal aspects of Michigan's action. "Every system of law with which we have any acquaintance," wrote Curtis, "and certainly the law of Michigan, makes no distinction between the case of these banks and that of bona-fide purchasers. We believe the principle to be universally admitted that whenever a purchaser of property acquires a title from the seller which he can transmit, although that title be tainted with fraud, if he sells to a bona-fide purchaser who parts with his money or any other thing of value on the faith of the property, such purchaser retains a valid title purged of fraud. This principle is not only well established but society could hardly get along without it and it is most often and most literally applied to the sales and transfer of negotiable securities. That the United States Bank of Pennsylvania had a title which it could transmit does not admit of a doubt. The sale negotiated by the Morris Canal and Banking Company might have been open to some objection as they were themselves the agents to sell and seem to have been in some way interested in the purchase, but surely it is too late to object after the Governor who was the immediately

[41] *London Times*, May 8, 1843.   [42] See Chapter IV.

authorized agent of the state had with a knowledge of all the facts ratified the contract and delivered the bonds and after the Legislature with all the facts before them had interposed no objection and had taken one-third of the purchase money. It would be monstrous to say that because property bought on credit has not been paid for, the holder cannot give a good title to it. Such a doctrine would overset half the sales made in this country. We cannot doubt the legal and equitable claim of the holders of these bonds to be paid what is due them to the extent of the amount for which they were pledged." [43]

In view of the criticism heaped upon Michigan by the eastern papers [44] and the exploitation of the situation for political purposes by the Whigs in the state, the Democratic state officials evidently felt called upon to justify their actions. The state treasurer and the auditor general jointly drafted a letter which they sent to the American Minister in England, Edward Everett. In this communication British holders of Michigan bonds were definitely told that the state would never recognize or pay the bonds for which the commonwealth had received no consideration and even if the state could be sued, no court of law would hold it liable. It was the part of wisdom, therefore, for the bondholders to avail themselves of the provisions of the act if they hoped to receive "a proper and patient hearing from the legislature" on the adjustment of their claims. [45]

In his message of January 6, 1845 Governor Barry also felt called upon to defend Michigan. "Of the justice of the claims presented by the holders of certain outstanding obligations of the state, amounting with interest, to about three millions for which no consideration has been received . . . I do not here design to speak. The information, however, that has been received seems to warrant the belief that the equity, originally existing between the state and the late Bank of the United States has been in no way affected by the transfer of the securities by that institution to their present holders. Of the justice of the indebtedness of the state recognized and provided for by the acts of February 17, 1842 and of March 8, 1843 no doubt exists." Nevertheless the governor did suggest to the legislature as worthy of inquiry "whether the amount of damages

[43] North American Review, Vol. 58, pp. 109-154.
[44] New York Commercial Advertiser quoted in London Times, May 8, 1843.
[45] Jenks, op. cit., pp. 614-615.

claimed under the first-mentioned law upon the unpaid installments of the five million loan were not greater than would be demanded or paid, had the action occurred between individuals and been wholly of a private character." [46] Later in the session the governor transmitted to the legislature three letters from the British holders of bonds protesting against the manner in which the legislature had dealt with them. The report of the joint committee of the Senate and the House to whom these communications were referred has been well characterized as worthy of a "pettifogging lawyer in behalf of a client with a bad case." The legislature adjourned without taking any action. [47]

When the legislature met in January 1846 the public debt again demanded attention. The Act of 1843 required the surrender of *all* the part paid bonds before new bonds should be issued after deducting 25 percent for damages on account of nonpayment. These provisions, as well as the hope entertained by the foreign bondholders that they might possibly be able to persuade the legislature to recognize their claims, resulted in the delivery of none of these securities. The governor in his message pointed this out and also raised the question of the sale of the state railroads in order to provide means for the liquidation of the recognized debt.

The only works of internal improvement which had yielded any income were the Central and Southern Railroads. The Central road already had cost the state $2,238,289.92 and the Southern, $1,125,590.65. To complete these works and to keep them in repair would call for additional expenditures. The governor therefore recommended the sale of these roads and the application of the proceeds of the sale to the discharge of the debt. The legislature promptly passed the necessary legislation carrying out the governor's suggestions. The Central road was sold for $2,000,000 to a company incorporated to build the Michigan Central and the Southern road for $500,000 to a company incorporated to build the Michigan Southern. The state treasurer was authorized to accept in payment from the purchasers full paid bonds and those issued for interest, and part paid bonds at the rate of $403.88 for $1,000 of principal and interest due January 1, 1846 and adding for subsequent interest at the rate of 6 percent upon $302.73 for each $1,000

[46] Fuller, *op. cit.*, pp. 504-518.   [47] Jenks, *op. cit.*, pp. 617, 618.

bond. By the sale of these roads the public debt of Michigan was materially reduced.[48]

Although the Act of 1846 providing for the sale of the Central Railroad reduced the rate of damages from 25 percent to 3 percent, the governor reported the following year that only $21,000 of part paid bonds had been received by the state.[49] The *London Times* had advised British holders of Michigan stock not to accept the proposition. The railroads were unfinished and the offer to take the acknowledged bonds at par, and the others at 40 percent in payment should not be entertained. "It is hoped," exclaimed the irate *Times,* "that European creditors will have firmness to refuse any terms short of their payment of their entire principal." Michigan, Indiana, and Illinois were in "a flourishing condition"; and with increasing wealth the desire of these states for something like a decent standing in the civilized world was certain to grow. It was only a question of time and the day was not far distant "if the parties interested would but wait for it with confidence when the people of these states, at all times sensitive to the imputation of inferiority will deem it a not disadvantageous transaction to lay out ten or twenty millions or whatever may respectively be the amount of their defalcations in purchasing a restoration of their forfeited respectability."[50]

There was no question that Michigan was anxious to dispose of this troublesome question. Both the governor and the auditor general in 1848 called the attention of the legislature to the requirement of the Act of 1843 that *all* the part paid bonds must be surrendered before new bonds were issued while the Act of 1846 permitted their reception in payment for the state railroads upon a reduction of 3 percent. In order to persuade the holders of these securities to turn them in to the state the legislature therefore passed a bill providing that upon the surrender of any of the part paid $5,000,000 bonds the holder was entitled to receive new bonds at the rate of $403.88 on each $1,000 of said bonds for principal and interest due thereon to January 1, 1846 and adding for subsequent interest 6 percent on $302.73 for each $1,000 to be computed to the first of January following the surrender. Furthermore the holders of the part paid

[48] Fuller, *op. cit.,* Vol. *II,* pp. 41-48; Michigan Laws, 1846, pp. 27-64, 170-194.
[49] Fuller, *op. cit.,* Vol. *II,* pp. 71-75.
[50] *London Times,* Dec. 3, 1846.

bonds were entitled by this act to demand and receive from the United States Bank and the Morris Canal and Banking Company whatever might be due from the bank and the company to the state.[51] On commenting on this law to the Barings James G. King wrote: "Michigan has passed a law which you will probably agree with us in thinking cunningly devised to slip their neck out of the noose and obtain from their creditor an acquiescence in their repudiation." [52] As many of the creditors evidently viewed the law in the same way, Michigan in exasperation finally passed a law in 1855 requiring the holders of the part paid bonds to present their securities within six months, otherwise they would receive no interest. This produced the desired result although the compulsory surrender was strongly protested by George Peabody, one of the largest creditors.[53] By 1859 Governor Bingham was able to report that most of the part paid bonds had been returned and new ones at the adjusted rate had been issued in their stead.[54] Forty years later the state treasurer was directed to advertise in the Michigan and New York papers for the return of all outstanding part paid bonds and if they were not returned within a specified time to declare them forfeited.[55]

Thus ended Michigan's relations with the holders of the part paid bonds. They were unable to persuade the legislature to recognize their claims and they were equally unsuccessful in recovering anything from the United States Bank. Both to Michigan and to the bondholders the flotation of the five million dollar loan had proved disastrous; and the treatment of the creditors by the state reflected the inability of the people of Michigan to deal dispassionately with a vexatious financial problem in a period of partisan politics and economic depression.

[51] Michigan Laws, 1848, pp. 228-232.
[52] King to Baring, May 24, 1848. Baring Mss.
[53] Jenks, *op. cit.*, pp. 627-629.
[54] Fuller, *op. cit.*, Vol. *II*, p. 304.
[55] Jenks, *op. cit.*, p. 629.

CHAPTER IX

THE PUBLIC DEBT OF LOUISIANA BEFORE THE CIVIL WAR

The establishment of land banks in Louisiana grew out of the mercantile needs of the community. There was a dearth of capital in the new commonwealth which materially retarded the growth of the sugar industry. Sugar was the staple crop of Louisiana; and during the first quarter of the nineteenth century the cultivation of sugar was rapidly expanded. This created a heavy demand for capital for the purchase of land and negroes which the meager financial resources of the state were unable to meet. To remedy this situation needy and influential planters in Louisiana began to urge the legislature to create banks for the purpose of loaning them the funds necessary to carry on their operations. The stock in these banks was subscribed by planters who paid their subscriptions by tendering mortgages equal to one-half to two-thirds the market value of their estates. Since the credit of the state was deemed more effective in attracting capital from the north or from Europe, the legislature was urged to issue state bonds in order to procure the working capital of these banks or to guarantee the bonds issued by the bank.

In 1824 Louisiana inaugurated her system of land banks by incorporating the Bank of Louisiana, with a capital of $4,000,000, one-half of which was subscribed by the state. For the state subscription the treasurer of the state delivered to the bank bonds bearing 5 percent interest at the rate of $100 in bonds for every $83⅓ of stock. These bonds were payable at intervals of from ten to twenty-five years from their date of issuance. They were to be sold by the bank for specie at the same rate at which they had been delivered to the bank. The faith of the state was pledged for the payment of the principal and interest of these bonds as well as the stock of the state in the banks. The interest was to be paid from the dividends upon the bank stock held by the state and in case of any deficiency the bank was to pay the amounts due and charge the same to the account of the state. The charter provided that $2,000,000 of the capital stock of the bank was to be appropriated for the sole purpose of being loaned upon notes or bonds secured by mortgages on immovable property; but no mortgage was to be taken upon uncultivated land and not more than one-half of the net value of the mortgaged property was to be lent by the bank.[1]

Within three years the facilities offered by this bank were found inadequate to meet the needs of the planters. The attention of the legislature again was directed to the wants of the agriculturists; and on March 26, 1827 the Consolidated Association of the Planters of Louisiana was chartered. The capital of this corporation was originally $2,000,000 which was to be procured through the issuance of bonds by the company bearing 5 percent interest. This loan was guaranteed by mortgages on real productive property amounting to $2,500,000; and only planters were entitled to subscribe for shares in the Consolidated Association. All subscribers were required to give mortgages on their estates equal to the number of shares for which they had subscribed. No stockholder was permitted to borrow from the corporation more than 50 percent on his stock; and this amount was to be returned by yearly installments to meet the payment of the bonds issued by the company. Dividends were to be declared only as the bonds were paid and in the same proportion. In the meantime the profits were to be retained as a sinking fund to meet the redemption of the bonds. By a subsequent act passed the following year the capital of the corporation was raised to $2,500,000; and the amount of subscriptions guaranteed by mortgages on cultivated estates was increased to $3,000,000. In order to facilitate the Consolidated Association in negotiating this loan, the faith of the state was pledged "for the reimbursement of the capital and interest of the said sum of $2,500,000." The state for its guaranty of the bonds of the company was considered to be a stockholder to the amount of $1,000,000 and was granted a credit of $250,000. The dividends arising from the stock of the state in the company were to be paid to the state in the same proportions and at the same time that the dividends accruing to other stockholders were paid. By this act six of the twelve directors were

[1] Louisiana Laws, 1824, pp. 92-130.

appointed annually by the governor and the expiration of the charter was extended to June 30, 1843.[2]

The Union Bank chartered in 1832 was established on the same general principles. The capital of this bank was $7,000,000, which was to be raised by means of a loan obtained by the bank. Books for the subscription of the sum of $8,000,000 divided into shares of $100 each and intended to secure the loan were to be opened; and only owners of real estate situated in Louisiana were entitled to subscribe for shares in the bank. In order to facilitate the bank in negotiating this loan the faith of the state was pledged for the capital and interest and state bonds bearing 5 percent, payable in 12 to 20 years were delivered by the governor to the bank. To secure the payment of the capital and interest of these bonds subscribers were to give mortgages equal to the amount of their respective stock; and when mortgages were offered on lands and slaves the value of the land was to equal at least two-thirds of the stock for which the mortgage was given. The board of directors were to appoint in each parish commissioners whose duty it was to ascertain and appraise the property of those who wished to become stockholders as well as those desirous of obtaining loans on mortgages. In consideration for the bonds issued by the state in favor of the bank the state was entitled to one-sixth of the net proceeds of the bank and was granted a credit of $500,000.[3]

The following year the legislature chartered another property bank. The capital of the Citizens Bank was $12,000,000, which was to be obtained through the issuance of 5 percent bonds by the bank payable in 14 to 50 years. These bonds were guaranteed by mortgages on estates valued at $14,400,000; and the law specifically stated that the mortgages given by the stockholders were to remain a perpetual pledge "to the holder or holders of said bonds until the expiration of the charter and the final liquidation of the affairs of the bank." In case of the nonpayment of either the principal or interest of the bonds, holders of these securities were entitled to enforce payment by the most summary process of law on the mortgages. In 1836 a supplementary act was passed by the legislature

[2] *Ibid.*, 1827, pp. 96-116; *ibid.*, 1828, pp. 30-36. Another amendatory act was passed in 1830. Louisiana Laws, 1830, pp. 68-70. A brief history of the Consolidated Association can be found in 5 Louisiana Reports, pp. 54-57.

[3] Louisiana Laws, 1831, pp. 42-72.

pledging the faith of the state for the security of the capital of the bank; and bonds for the sum of $3,000,000, with the privilege of extending the amount to $12,000,000 were issued by the state in favor of the bank. The bank was also permitted to grant loans for twelve months with the privilege of renewing them at the end of each year for fourteen years on the payment of one-fourteenth of the original amount borrowed at each period of renewal.[4]

In negotiating these loans, the Louisiana banks naturally turned to the London and Amsterdam money markets. The Barings of London and Hope and Company of Amsterdam were either approached through their American representatives in this country or duly authorized commissioners of the banks visited Holland to deal directly with these houses. Although the credit of Louisiana was held in high estimation at the time these loans were authorized, and there was an eagerness upon the part of European investors to purchase American securities, the bank commissioners found it necessary to remove certain doubts in the minds of European financiers before they were able to dispose of the bonds. The fact that Louisiana was a slave-holding state was a disadvantage. To remove any fears on the part of the bankers, Edmund J. Forstall of New Orleans pointed out to T. W. Ward that Louisiana had only 110,000 blacks in 1832 "scattered among at least an equal number of whites." Forstall stressed the commercial importance of New Orleans and the fact that the six slave-holding states contained a white population of 1,600,000, all equally interested "in the tranquillity and prosperity of this capitol of the west." The whole black population of the Mississippi Valley amounted only to 600,000 while that of the whites exceeded 3,000,000. "London and Paris," wrote Forstall, "have much more to dread from their rabble than Louisiana will ever have from her blacks."[5]

The increasing number of loans authorized by Louisiana also tended to make European capitalists cautious. Louisiana commissioners stressed the security behind the bonds and the purposes for which they were issued. Representatives of the Consolidated Association called the attention of the Barings to the acts of 1827 and 1828 whereby the capital of the corporation was to be loaned "solely

[4] *Ibid.*, 1833, pp. 172-192; *ibid.*, 1836, pp. 16-24.
[5] Forstall to Ward, Nov. 19, 1832. Baring Mss. Forstall was a director of the Citizens Bank and later the representative of the bondholders in Louisiana.

on the most undoubted, productive real estate"; and that such loans could never exceed half the ascertained cash value of the mortgaged property. In addition to these ample securities, the commissioners pointed out that no dividends were to be made until the end of the charter. The private fortune of every stockholder and every director was "irrevocably pledged to the amount of his stock, or shares, for the faithful performance of all the contracts of the Association." It should be recalled that the directors of the corporation were well acquainted "with the nature and value of the properties offered as securities" and that each of them had "a deep personal interest in the success of the institution." The commissioners claimed there was no reason to fear losses from the persons to whom the Association might grant loans because the laws of Louisiana required "all titles, transfers, and mortgages of real estate to be on public record." They also claimed that wealthy and respectable planters of Louisiana were subscribers to the Association solely for the purpose "of benefiting the country" because, according to the commissioners, these planters had no need "of any money from the Association." "In fact," stated the commissioners, "the whole body of planters of Louisiana are remarkable for their good faith in money transactions, and, extraordinary as the fact may appear, we state, without fear of contradiction, that under the different forms of government to which Louisiana has been subjected, it would be difficult to cite an instance of pecuniary loss arising out of the default of payment by a Louisiana planter." The same views were set forth by Forstall in a letter to Ward concerning the Union Bank bonds; and at a later date when conditions in Louisiana were becoming serious the president of this bank assured the Barings that the different corporations would be able to meet their engagements.

The Union Bank president emphasized in his letter to the Barings the difference between the loans of Louisiana and those of other states. He pointed out that in Louisiana the state was guaranteed against "any loss by mortgages on property and landed estates in value double the amount of the bonds issued." The bonds issued by other states were dependent upon the profit realized from the improvements, created and carried on, by the sale of such securities. In the case of Louisiana, he claimed, the state debt was merely nominal; in the other states it was really a state debt. He definitely declared that in Louisiana the bonds were to be redeemed by the corporations; whereas the bonds of the other states were to be redeemed by the commonwealths.[6]

Notwithstanding the statements made by the bank officials, European capitalists were not always satisfied as to the security of the loans. The Barings suggested that the act incorporating the Bank of Louisiana should be so amended that the state should appear the borrower instead of the bank since people in Europe could not understand how banks that were solvent should ever want to borrow money. This might be done by modifying the wording of the state bonds in such a way as to make any special arrangement between the purchaser of the bonds and the bank binding upon the state. Furthermore the price of 83⅓ as fixed by the legislature was considered too high by the Barings unless the dividends on the stock were made payable in England at a given date. Since the legislature would probably consider it derogatory to their dignity to alter the price in the law, the Barings proposed that the bank should agree to pay the principal and interest in London at a stipulated rate, preferably 4 shillings 6 pence to the dollar, or if that rate for the dollars was unsatisfactory, any other rate might be agreed upon as long as the rate was "a determined one and was not subject to the fluctuations of exchange." Although these changes were not made in the original statutes, the correspondence of the Barings reveals the importance placed by European financiers upon the necessity of state guaranties in order to induce the investing public to take the bonds. It is also indicative of the care with which the Barings tried to protect their clients from any unfavorable fluctuations in exchange. The failure of many of the American negotiators to exercise the same caution was the basis of many of the later state debt controversies.[7]

Information transmitted by American correspondents of European banking houses to the home offices also tended at times to make some of these firms hesitant in accepting certain Louisiana bonds. The negotiation of the loan for the Citizens Bank in Europe

[6] Lavergne and Gordon to Baring, Aug. 19, 1828; Forstall to Ward, Nov. 19, 1832; Gordon to Baring, March 21, 1839. Baring Mss.
[7] Nolte's Memorandum on Louisiana State Bonds, Aug. 16, 1824. Baring Mss. Cf. also memorandum dated 1824 in Baring Mss. on bond of Bank of Louisiana; Acts Louisiana, 1824, pp. 92-130.

illustrates this point; and in view of the subsequent controversy between the State of Louisiana and the foreign bondholders, it is necessary to relate the circumstances surrounding the sale of these bonds.

In 1834 the Citizens Bank appointed commissioners to negotiate a loan in Europe of $9,000,000. The following February a conditional contract was entered into between the commissioners and the banking house of W. Willinck of Amsterdam whereby the entire loan was tendered by this firm to European capitalists. This loan, however, remained without takers on the days fixed for subscription largely due to the failure of the bank to transmit the bonds to Europe. Upon the transmission of the bonds a new contract was signed on July 3, 1835. A prospectus was issued in Amsterdam by Willinck tendering the loan of $9,000,000 at the rate of 40 cents to the guilder and enumerating all the guards and checks provided by the charter. In the meantime the bank appointed other commissioners to negotiate the loan in Europe providing no engagements had been entered into by their predecessors. One of the new commissioners arrived in Amsterdam late in August; and upon the failure of the second attempt by Willinck to find takers for the loan, a conditional contract was entered into by this commissioner and Messers Hope and Company. By the terms of this contract Hope and Company agreed to take $3,000,000 of the bonds, or 6,750 bonds of £100 sterling each, at the rate of 1,200 florins for each bond of £100 sterling, which Hope and Company later contended was 8 percent higher than the offer of Willinck and made a difference in the favor of the stockholders on $9,000,000 of $720,000. The contract stipulated that the commission allowed Hope and Company on the loan was 2 percent instead of 5 percent as originally allowed Willinck, which was a difference of 3 percent in favor of the stockholders, amounting on $9,000,000 to the sum of $270,000. Furthermore the commission allowed Hope and Company for paying the running interests during the currency of the charter and on the reimbursement of the capital was ½ of 1 percent instead of 1 percent agreed to in the Willinck contract, which was a difference in favor of the Citizens Bank of 50 percent in commissions. The *sine qua non* demanded by Hope and Company for these considerations was that the Citizens Bank should obtain the following amendments to its charter: (1) the repeal of the power given to the bank to subscribe to the stock of the late Borgne Navigation Company; (2) the issuance of the bonds of the state in lieu of the bank. With the combination of real estate security and state guaranty and supervision, Hope and Company evidently believed the investment would be safe. On December 28, 1835 the conditional contract entered into with Hope and Company was submitted to both houses of the legislature, accompanied by a petition from the directors of the bank requesting the amendment of the original act of incorporation. An act was accordingly passed on January 30, 1836 embodying these provisions in the charter of the bank.[8]

While these negotiations were being carried on, the Barings were warned by Ward not to take the Citizens Bank bonds. "I have examined the charter of the Citizens Bank," wrote Ward on June 22, 1835, "and have come to the conclusion to have nothing to do with it on this side. . . . Under this charter I do not see but that the bank may do just what it pleases and to any extent within the limits of double the amount of its capital." Ward therefore notified the bank commissioners who had approached him that he would not agree to have it come out under the Baring sanction, or to take any interest in it unless some modifications in the law were made. Ward confessed to the Barings that the success of the bank "depended to be sure, as in other banking institutions, upon the manner in which it was conducted" but in his estimation the charter afforded too many opportunities for abuse. Evidently the insistence of Ward upon changes in the charter convinced the commissioners of the advisability of accepting the terms set forth by Hope and Company. When Ward learned that the Dutch financiers had agreed to take the loan he was convinced that they had done so only because of the state guaranty. This presumably was the interpretation held by Hope and Company.[9]

If the bankers of Europe were somewhat dubious of the Louisiana bonds, there was no such anxiety upon the part of investors. The Barings were pressed by some of their clients to allow them to take some of the Louisiana bonds which the house held. "I have

[8] This account is based on a copy of Forstall's Memorial to the legislature, Feb., 1844. Baring Mss. This memorial with accompanying documents is published in Senate Journal Louisiana, 1843-1844, App. *LI-LVIII*.

[9] Ward to Baring, June 22, 23, Oct. 13, 1835. Baring Mss.

no doubt," wrote one eager buyer, "that you are aware that the capitalists who regulate the American stock market are but few and that some of them have a good deal in their power to support prices by their being consulted by others in making investments. I have been consulted by many both in town and down here, and I have invariably seen my example oftener followed than my advice. The question always put is, are you a holder yourself?" Other purchasers of Louisiana bonds notified the Barings that they had brought pressure to bear upon the *London Times* to refer favorably in its columns to the Louisiana loans. All of the London papers, however, did not need to have influence brought to bear upon them to point out the advantages of purchasing Louisiana securities. "The capital now about to be invested in the State of Louisiana," announced the *Circular to Bankers,* "is not only safe so far as the English contributors to it are concerned, but it is certain to yield a good return to the projectors and undertakers. . . . According to the testimony of well informed Americans, the State of Louisiana is politic and wise in borrowing, and the contractors are prudent and judicious in lending money for public improvements." With such notices in the daily press, and with the issuance of prospectuses quoting almost verbatim the statements of American negotiators, Louisiana bonds found a ready sale in the London and Amsterdam investing circles.[10]

Unfortunately the State of Louisiana was not "as politic and wise in borrowing" as the *Circular to Bankers* claimed. When the bonds of the Consolidated Association were negotiated the whole amount of state taxes was a little over $263,000 and barely sufficed to defray the current expenses of the administration. By the census of 1830, the population of the state was about 215,739 "or less than half the population of a small French department and more than half that number were slaves."[11] These facts did not warrant the prodigal use of the public credit which the legislature loaned to numerous banking institutions and railroad corporations. By 1841 Louisiana had issued over $21,000,000 of bonds in favor of various banks and other companies.[12] As long as the state was able to

---

[10] Ferguson to Baring, Sept. 10, 1832; Cotterill to Baring, Oct. 21, 23, 1832. Baring Mss.; *Circular to Bankers,* Oct. 5, 1832; Prospectus of Louisiana State Loan, 1833, in Baring Mss.

[11] Senate Journal Louisiana, 1843-1844, App. *XXI-XXVI*.

[12] House Journal Louisiana, 1840-1841, App. C.

borrow from the banks and these institutions were apparently in a flourishing condition, the legislature paid little attention to the management of their affairs.

The banks of Louisiana, however, do not seem to have been conducted any better than many others in different sections of the country. They speculated in real estate and cotton, expanded their circulation, and granted unwise loans. In the spring of 1837 all the New Orleans banks with the exception of the Citizens Bank and the Consolidated Association suspended specie payments. The legislature attempted to force resumption the following year; but on October 19, 1839 all the New Orleans' banks were forced to suspend specie payments with the exception of the Merchants Bank.[18]

In his message of January 1840 Governor Roman discussed at length the financial ills of Louisiana. In his estimation the present financial crisis was largely due to the unwise policy of some of the banks increasing their circulation beyond their active means. To remedy this situation, Governor Roman recommended to the legislature that they force the weaker banks to liquidate. As long as these unsound institutions continued to exist, the governor was convinced that it would be impossible to establish a sound circulation. The legislature refused, however, to adopt such drastic measures; and nothing was done at this time to reorganize the banking system. The governor's advice regarding the issuance of more state bonds was also disregarded by the legislature. The governor confessed that it was practically impossible to dispose of any of the state bonds in Europe since all American credits had been affected by the present financial stringency. Nevertheless he was confident when the storm had subsided and affairs had resumed their normal course that Louisiana bonds would be in immediate demand. But the governor cautioned the legislature not to authorize an excessive amount of bonds for internal improvements if they hoped to be able to sustain the credit and faith of the state and not run the risk of burdening the people with additional taxes. In absolute disregard of the governor's suggestions, the legislature increased the appropriations and passed numerous bills for the issuance of more bonds. All of these bills were vetoed by the governor and, with the excep-

[18] *Ibid.*, pp. 105-108; *London Times*, Feb. 23, 1838.

tion of $500,000 of bonds granted to the Port Hudson and Clinton Railroad, none of these measures became law.[14]

When the legislature assembled the following year the financial embarrassment of Louisiana was more serious. The same recommendations were repeated by Governor Roman with no better success. The governor called the attention of the legislature to the dangerous condition of the public treasury. He pointed out that the income of the state was considerably below its expenditures; and that for many years the state had paid its debts by borrowing from the banks. The prostrated condition of these institutions made it impossible for them to lend any assistance. The governor urged the legislature to exercise all possible economy in making appropriations for carrying on the administration of the state without impairing its efficiency; and at the same time he suggested increased taxes. Holders of Louisiana bonds were assured by the governor that they would "never have cause to repent their confidence in the state. The resources afforded by the inexhaustible fertility of our soil and by a position which makes us the great mart for the produce of the Mississippi," declared Governor Roman, "will enable us honorably to meet our engagements; and nowhere is it better felt than in Louisiana that if it is difficult to compel a recusant state to pay its debts, the honor of the people will be prompted by that very difficulty to observe conscientiously and religiously its pledged faith." This statement was quoted in the English newspapers as evidence of the good intentions of Louisiana to meet its engagements.[15]

When this message was delivered the public faith and credit of Louisiana was as yet unimpaired. The property banks were paying the interest on the state bonds issued in their favor. But it was evident that the banking system of Louisiana needed reform. The only banks then paying specie were the Bank of Louisiana and the Citizens Bank; and there was a division of opinion among the banking institutions as to the propriety of resuming specie payments. Some of the banks openly acknowledged that they were in no condition to resume without assistance; many were desirous of continuing the suspension until November 1842. But shortly after the legislature assembled in 1842 there was a depreciation of the paper

[14] House Journal Louisiana, 1840-1841, pp. 2-4.
[15] Senate Journal Louisiana, 1841-1842, pp. 3-5; *Circular to Bankers*, Jan. 21, 1842.

currency of Louisiana on account of the refusal of some of the banks to receive, either in payment or in deposit, the notes of those institutions whose insolvency was suspected.[16]

In order to remedy this situation, the legislature on February 5, 1842 passed a banking act which Horace White later declared was "in nearly all respects, a model for other states and countries." According to the provisions of this act the charters of the incorporated banks of New Orleans were severally revived providing each bank immediately prepared for a general resumption of specie payments and strictly observed the following rules in its operations. Each bank was to maintain a specie reserve equal to one-third of all of its cash liabilities; the other two-thirds of its liabilities were to be represented in satisfactory commercial paper, payable in full at maturity and within 90 days. Bank directors were personally liable for all loans and investments made in violation of the law, unless they could show that they had voted against the same, if present. All commercial paper was to be paid at maturity; and if it was not paid or an extension of time was requested, the account was to be closed and the name of the delinquent party was to be sent to the other banks. The governor was to appoint a board of currency whose duty it was to supervise the execution of this act. This board was to examine thoroughly the affairs of any bank whenever they might deem it expedient to do so and at least quarterly. No bank was to have less than 50 shareholders holding at least 30 shares each; and no bank was to pay out any notes but its own. All the banks were required to pay their balances to other institutions every Saturday in specie under the penalty of being placed immediately in liquidation. No bank was to purchase any shares of its capital stock; and, with the exception of the property banks, none were to loan on a pledge of their shares more than 30 percent of the amount paid in on the shares. Some loans on mortgage securities were permitted but these were restricted to the bank's capital. Whenever a bank was placed in liquidation the board of currency was to require the board of directors to make a statement of its cash assets and liabilities; and it was made the duty of banks not in liquidation, as a consideration for the restoration of their charters to receive at par in payment of all debts and obligations due them the circulation of

[16] House Journal Louisiana, 1843, pp. 3-5.

any bank or banks that might enter into liquidation; and the circulation and cash assets of these liquidating banks were to be distributed according to a fixed ratio among the several banks not in liquidation.[17]

By a subsequent act passed on March 14, 1842 the legislature provided for the liquidation of banks under certain contingencies. In case of a forced liquidation the commissioners appointed to control the operations of such institutions were to take possession of the property of the bank in liquidation and the board of currency was to distribute as equally as possible the available cash assets among the banks which had received its circulation and the commissioners were to redeem the notes of the bank in circulation. Section 28 of this law specifically provided that in the case of property banks placed in liquidation the board of currency was to convert the available assets into a sinking fund applicable exclusively to the payment or purchase of the state bonds in favor of such institutions.[18]

In his last message to the legislature Governor Roman was forced to confess that these laws had not produced the desired results although he refuted the charge that they were entirely responsible for all the evils laid at their door. In his estimation their greatest fault was that they had been passed "to remedy those abuses which it would have been wiser to have prevented." Nevertheless in adopting the law for the liquidation of banks and in creating a board to control these institutions and to examine and publish their real condition, the governor acknowledged the legislature "without being the primary cause" had rendered inevitable the failure of those banks "whose credit had no other foundation than the confidence inspired by other institutions which received their paper at par." On the other hand the governor accused the banks of not faithfully carrying out the provisions of the law; and not perceiving that "the failure of one endangered the fate of all." Furthermore, the governor declared the inability of the banks to harmonize their differences in the mode of settling their balances had led the banks to resume specie payments in May "more than six months before the period fixed by law." Since most of these institutions had not

---

[17] Louisiana Laws, 1842, pp. 34-63; Knox, J. J., A History of Banking in the United States, pp. 613, 614.

[18] Louisiana Laws. 1842, pp. 234-254.

prepared themselves for resumption, the banks, with one or two exceptions, had been forced again to suspend, after having lost all the specie which constituted their strength.

Among the banks which had been placed in liquidation in the fall of 1842 were the Citizens Bank and the Consolidated Association. Governor Roman called attention to the failure of these institutions; but he assured the legislature that the stockholders of these institutions were bound by the charters granted them to pay the interest and principal of the state bonds. He declared that the value of the mortgages on real estate given as security exceeded the amount of the debt contracted by the state. The bondholders need not be alarmed, however. The governor assured them that Louisiana would not shrink from keeping her plighted faith. Louisiana would maintain the "purity of her honor" and "never furnish the enemies of popular governments with a new cause to charge them with dishonesty." [19]

Unfortunately Governor Roman proposed no changes in the laws which would make it easier for these banks to meet their engagements. He made no reference to the statute which authorized the state to take possession of the assets of property banks in liquidation and authorized the board of currency to apply the assets as they became available to the payment or purchase of the state bonds while at the same time there was another statute which required these banks to receive in payment for all debts due them their own depreciated notes.[20] On the contrary Governor Roman told the legislature "in case of non-payment by those two banks of the capital or interest of the bonds issued in their favor you will not be under the necessity of imposing additional taxes, which, in no event could be collected within the year, and which cannot be required to meet your obligations. Between the holders of the bonds and the state, stand the stockholders of the institution for whose benefit they have been issued. You have only to see that the engagements they have contracted be complied with, in all their strength, and to their full extent. Being myself one of those stockholders I deem it my duty to declare, as my opinion, that the state should demand nothing from those of her citizens who have derived no direct profit

[19] House Journal Louisiana, 1843, pp. 3-5.
[20] Senate Journal Louisiana, 1843-1844, App. *XXI*.

from the sale of the bonds issued, without having first exhausted the whole property mortgaged to secure their punctual payment." The governor declared that the situation of the Citizens Bank and the Consolidated Association was not so desperate as to ruin the stockholders who should realize that it was to their interest "to anticipate the necessity of coercive measures by using every exertion in their power to comply punctually and in good faith with all their engagements." On the other hand, the governor expressed the hope that the holders of the bonds would not "exercise a rigor which might injure the debtors without hastening the recovery of the debts." If they would coöperate with the state the governor was confident that they would soon begin to receive their regular interest payments.[21]

Upon his inauguration in January 1843 the new Democratic governor, Alexander Mouton, found the finances of the state in a deplorable condition. The governor informed the legislature that the state owed the banks about $1,200,000; that there was due for salaries and other ordinary expenses another $200,000; that there were state bonds, for the payment of which the state had no guaranty, to the amount of $1,273,000 on which the interest was unpaid; that in all probability the interest on the state bonds issued in behalf of the insolvent property banks, the Citizens Bank and the Consolidated Association would not be paid; that the current expenses of the government exceeded its income by more than $200,000; that the funds in the treasury were exhausted; and that the state was no longer able to borrow from the banks or the people bear heavier taxes. The governor urged the legislature in view of this situation to devise means of meeting these engagements and to restore the credit of the state. He suggested that a thorough investigation be made of the debts and resources of the commonwealth; and especially the affairs of the property banks in which the state was interested.[22]

Governor Mouton performed a useful service in revealing the chaotic condition of Louisiana finances. But it was soon evident that the policy to be pursued by the new administration was different from that of its predecessor. Whereas the Whig Governor Roman had believed in regulating the banks and that the weaker

---

[21] House Journal Louisiana, 1843, pp. 3-5.   [22] *Ibid.*, pp. 25-28.

banks were primarily responsible for the financial ills of the state, Governor Mouton was hostile toward all banking institutions. Furthermore it was apparent that the planter interests were as desirous of relieving themselves of their debts to the banks as the governor and the legislature were anxious to free the state from some of its pressing obligations.

It was under these circumstances that the legislature on April 5, 1843 passed a law which brought discredit upon the state.[23] By the provisions of this act whenever any stockholder in any of the property banks in liquidation should offer to the state managers supervising these institutions any of the outstanding bonds of the state, he was entitled to have the property mortgaged by him to secure the stock released from such mortgage for the amount of the capital and accrued interest on these bonds. In lieu of these bonds, certificates were to be issued to the stockholder which were not to be secured by mortgage nor by the faith of the state. But the assets of the Citizens Bank and the Consolidated Association were to remain in the possession of the state until the final payment by each of them of all the state bonds issued in their favor. The Citizens Bank and the Consolidated Association were authorized to extend the time of payment of any of their outstanding bonds for a period of fifteen years with the privilege of making further arrangements with the holders of such bonds for an additional extension of the time of payment.[24]

Upon the publication of the Act of April 1843 a storm of protest arose from the foreign bondholders. The Barings issued a circular to the foreign creditors of the Consolidated Association in which they called attention to the fact that neither the bank nor the state had provided funds for the state bonds due June 30, amounting to $763,000, which formed the remainder of the loan negotiated by them, or for the semi-annual interest due on that day. The Barings definitely declared that "without doubt" these were engagements for which Louisiana was bound to provide whatever might be the fate of the banks. Up to this time the banks had regularly met all payments but this had been rendered impossible by forcing the institutions into liquidation. The Barings therefore declared that

[23] Democratic Review, Vol. 14, new series, p. 14.
[24] Louisiana Laws, 1843, pp. 56-59.

the state was now liable for these payments. "The recent conduct of the legislature," stated the Circular, "has had the effect of embarrassing the banks, of depreciating the value of their assets, of lowering the credit of the state, and by the non-payment of the interest or capital of the bonds of greatly depreciating the prices of these securities; and as at the same time the banks had been compelled to receive in payment of debts the bonds issued by the state in their favor at par or the nominal value indicated in the bond, the result has been that the domestic debtors are benefitted at the expense of the honor of the state and of the just claims of its foreign creditors." Since the notes in circulation of the Consolidated Association were then at about 30 percent discount the overdue bonds if sent to New Orleans would be classed with the notes in price, and if a large amount were forwarded for sale, the increased supply of the bank's paper would lower the price, as, in view of the pecuniary embarrassments of Louisiana, no eagerness was shown by the debtors of the bank to avail themselves "even of the existing depreciation to make their payments." The Barings therefore recommended that the bondholders retain their securities in England where each owner could "better direct and control the price at which he would be disposed to sell them." [25]

In addition to this advice, the Barings began an active campaign to educate the citizens of Louisiana to the claims of the foreign bondholders. Editorials of the *Boston Advertiser* were inserted at Ward's expense in the columns of influential Louisiana papers; special articles were written and published in the *New Orleans Bee* in both French and English; and representatives of the foreign bondholders interviewed the committee of the legislature which had introduced the bill at the last session. [26]

In the excellent article prepared by B. R. Curtis, at Ward's suggestion, for the January 1844 number of the *North American Review* particular stress was laid upon the injustice to foreign bondholders by the Act of April 1843. In this article Curtis pointed out that all debts due to the liquidating banks must be paid in state bonds issued by the banks which bonds were to be received in payment at par. Yet the capital stock of these institutions consisted

[25] Circular of the Barings, July 8, 1843. Baring Mss.
[26] Ward to Shepherd, Nov. 23, 1843; Shepherd to Ward, Dec. 14, 1843; Forstall to Ward, Jan. 3, 1844. Baring Mss.

of the obligations of those who subscribed to the stock to pay the sums for which they subscribed secured by mortgages on real estate; and the law providing for the issuance of these bonds specifically stated that these mortgages were a "guaranty for the reimbursement of the principal and interest of the bonds to be issued by the state. . . . Now there is not the smallest doubt," wrote Curtis, "that this law amounted to a contract made by the state and the banks with every bondholder that these mortgages should be held by the banks in trust to secure the payment of the money loaned on the bonds. There is not a court in the country which would hesitate so to declare upon these facts. And when the state placed these banks in liquidation and thus took control of their affairs it was bound to guard this trust strictly and faithfully. It had no right to receive depreciated bonds at par in payment for well secured debts which it held in trust for third persons. What would the law of Louisiana, or the courts of Louisiana say to a tutor or guardian who should receive depreciated paper in payment of a debt due to his ward secured by mortgage? Undoubtedly, they would say it was unfaithful administration; and would order him to make good the difference. And may the legislature itself justly do what its own laws condemn as unfaithful and unjust? As a question of right this matter admits of no doubt. As a question of the constitutional power of the legislature it is equally clear. This law impairs the obligation of a plain contract between the state and the banks on the one part and the bondholders on the other; and it is therefore in conflict not only with the Constitution of the United States but with the fundamental law of Louisiana which prohibits the legislature from enacting any law impairing the obligation of a contract." [27]

A memorial was presented to the legislature on February 19, 1844 by Forstall for Hope and Company in behalf of the holders of Citizens Bank bonds. In this memorial Forstall recounted the negotiations surrounding the sale of $6,099,939 of Citizens Bank bonds to Hope and Company; and called attention to the nonpayment by the bank or the state on the interest due on these bonds since February 1, 1843. Forstall declared that he had filed a protest on March 24, 1843 with Governor Mouton and the president of the board of managers of the bank. But his communication was ignored.

[27] North American Review, Vol. 58, pp. 137-140.

When no provision was made for the August interest a second protest had been filed with the governor; and when payment was demanded the notary public representing the Dutch bondholders had been informed the governor and the secretary of state were absent from the city and had left no instructions concerning the nonpayment by the state or the bank. Again on February 1 no provision had been made for the overdue payments. By the nonpayment of these three installments, Forstall declared that a sum amounting to upwards of $512,000 was now in arrear for which the state had made no provision; and the attention of the legislature was called to the fact that a petition signed by more than 120 stockholders representing upwards of $2,000,000 was on file in the archives of both houses of the legislature "praying for legislative action to enable the managers of the bank to meet the interest on the bonds." [28]

About the same time a series of articles appeared in the *New Orleans Age* violently attacking Governor Mouton and the legislature. This paper openly charged Governor Mouton with being "instigated by a set of unprincipled men" to bring repudiation to Louisiana. To substantiate this accusation the *Age* declared that the governor had referred the correspondence of the foreign creditors to the board of currency; and this board "composed of partisans of the governor" had actually drawn up a report which the governor refused to make public recommending state repudiation. Furthermore the *Age* asserted that Governor Mouton having broken the Consolidated and Citizens banks was also desirous of breaking the Union Bank; and had only been deterred from carrying out this plan when upon examination it was found that the assets of the Union Bank exceeded its liabilities. [29]

In addition to the protests, memorials, and articles published in the New Orleans papers in behalf of the foreign creditors, the London press sharply criticized Louisiana. The *London Morning Chronicle* characterized the Act of 1843 as "a more heinous breach

---

[28] Senate Journal Louisiana, 1843-1844, App. *LI-LVIII*. There is a copy of this memorial in the Baring Printed Documents.
[29] *New Orleans Age*, March 11, 12, 13, 1844. Copies of these articles are in the Baring Printed Doc. Gov. Mouton did request the Board of Currency on Apr. 26, 1843, for information regarding the property banks; but it was not until May 6, 1844 that the chairman of the board replied. In his report, subsequently printed, there is good ground to substantiate the suspicions voiced in the *New Orleans Age*. For this report consult Senate Journal Louisiana, 1843-1844, App. *XXI-XXVI*.

of faith than repudiation." The *London Times* strongly approved of the advice given by the Barings to the foreign bondholders to retain possession of their securities.[30]

As in the case of other indebted American states, these attacks upon the integrity of the citizens of Louisiana were vigorously denied by the defenders of the state. The board of currency publicly declared that the British public was "designedly misinformed" as to the real causes of Louisiana's defalcation.[31] A strong defense of the state was published in the columns of the *New Orleans Bee*. "The writer in the *London Morning Chronicle*," stated the *Bee*, "either did not understand the circumstances under which the law was passed or had grossly misrepresented them. It would be just as well for European journalists to be chary of their abuse in noticing matters of this sort, for people of this section of the Union are just the very last men in the world who could be bullied or blackguarded into measures. . . . Now we would ask the *Morning Chronicle* or the *Boston Advertiser*, . . . if by any convulsion in business or revolution in monetary affairs, or imprudence if they like, either Great Britain or Massachusetts was suddenly and without previous suspicion of the crisis, called upon to provide for a debt, the interest of which alone required twice as much revenue as the ordinary receipts of the treasury, would or could either of them at once meet it? And if the amount of the obligation for which they would have ultimately to provide depended upon the value of the assets of insolvent corporations for which they had indorsed, would they not make a schedule of their effects and arrive at a reasonable appreciation of the deficit they would have to make good before adopting a system of taxation for that purpose? . . . We know of no surer way to blunt the sensibilities of a people to the obligations of contracts," concluded the article, "than for the press and more especially for foreign journalists to assail their honesty, when they have done the best thing, at the time, in their power to do, for the public creditors."[32]

Nevertheless there was a noticeable change in the attitude of the legislature with regard to the payment of debts when it assembled in January 1844. Whether this was due to domestic or foreign

[30] *London Morning Chronicle*, Nov. 3, 1843; *London Times*, July 19, 1843.
[31] House Journal Louisiana, 1844, App. *V-VIII*.
[32] *New Orleans Bee*, Dec. 23, 1843. Baring Printed Doc.

criticism, or to the improved economic condition of Louisiana, it is difficult to determine. In all probability both contributed in bringing about a clearer realization upon the part of the people of Louisiana to make some provision for the payment of their obligations. In his message to the legislature Governor Mouton recommended the sale of a number of the public works undertaken by the state and the payment of the public debt.[33]

Shortly after the delivery of this message the finance committee of the lower house presented a detailed report on the debts of the state. The committee estimated the public debt amounted in the aggregate to $21,433,523.03, exclusive of interest. These liabilities were divided into two classes. Such as were incurred by the state for administrative purposes, for public works, and for the purchase of stock in certain banks, amounting in the aggregate to $3,898,000, were designated the debt proper of Louisiana. For these debts the committee held the state alone was responsible; and they recommended that the legislature execute new state bonds to an amount equal to the capital and interest due and unpaid on those already issued. These bonds were to bear the same interest rate as those originally issued and were to be payable within fifteen years. Property of the state, valued at $4,860,000, should be set aside as a pledge for the payment of the capital and interest of these new securities. The second group of liabilities, the committee pointed out, had been incurred by the state in providing the capital of the property banks through the issuance of state bonds. The aggregate amount of this indebtedness was $16,500,000. If new state bonds were issued the committee declared that the Union Bank would be able to pay the amounts due on its bonds; therefore the committee confined themselves to the bonds issued for the Consolidated Association and the Citizens Bank. Although these banks were in liquidation, the committee asserted their assets were "still very considerable." But the amount of interest due on February 1, 1844, on the bonds of the state in favor of the Citizens Bank was $447,-602.98, not one cent of which had been paid; and the amounts due on bonds of the Consolidated Association was $120,500. "The non-payment of the interest on the bonds of the state has thrown a shadow upon her reputation," declared the committee. "But she will

[33] House Journal Louisiana, 1844, pp. 2-5.

not suffer it to darken into dishonor. The rights of the creditor, her bondholder, must be upheld." In their opinion the cause of non-payment was due to the law which allowed debtors of these institutions "to pay a large proportion of their debts in state bonds not yet matured." These bonds were greatly depreciated and could be purchased at a great discount in the market. As long as this was permitted depreciated bonds not yet due would constitute the only medium of payment to the bank. Therefore, the committee recommended that a law be passed prohibiting the banks from accepting these state bonds.[34]

These recommendations were carried out in part by the legislature. On March 25, 1844 an act was passed to provide for the adjustment and liquidation of the debt proper of the state. The state treasurer was authorized to sell a sufficient amount of the stock owned by the state in the Bank of Louisiana for the purpose of extinguishing the two series of bonds each for $600,000, issued by the state in favor of that institution. The treasurer was also authorized to sell 8,000 shares of the capital stock of the Bank of Louisiana owned by the state and apply the proceeds of the sale to the payment of various other debts and obligations of the state. This measure, it was hoped, would liquidate about $2,500,000 of the debt proper of the state.[35] But the legislature made no change in the mode of payment of debts due the property banks in liquidation. Even though the pamphlets and other publications issued by the foreign bondholders had not brought about any favorable legislation, Forstall was convinced that they had "at least rendered repudiation impossible by making repudiation look like robbery. Yet the executive and his party, in both houses," wrote Forstall to Ward, "were in favor of it a few months ago. Now only bankrupt debtors and disorganizers are for it."[36]

During the next two years Louisiana made rapid strides in the settlement of her public debt. In his message to the legislature in 1845 the governor reported that $1,754,000 of Union Bank bonds which had matured the preceding November had been redeemed. Certain modifications were made by the legislature in the acts pro-

[34] Ibid., pp. 57-59; Niles, March 16, 1844. See comments in Boston Advertiser and Patriot, March 14, 1844. Baring Printed Doc.
[35] Louisiana Laws, 1844, pp. 49-52; House Journal Louisiana, 1845, pp. 10-12.
[36] Forstall to Ward, March 22, 1844. Baring Mss.

viding for the adjustment of the debt proper; and on March 10, 1845 the legislature passed an act providing that after May 1, 1845 it should be unlawful for the Citizens Bank and the Consolidated Association to receive their "unmatured coupons, or bonds, or other unmatured debts in payment of debts due to them." As a result of these acts Governor Mouton was able to report in his last message that the debt proper had been reduced to about $1,300,000; and that there was a cash surplus of $225,000 in the treasury. But the governor made no mention of the unpaid interest on the Citizens Bank bonds. In a memorial to the legislature in behalf of Hope and Company, Forstall called attention to this omission. He raised the question why the interest on these bonds remained under protest while the arreared interests on the state bonds issued for numerous railroad companies had been paid as well as the redemption of a large portion of their bonds, some of which did not mature until 1870.[87]

Forstall's memorial was referred to the finance committee in the lower house for consideration. On April 28, 1846 this committee submitted a report on the condition of the Citizens Bank and the Consolidated Association. In their estimation the inability of these institutions to meet their engagements was largely due to the operation of the Act of April 1843 which had required the banks to accept a large amount of their unmatured bonds in payment of debts. The committee held that in all probability the state would not be called upon to meet any losses incurred by the Citizens Bank since an assessment of not more than $25 per share would be sufficient to cover the bank's liabilities. The committee therefore recommended that the stockholders of the Citizens Bank should be allowed to elect three managers to represent their interest in the liquidation of the bank. They also suggested that authority be given to the board of bank managers to renew the bonds falling due in 1850 in four installments; and that the stockholders be required to pay up such amounts on their stock as would extinguish any deficiency in the assets of the bank to meet its liabilities. They thought that it was necessary to renew the bonds because of the responsibility of the state for their redemption. A renewal would give the stockholders an opportunity to pay up a sufficient amount of their stock mort-

[87] House Journal, Louisiana, 1845, pp. 2, 3, 81; Louisiana Laws, 1845, pp. 29, 30, 33-37; Forstall's Memorial, Feb. 26, 1846. Baring Printed Doc.

gages to cancel the deficit of the bank and relieve the credit of the state. The committee also recommended that the bank managers fund or settle in any practical way the arrearages of interest in coupons on the bonds and set aside a specific portion of the assets of the bank to pay the interest. Practically the same suggestions were made with regard to the Consolidated Association with the exception that its bonds should be renewed payable in installments of one to fourteen years.[38]

The legislature refused to carry out these recommendations.[39] But at the next session of the General Assembly an act was passed on April 6, 1847 embodying the main provisions of the committee's report. A month later, however, the legislature passed a supplementary act which allowed the stockholders to pay off their stock mortgages in bonds of the state after making due allowance for the difference of interest that the debt to be paid might bear and which the bonds might bear.[40] By the passage of these acts the state protected itself against any loss on account of its liabilities for the bonds issued in favor of these banks while the domestic stockholders were aided.

The following year the legislature found it necessary to enact new legislation with regard to the state debts. In order to provide for the gradual payment of the debt proper, an act was passed setting aside certain specific funds for the purchase of the outstanding state bonds; while another law was passed requiring the stockholders of the Consolidated Association to pay all debts due the bank, except their stock mortgages, in specie. When the managers of the Consolidated Association, however, levied an assessment of $6 on each share of stock and applied to the legislature to appropriate $12,000 as a contribution due from the state on its 2,000 shares, the legislature questioned the liability of the state. In order to test the question an act was passed authorizing and empowering the Consolidated Association to sue the state. A decision was

[38] House Journal, Louisiana, 1846, pp. 120-122.

[39] The House and Senate were unable to agree on the terms of the proposed bill. During the discussion one of the members of the House offered a motion as a substitute for the title of the act: "An act to protect the interest of Hope and Company and other European bondholders by violating the constitution of this state and sacrificing the embarrassed stockholders of the Consolidated Association of the Planters of Louisiana." This motion was tabled. House Journal, Louisiana, 1846, p. 166. On May 27, 1846 the legislature passed an act restricting banks or other corporations of any other state or of any foreign country from enforcing the collection of debts. Louisiana Laws, 1846, p. 161.

[40] Louisiana Laws, 1847, pp. 76-78, 158.

rendered against the state in the lower court; but upon appeal the Louisiana Supreme Court reversed the judgment.[41]

The State of Louisiana was determined to free itself from all liability for losses incurred by the property banks. By 1852 the board of bank managers reported that the Consolidated Association had gradually accumulated a sufficient fund by means of contributions from the stockholders to enable it to meet at maturity the state bonds; but the Citizens Bank was not in such a prosperous condition. In order to protect the state for the payment of the state bonds issued in favor of this bank, amounting to a sum exceeding $6,000,000, together with accrued interest, the legislature on March 10, 1852 passed over the governor's veto an act to relieve the bank from the decree of forfeiture rendered against it in October 1842. The bank was restored to the stockholders with its former rights and privileges; and three commissioners elected by the stockholders were given the power to negotiate with the bondholders for the surrender of the whole or any part of their bonds and receive in exchange bonds of the bank or certificates of stock. The rehabilitation of the bank was coupled with the condition that the bank should restore "to the governor of the state, bonds of the state to the amount of $800,000. The requirements of the law were complied with by the exchange of $800,000 of bank bonds for the bonds of the state, which were cancelled, and an additional capital of $984,430 was raised by the stockholders by means of a contribution of $7 per share." As soon as the stockholders were in charge of the bank, the available capital of the bank was increased by obtaining the payment in cash of ten thousand of the shares composing the capital stock of the bank. By this arrangement it was hoped that the redemption of the liabilities of the mortgaged stockholders would be secured while at the same time the state would be secured to a corresponding extent against the eventual liability upon the bonds issued to the bank. Thus the state attempted to relieve itself of all liability for the payment of the bonds issued in favor of the property banks. On the eve of the Civil War, however, the finance committee in the House listed among the liabilities of the State of Louisiana, $5,398,533.33 of bonds issued to the property banks.[42]

[41] *Ibid.*, 1848, pp. 16, 17, 34; 5 Louisiana Reports, pp. 44-60.
[42] Senate Journal Louisiana, 1852, App., p. 9; Louisiana Laws, 1852, pp. 109-111; House Journal Louisiana, 1854, p. 4; 10 Census, Vol. 7, p. 598.

CHAPTER X

BONDS OF THE STATE OF MISSISSIPPI

ALMOST a century has elapsed since the State of Mississippi repudiated the Union Bank bonds. Nevertheless, the discussion over these bonds and those of the Planters' Bank which were subsequently repudiated, never ceases. Unfortunately the same polemics are indulged in by the creditors and debtors today as aroused those who were active participants in the original dispute with the result that the flames of passion are once more rekindled. In view of the present discussion over the collection of private and intergovernmental debts a recital of the circumstances surrounding the inception of the Mississippi debt may help to throw some light on the problems which confront foreign investors; the dangers inherent in a weak banking system; and the difficulties encountered by debtors and creditors in attempting to understand each other in periods of universal distress.

The fundamental cause of most of Mississippi's later difficulties was a lax state banking system. In 1818 Mississippi granted the Bank of the State of Mississippi exclusive banking privileges. The conservative policy pursued by this bank established the credit of the state. In time, however, dissatisfaction arose from the limited extent of the accommodations afforded by the state bank. It was claimed that the bank did not furnish the people with sufficient banking facilities commensurate with their needs.[1] In response to public pressure the legislature in 1830 chartered the Planters' Bank for the express purpose of promoting agriculture. The capital stock of this institution was $3,000,000, two-thirds of which was subscribed by the state and paid for by the issuance of state bonds.

[1] Mississippi Senate Journal, 1841, pp. 324-325. There are sketches of the history of the Planters' and Union Banks in Brough, C. H., History of Banking in Mississippi, Mississippi Historical Society Publications, Vol. III, pp. 317-341; Lowry, R., and McCardle, W. H., A History of Mississippi (Jackson, 1891) passim; Rowland, D. (editor), Encyclopedia of Mississippi History (Madison, 1907) passim.

The faith of the state was pledged for the payment of the principal and interest of these bonds as well as the stock of the state in the bank. A sinking fund was created for the redemption of the bonds; and the bank was authorized to loan upon mortgages not more than one-half of the capital annually paid in.[2] In 1831, $500,000 of Mississippi state bonds, bearing 6 percent were disposed of to New York brokers at a premium of ⅛th percent; and two years later the remaining $1,500,000 were sold to Eastern capitalists at a premium of 13¼ percent.[3] The premium might have been even larger if it had not been for the fact that Mississippi was practically unknown in the stock market; foreign capitalists disliked to touch loans of slave states; and the rumor had spread that the state had violated its pledge to the state bank in chartering the Planters' Bank.[4] The careful management of the Planters' Bank for a number of years reflected the confidence reposed in it. On the eve of the panic of 1837 the bank was paying annual dividends of 10 percent and was recognized as one of the best regulated institutions in the country.[5]

The apparent success of the Planters' Bank stimulated the desire for more banks; while the certainty that the United States Bank would not be rechartered furnished a plausible excuse for their incorporation. The withdrawal of the branch of the United States Bank from Mississippi would leave the state with a banking capital of little more than $6,000,000. This was deemed inadequate to carry on the marketing of cotton crops valued at $15,000,000. It was, therefore, proposed that a bank should be established the stock of which should be subscribed by planters secured by mortgages on their estates. To procure the working capital for such a bank it was suggested that the state issue bonds. The constitution of the state, however, prohibited the pledging of the faith of the state for such a loan unless the act was passed by two successive legislatures and had received the approval of the electorate at the polls.[6]

Notwithstanding the constitutional obstacles and the economic dangers lurking in such legislation, the legislature in January 1837

[2] Mississippi Laws, 1830, pp. 92-109. For subsequent minor amendments of the original charter cf. Mississippi Laws, 1830, pp. 1-9; 1831, pp. 28, 29; 1833, pp. 104-110.
[3] Mississippi House Journal, 1831, pp. 11, 12; Bankers Magazine, Vol. 8, pp. 89-109.
[4] Mississippi House Journal, 1831, pp. 11, 12; Hope to Baring, Aug. 16, 1833. Baring Mss.
[5] Mississippi House Journal, 1836, p. 30.
[6] Mississippi Senate Journal, 1835, p. 21; Poore, B. P., The Federal and State Constitutions, Pt. 11, pp. 1076, 1077.

chartered the ill-fated Union Bank with a capital of $15,500,000. The capital was to be obtained by means of loans negotiated through the sale of 5 percent state bonds payable in four installments covering twenty years. The faith of the state was pledged for the payment of the principal and interest of these bonds; and the security behind the bonds was the mortgages offered by the stockholders. Commissioners were appointed to appraise the property of those desirous of becoming stockholders; and the section of the law pledging the faith of the state for the payment and redemption of the loan was referred to the next legislature for approval.[7]

By the time the fall elections occurred, the banking institutions throughout the country were in bad repute. Mississippi was already engulfed in the throes of the panic of 1837; estates formerly valued at $30,000 were selling for $3,200; whole plantations were falling under the sheriff's hammer.[8] The people forgetful of their own past follies of reckless speculation were blaming the banks for their insolvency and ruin. During the campaign the Democratic candidate for governer, Alexander McNutt, fanned the flames of popular hostility to the banks and owed his election to an electorate avowedly antagonistic to all banking institutions.[9] His first message to the legislature was directed against the abuses of the credit system. He pointed out that the present distress was largely due to the desire of bank officials to make large dividends for their stockholders; that a few individuals controlled the banks and granted loans to speculators and to bank officials; and that the Planters' Bank had failed to aid agriculture and had refused to allow the state commissioners to examine its books.[10]

In the midst of this tense excitement, the legislature reënacted the charter of the Union Bank; and Governor McNutt signed the bill. Ten days later the legislature passed a supplementary act which materially changed the relation of the state to the bank. By the provisions of this act the governor was instructed to subscribe for 50,000 shares of the capital stock; and pay for the same out of the proceeds of the sale of the state bonds.[11]

The new bill encountered vigorous opposition in the Senate.

[7] Mississippi Laws, 1837, pp. 34-57.
[8] Claiborne to Van Buren, April 10, 1837. Van Buren Mss.
[9] *Mississippian*, June 23, Oct. 13, 1837.
[10] Mississippi Senate Journal, 1838, pp. 112-117.
[11] Mississippi Laws, 1838, pp. 33-44.

Opponents of the measure called attention to the rapid increase of banks in Mississippi within recent years. Particular stress was laid upon the danger of allowing the state to become a stockholder in the bank. The original act protected the state from possible losses by holding the stock and mortgages of the stockholders as security for the loans; the only security for the redemption of the bonds by the supplementary act was what the state stock might afford. An unsuccessful attempt was made to hold the stockholders liable for the state bonds; and even though the bill was passed a protest was entered upon the Senate Journal questioning the constitutionality of the law since it had not been enacted in conformity with the provisions of the state constitution.[12] The new bill was also denounced by the Democratic newspaper, the *Mississippian*. The Union Bank would never be a "people's bank" as all the stock was not owned by the state. It would be managed for the benefit of a few speculators and brokers to the disadvantage of the planters' interest; and as the law was not passed in accordance with the intentions of the framers of the constitution, the faith of the state was not pledged for the redemption of the bonds.[13] Notwithstanding these protests and even though the governor had declared in his annual message that all the banks in the state had exceeded their powers and were conducted by their managers with the sordid desire to make large dividends for the stockholders, Governor McNutt later confessed he signed the bill without any constitutional scruples.[14] Five millions of dollars of state bonds were duly executed and delivered to the bank by the governor in accordance with the provisions of the law.

Much of the subsequent controversy centered around the sale of these bonds. The bank appointed three commissioners to negotiate the loan. They were specifically instructed not to dispose of the bonds below par estimated in the currency of the United States. In negotiating the sale of the bonds they were to point out that Mississippi, although temporarily laboring under pecuniary embarrassments, had ample resources to meet all its obligations for it was one

[12] Mississippi Senate Journal, 1838, pp. 230, 312, 347; *Mississippian*, Feb. 2, 1838; Bankers Magazine, Vol. 8, pp. 491-503. The protest was signed by Hanson Alsbury and Tillman M. Tucker.

[13] *Mississippian*, Jan. 12, 1838.

[14] Mississippi Senate Journal, 1839, pp. 20, 21.

of the largest cotton growing states in the Union. The charter was not the result of premature legislation as it had been passed by two successive legislatures and had been approved by the people; while in addition to the guaranty of the state the bonds were secured by mortgages on the most productive cotton growing estates which yielded a revenue sufficient in any one year to redeem the entire amount of the bonds.[15] Unable to negotiate a sale in New York, owing to the prevailing low market prices, the commissioners proceeded to Philadelphia where on August 18, 1838, they sold the entire lot to Nicholas Biddle.

In their eagerness to place their bank in operation the commissioners either were hoodwinked by the shrewd financier or they connived with him in breaking their instructions. The contract specified that the bonds were to be paid for in five equal installments; but the interest began from the date of the sale. To make them negotiable abroad, they were made payable in England at the rate of four shillings six pence on the dollar. By this transaction Biddle gained two advantages. As the bonds were bought on credit while the interest began immediately, he received the difference of interest during the interval on all that remained unpaid; and by making them payable in England in pounds sterling a $2,000 bond at the current rate of exchange was equivalent to $2,189.92.[16] Nevertheless, the news of the sale was received in Mississippi with wild enthusiasm. The Senate congratulated the commissioners on the successful completion of their negotiations "in accordance with the injunctions of the charter"; but the governor in his message refused to sanction the violation of the charter in disposing of the bonds below par although he acknowledged the overzealous commissioners "no doubt had obtained as much as they could for the bonds." [17]

Biddle sent the bonds to his agent Jaudon in England. In recommending their sale the Philadelphia financier stressed the agricultural resources of Mississippi and the high character of Wilkins, one of the commissioners, as the best guaranty that the state would fulfill

[15] *Ibid.*, pp. 148-151.
[16] Mississippi Senate Journal, 1839, pp. 20, 21; Democratic Review, Vol. 10, pp. 371-375.
[17] Lowry and McCardle, History of Mississippi, pp. 280-285; Mississippi Senate Journal, 1839, pp. 20, 21, 135.

its engagements.[18] Jaudon succeeded in disposing of $2,000,000 of these bonds in November, 1838, and "the remainder were pledged by him as collateral for loans made by that bank in November and December of 1839 and January and February of 1840." There is no evidence that anyone in England had knowledge that the bonds had been sold to the United States Bank on credit or that the state had not received the whole of their value until Governor McNutt in his message of 1839 stated the terms of the sale.[19] When conditions began to grow serious in Mississippi, Jaudon assured the English bankers, Huth and Company, that there was no cause for alarm quoting Biddle's endorsement verbatim and Governor McNutt's statement that "the honor of the state must be preserved unsullied" as proof there was not "the shadow of doubt as to the solidity of the Mississippi state stock."[20] Even if the Union Bank should liquidate, English bankers believed that the Mississippi state stock would be good for, as Huth was informed by one of their partners, then traveling in the United States, "the mortgages held by this institution" would "pass into the hands of the state" and would "be worth a great proportion of the amount loaned on them." While there might be some "irregularity in remitting the interest, the stock would eventually be good and if," continued the writer, "I should be right in my conjecture that the United States Bank has guaranteed the interest to the foreign holders, I think all will go right, as the bank would advance the interest, and recover it as soon as the state could make new provisions."[21]

Meanwhile popular hatred of the banks in Mississippi was growing. The governor stimulated this antagonism as he recounted the nefarious conduct of the banks in his annual messages. In 1839 he pointed out that nearly all the banks had forfeited their charters by misusing their privileges. Some had increased their circulation more than their acts of incorporation permitted, others held more prop-

[18] Biddle to Jaudon, Oct. 2, 1838. Huth Mss.
[19] Memorandum on Mississippi bonds in Huth Mss.
[20] Memorandum on Mississippi stock sent by Jaudon, Feb. 25, 1840. Huth Mss. Throughout this period, the *London Times* was calling the attention of the public to the chaotic banking situation in Mississippi (*London Times*, Oct. 26, 1838; Jan. 19, July 30, Aug. 30, Dec. 31, 1839). The *New York American* on May 21, 29, 1839, likewise commented on this subject. The Barings were somewhat doubtful about Mississippi stock as they were warned that "Mississippi, Alabama and Louisiana are gambling in their stocks." (Cf. Baring to Prime, Ward and King, Nov. 23, 1838; Baring to Hope, May 17, 1839; Ward to Baring, Aug. 15, 22, 1839. Baring Mss.)
[21] Kindermann to Huth, Jan. 19, 1840. Huth Mss.

erty than they were authorized to hold. Many had exceeded their powers by dealing in cotton; and all had suspended specie payments. Particular attention was called to the management and conduct of the Planters' and Union banks since "the faith of the state" was "pledged for the redemption of the two millions of dollars of bonds sold to take stock in the Planters' Bank and for the whole of the capital of the Union Bank." Both of these institutions had refused to allow the bank commissioners to examine their books, the Union Bank claiming that the state officials could not be trusted as "their minds were biased." It was well known, however, that the Union Bank had added to the quantity of depreciated paper in circulation by issuing a large amount of post notes and was endeavoring to monopolize the cotton crop of the state.[22]

The governor should have revealed these misdemeanors of the bank; but beyond launching these tirades, he did nothing. If he had any doubt as to the validity of the contract signed by the United States Bank for the purchase of the Union Bank bonds he should have stopped further action on it. Instead of doing so, he distinctly declared that the state was pledged for the payment of the whole of the bonds and allowed the United States Bank to pay over to the Union Bank the remainder of the three installments due in 1839. In his message of 1840 the governor intimated that some of the states might find it difficult to meet their engagements; and raised the significant question whether one generation had the right to saddle posterity with a heavy debt.[23] Two months later he issued a proclamation "warning all persons and corporations not to advance money or securities or credit on the hypothecation" of Union Bank bonds. The United States Bank had already, however, hypothecated these bonds with European capitalists and the proclamation did not, as the governor later claimed, have the desired effect in preventing the disposal of the bonds.[24] Two months after the governor's proclamation the Barings were assured by their American representative, T. W. Ward, that although the credit of Mississippi was low and the Union Bank should not be trusted, the Mississippi stock would ultimately be good as the resources of the state were

[22] Mississippi Senate Journal, 1839, pp. 21-32.
[23] Mississippi House Journal, 1840, p. 27.
[24] The governor discussed this subject in his message of 1841. Mississippi Senate Journal, 1841, pp. 17-21.

great and the people, though "reckless," should "have a sense of justice sufficient to bring them right." [25]

It was not until 1841 that Governor McNutt definitely advocated the repudiation of the Union Bank bonds. He claimed that the sale of the bonds was illegal and fraudulent because the charter of the United States Bank prohibited the institution "from purchasing stock either directly or indirectly"; and even though the contract was in the name of Nicholas Biddle, the sale had actually been made for the benefit of the bank. Furthermore, "the sale was illegal in as much as the bonds were sold on credit" and for less than their par value since interest amounting to $170,000 had accrued before the purchase price was paid. To meet the interest payments, the governor declared it would be necessary to raise the taxes. This would increase insolvencies and if the taxation became intolerable would depopulate the state. If new subjects of taxation were not resorted to, each taxpayer would have to pay twenty times as much taxes as he then paid. Such an enormous tax could never be collected from the hard earnings of the people. "They will not elect representatives," the governor stated, "who will impose it or tax collectors who will collect it." Many of the tax collectors were already in default upon their payments. The whole system of assessing and collecting the revenue needed revision for "not more than one-half of the taxable property in the state" was "ever assessed and large portions of the taxes collected" were "never paid into the state treasury." [26]

Governor McNutt's message gave the timid legislators the opportunity they were looking for. They were afraid to impose heavier taxes upon their constituents. One member of the legislature publicly declared an increase in taxation would be the "signal to arms" in his constituency; another announced he would resign his seat before he would vote to tax the people.[27] Democratic papers applauded these statements. The *Mississippian* agreed that all debts contracted honestly should be paid, if the debtors were able to pay; "but common sense and common justice" taught "that the good people of this state" were "not bound to pay a debt not founded in justice and which the perfidy of bankers and not the majesty of the

[25] Ward to Baring, June 22, 1840. Baring Mss.
[26] Mississippi Senate Journal, 1841, pp. 8-21.
[27] *Mississippian*, Jan. 29, Feb. 12, 1841.

law" was "endeavoring to impose upon them. Let the bondholders look to the banks for pay; with them they contracted and not with the people of Mississippi."[28] To pay the bonds in gold and silver the people were told by the Columbus *Democrat* "the beds on which your wives and children sleep, the tables on which you eat your daily bread will be taken by the excise men for the benefit of those who sleep in splendid brick palaces, who sleep in mahogany bedsteads, eat with gold knives and forks, and drink champagne as the ordinary beverage of the day."[29] It is true the Whigs as a party were for paying the debt; and a few Democrats believed that the state had created a moral if not a legal obligation to pay; but beyond passing perfunctory resolutions condemning the insinuation that Mississippi would violate her plighted faith, the legislature refused to act. The governor did not intend, however, that the legislature should throw all the blame upon his shoulders for suggesting repudiation. He promptly vetoed these resolutions on the ground that they were a censure on the executive; and then in Billingsgate language vehemently attacked Baron Rothschild, who held some of these bonds. Let the Baron, in whose veins "the blood of Judas and Shylock" flowed, exact his pound of flesh of Mr. Jaudon and the Bank of the United States and let the latter "institution of our country exact the same of the Mississippi Union Bank." Thus adroitly the governor gave the public the impression the contest was a "bankers' war" in which "the honor, justice, and dignity of the people" of the state was not involved.[30] With the governor beclouding the issue, the press stirring up the people, the masses overwhelmed by their own personal obligations, and a leaderless legislature unwilling and unable to act, the case of the foreign bondholders soon began to appear hopeless.

The threat of repudiation and the nonpayment of the Mississippi dividends in 1841 alarmed European capitalists. They realized that their clients would hold them partly responsible in case Mississippi disavowed her bonds. The *London Times* was not hesitant in warning the bondholders they would have to prove they had not purchased the bonds for less than their par value before they could hold the state responsible. To be sure, the bonds specifically stated the

[28] *Ibid.*, Jan. 22, 1841.   [29] *Columbus Democrat*, Feb. 20, 1841.
[30] Mississippi House Journal, 1841, pp. 234-249, 491-504; *Mississippian*, Jan. 18, 1841.

faith of the state was pledged for the payment of principal and interest. But the caustic *London Times* reminded its readers that in all probability the people of Mississippi had never imagined they would be called upon to redeem this pledge when the bonds were issued. As long as the Union Bank was prosperous, the state had paid little attention to it. The dividends had been paid by the bank, not by the state. Not until the bank was unable to meet its obligations did the people of Mississippi awake to the fact that they might be called upon to meet these engagements. There was great danger, however, the people would feel they were not bound to pay for rotten and ill-managed institutions especially as their political leaders were telling them the state credit had been pledged by a group of speculators and not by the legitimate voice of the state.[31]

This was a fairly accurate diagnosis of the situation in Mississippi; and although banking organs of the press tried to quiet the fears of the bondholders by discounting these statements,[32] European capitalists appreciated the need of acting promptly to safeguard their clients' interests. A memorial was drafted by the Rothschilds to send to Mississippi setting forth the claims of the bondholders. Before it was despatched a copy was presented to Lord Palmerston, the British Foreign Secretary, with the request that it be presented through the medium of His Majesty's minister at Washington. Lord Palmerston curtly refused to do this on the ground that "British subjects who buy foreign securities do so at their own risk and must abide the consequences."[33] Whereas the British government refused to serve as the channel of communication for European financiers, Hope and Company of Amsterdam found Webster, the Secretary of State, quite willing to act as their diplomatic agent. This was a blunder upon the part of the Dutch financiers for the *Globe* did not fail to call attention to the manner in which the federal government presumably was aiding the foreign bondholders.[34]

[31] *London Times*, May 6, 8, 1841.
[32] *Morning Chronicle*, May 17, 1841.
[33] Rothschild to Palmerston, May 21, 1841; Bidwell to Rothschild, June 3, 1841. F. O. 5, 372,373 in Public Record Office. Bidwell wrote at Palmerston's suggestion and to the above in Palmerston's handwriting was added "Of any speculation of this kind which they may enter into."
[34] *Globe*, Aug. 4, 1841.

In his reply to Hope and Company Governor McNutt not only reiterated his old arguments but in addition advanced two new ones. In the first place the governor pointed out that the bonds had been issued under the terms of the supplementary act which had not been passed by two successive legislatures and approved by the people as the constitution required. Furthermore, the charter had been violated by changing the currency in which the bonds were made payable from current money of the United States to pounds sterling of England. By selling the bonds on credit and by changing them from dollars to pounds sterling the governor estimated that the enormous sum of $1,084,781.30 had been lost. To make matters worse, Hope and Company replied reminding the governor that foreigners should not be made to suffer for disputes "between corporations and individuals" especially as the executive's opinion on the subject was "in opposition to the great majority of the last legislature of the state and to that of the people of Mississippi." [35] Such statements were not apt to calm the crusading fervor of the governor; and when in the fall elections the anti-bondman Tucker was elected governor, even though the wealthiest counties in the state voted in favor of paying the bonds,[36] both English and American newspapers added fuel to the flames of popular passion by excoriating the Mississippians. The *London Standard* characterized the anti-bondmen as "a set of atrocious scoundrels." The *London Morning Chronicle* stigmatized Governor McNutt "a pettifogging attorney"; and defiantly declared that the bonds "must be paid, principal and interest." To this the Americans might "as well make up their minds for they" were "perfectly able to pay their debts." Until the Mississippians could "rail the seal from off the bonds" and until they could show cause why the signature of Governor McNutt on the bonds did not bind the state, "they not only offend their own lungs, but the public sense, by mouthing about repudiation," thundered the *New York American.*[37]

[35] For this correspondence consult *Niles*, Aug. 21, 1841; *National Intelligencer*, Feb. 4, 5, 1842.
[36] *Arkansas Shield*, Dec. 25, 1841.
[37] *London Standard* quoted in *Circular to Bankers*, Dec. 10, 1841; *Morning Chronicle*, Dec. 14, 1841; *New York American*, Nov. 30, 1841.

Governor Tucker in his inaugural address interpreted his election as a vote in favor of repudiation; but he made a clear distinction between the Planters' and the Union Bank bonds. The former were legally and morally binding on the state as they had been issued in accordance with the provisions of the constitution.[38] The legislature tacitly subscribed to this omission; and on February 26, 1842 the governor approved the famous resolution repudiating the Union Bank bonds.[39] It is interesting to note that the report of the state treasurer for that year showed a balance in the treasury of thirty-four cents and receipts for the claims upon broken banks and notes of insolvent railroad companies.[40] It is also significant that in the Mississippi legislature which voted for repudiation the anti-bond paying members owned 772 shares of stock in the Union Bank while those in favor of sustaining the state's credit owned 462 shares. By the state canceling the bonds the stockholders were relieved of their liabilities to the bank. It is claimed that the anti-bond paying members owed more than $119,000 on their personal accounts to the bank. Thus the debtor legislators protected their own interest while they brought dishonor to the state.[41]

The doctrine of repudiation did not have the sanction, however, of all the press or of the entire electorate of Mississippi. Senator Henderson was an outspoken opponent of repudiation. The Whig party did not subscribe to the doctrine; and within the Democratic party there was a division of opinion upon the wisdom of such a move. At Natchez a large number of old and wealthy citizens advocated the payment of the bonds. A weekly newspaper was established at Jackson by the bondmen for the purpose of disseminating their views. On the other hand, the *Vicksburg Sentinel* boldly set forth the theme of repudiation with exultation and predicted the day would come when the *London Times,* "the organ of Jew brokers," would be held up to execration for advocating the cause of the foreign bondholders. The Mississippi bar was also denounced by

[38] Mississippi House Journal, 1842, pp. 374-375; cf. Mississippi Senate Journal, 1843, pp. 26-29.
[39] Mississippi Laws, 1842, pp. 260-262.
[40] Governor's message quoting State Treasurer's Report, Miss. Senate Journal, 1843, p. 26. See also unsigned memorandum on state debts, Dec. 12, 1839. Baring Mss.
[41] Republican (Woodville, Mississippi), Mar. 5, Dec. 3, 1842; see also Alexander, C. C., A History of State Banking in Mississippi, pp. 138, 139. Unpublished thesis, University of Mississippi.

the Democratic press and by some of the clergy for sponsoring the case of the creditors.[42]

In order to check the spread of repudiation doctrines to other states and in the hope of inducing the Mississippians to reconsider their decision, the foreign creditors redoubled their efforts. Huth and Company of London drafted a memorial to the Mississippi legislature and an address to the people of Mississippi setting forth the justice of the claims of the foreign bondholders.[43] At Webster's suggestion Ward, the American representative of the Barings, engaged Senator Robert J. Walker and Judge Montgomery, both of Mississippi, to carry a suit on the Union Bank bonds through the Mississippi courts and Webster to argue the case in the United States Supreme Court if it reached that tribunal. Walker was to receive $200 as his legal fee and Judge Montgomery and Webster $100 each; and 15 percent of whatever was recovered was to go to Walker and Montgomery while Webster's share was to be 5 percent. Judge Montgomery declined to serve; and when Walker became Secretary of the Treasury his services were discontinued.[44] Reid Irving and Company of London secured the services of Edmund J. Forstall of New Orleans to agitate the claims of their clients in Mississippi. Forstall secured the publication of a series of articles in a Jackson paper which he had later bound in a volume entitled "Nine Years of Democratic Rule in Mississippi." A copy of this pamphlet was sent to every congressman and department head in Washington. Then convinced he had done all that could be accomplished, Forstall discontinued his work.[45] The isolated, haphazard attempts of the foreign creditors were unable, however, to produce the desired results because of the confused state of Mississippi politics.

Just as the foreign bondholders were becoming somewhat disheartened, a plan for liquidating the debt was presented to them by a group of Mississippians. In 1847 Jefferson Davis and Thomas E. Robins devised a scheme whereby the Union Bank bonds were to be

---

[42] *Niles*, Dec. 4, 1841; *National Intelligencer*, Jan. 15, Feb. 5, Mar. 29, 1842; *Mississippian*, Jan. 18, 1841; *London Times*, Mar. 4, Apr. 16, 1842, June 22, 1843; Nine Years of Democratic Rule in Mississippi (Jackson, 1847), pp. 115, 116.

[43] Copies of these can be found in the Huth Mss., Nov., 1843.

[44] Ward to Baring, Sept. 16, Nov. 28, Dec. 27, 1843; Mar. 30, 1844; Nov. 22, 1848. Baring Mss.

[45] Reid, Irving and Company to Forstall, Aug. 4, 1845; Forstall to Baring, Apr. 12, 1853. Baring Mss.

paid by the private subscriptions of individual Mississippians. Robins journeyed to London with letters of introduction from Buchanan, Secretary of State; but he found the English indisposed to accept his proposal.[46] Since Robins refused to acknowledge the legality of the bonds and insisted upon considering the debt a matter of honor, the English bondholders were afraid if they handed over their bonds and subsequent difficulties arose over their payment they would have tacitly admitted the illegality of their claims.[47] Both the Barings and the Rothschilds were skeptical of the practical feasibility of the plan; while the *London Times* sneered at the roundabout manner in which the Mississippians tried to avoid their legal obligations.[48] At the request of Thomas Ritchie, Jefferson Davis prepared a statement published in the *Washington Union* defending the stand taken by Mississippi. Davis ridiculed the "crocodile tears" which had been shed over the "ruined creditors" and defiantly asserted that Mississippi, "conscious of her rectitude," was not afraid of the "verdict of the civilized world." The abusive reply of the *London Times* only widened the chasm between the foreign creditors and their debtors.[49]

A ray of hope, however, dawned upon the gloomy horizon. When the Planters' Bank was created a sinking fund had been established. The state had never repudiated these bonds and in 1848 there was a balance of $94,000 in the sinking fund. In that year the legislature passed an act that this sum should be applied to the discharge of the first overdue coupons on these securities. At the same time a bill was passed providing for the sale of 500,000 acres of land granted the state by the federal government for internal improvement purposes and making the Planters' Bank bonds receivable in payment for these lands at par.[50] The passage of these acts stimulated the demand for these bonds; and the Barings were requested

---

[46] Rowland, D. (editor), Jefferson Davis, Constitutionalist, Vol. 7, pp. 248-251, 266, 267; Vol. 8, pp. 116, 117.

[47] *London Times*, Feb. 11, 1848. C. & J. Fallon of Philadelphia advised Huth the "holders of bonds should not for a moment think of abandoning their high ground." Fallon to Huth, July 1, 1848. Huth Mss.

[48] James G. King informed the Barings "the plan could not be relied upon to accomplish its object." King to Baring, Dec. 7, 1847, Baring Mss. The Rothschilds' reaction is given in the letter of Robins to Palmer, MacKillop, Dent and Company, Jan. 13, 1848. Huth Mss. (enclosure). The *London Times* comment can be found on Feb. 11, 1848.

[49] Bankers Magazine, Vol. 4, pp. 363-371; *London Times*, July 13, 1849.

[50] *London Times*, March 28, 1848; Nov. 14, 1850.

by Robert J. Walker to purchase some of these securities for him. They were unable to do so as the holders of these bonds declined to part with them since they believed that the state would soon redeem her obligations.[51] The *London Times* cautioned the bondholders not to press too eagerly for a settlement of their claims. "Let the tide of American prosperity roll on for a short period longer," the *London Times* advised its readers, "and these people will only be too glad to cancel by a full return to honesty the doom which now excludes them from a place amongst civilized communities."[52] Whatever adjustments might then have been made of the Planters' Bank debt was lost by the foolish advice given the security holders by the *London Times;* the tactless policy of the agent of the foreign bondholders in Mississippi of "giving oyster suppers and champagne parties to the members of the legislature" which was viewed as "a direct attempt at corruption"; and the state auditor's refusal to comply with the terms of the law.[53] This caused the agent of the bondholders to obtain a mandamus against him which the latter met with an appeal to the courts.[54]

Notwithstanding the unfortunate state of affairs which had risen in connection with the Planters' Bank bonds, the bondholders soon realized that there were new forces working in Mississippi to rehabilitate the state's credit. The high prices of cotton had changed the economic conditions within the state. A surplus was piling up in the state treasury; and the people were beginning by the 'fifties to think of building railroads. The richer the Mississippians grew the more they felt the sting of riches without a reputation for integrity. How could the state borrow money to undertake these enterprises as long as the stain of repudiation rested upon her escutcheon? How could she offer her bonds in Europe until she redeemed

[51] Walker to Ward, Oct. 3, 1849; Baring to Ward, Oct. 26, 1849, Feb. 22, 1850. Baring Mss. Walker wanted the bonds to be purchased in the name of the Barings and by them sent to Ward, their American representative, from whom Walker would buy them. Walker said he wanted to purchase these bonds not for speculation but to pay a debt.

[52] *London Times,* Nov. 14, 1850.

[53] Claiborne to Latrobe, Oct. 23, 1850. Baring Mss.

[54] $500,000 of Planters' Bank bonds were issued without coupons. It was these bonds which the law of 1848 specified should be paid first. The High Court of Errors and Appeals finally ordered the auditor of the state to pay the coupons of interest "amounting to $45,000." British creditors naturally inquired how the sum of $94,000 had dwindled to $45,000 (*London Times,* Feb. 2, 1853). Not many bondholders availed themselves of the opportunity of purchasing land. On this subject consult Rowland, Encyclopedia of Mississippi History, Vol. I, 203.

her old obligations? Would even American capitalists trust her?

In order to raise the state's credit, F. L. Claiborne, of Natchez, on his own initiative, inaugurated a movement in Mississippi to redeem the Planters' Bank bonds. Claiborne wrote to John D. Freeman, former attorney general of the state, and to General Felix Huston, one of the founders of the Planters' Bank, as to the best way to proceed. Freeman suggested that the bondholders sue the state. Huston advised the publication in the press of temporate and practical arguments pointing out to the people the indebtedness of the state, her ability to pay, and possible easy methods of liquidating the debt. Just enough should be done through the press prior to the next election "to give it the character of a question and after the election a clear headed agent or agents should visit every member of the legislature and fix him." The details of the bill should be liberal but means should be provided for the regular payments of the debt. Claiborne sent these suggestions to his friend, J. H. B. Latrobe, of Maryland, who was in touch with the Barings, endorsing Huston's scheme. Claiborne proposed that a strong circular, "full of facts and calculations" should be printed and placed in the hands of every candidate for the legislature. When the legislature met a bill should be introduced by "certain *prominent members*" providing for the funding of the debt and "for the annual instalments without fail." "To accomplish this," wrote Claiborne, "it will be necessary to spend some money. Men neither write for nothing, nor can printers work without pay. In Mississippi the press forms and controls public opinion. To accomplish any object, the press must be conciliated." "I do not advise," continued the writer, "any corrupt measures—such as the wholesale purchase of presses—the bribing of public men—the purchase of the legislature either with money, wine, or oysters. But I do advise the putting the machinery of the press in honorable motion—that is, to pay the editor and publisher for services fairly rendered in an honorable way. Also to have one or more agents and pay them for their services." It would also be wise for Latrobe to visit Mississippi "as the open and *avowed attorney of the bondholders, authorized to make liberal terms with the state.*" But Claiborne warned that no movement must be made in favor of the Union Bank bonds "*until one year after the Planters' bonds"* were funded as there was still a "deep rooted" hostility to these bonds. "As to my services," concluded Claiborne, "let me be candid. I will do what all good citizens should to have the state erect on the Planters' Bank bonds. There I would stop. . . . For such aid as I could bring . . . I would expect pay. I neither work for glory or praise—much as both are to be desired I prefer something more solid. My blunt manner of telling what I mean in all things may not be agreeable to some, but if I am employed by men or corporations, they will not receive guilded pills." Without waiting for a reply, the impetuous Claiborne proceeded to enlist the services of prominent men in the cause; and a few days later sent Latrobe another letter which, according to Claiborne was "worth *thousands* to the bondholders" from the Speaker of the House of Representatives, John J. McRae, expressing his willingness to coöperate. Since the slavery question was then agitating the legislature, Claiborne doubted, however, whether they would be willing to part "with one dollar"; and so he suggested that Latrobe postpone his visit to the state to January 1852 when the legislature met. In the meantime Claiborne declared if he was to be engaged in the services of the bondholders he must know one or two things promptly; (1) if Latrobe was to be benefited, then Claiborne was willing to work for nothing; (2) but if he was to be the actual agent he must be paid. He desired a certain sum should be placed in his hand and "in the event of success to leave the consideration to the liberality of the person who engages my services." [55]

Latrobe forwarded Claiborne's suggestions to Ward, the American representative of the Barings, who transmitted them to the house in London. According to Latrobe, Claiborne was as "honest as the sun," "warm hearted" and "apt to be sanguine and take people somewhat on their own representations of themselves." He considered General Huston "a clever man in the English sense"; and Latrobe confessed he did not know how he "would like to deal with him" as he thought Huston was "a politician." The governor, Gen-

[55] Ward to Baring, Nov. 5, 1850; Claiborne to Latrobe, Nov. 14, 17, Dec. 1, 10, 12, 1850. Baring Mss. F. L. Claiborne was one of the editors of the *Natchez Free Trader* (*Niles*, Jan. 8, 1842). John H. B. Latrobe was the representative of the Barings who was largely instrumental in getting Maryland to pay its debt. For a sketch of his life consult Semmes, J. E., John H. B. Latrobe and his Times (Baltimore, 1918) *passim*.

eral Quitman, Latrobe felt was a small man for his place, vain, a popularity seeker, but a gentleman and brave. Since the Mexican War, however, his head had been turned "topsy turvey" and he fancied "himself Napoleon, Wellington, and Alexander the Great stewed into an essence." [56] Perhaps, it was the comments of Latrobe as well as the fact that the Barings had no personal interest in the Planters' Bank bonds which caused the English financiers to take so little interest in the proposal. The Barings confessed their willingness to coöperate with others in rescuing "any state from the stigma of repudiation." As the plan interested only Planters' Bank bondholders, it was not clear to the Barings how a fund of 4,000 or 5,000 pounds could be raised to carry out the proposed plan. Latrobe, therefore, advised Claiborne to suspend his operations.[57]

The foreign holders of the Mississippi bonds wanted the state to redeem all of her outstanding obligations, not a part of them. For this reason they were more interested in the proposition submitted to them by G. W. Billings of Illinois. At a called meeting of the Mississippi bondholders in London, July, 1851, Billings informed them the federal government had granted the state certain lands for internal improvements. The most important of these grants was for a railroad from Chicago to Mobile which would pass through the eastern portions of Mississippi for a distance of 250 miles. Charters had already been obtained from Alabama, Mississippi, Tennessee and Kentucky and consolidated into one grant called the Mobile and Ohio Railroad. As the credit of Mississippi was prostrate it might fairly be presumed that no legislative action upon her part would be available in granting these lands to private companies or in using them in any form for the construction of public works as long as the repudiation of former contracts was the law of the land. The eastern portion of the state through which the

---

[56] Latrobe to Ward, Dec. 2, 1850. Baring Mss.

[57] Latrobe to Ward, Dec. 13, 1850; Baring to Ward, Jan. 3, 7, 1851. Baring Mss. Ward thought the time was favorable to work on Mississippi and suggested Latrobe be made agent because "of his experience, patience, good nature, social qualities, gift of speech, and residence in a slave state." (Ward to Baring, Dec. 5, 1850). In writing to Ward about Claiborne's activities, Latrobe confessed: "These southern men jump into things right off—which people in our part of the world and yours too, would skirt around several times before they went into them." Latrobe to Ward, Dec. 13, 1850. Baring Mss.

railroad would pass was the stronghold of repudiation; and Billings proposed to make repudiation a test question at the next November election. He intended to point out to the people of Mississippi that "it was for their interest to restore the credit of the state" by paying her debts, otherwise there would be difficulty "in inducing persons in New York and elsewhere to subscribe toward public works in Mississippi." He planned "to procure the passage of a law at the coming session of the legislature acknowledging the old debt and interest, also authorizing new bonds to be given for arrears of interest, and fixing a definite amount of taxation to be annually applied to the payment of the interest." He was confident that he could secure a tax law of two mills, perhaps, even of three or three and a half mills. Billings did not ask for any remuneration in money for such services but if he succeeded his compensation should be a certain amount of the coupons of arrears of interest upon the bonds. At the close of the meeting a committee representing the bondholders was chosen and the bondholders were requested to sign statements to hold two coupons of the 6 percent Planters' Bank bonds and four coupons of the 5 percent Union Bank bonds until June 1, 1853 on the conditions specified by Billings.[58] The latter immediately proceeded to New York where he met General Foote, the governor-elect of Mississippi who "expressed himself very decisively in regard to paying the Union Bank bonds." According to Billings General Foote declared that he would "use all his influence in the legislature in favor of resumption" and would sign "any bill passed for the collection of revenue to pay the interest." Even though General Foote should be elected to the Senate, Billings did not fear of success as the lieutenant governor was "also a strong bond paying man."[59] After his arrival in Mississippi, however, Billings decided it was inadvisable to bring forward the question at

[58] George W. Billings to Creditors of Mississippi, July 11, 1851; Stokes to Ward, Apr. 8, 1853. Hope Mss. The members of the London Committee were Thomas Baring, David Barclay, John P. Heywood, D. Meinertzhagen, George Peabody, Baron Lionel de Rothschild, and Alexander Trotter. Ward made various inquiries regarding Billings at Springfield and one Judge of the Illinois Supreme Court declared "he would not recognize Billings—that he had been *impeached as a witness* and indeed that his want of character for truth was so notorious that it became unnecessary to impeach whatever he might swear to." Ward to Baring, Aug. 5, 14, 1851. Baring Mss.
[59] Billings to Stokes, Dec. 30, 1851. Hope Mss. Stokes was the secretary of the London Committee.

the election in November, 1851; but in May 1852 commenced the suit of Hezron A. Johnson vs. Mississippi in the Chancery Court of Mississippi on the Union Bank bonds.[60]

In the meantime the Mississippi legislature decided to refer to the people at the November election of 1852 the question of paying the Planters' Bank bonds. As soon as this was announced the belligerent *London Times* burst forth in righteous indignation. "For the first time in the civilized world," exclaimed the *London Times*, "the question of the payment or the nonpayment of state obligations" was to be submitted "to the inhabitants of a country by its government as a point upon which they may please themselves. They promised to pay when they borrowed the money; but it is suggested that they may have changed their minds, and that, at all events, it would not be proper for the executive to fulfil the bargain without first ascertaining whether a contingency so probable has or has not actually occurred." Hence a contest was pending "in which the rallying cry on one side" would "be defiance to the foreign creditor, and on the other, taxation and payment." There could be little doubt as to which would prove "more powerful at the polling booths"; and consequently, "instead of having to blot out, as was anticipated, at an early period, a history which all who speak the English tongue would be anxious to forget, we may have to consummate it by recording an act such as has never yet found a place in the annals of public demoralization." [61]

The fears of the British were verified in the fall election although the heaviest tax-paying counties voted for payment.[62] One Mississippian wrote Ward the defeat was due to the lack of energetic and unanimous action upon the part of the Planters' Bank bondholders. If they had entrusted the affair "to one or two persons" resident in Mississippi, "persons of good judgment, probity, general acquaintance with the men who lead, and the habits which obtain in political matters in the state" and "such agents by quietly agreeing to sell to about a dozen leaders from $10,000 to $50,000 apiece of these bonds at from 30 to 50 cents, payable when the state 'commenced' paying the bonds, by influencing, even buying up, if necessary, one or two leading Democratic journals, *the thing could have been done*." The

[60] Stokes to Ward, Apr. 8, 1853. Hope Mss.
[61] *London Times*, March 26, 1852.
[62] *London Times*, Dec. 14, 1852; Bankers Magazine, Vol. 7, pp. 497-500.

reason for the failure of the former agent of the bondholders was "because he could offer no inducements to politicians" such as had been indicated. *"The small and sole chance for the Union Bank bonds"* was *"to make a powerful effort to have the Planters' Bank bonds taken up."* Prosperity and the advancement of new men might ultimately help the Union Bank bonds but even this was doubtful; and the frequent connection of the two debts only played into the hands of the anti-bond party. "In the differences between the Foote and the Davis sections of the Democratic party, in the revival of States rights and Union parties, the bond question might be used to advantage." As a result of the election the case of the Planters' Bank bonds looked bad; but these bonds were in a better position than the Union Bank bonds as "no *prominent Democratic politician*" was "against them," while "every one of that party of any note" was decidedly opposed to the Union Bank bonds. Yet it was only by operating with the Democratic party that the bonds would be paid, for the Whigs were not sound on the question and to "make it a purely Whig measure" would mean failure. If the bondholders, however, followed the advice of the *London Times* and awaited "the returning sense of honor," the writer of this letter was convinced that they would wait "until time will be no more. The truth is," stated this outspoken correspondent, "that public opinion or the opinion of the civilized world has no more effect upon our state in this regard than it has upon the Emperor of Japan." [63]

It was this state of affairs which probably induced Billings and his associates to entrust the case of the Union Bank bonds to the courts rather than to the verdict of the polling booth. The complexion of the courts also favored them for the Chancellor of the Superior Court of Chancery was Charles Scott, a former attorney of the Union Bank, who in 1841 had assured the president of the bank that the bonds were legal obligations of the state. [64] It was not strange, therefore, that the Chancellor decided in December 1852 in favor of the bondholders. The Attorney General appealed the case to the High Court of Errors and Appeals; but, as the *New Orleans Commercial Bulletin* remarked, the decision of the Superior Court

---

[63] Cochran to Ward, Dec. 20, 1852; Ward to Baring, Jan. 1, 1853 (with enclosure). Baring Mss.

[64] Elliott to Hope, July 17, 1841. Hope Mss. Elliott was president of the Mississippi Union Bank.

would be sustained for the majority of the higher court were known to be in favor of paying the bonds. The Chief Justice had published nearly ten years previously "a masterful and unanswerable argument in favor of payment" and had showed "conclusively the legal and moral nature of the liability resting upon the state." Justice Yerger had always been a decided bond payer and had denounced repudiation all over the state; while the third member of the court was likewise believed to be a bond payer.[65]

The decision of the lower court elated the bondholders while it placed the people of Mississippi in a very awkward predicament. The people had voted not to pay certain obligations while the highest tribunals of their own creation, especially authorized to pronounce upon such subjects had declared that they were legally and constitutionally bound for their redemption and payment. In order to avoid unnecessary delays by referring matters requiring prompt decision to England, the London Committee passed a resolution appointing S. G. Ward of Boston, agent of the Barings, Fallon of Philadelphia, agent of Frederick Huth and Company, and August Belmont, agent of Rothschild, to associate with other parties in America, reëngage Billings whose contract had expired, and appoint other agents if they thought proper to coöperate with him upon the same terms as Billings had been hired. As it would be necessary to engage writers for the Mississippi press and other persons to advocate the cause of the bondholders a subscription of 1,300 pounds was placed at the disposal of the American committee.[66] An attempt was made by this committee to locate American holders of Mississippi bonds; but beyond locating $100,000 to $150,000 presumably held by Corcoran, and another sum of $25,000 owned by various individuals in amounts not exceeding $5,000 each, it was found almost impossible to unite the interests of the domestic bondholders. For a time Robert J. Walker was considered the best man to appoint as agent of the creditors; but at last Edmund J. Forstall was placed in charge of operations with Billings as his lieutenant. The latter had clearly demonstrated his unfitness to direct operations.[67]

[65] The decision and newspaper comments are given in Bankers Magazine, Vol. 7, p. 829.

[66] Stokes to Ward, Apr. 8, 1853, Hope Mss.; Stokes to Baring, Aug. 30, 1853 gives the list of contributors to the fund. Baring Mss.

[67] Ward to Baring, Apr. 14, 15, 22, 1853; King to Baring, May 14, 1853. Baring Mss.

The bondholders looked forward to the final decision with great hopes; but they did not prepare adequately to utilize the advantage they had gained. This was due in part to the friction between Billings and Forstall; and also to a lack of sufficient funds which prevented Forstall and the bondholders attorney, D. W. Adams, from giving the greatest publicity to the court's decree. Billings was a constant trial to his associates. It was with the greatest difficulty he was restrained from presenting communications from President Fillmore and Webster to the governor of Mississippi. Any attempted interference upon the part of the federal government at this particular moment would have been fatal to the cause of the creditors. Adams finally induced Billings to refrain from an act so injudicious; but he urged upon him the importance of the bondholders being ready to act immediately the moment the court decree was obtained. The greatest publicity should be given to the decision; and to do this it was necessary to secure the support of the Mississippi press. Billings pretended that he had sufficient funds at his disposal for such purposes; and when forced to confess his means were very limited he boldly announced his intention of raising funds by contributions from the presidents of the three railroad companies, who were very desirous of reëstablishing the credit of the state. This destroyed whatever confidence Billings' associates may have had in him; Forstall immediately wrote the Barings that at least $20,000 was needed to carry out the proposed plan of publicity as there were "forty papers edited in Mississippi" and it would be necessary "to subscribe for 100 papers" from each of these presses "for free distribution over the state." [68]

Before a reply to this request was received, the High Court of Errors and Appeals rendered its decision. The court unanimously declared that the Union Bank bonds were valid obligations and that the State of Mississippi was held liable for the payment of the principal and interest.[69] As soon as the opinion of the court was publicly announced, Adams had it sent to all the principal papers in the United States, particularly the Democratic papers in Mississippi, Alabama and Tennessee. He then proceeded to New York where he laid before the American committee a scheme of future

[68] Forstall to Baring, Apr. 12, 1853. Hope Mss.
[69] Mississippi Reports, Vol. 25, pp. 697 et seq.

operations. He suggested that a plan for the redemption of the bonds should immediately be agreed upon by the London committee. This should be transmitted to Forstall who would put it into the form of a law. The proposed measure should be published "section by section" in the press and agents should be selected who in public addresses should advocate the election of members of the legislature pledged to the passage of such a bill. It was necessary to do this for two reasons. In the first place Adams declared that the state could not with propriety propose an arrangement to pay less than the whole of the debt after the court's decision but it might easily accede to such a proposal from the creditors. The Mississippians expected a compromise proposition as the English papers were teeming with praises of the Indiana and Illinois compromises of their public debt and Mississippi had been defrauded as well as these states. In the second place it was understood that the Queen of Spain was the owner of a large amount of bonds represented by Huth and Company. Adams pointed out that a foreign royal personage could sue a state in the United States Supreme Court and if judgment were obtained could attach state property. Since the decision of the Mississippi courts in favor of the validity of the bonds such a suit might be successful; but it would fatally embarrass any arrangement for the remainder of the bonds. As Huth and Company, however, was represented on the London committee, it was to be presumed they would not take unfair advantage of their colleagues. Nevertheless, Adams declared that he had heard privately within the last two or three months of offers to parties to undertake such a suit which were declined at the time as the verdict of the higher court was then unknown. To prevent possible contingencies, Adams requested that a definite agreement such as he proposed should be agreed upon by all the bondholders.

It was also important that the public should be educated on the subject. The people could be trusted to decide intelligently on the question more than the legislature or politicians if it only could be isolated from party politics. To accomplish this Adams arranged with a former confidant of Governor McNutt to establish a bond-paying paper which would possibly cost four or five thousand dollars. He also felt confident that at least three Democratic papers would take the risk of sponsoring the creditors cause if they were compensated with some two thousand each; and four agents should be secured, men of character and standing, to travel throughout the state as the avowed and acknowledged representatives of the bond-holders. To carry out all these plans, Adams asked that at least $30,000 should be placed at the disposal of the American commit-tee. Adams' suggestions were forwarded to the Barings with the endorsement of one of the American committee. "I can see no ob-jection to such a course," wrote King. "The corn law league in Eng-land was of a similar character—under a less elevated moral standard." [70]

The reply of the Barings to these requests for funds was not encouraging. As the plan of operations must be kept secret, the Barings could not appeal publicly to the bondholders for subscrip-tions. They were forced to turn to a few leading houses or capital-ists for aid; and almost everyone they approached either refused to contribute or threw cold water on the proposition. There was no assurance that the Mississippi legislature would make a favorable settlement even if more money was expended; and for this reason the capitalists were extremely reluctant to make additional advances. Hope and Company declared $30,000 was a very large sum to spend on newspaper publicity. They were unwilling to contribute as they personally had no great interest in Mississippi stock, for their holdings consisted chiefly of stock deposited with them by the United States Bank as security for loans. The bank could not be charged for any contributions they had already made. The Barings realized the importance, however, of continuing the campaign for they did not want to see all that had been accomplished lost because of lack of funds. At last they induced Frederick Huth and Com-pany to join with them in subscribing to a sum of 1,000 pounds, each firm advancing 500 pounds. The American committee was authorized to draw upon this amount; and more if they thought it really useful and important. But they were cautioned to practice all practical economy in the expenditure of this sum for "no long purses could be relied upon." [71]

The unpreparedness of the bondholders to follow up the advan-

[70] Ward to Baring, Aug. 9, 12, 17, 1853; King to Baring, Aug. 10, 1853, Baring Mss.; Forstall to Baring, Apr. 12, 1853. Hope Mss.
[71] Hope to Baring, Sept. 13, 1853, Baring Mss.; Baring to King, Sept. 23, 1853. Hope Mss.

tage they had gained by the court decision proved fatal to their cause. Valuable time was wasted in procuring the additional funds with which to carry on the campaign and in proposing a definite compromise scheme for settling the debts. While the bondmen remained inactive, the anti-bondmen and the press violently attacked the court decision. The judges were denounced; and leaders in the Democratic party found it impolitic to stand out against the popular furor. General Foote quickly announced it was absurd and malignant to charge that he and his supporters were in favor of appropriating public money for the payment of the Union Bank bonds. Adams, the bondholders' attorney, tried to stem the popular furor by proposing a method for paying the bonds; but since he insisted the court decision had definitely shown that the state was legally responsible for the payment of the bonds, although the bondholders were willing to accept a compromise, his offer seemed only to arouse greater opposition. In the ensuing elections J. J. McRae, now on the side of the anti-bondmen, was elected governor; and Judge Yerger was defeated for reëlection.[72] The *London Times* claimed the defeat of the Judge was due to the fact that he was on the same ticket with Governor Foote whose political enemy, Jefferson Davis, the Secretary of War, had brought all the official patronage and power of the administration to bear directly against his old antagonist.[73]

Nevertheless, the victory of the anti-bondmen at the polls did not dispose of the troublesome bond question. Upon the eve of the Civil War the governor once more raised the question of paying the Planters' Bank bonds and suggested that the question be again referred to the people. A committee of both houses of the legislature was appointed to consider the matter and a majority report was submitted. The majority report stated that it was impolitic to agitate a question of such magnitude and "divert the attention of the people from more important questions of state policy" at such a time. The minority of the committee held that the strained relations of the state and the federal government was the very reason the subject should be given careful consideration. They pointed

---

[72] Adams to King, Sept. 9, 1853; Forstall to Ward, Sept. 23, 1853, Hope Mss.; *New Orleans Picayune*, Oct. 29, 1853; Bankers Magazine, Vol. 8, pp. 431-433; Ward to Baring, Nov. 11, 15, 1853, Baring Mss.

[73] *London Times*, Dec. 13, 1853.

out that should there be a separation of the slave and free states and Mississippi became a free and sovereign state, she would need friends to uphold her in her new position. Mississippi would want all the character, her resources, her wealth, and her people could give her. She now lacked character for good faith and fidelity in her transactions. As long as Mississippi remained in the Union this "want of character" was not felt by her; but out of the Union, "left to defend herself, thrown upon her own resources," Mississippi would not only find the payment of her just debts "a tower of strength to her"; but she might further find that her independent position exposed herself and her people to the demand of instant payment of this debt by foreign governments.[74] No action was taken, however, upon these reports for the legislature was too engrossed in discussing other matters which ultimately terminated in an appeal to arms. During the war, R. J. Walker visited England and issued pamphlets denouncing Jefferson Davis, as the arch-exponent of repudiation, in order to weaken the financial standing of the Confederacy.[75]

When the war was over and Mississippi lay prostrate under negro rule, a movement originated outside the state, instigated by New York brokers, to get "the motley crew of Senators and Representatives of all shades of coffee and chocolate," to do honor to themselves and Mississippi by bringing about a recognition of the old debts. To accomplish such a result, it was claimed "almost any means would be warrantable." Governor Alcorn and a few other high functionaries of the old school were said to be ready to promote the measure; and in anticipation of success August Belmont, as the Rothschild agent, began quietly buying up the old bonds. But the schism within the radical party enabled the conservatives in Mississippi to carry the election of 1875; and an amendment to the constitution was ratified by the people prohibiting the state from ever redeeming or paying the Union Bank bonds and the Planters' Bank bonds.[76] Henceforth, the bond question was over so far as the Mississippians were concerned. The Council of Foreign Bondholders

[74] Bankers Magazine, Vol. 14, pp. 509, 861-867.
[75] Cf. Letter of Robert J. Walker on Jefferson Davis and Repudiation (London, 1863) *passim.*
[76] Haslewood to Hope, Aug. 13, 1870; King to Hope, Nov. 1, Dec. 20, 1870; Randall to Sellers, Oct. 13, 1870, Hope Mss.; Garner, J. W., Reconstruction in Mississippi, pp. 372-398; Poore, Federal and State Constitutions, Pt. II, p. 1096.

seldom fails, however, to remind the Mississippians of their past delinquencies.

In September 1933 the Principality of Monaco came into possession of $100,000 of the repudiated bonds of Mississippi. The holders of these bonds transferred and delivered them to the Principality at its legation in Paris, France, as an absolute gift. In a letter accompanying the donation, the owners stated that the bonds "had been handed down from their respective families who purchased them at the time of their issue by the State of Mississippi." The donors declared that they had waited "for some ninety years in the hope that the state would meet its obligations and make payment." They had been advised "that there was no basis upon which they could maintain a suit against Mississippi on the bonds, but that 'such a suit could only be maintained by a foreign government or one of the United States.'" Under these circumstances the bondholders had made "an unconditional gift of the bonds to the principality to be applied 'to the causes of any of its charities, to the furtherance of its internal development or to the benefit of its citizens in such manner as it may select.'"

The following December the Principality of Monaco asked leave to bring suit in the Supreme Court of the United States against the State of Mississippi. The State of Mississippi, in its return to the rule to show cause why leave should not be granted raised the following objections: (1) that the Principality of Monaco was not a "foreign State" within the meaning of Section 2, Article III of the Constitution of the United States; (2) that Mississippi had not consented and did not consent to be sued by the Principality of Monaco and that without such consent the state could not be sued ; (3) that the Constitution by Section 10, clause 3, Article I, "forbids the State of Mississippi without the consent of Congress to enter into any compact or agreement with the Principality of Monaco, and no compact, agreement or contract has been entered into by the State with the Principality"; (4) that the proposed litigation was an attempt by the Principality "to evade the prohibitions of the Eleventh Amendment of the Constitution of the United States"; (5) that the proposed declaration did not state a controversy which was "justiciable under the Constitution of the United States and cognizable under the jurisdiction of this Court"; (6) that the alleged right of action "has long since been defeated and extinguished" by reason of the statute of limitations of April 19, 1873; and that the right to sue the state had been taken away by the Code of 1880.

' In reply to these objections the Principality asserted that she was a foreign State recognized as such by the Government of the United States; that the consent of the State of Mississippi was not necessary to give the Court jurisdiction; that the obligation of the State of Mississippi to pay her bonds was not an agreement or a compact with a foreign power; that the action was not a subterfuge to evade the Eleventh Amendment; that the cause of action was justiciable; that no statute of limitations had run against the plaintiff or its predecessors and that neither had been guilty of laches.

On May 21, 1934, Chief Justice Hughes delivered the opinion in which the Court unanimously held that the Principality of Monaco could not sue the State of Mississippi. The Chief Justice held that the suit could not be begun without the consent of Mississippi which the State argued had been rescinded by the Code of 1880. In denying to the Principality the right to file a declaration against Mississippi, Chief Justice Hughes said: "We conclude that the Principality of Monaco, with respect to the right to maintain the proposed suit, is in no better case than the donors of the bonds, and that the application for leave to sue must be denied." In discussing the question of the immunity of American states from suits brought by a foreign state, Chief Justice Hughes said: "The foreign State lies outside the structure of the Union. The waiver or consent on the part of a State, which inheres in the acceptance of the constitutional plan, runs to the other States who have likewise accepted that plan, and to the United States as the sovereign which the Constitution creates. We perceive no ground upon which it can be said that any waiver or consent by a State of the Union has run in favor of a foreign State as to suits brought by a foreign State, we think that the States of the Union retain the same immunity that they enjoy with respect to suits by individuals whether citizens of the United States or citizens or subjects of a foreign State. The foreign State enjoys a similar sovereign immunity and without her consent may not be sued by a State of the Union.

"The question of the right of suit by a foreign State against a State of the Union is not limited to cases of alleged debts or of obligations issued by a State and claimed to have been acquired by transfer. Controversies between a State and a foreign State may involve international questions in relation to which the United States has a sovereign prerogative. One of the most frequent occasions for the exercise of the jurisdiction granted by the Constitution over controversies between States of the Union has been found in disputes over territorial boundaries. Questions have also arisen with respect to the obstruction of navigation, the pollution of streams, and the diversion of navigable waters. But in the case of such a controversy with a foreign power, a State has no prerogative of adjustment. No State can enter 'into any Treaty, Alliance, or Confederation' or, without the consent of Congress, 'into any Agreement or Compact with a foreign Power'—Const., Art. I, sec. 10. The National Government, by virtue of its control of our foreign relations is entitled to employ the resources of diplomatic negotiations and to effect such an international settlement as may be found to be appropriate, through treaty, agreement of arbitration, or otherwise. It cannot be supposed that it was the intention that a controversy growing out of the action of a State, which involves a matter of national concern and which is said to affect injuriously the interests of a foreign State, or a dispute arising from conflicting claims of a State of the Union and a foreign State as to territorial boundaries, should be taken out of the sphere of international negotiations and adjustment through a resort by the foreign State to a suit under the provisions of Section 2 of Article III. In such a case, the State has immunity from suit without her consent and the National Government is protected by the provision prohibiting agreements between States and foreign powers in the absence of the consent of the Congress. While, in this instance, the proposed suit does not raise a question of national concern, the Constitutional provision which is said to confer jurisdiction should be construed in the light of its applications." [77] Thus the rappings of the ghosts of the repudiated bonds continue to the present day.

[77] Principality of Monaco vs. The State of Mississippi, United States Supreme Court Reports, pp. 1-12.

CHAPTER XI

THE TERRITORIAL BONDS OF FLORIDA

FLORIDA is accused of having repudiated upon two separate occasions bonds issued by its legislature. Defenders of Florida integrity assert that these are unjust charges. They claim that the unpaid so-called "Faith Bonds" were issued by a territorial legislature that did not possess the authority to pledge the faith of the territory for their redemption; while the bonds issued in behalf of the Jacksonville, Pensacola, and Mobile Railroad and Florida Central Railroad in the 'seventies were later declared unconstitutional and void by the Supreme Court of Florida. In view of the controversy over the Florida bonds it may be advantageous to reëxamine the origin of these debts; the inducements offered to investors to purchase these bonds; the unsuccessful efforts of the creditors to recover their funds. In this section we will deal only with the territorial bonds of Florida.

In 1822 Congress established the Territory of Florida. By the provisions of the organic law the legislative power was vested "in the Governor and in thirteen of the most fit and discreet persons of the Territory to be called the Legislative Council." The legislative powers of the council extended "to all the rightful subjects of legislation" with certain exceptions enumerated in the law. The governor was required "on or before the first day of December in each year" to report to the President of the United States all laws passed by the legislative council; and any laws which might be disapproved by Congress were henceforth null and void.[1]

Within two years after the passage of this law the question of chartering banks in Florida arose. In 1824 the governor vetoed a bill incorporating certain banks because in his judgment they were unsuited to the "genius and spirit of our free institutions."[2] With

[1] Poore, B. P., Federal and State Constitutions, Part *I*, p. 313.
[2] Rerick, R. H., Memoirs of Florida, Vol. *I*, p. 157.

223

the growth of the territory, this fear of banks gradually subsided. Cotton planters strongly advocated the establishment of banking institutions and in response to public pressure the Bank of Florida was chartered in 1828. Within the next few years numerous other banks and insurance companies were incorporated; and among those chartered were the Bank of Pensacola, the Union Bank of Florida, and the Southern Life Insurance and Trust Company.

In 1831 the Bank of Pensacola was incorporated over the governor's veto. The original capital of the bank was $200,000. Amendments were made to the charter in 1832 and 1833 extending the time allotted to obtain subscriptions and on November 28, 1833 the bank began operations. By an amendment passed February 13, 1835 the capital stock was increased to $2,500,000 and the bank was authorized to purchase as many shares of the stock of the Alabama, Florida, and Georgia Railroad as the directors might deem expedient. In order to make these purchases the bank was empowered "to issue bonds, payable to the Territory of Florida for a sum not exceeding $500,000." These bonds were to be endorsed by the governor and were in denominations of $1,000 each. They bore interest at the rate of 6 per cent, payable semi-annually and the bonds themselves were payable after January 1, 1860. The territory guaranteed the payment of the principal and interest of these bonds and the faith of the territory was pledged for their redemption. As the bank might have occasion for further funds, in order to pay the installments on its railroad stock, it was authorized to issue additional bonds which upon the endorsement of the governor were guaranteed in like manner by the territory. To indemnify the territory for guaranteeing the bonds, the bank executed and delivered to the governor an hypothecation of its capital stock, as well as its real and personal property and assets in the railroad. Section 8 of the Act of 1835 provided that the stockholders of the bank and the railroad were "individually and personally liable for the redemption" of the bonds;[3] but on February 9, 1838 an amendment was "clandestinely" passed which repealed this section.[4] The Act of 1835 was laid before Congress on the last day of the session; and as no adverse action was taken $500,000 of bonds

---

[3] Florida Laws, 1831, pp. 47-52; 1832, pp. 5, 6; 1833, p. 65; 1835, pp. 303-307.
[4] Gamble to Hope, June 29, 1841, Hope Mss.; Florida Laws, 1838, pp. 52, 53.

were sold on December 2, 1835 by the agent of the bank to Thomas Biddle, Samuel Jaudon, and Elihu Chauncey.[5]

In 1833 the Union Bank of Florida was chartered with a capital of $1,000,000 and with the privilege of increasing this amount to $3,000,000. The capital was to be raised by the sale of territorial bonds loaned to the bank. These bonds carried 6 percent interest and were payable in twenty-four to thirty years. In order to facilitate the sale of the bonds, the faith of the territory was pledged for the payment of the principal and interest; but the charter specifically prohibited their sale or negotiation at a discount. The shareholders, exclusively citizens and owners of real estate in Florida, were required to give bond and mortgage on their lands and negroes equal to the amount of their stock subscription. Each stockholder was entitled to a loan from the bank equal to two-thirds of the amount of his stock. Appraisers were appointed by the governor to value the property offered to be mortgaged.[6]

Two years later the Southern Life Insurance and Trust Company was incorporated with a capital stock of $2,000,000 which might be increased to $4,000,000. The whole of the capital was secured by bonds and notes on unencumbered real and personal property located in Florida. The company was required to make an annual report to the Court of Appeals which was laid before the Council. In order to enable the company to make loans and discounts beyond the amount of their capital they might issue certificates of $1,000 each bearing 6 percent interest. Upon the presentation of these certificates to the governor they were to be endorsed by him as "guaranteed by the Territory of Florida." The faith of the territory was pledged as security for the faithful payment of the certificates; but no greater amount was to be endorsed at any time than might be equal to the debts placed under mortgage to the company. In case of default in the payment of the principal or interest of the certificates, the Court of Appeals was to instruct any marshal of the territory to take possession of the assets of the company. In 1839, $400,000 of these certificates were issued. None were sold but in 1840 it was claimed that 150 were in London and the residue in New York.[7]

[5] Senate Doc. No. 447, 26 Cong., 1 Sess., Vol. 7, p. 145.
[6] Florida Laws, 1833, pp. 73-84.
[7] Ibid., 1835, pp. 265-272; House Doc. No. 111, 26 Cong., 2 Sess., Vol 4, p. 484.

The power of the territorial legislature to grant franchises to such corporations and the wisdom of pledging the faith of the territory for the issuance of these bonds was questioned at the time of the chartering of these institutions. The secretary of the territory opposed the establishment of the Union Bank because he doubted the authority of the territorial legislature to create such a corporation. Others objected to the provision in the charter allowing the stockholders to borrow a large part of the capital which the bank originally had borrowed from the territory. There was also objection upon the part of some to the bank lending money for long terms on mortgages of real estate; and that the bondholders had no power to restrain the managers of the bank from wasting the capital as long as the interest on the bonds were paid.[8] Whether Florida by becoming a state could release herself from obligations entered into as a territory also aroused some discussion. To set at rest all doubts upon this matter, the legal advice of Chancellor Kent, Horace Binney, Peter A. Jay and Daniel Webster was obtained upon this technical point. It was the unanimous decision of these lawyers that contracts entered into by the territory would be binding upon Florida when she became a state.[9] Governor Eaton in discussing the incorporation of the Southern Life Insurance and Trust Company significantly declared: "The guaranty of a State or Territory is nothing more than a mere promise to do a particular act. There is no compulsory authority whereby the fulfilment of the promise can be enforced; it is but the assurance of plighted faith; though it is that which the sovereignty making it will always be careful to redeem."[10] It is, therefore, evident that while some doubted the validity of the Florida bonds when they were issued, prospective purchasers were given many assurances of their unquestionable security. Thomas W. Ward assured the Barings that in Chancellor Kent's opinion Florida, either as a state or territory, was bound to redeem the Union Bank bonds. But Ward warned the Barings, however, that Florida was assuming too many obligations for its limited resources and population.[11]

[8] Brevard, C. M., History of Florida, Vol. *I*, pp. 210-214.
[9] House Doc. No. 111, 26 Cong., 2 Sess., Vol. 4, pp. 269-277.
[10] Senate Doc., No. 447, 26 Cong., 1 Sess., Vol. 7, p. 7.
[11] Ward to Baring, July 21, 1835. Baring Mss.

With the exception of a few carping critics the establishment of these banks was acclaimed by the people of Florida. Advocates of the Union Bank enthusiastically hailed its incorporation. Many of the settlers had bought land at very low prices, ranging from $1.25 to $2.00 per acre. They wanted slaves to clear and cultivate their land and they eagerly availed themselves of the facilities offered by the bank. The appraisers valued the uncultivated land at $5 per acre, other lands in proportion, and thus the advances from the bank were fifty and one hundred percent more than the whole capital invested. Perhaps the appraisement was justified in view of the rapid growth in population and prosperity of the country. Some years later, however, when it was determined to increase the capital to three millions, a ruinous course was adopted. By vote of the directors the old shareholders were given a preference in the appropriation of the new stock. Since the stockholders had no additional property to pledge it was decided to reappraise the former mortgages. This happened at a time when there was a feverish excitement for real estate in Florida. Thus lands which originally had been valued at $5 an acre and which all the time had remained totally unproductive, were now appraised at $15 and more an acre and the advance of the bank was raised to $10 per acre.[12]

Enthusiastic supporters of the bank explained its operations in glowing terms. All that was necessary, declared one, was for a man to mortgage "his lands and negroes; draw from the bank two-thirds (in money) of their value, which will be reinvested in more land and more negroes. One or two crops of cotton will redeem all obligations to the bank; so you see it is the best thing afloat; a man can go to sleep and wake up rich."

"Going to sleep," remarked one, "is a good suggestion, but unfortunately too many are wide awake, spending money in display when the very shovel and tongs in the kitchen belong to the bank. But asleep or awake, there will be nightmare with some, before they shuffle off that coil."

"Oh, no; the bank gives the greatest possible opportunity for relief. In a few years every man will be so independent, that he

[12] Meinertzhagen to Huth, Apr. 8, 1843. Huth Mss.

will have a surplus of means to expend in public enterprises, and Florida will then become a state of which the Union will be proud." [13]

Since the terms upon which the Union Bank bonds were sold caused much discussion in later years it is essential to examine the manner in which they were marketed. On April 16, 1834 the bank received from Governor Duval 360 "faith bonds." The following February Governor Eaton issued 640 which completed the first million of the capital of the bank. These were sold by Colonel John Gamble, the president of the bank, to New York and Philadelphia brokers at an average premium of one percent. In March 1838 Governor Call delivered 2,000 bonds to increase the capital of the bank to $3,000,000 as the charter provided. [14]

The following June Colonel Gamble set out for New York to dispose of the bonds. By the terms of the charter the bonds could not be sold or negotiated at a discount; and Colonel Gamble was instructed "to sell at the best price attainable which would produce not less than *par* at Tallahassee." He succeeded in selling 200 bonds to the American Life Insurance and Trust Company in New York; and in August sailed for Europe with a letter of introduction from Prime, Ward, and Company to Hope and Company in Amsterdam. In London Samuel Jaudon, the London agent of the United States Bank of Pennsylvania gave Colonel Gamble another letter of introduction to Hope and Company in which the Union Bank bonds were claimed to be "as solid and desirable a security as any in the market." Jaudon called the attention of the Dutch financiers to the admirable administration of the bank, the creditable manner in which it had passed through the crisis of 1837, the large accumulated surplus, and "the high personal character and standing of Colonel Gamble." [15]

Equipped with this strong endorsement by a bank that enjoyed the confidence of European financiers, Colonel Gamble visited Amsterdam, Bremen, and Hamburg. In Amsterdam he succeeded in selling 100 bonds to Hope and Company at 97. By the terms of the contract the bonds were made payable in Holland at the rate

[13] Long, E. C., Florida Breezes, p. 84.
[14] House Doc. No. 111, 26 Cong., 2 Sess., Vol. 4, pp. 249, 299.
[15] Prime, Ward and Company to Hope, Aug. 15, 1838; Jaudon to Hope, Sept. 12, 1838. Hope Mss.

of two and one-half florins on the dollar; and the interest began from the date of the sale. Hope and Company were allowed a commission of one-half of one percent for their services in paying the interest and principal when such payments were not made from the net proceeds of produce consigned to them; and if bills of exchange were remitted they were allowed brokerage in addition to their commission.[16]

In order to induce Hope and Company to take these bonds, Colonel Gamble drew up a lengthy statement which he presented to the Dutch financiers setting forth the advantages of the Florida investments. The arguments employed by Colonel Gamble in persuading the Dutch to take a portion of the Florida loan are illuminating in view of the subsequent controversy between Dutch holders of these bonds and the authorities of the territory. Colonel Gamble called particular attention to the fact that the bonds were executed in the name of the Territory of Florida, signed by the governor and treasurer, and sealed with the seal of the territory. They were endorsed by the cashier of the bank and would be endorsed by the president. The principal and interest, payable in florins, would be made by the bank. Shares in the stock of the bank were secured by mortgages on the property of the respective shareholders; and the Dutch were assured that the value of the property offered for mortgage had been so carefully appraised that it was "worth thrice the money for which it was mortgaged." With the growth of population and the improvements made on these estates, their value would annually be increased.

Turning to the financial standing of the bank, Colonel Gamble pointed out that the Union Bank was the only bank in middle Florida. This gave the bank control of the exchange business of that section; and "availing itself of the existing state of things the *surplus profits*" had "already risen to $250,000"; and would "certainly exceed $300,000 before the end of the year." While it was neither expected nor desired that similar profits would accrue in the future, past experience proved "that an annual surplus profit of four percent" might be relied upon; which profit, compounded at bank interest, would "double the capital in fourteen years." Even if the surplus profit should be reduced to 2 percent per year it would

[16] Gamble to Hope, Sept. 27, 1838. Hope Mss.

double the capital in twenty-one years, whereas the bonds had an average of twenty-seven years.

There was no cause for alarm over the management of the bank. With a single exception, the stockholders were planters residing upon and cultivating their own estates. They felt "that their *all*" was ventured upon the prudent management of the bank. "No person having any control or influence over the operations of the bank" was engaged "in commerce or in hazardous speculation." As the bank "must and will be managed with prudence," holders of the bonds would have "a four fold security for their payment viz.: (1) the capital of the bank derived from the sale of the bonds; and unless this capital shall be impaired by bad debts, this fund will remain a sufficient security for the bonds; (2) the accumulating surplus profit which in fourteen years will equal the amount of the bonds to be paid; and which if even reduced to an annuity of 2 percent will double the capital in twenty-one years; (3) the property of the stockholders mortgaged to secure their respective shares. A security even now equal to thrice the amount of the bonds. And if any unforeseen and improbable cause shall ever render necessary a resort to this security the holders of the bonds may confidently rely upon the government enforcing their payment from this fund—which must also be paid out of the coffers of the state; (4) the faith and responsibility of the Territory or State of Florida. She will become a state next year. A convention has been called by direction of Congress in St. Joseph in November next to frame a constitution. The constitution will be submitted to the people and then to Congress. The change from a Territory to a State will in no manner affect the security of the bonds, it being a well-established principle of national law 'that a change in the form of its government, operates no change in the rights or responsibilities of a community.' "

Colonel Gamble then dwelt upon the wonderful economic possibilities of Florida. Her soil and climate were adapted "to the profitable production of all the agricultural staples of the southern states; as well as many of those of the tropics." Like that of the other southern states the soil of Florida was much diversified. She possessed millions of acres of the most fertile land, "the hundredth part of which has not been subjected to cultivation." "So great are her advantages of soil and climate that the query is not 'what can

Florida produce?' but 'what production will yield the greatest profit with the least labor?' " The present population and resources of Florida furnished "little information by which to decide what they will be before the maturity of her bonds."

Due to her position on the Gulf and her excellent harbors, Florida was destined "to become a great commercial state." She possessed "the only good harbors on a coast of 2,000 miles from Cape Florida to Mexico." The country was rapidly filling up with a white population and it might confidently be assumed that "before the end of ten years" the exports of cotton will exceed 250,000 bales.

The people of Florida were energetic and wide awake. Four railroads were already under construction; and these improvements had been made "by the Floridians without the aid of foreign loans." They served to show the "go-ahead spirit which actuates a new country."

When these bonds were sold, it would appear that Florida had a debt of $3,500,000. "But although responsible for her bonds to that amount, it is not a debt which she will have to pay from her own coffers. The bank and railroad of Pensacola will pay the half-million; and the Union Bank will pay $3,000,000. Florida has taken ample security to indemnify and protect herself from loss. And if the expectations, already realized, be not falsified she will in fourteen years be in the annual receipt of $60,000 from the profits of the Union Bank of Florida as a remuneration for the aid offered by the loan of credit by the issue of the bonds."

To this already lengthy document Colonel Gamble added a postscript in order to remove "an erroneous opinion" that a territory was something "of a political infant incapable, in law, of acting for itself or of contracting with others without the assent of a guardian." By the terms of the organic law organizing the territory, "the legislative power of the territorial legislature 'extends to all rightful subjects of legislation.' " "And in the case of the Bank of Michigan (chartered by the *Territory* of Michigan) vs. a citizen of New York it has been judicially decided that the creation of a bank is 'a rightful subject of legislation.' And that a corporate body, created by an act of territorial legislation possesses the same legal rights and qualifications as if it owed its being to a state legislature." While Congress possessed the right to review or annul any act of a territorial legislature, the Constitution of the United States forbade the passage "of any post facto law or any law which will impair the obligation of contracts." The Union Bank had been chartered in 1833. The stockholders had acquired certain rights under it. Contracts had been made and consummated by the execution of the bonds of the territory payable to the bank and to its officers. "And over these rights and these contracts the power of Congress has ceased." The "feeling of Congress" towards the Union Bank might be inferred from the fact that "in the session of 1836 Webster as chairman of a committee of the Senate had submitted a report in relation to the several banks which had been incorporated by Florida." Certain provisions in the charters of the Southern Life Insurance and Trust Company and the Bank of Pensacola had been censured; and an act had been passed declaring "that no future act of a territory for the incorporation of a bank should have any validity until after receiving the express sanction of Congress." But an attempt to restrain the governor of Florida from issuing the two million dollars of bonds now offered for sale had met "with no favour in Congress." It had "slept the sleep of death." [17]

A résumé of Colonel Gamble's arguments clearly shows that the Dutch financiers were given every encouragement to believe that the Florida bonds were a safe investment. Particular stress had been placed upon the power of the territorial legislature to issue these bonds and that Congress had sanctioned their issuance. Attention had been called to the four fold security behind the bonds and among these had been cited "the faith and responsibility of the Territory or State of Florida" for their redemption; but it is evident that Colonel Gamble never thought the people of Florida would be called upon to meet this obligation. What effect the high-pressure sales arguments of Colonel Gamble had upon the Dutch financiers cannot be definitely stated. It was later claimed that a member of Hope and Company purchased the bonds on his private account in order to thwart a rival house. [18] While Hope and Company were negotiating for the bonds, they were in direct communication with the Barings in London. As stated above, the Barings had been

[17] Memorandum by Gamble on subject of the Florida bonds. Hope Mss. On Webster report on Florida banks and discussion in Congress consult Cong. Debates, 24 Cong., 1 Sess., Vol. 12, pp. 1447, 1847.
[18] Meinertzhagen to Huth, Apr. 8, 1843. Huth Mss.

warned not to handle Florida securities and this information was passed on to the Dutch financiers. On December 4, 1838 Hope told the Barings that they would be more inclined to deal with Colonel Gamble if Florida were raised to the status of a state; and on January 6, 1839, after refusing an option on an additional 400 bonds, Hope acknowledged to the Barings that "with so many good investments being now offered we may set aside the more dubious." [19]

In the meantime Colonel Gamble had succeeded in negotiating a contract with Palmer, MacKillop, Dent and Company of London for the remainder of the Florida bonds. Nine hundred and fifty bonds were sold to this firm at 91 payable in four installments beginning March 1, 1839; but the interest on the bonds commenced on the preceding January 1. The remaining 720 bonds were left for sale with this house and sixteen were later sold at 10 percent premium. The 704 unsold bonds were hypothecated to Palmer, MacKillop, Dent and Company to secure the payment of $533,-333.33 borrowed by the Union Bank from the Bank of the United States of Pennsylvania. Palmer, MacKillop, Dent and Company were instructed not to sell these bonds for less than 95; but this restriction was removed by later instructions. For their services they were allowed a commission of 2 percent in addition to their customary brokerage fees. [20]

British investors were urged to purchase the Florida bonds. Palmer, MacKillop, Dent and Company issued a prospectus citing the four-fold security mentioned by Colonel Gamble in his statement to Hope and Company. [21] The *Morning Chronicle* in a lengthy article on the Florida loan told its readers that in every way "purchasers of Florida bonds were amply secured." The agricultural resources of the territory were listed as proof that Florida was "a very rising and prosperous country." "We should not have dwelt so much upon this subject," concluded the writer of this article, "were we not aware that great efforts are making to alarm English people most unjustly in reference to the solidity of American securities and we feel convinced that persons desirous of investing money in any of the principal American securities will find on

[19] Hope to Baring, Dec. 4, 1838, Jan. 6, 1839. Baring Mss.
[20] House Doc. No. 111, 26 Cong., 2 Sess., Vol. 4, p. 299.
[21] Senate Doc. No. 103, 34 Cong., 1 Sess., Vol. 15, pp. 297-300.

inquiry that we have never overrated the honor and good faith which have always been shown by the United States to her creditors." [22] About the same time the governor of Florida was telling the legislature that perhaps "in no part of the world" was there "greater punctuality in the discharge of pecuniary obligations" than was to be found "among the people of this territory." In the midst of the universal destruction of credit not a single commercial house had failed in Florida. This condition of affairs was attributed to the liberal policy of the banks in accommodating the people with funds to purchase property which had resulted in increasing the value of every article. [23]

Within a year, however, the banks in Florida were being severely censured for their loan policies. English capitalists were privately informed that the currency of the Union Bank was at a discount of twenty-five percent. It was common knowledge that the planters to whom the bank had made loans offered "very little security" for their payment and the improper management of its affairs was "freely reflected upon." [24] These rumors were verified in the governor's message of 1840 where the financial difficulties of the Florida banks were discussed at length. [25] In the House the Committee on Banks were instructed to investigate the affairs of the Union Bank; while the Judiciary Committee was ordered to report on "the power of the Governor and Legislative Council to create banks and to pledge the faith and credit of the people of Florida."

On February 25, 1840 the Committee on Banks submitted its report on the Union Bank. They found no irregularity in the sale of the first issue of bonds; but the directors and shareholders were sharply criticized for the unwise and imprudent management of the bank as soon as these funds were obtained. The bank had "not only distributed all its borrowed capital among shareholders and others, upon terms which precluded the possibility of its being repaid within any reasonable time"; but it had likewise "extended these imprudent loans upon the capital based on circulation and floating deposits." On January 2, 1836 the liabilities of the bank were $1,675,705; its presumed resources $1,728,605. Of these only

[22] *Morning Chronicle*, Feb. 19, 1839.
[23] Florida Senate Journal, 1839, p. 17.
[24] Kindermann to Huth, Dec. 27, 1839. Huth Mss.
[25] Florida Senate Journal, 1840, pp. 7, 8.

$110,179 was in cash or immediately available; while the bank might be called upon to meet immediate liabilities of $675,704. Subsequent experience had proved that the bank could place small reliance upon its discounted paper to produce funds requisite to meet its engagements.

Furthermore the bank had engendered a reckless spirit of extravagance by its profuse loans. Before the establishment of the Union Bank, a bank founded on borrowed capital had not been understood; now it was perfectly comprehensible. "To become suddenly rich, to become off-hand the proprietor of lands, negroes, houses, and equipages, simply by pledging property on a loan, with thirty years credit, which property could be bought with money thus obtained, was to enjoy in reality the vision of fiction." In fact, the character of the bank was an Eldorado, for it authorized a further issue of 2,000 bonds.

It was the sale of these bonds which the committee especially criticized. Colonel Gamble stated that he had sold 1,280 bonds abroad on terms which he claimed produced in Tallahassee a premium of 7.41 percent, and 16 bonds had been sold in London since his return. He acknowledged that 30 of these bonds had been sold at par; 100 at a nominal discount of 3 percent; 201 at 8 percent discount; 950 at 9 percent; and 15 at 10 percent. But the committee claimed that the only par which could be recognized in computing the value of state securities was "the constitutional currency of the Union when payable in the United States or the legal currency of England when made payable in London." Therefore, the committee held that the bonds disposed of in England had been sold at 10½ percent discount instead of 9 percent since the purchasers by the terms of payment, had gained $14,960 of interest which was equivalent to a "further reduction of 1½ percent." But the charter provided that all bonds sold at a discount were "null and void"; and in insisting upon this the committee declared that they were insinuating "nothing of which the purchasers were not before aware." A house as extensively engaged in the negotiation of American securities as Palmer, MacKillop, Dent and Company must have understood "the constitutional difference between a Territorial bond and the obligation of a State sovereignty." They must have seen that by the eleventh section of the charter "the *principal* and interest were to be paid by the *bank* and not by the *Territory.*" Moreover, Colonel Gamble was on the ground to explain all such matters. It was evident, therefore, that "the European purchaser instead of being a quiet easy man, duped into an unfortunate purchase by a reliance on the honor and faith of Florida" had made "his *calculations* before he *parted with his funds.* Should speculators abroad hereafter complain of having suffered loss by their transactions in these bonds, it must not be forgotten that it was themselves who, for purposes of their own, induced sales at a rate which they were aware destroyed any guaranty of public credit implied by the law." [26]

A month later the Judiciary Committee reported upon the power of the territorial legislature to create banking institutions. The committee granted the authority of the Legislative Council to establish banks; but they denied the power of the legislature to bind the sovereign people of Florida. To concede the attributes of sovereignty to the Legislative Council was to deprive the people of their birthright as freemen and make them slaves. The Legislative Council had incorporated banks and issued bonds purporting to be guaranteed by the territory to the amount of $3,900,000. With a population less than 50,000, every man, woman, child, white or black, in Florida was already burdened with an imputed debt of near $200. The annual interest charges on this debt was upwards of $230,000. To pay this sum taxes must be levied vastly beyond the ability of endurance of the people of Florida. The committee declared that it was not their intention in revealing these facts to endeavor to influence the final decision upon this subject. If the obligations had been rightfully contracted, the people of Florida would submit "to any loss rather than that of their honor." Nevertheless, as the Legislative Council had assumed powers of sovereignty which it did not possess, the committee was forced to declare "that such pledge of the faith and credit of the people of Florida is null and void." [27]

The controversy over the payment of the Florida bonds began with the publication of these reports. The Senate passed resolutions protesting against the doctrines set forth as calculated "to destroy all confidence in the honor, integrity, and good faith of the people

[26] Journal Proc. Leg. Council, 1840, App., pp. 27-42.
[27] *Ibid.,* App., pp. 1-17.

of Florida."[28] Colonel Gamble issued a statement in which he declared that the increasing disposition of Europeans to invest in American stocks was due to the "strong feeling of confidence in American honor and honesty."[29] But he did not tell the people he had informed Dutch financiers that the bank was responsible for the payment of the principal and interest on the bonds; nor could he deny that they had been sold under par in direct violation of the provisions of the charter. But Colonel Gamble had given Hope and Company to understand that the faith of the territory was pledged for their redemption; and the prospectus issued by Palmer, Mac-Killop, Dent and Company had listed this as one reason why the British should purchase these bonds. The banks were in no position, however, to defend the interest of the bondholders on account of their own misdemeanors; and without direct representatives on the ground to present the case of the creditors, public opinion was mobilized against payment. Suppose Palmer, MacKillop, Dent and Company did not lend Florida any more money. "Well, who cares if they don't," thundered the *Floridian*. "What harm will it do to stop our credit? None in the world. We are now as a community heel over head in debt and can scarcely pay the interest. We must retrench and reform."[30] In such an atmosphere in the fall of 1840 a constitution was ratified rigidly controlling banks and a Democratic majority hostile to all banking institutions was elected to the territorial legislature.[31]

The doctrine of repudiation was set forth in Governor Reid's message of January 11, 1841. The governor admitted that the bills of the three banks in operation were depreciating and that every section of Florida was suffering from the universal indebtedness. There were no funds in the treasury to pay the salaries of officials; specie had disappeared and exchange had gone up to a high rate; the court dockets were thronged with suits; the necessities of life were selling at enormous prices. These misfortunes were due to the passion for chartering banks. But these institutions had been created and it was unnecessary to enter into a discussion of the authority of the territoral legislature to establish them. The important

[28] Florida Senate Journal, 1840, p. 126.
[29] House Doc. No. 111, 26 Cong., 2 Sess., Vol. 4, p. 384.
[30] *Floridian*, March 14, 1840.
[31] Davis, W. W., The Civil War and Reconstruction in Florida, p. 27.

question was the liability of the territory for the bonds issued in behalf of these banks. The governor suggested that these bonds should be called in and cancelled and bonds of the stockholders substituted for these obligations; but it was evident that the governor was disposed to repudiate entirely the territorial bonds. To repudiate these bonds was no evidence of "bad faith or want of honor or honesty" for they had been obtained "through legislation partial and unjust. What right had a few hundred stockholders to make the whole people . . . and their posterity . . . groan under a load of debt for these institutions?" The banks had brought no money into the treasury; they had produced only appearances of prosperity. The holders of these bonds should be informed that "they possess bonds which they never can collect from the Territory." [32]

The threat of repudiation alarmed the Florida bondholders. Hope and Company despatched a letter to Governor Call in behalf of holders of Bank of Pensacola bonds informing him that the interest due on January 1, 1841 had been refused and calling upon the government of Florida to redeem its pledge. In his reply Governor Call admitted that the territory had guaranteed the payment of the principal and interest on these bonds; but he insisted that the territory was a remote and contingent endorser whose responsibility did not arise until all legal measures had been exhausted against the bank and the stockholders. By the amended charter of the bank the stockholders were "individually bound in their private fortunes to pay both the principal and interest of these bonds." They were wealthy men residing in New York, Philadelphia, and Louisiana, and the laws of these states afforded ample relief to their creditors. The governor recommended that the bondholders proceed at once to attach the assets of the bank as well as take action against the individual stockholders since he had "every reason to believe that the stockholders abroad" were "withdrawing the funds of the bank beyond the jurisdiction of this territory." If the bondholders were disposed to pursue this course, the governor offered to aid them in securing faithful competent agents to protect their interests. But he had no power to authorize the payment of the principal or interest on the bonds unless instructed to do so by the legislature. [33] The

[32] Florida Senate Journal, 1841, pp. 12, 13, 17; consult also comments on this message in *London Times*, Feb. 20, March 8, 1841.
[33] Call to Hope, June 28, 1841. Hope Mss.

governor must have realized that it was useless to bring action against either the bank or the original shareholders as neither were "worth the expense of being sued." This was especially true of the latter who were located in different parts of the Union which would necessitate separate suits in various courts.[34]

The views held by Governor Call were reiterated in a private letter of Colonel Gamble to Hope and Company. "You will perceive by inspection of the Pensacola bonds," wrote Colonel Gamble, "that they are not the bonds of the Territory of Florida; but the bonds of a railroad and banking company which have been *endorsed* by the governor of the Territory. It is as *endorser* then that the Territory is bound; and in that light the Territory will consider itself as only bound in the event that after using due diligence the holder of the bonds do not recover their amount from the parties liable." By the Act of 1835 the stockholders were "individually and personally liable for the redemption of said bonds." In 1838 this provision in the charter had been "clandestinely" repealed, "the legislature being ignorant of the contents of the section." But this repeal would not "operate to the prejudice of the holders of the bonds since it would be to them 'ex post facto' and would 'impair the obligation of the contract' existing between the holders of the bonds and the stockholders who were bound for the payment—both of which things are forbidden by the Constitution of the United States. . . . The only bonds issued in the name of the Territory of Florida," declared Colonel Gamble, "are those issued to and sold by the Union Bank of Florida."[35]

Upon the receipt of these letters and at the suggestion of their legal advisers, Hope and Company determined to send a stronger note to the governor. At the same time their lawyers induced Jaudon "to write to Webster to use his influence not officially but indirectly to obtain an equitable settlement of the business";[36] and Edmund J. Forstall of New Orleans was retained by Hope and Company to look after their interests in Florida. In their second communication to Governor Call, the Dutch financiers declared that they did not care to prosecute the bank and the stockholders. Holders of

---

[34] Gowan and Marx to Hope, Sept. 17, 1841. Hope Mss. Gowan and Marx of London were the legal advisers of Hope and Company.

[35] Gamble to Hope, June 29, 1841. Hope Mss.

[36] Gowan and Marx to Hope, Sept. 17, 1841. Hope Mss.

the bonds of the Bank of Pensacola had purchased them relying upon the good faith of the territory. They supposed the territory would "immediately indemnify them in case of any default on the part of the bank." Now they were given to understand that legislative guaranty was different from that universally recognized in commercial transactions. They had confidently believed that "the immunity enjoyed by a sovereign state" from court proceedings would only make it "more scrupulous in fulfilling its engagements." They might also suggest that any delay in the payment of this interest would be "an additional and disastrous blow" to the credit of the nation; while the territory, if it should in the future resort to loans would be obliged "to submit to a sacrifice greater than any now required." The bondholders should not be held responsible for the negligence or violation of any trust upon the part of those to whom the law confided the management of these funds. "They had no influence over and have derived no benefit from this expenditure and if the government with all its powers did not discover and could not prevent any proper proceedings which may have taken place surely those at a distance without any means to borrow or prevent any malpractices cannot be considered blameable." [37]

The second appeal was as ineffective as the first. Governor Call refused to change his opinion. He also declined to pay the interest of $30 each due on 225 coupons held by Hope and Company which Forstall presented for payment.[38]

It was Forstall's conviction that the national government must assume the debt. Forstall wrote Hope and Company that the federal government was responsible for the debt because the governor of Florida was a federal officer; because the legislative council who created the Bank of Pensacola was composed of federal officers appointed by the federal government; and because the bonds had been approved by the governor of the territory, an agent of the national government and by Congress. In this he was sustained by the legal opinion of the United States District Attorney of Pensacola who drew up a lengthy brief for Forstall on the federal government's responsibility for the bonds. The district attorney held that the bondholders had a claim upon the federal government because

[37] Williams to Call, Oct. 13, 1841. Hope Mss.
[38] Forstall to Call, Oct. 29, 1841; Call to Forstall, Nov. 12, 1841. Hope Mss.

the whole machinery of government of Florida had been created and set in motion by Congress. Moreover, Congress had notoriously and flagrantly neglected its duty by allowing Florida to become involved in financial difficulties "not so much by her own acts as by the acts of the agents of the United States" who both made and executed her laws. In her character as guardian Congress should have seen that the means of the banks were not squandered. Instead of doing so, "the most shameless and wanton career of wastefulness and folly had been suffered to pass unheeded and unrebuked in spite of the earnest and repeated appeals to Congress." The convention which had drafted a constitution for Florida had addressed a memorial to Congress "anxiously soliciting its attention and invoking its interference." Subsequently a report on the Bank of Pensacola had been prepared by the legislature and had been laid by the governor before Congress and yet nothing had been done "to arrest the work of destruction and protect the interest of the bondholders." Furthermore, it should not be forgotten that the national government owned "seven-eighths of the whole territory" and the value of that land had been greatly enhanced by the money which the sale of the bonds "had brought into the territory." This consideration certainly added to the moral obligations of the federal government; while the destruction of the credit of Florida and the imposition of heavy taxes would vastly impair the property of the United States.[39]

In January, 1842 Governor Call laid his correspondence with Hope and Company before the legislature. He repeated his former arguments and quoted the inscription on the bonds to show that the stockholders were "individually and personally liable" for their payment; but he made no reference to the repeal of this section in the Act of 1838. The governor denied the direct liability of the territory for the bonds of the Bank of Pensacola and the Southern Life Insurance and Trust Company but he acknowledged that the territory was responsible for the Union Bank bonds. He declared that the names of such stockholders as Biddle, Jaudon, Chauncey, and others of the Bank of Pensacola were "worth more in the European market than the faith and responsibility of the territory; and it was the liability of these persons which induced foreign capitalists to make the investment." Undoubtedly the names of these persons

[39] Anderson to Forstall, Nov. 20, 1841. Hope Mss.

had caused foreign bankers to agree to handle the bonds but, as shown above, Hope and Company had been particularly solicitous whether the territory or the "state" of Florida was going to guarantee the Union Bank bonds. The governor was undoubtedly correct in inferring that the European capitalists hoped by getting the federal government to acknowledge its responsibility for the Florida bonds to prepare the way for assumption by the federal government of all state debts.[40]

Within a month of the receipt of this message the legislature cleared the way to release the territory of all obligations to pay the Florida bonds. In February, 1842 the legislature passed a resolution declaring "that the Territorial legislature does not possess, nor was it ever invested with the authority to pledge the faith of the Territory, so as to render the citizens of the Territory responsible for the debts, or engagements of any corporation chartered by said Territorial legislation."[41] By this action the legislature repudiated its bank debts.

It was quite evident, however, that the Union Bank could not meet the payments on its bonds owing to the failure of the last two crops of cotton. In endeavoring to meet its liabilities the bank had suffered severe losses in attempting to purchase cotton as a substitute for exchange. In the competition, for the short crop of cotton prices had been run up "to more than double the New York prices." Florida merchants had competed with agents of northern houses who had become possessed of the bank's paper, "some in payment of debts, others by purchases in Wall Street at discounts varying from 35 to 50 percent." This had resulted in Florida merchants trying to protect themselves "by demanding payment for their goods in bank paper at fifty cents on the dollar, while another fifty percent had been added to the price of the goods." It was impossible, according to Gamble, for Florida to pay any large amount of its debt. The people had no money as was evidenced by the fact that property purchased two years previous for $13,000 was selling under execution for $900.[42]

The bondholders soon realized that there was no hope of recovering their funds. Congress refused in 1842 and 1843 to take any

[40] Florida Senate Journal, 1841, pp. 6-27.
[41] Florida Laws, 1842, p. 53.
[42] Gamble to Jaudon, May 14, 1842. Huth Mss.

action upon memorials presented by the Florida bondholders.[43] The chargé d'affaires at the Hague, in replying to the petition prepared by Hope and Company in behalf of holders of American loans, was instructed by the State Department to declare "in the most formal and explicit terms, as the clear and unalterable determination of the general government, that it will not consent to be held, in any wise, or to any extent, responsible for any default, actual or eventual, in the execution of these engagements." [44] The Florida legislature considered it inexpedient to take any notice of resolutions passed by the Georgia legislature which were sent to the governor of Florida. These resolutions declared "that there is a moral obligation upon every government to discharge its pecuniary obligations, and any state refusing to do so, or to provide the means of payment, is false to the principles of common honesty, and an enlightened civilization, and is unworthy of the confidence of its sister states." [45] On February 2, 1843 the lower House of the Florida legislature passed a resolution announcing "that the people of Florida are not legally or morally responsible for the three millions of dollars of bonds issued to the Union Bank of Florida, $500,000 to the Bank of Pensacola, and $400,000 to the Southern Life Insurance and Trust Company," and, "will not pay the amount or any part thereof of the aforesaid bonds." This resolution was adopted with an amendment stating that "the only responsibility for the payment of the said bonds, and interest thereon, are the said banks and stockholders thereof." [46] The Senate tabled these resolutions [47]; but on February 24, 1843 passed a series of resolutions declaring that it was "inexpedient to renew or repeat the sentiment and opinion" of the resolutions passed at the preceding session of the legislature. In case it should become necessary to levy a tax "to meet the engagements on account of said banks," the Senate held that "the same should be assessed on the stockholders only," and "not on other people who have known these institutions only by the mischief

[43] A memorial was presented on June 24, 1842, and referred in House of Representatives to Committee on Foreign Affairs. As no report was rendered, the memorial was taken up at the next session, again referred to the same committee and held there without being reported. Statement in Forstall Memorial, Jan. 22, 1847. Hope Mss.
[44] Hope to Baring, July 17, 1843, enclosing reply of chargé d'affaires of July 10, 1843. Baring Mss.
[45] Florida Senate Journal, 1843, p. 64.
[46] Journal of Legislative Council of Florida, 1843, pp. 41, 74, 75.
[47] Florida Senate Journal, 1843, p. 105.

and injury they have brought upon the country." The House tabled the Senate resolutions and the subject was dropped.[48] At the same time these resolutions were passed the legislature enacted a stay law allowing debtors of the banks to extend the payment of their debts over a period of two years.[49] This made it impossible for the banks to collect their outstanding debts in order to meet their own engagements. In protecting the domestic debtor, the legislature had only made it more difficult for the foreign creditor to recover his funds.

In desperation the foreign creditors sought to induce the federal government to assume the debts. In 1847 Forstall presented another memorial to Congress in behalf of Hope and Company and other holders of Bank of Pensacola bonds. This was referred to the Senate Judiciary Committee who reported that "neither the United States nor the State of Florida" were "in anywise responsible for these bonds." The committee recommended that the memorial be referred to the attorney general and secretary of the treasury for investigation; but no report was ever rendered by these officials.[50]

When the Anglo-American Claims Convention of 1853 met to settle the claims of British and American subjects, the case of the Union Bank bondholders was presented by Palmer, MacKillop, Dent and Company. Their claim was denied by the umpire, Joshua Bates. He quoted the four securities enumerated in the prospectus issued when the bonds were sold as showing that "not the slightest allusion" had been made at that time "to the liability of the United States." "The bondholders have," continued Bates, "a just claim on the State of Florida; they have lent their money at a fair rate of interest and the State is bound by every principle of honor to pay interest and principal; and it is to be hoped that sooner or later the people of Florida will discover that honesty is the best policy; and that no State can be called respectable that does not honorably fulfil its engagements." [51]

[48] Florida Legislative Council Journal, 1843, pp. 41, 74, 75, 162, 163, 174, 175; Florida Senate Journal, 1843, pp. 105, 117, 144, 145.
[49] Meinertzhagen to Huth, Apr. 8, 1843. Huth Mss.
[50] Senate Doc., 29 Cong., 2 Sess., Vol. 3, p. 163.
[51] Senate Doc. No. 103, 34 Cong., 1 Sess., Vol. 15, pp. 297-300.

CHAPTER XII

ARKANSAS AND FOREIGN INVESTORS

THE public debt of Arkansas in the 'forties was incurred through the issuance of state bonds in favor of the Real Estate Bank and the State Bank of Arkansas. These banks subsequently failed; and foreign creditors called upon the state to meet the payment of the bonds issued in favor of these institutions. One of the large holders of the Real Estate Bank bonds was James Holford of London. Arkansas denied her liability for the payment of the bonds held by Holford on the ground that the Real Estate Bank in negotiating the sale of these securities had violated the state statute authorizing their issuance. At the close of the Reconstruction period Arkansas repudiated a large portion of her public debt; and among the bonds disallowed by the state at this time were those held by the administrators of the Holford estate. No attempt will be made in this chapter to discuss the financial troubles of Arkansas after the Civil War or the forces which impelled the state to disavow the Reconstruction debts or the Holford claims. But in order to understand the final adjustment of the indebtedness of Arkansas in the 'eighties it is necessary to review the origin of the Holford debt and the earlier financial misfortunes of Arkansas. Such an account reveals the extent to which some American bankers evaded the provisions of state statutes in the disposal of state stocks; the assurances given foreign capitalists of the undoubted security behind Arkansas bonds; the lack of careful investigation by some European financiers in accepting these securities; and the difficulties encountered by a typical frontier community in attempting to deal with monetary questions in a period of economic and political unrest.

The Real Estate Bank and the State Bank of Arkansas were established in response to a popular demand for banking institutions. Like all frontier communities, there was a dearth of circulating medium in Arkansas. Other western states had remedied this situation by creating state banks of issue; and naturally the example set by her neighbors reacted upon the inhabitants of Arkansas and increased the clamor for similar institutions. It is not strange, therefore, that the constitution adopted by Arkansas upon its admission into the Union provided that "the General Assembly may incorporate one State Bank, with such amount of capital as may be deemed necessary, and such number of branches as may be required for public convenience, which shall become the repository for funds belonging to or under the control of the state; and shall be required to loan them throughout the state and in each county in proportion to representation. And they shall further have power to incorporate one other banking institution calculated to aid and promote the great agricultural interests of the country; and the faith and credit of the state may be pledged to raise the funds necessary to carry into operation the two banks herein specified." [1]

When the first legislature assembled, Governor Conway urged the establishment of banks in accordance with the constitutional requirements. A joint committee on banking was appointed by the legislature and the report submitted by this committee dwelt upon the anticipated advantages of a banking system. The committee maintained that the creation of banks would benefit the agricultural, manufacturing, and commercial interests—in fact, all classes of the community. Had not South Carolina, Georgia, and Alabama established banks; and had they not derived great advantages from such institutions? Why should Arkansas, therefore, hesitate? Certainly the present period was "a most auspicious" moment, for the state could "borrow any desirable amount of capital at an annual charge of five percentum" and loan it out "at eight percentum per annum." If the legislature did not charter the banks asked for, Arkansas would be set back "at least twenty years." There was no question that a State Bank would be of "infinite value to the State"; and when all things were considered it was evident that the only objections to banks were "idle prejudices so commonly entertained against banking institutions" which were founded upon a "want of sufficient information" of their "beneficial effects." Notwith-

---

[1] Poore, B. P., Federal and State Constitutions, Pt. I, p. 114.

standing this enthusiastic endorsement of the proposition, three senators objected; but their opposition was silenced by the popular clamor for banks.[2]

To meet this demand the first act passed by the legislature was an act to establish the Real Estate Bank; and the second was an act to establish the State Bank of Arkansas. On October 26, 1836 the governor approved the act for the establishment of the Real Estate Bank. By the provisions of this law the original capital of the bank was $2,000,000. This was to be raised by "loans or negotiations on the security of real property at its cash value, with the guaranty of the public credit." To secure the loan of $2,000,000 the books of the bank were to be opened for subscriptions to the sum of $2,250,000, divided into shares of $100 each. The institution was to consist of a principal bank and three branches until such time as the legislature, or petition of the stockholders might deem it expedient to enlarge its capital and establish other branches. In order to facilitate the bank in negotiating the loan of $2,000,000, the faith and credit of the state was pledged for the security of the capital and interest; and the governor was authorized to issue two thousand bonds of $1,000 each, payable in twenty-five years, and bearing interest at the rate of 5 percent. Both the capital and interest of these bonds were to be paid by the bank; and the law specifically stated that the bonds should not be disposed of below their par value.

On November 2, 1836 the governor approved the act for the incorporation of the State Bank of Arkansas. The capital of this bank was to be $1,000,000; and was to be raised by the sale of bonds of the state. The faith and credit of the state was pledged for the payment of the principal and interest of the million dollar loan. When the legislature passed these acts the population of Arkansas was about 50,000 and the total value of its wealth was not in excess of $15,000,000. The entire debt of Arkansas at the beginning of the legislative session was less than $9,000; but before the legislature had adjourned, it had involved the state in debt to the extent of more than $3,000,000 and "had created a debt for each

---

[2] Journals of the General Assembly of Arkansas, 1837, p. 52; Messages and Doc. of Arkansas, 1856, pp. 11, 12.

white person in the State, man, woman, and child of over $63 per capita." [3]

Unfortunately the time was inauspicious for the launching of new banks. In the spring of 1837 all the banking institutions in this country suspended specie payments. This closed both the domestic and foreign markets for all American securities. The Commissioner of Indian Affairs had agreed to take 300 of the State Bank bonds; but on account of the financial stringency he purchased only 100. [4] The Arkansas banks were further handicapped in the disposal of their bonds because the state was a newcomer in the money markets. As Frederick Huth, the English banker, wrote one of his American correspondents the stock of Arkansas was unknown in London and it would be difficult to dispose of any of the Arkansas bonds unless the interest and capital were made payable in London and a favorable report was received of the financial condition of the state. [5]

At a special session of the legislature in November 1837 the governor commented upon the difficulties encountered by the Arkansas banks in disposing of the state bonds. To assist the Real Estate Bank, the governor suggested that the rate of interest be raised from 5 percent to 6 percent. At the same time the president of the bank in a report to the legislature assured the public that they would "never be called upon to pay either the principal or the interest of these bonds." He pointed out that the stockholders had mortgaged to the state 127,500 acres of land valued at $2,603,000. "When it is taken into consideration," wrote the president, "the State has a lien on $603,900 worth of property, more than her own guaranty amounts to, and against which she could have recourse at any time, in the event of that necessity. And when it is further taken into consideration that these lands which stand as permanent security to the state, are among *the very best in the United States* . . . it cannot be doubted . . . that every candid individual of this community will be fully satisfied that the security furnished by the stockholders of the Real Estate Bank is so full and ample, that, had it not been cheerfully offered by the stockholders themselves, it could in truth be said it is so far beyond what is actually necessary for that secu-

[3] Worthen, W. B., Early Banking in Arkansas, 1837, pp. 5-18, 43-51, 55, 56; Thomas, D. Y., Arkansas and its People, Vol. 1, p. 355.
[4] Arkansas House Journal, 1837, pp. 182, 238; Thomas, *op. cit.*, Vol. 1, p. 357.
[5] Huth to Perit, Nov. 22, 1837. Huth Mss.

rity, that it would be injustice in the State to ask it from the citizens." Probably influenced by these statements the legislature on December 19, 1837 not only raised the rate to 6 percent; but on February 24, 1838 established a new branch in the western part of the state. To supply the working capital for the new member, the governor was authorized to issue 500 bonds of $1,000 each and to pledge the faith and credit of the state for their payment.[6]

In May 1838 the New York and New England banks resumed specie payments. This helped to restore confidence in the money markets; and in August of that year the State Bank of Arkansas succeeded in selling $1,000,000 of its bonds to the North American Trust and Banking Company of New York. By the terms of this contract the company agreed to pay $103.67½ for each $100 of stock, making in the aggregate the sum of $1,036,750. Fifty thousand dollars was to be paid in specie and $250,000 was to be placed to the credit of the principal bank and its three branches upon the execution of the contract. The remainder was to be paid in 14 monthly installments ranging from $51,000 in January 1839 to $54,250 in February 1841. Seven-nineteenths of the last 14 payments were to be placed to the credit of the principal bank and the residue, in equal proportions, to each of the three branches at the time specified.[7] A month later the Real Estate Bank disposed of 1,530 of its bonds at par. Five hundred of these bonds were taken by the Secretary of the Treasury of the United States to be held in trust for the Smithsonian Institute. One thousand bonds of $1,000 each were taken by the North American Trust and Banking Company and thirty bonds were purchased by Richard M. Johnson of Kentucky.[8] At the November session of the legislature, the president of the State Bank reported the sale to the North American Trust and Banking Company and congratulated the negotiators upon receiving "terms even better than anticipated."[9]

On December 12, 1838 the principal office of the Real Estate

---

[6] Messages and Doc. of Ark., 1856, pp. 11-19; Worthen, *op. cit.*, p. 22.

[7] Journals of the House and Senate of Arkansas, App. E, 1838.

[8] Messages and Doc. of Arkansas, 1856, pp. 11-19; Bolcher, W., Early Banking in Arkansas, pp. 5, 6. In 1876 Bolcher declared that the Real Estate Bank bonds purchased by the Secretary of the Treasury were still in the possession of the federal government, with unpaid interest from 1842 to the present time, with the exception of such amounts as have been retained by the government due the state on account of the five percent fund arising from the sale of the public lands.

[9] Journals of the House and Senate of Arkansas, 1838, pp. 350-357.

Bank opened its doors for business; and in less than a month had made loans and discounts to the amount of $568,290.92. Within a few months the branches began operations; and by October 31, 1839 the combined loans and discounts of the main office and branches amounted to $1,585,190.80. The following month the principal bank at Little Rock suspended specie payments; and similar action was quickly taken by the branches. According to a proclamation issued at this time by the cashier of the bank this move was taken in order to carry into execution "a prudent expansion of the currency" and "to avoid a too stinted accommodation to the public," which would be necessary "as long as the bank paid specie." [10]

Years later William M. Gouge and W. R. Miller, state accountants appointed to investigate the affairs of the Real Estate Bank, claimed that the bank suspended specie payments for entirely different reasons from those given by the cashier. The accountants pointed out that the suspension occurred at the time "the first installment on the stock notes was falling due. The stockholders and others owed also on accommodation notes many of which were overdue. It had been very easy to borrow from the bank. It was not so easy to pay back even a part of what had been borrowed." By suspending specie payments the bank "need not press for payment what had been lent"; on the contrary the bank "could grant new accommodations to its customers." To substantiate these charges the accountants called attention to the rapid expansion of the bank's circulation and the increasing number of loans and discounts made during the period of suspension. By November 1, 1840 the loans and discounts amounted to $2,158,869.57 while the preceding November they were only $1,585,190.80. [11]

While the Real Estate Bank pursued its policy of a "prudent expansion of the currency," the collection of sufficient funds to pay the interest on the state bonds became increasingly difficult. To meet this and other pressing demands, the officials of the bank evolved a scheme to dispose of the remaining unsold bonds without violating the letter of the state statute which prohibited their sale below par. On July 20, 1840 the cashier of the bank was instructed to proceed to New York and "to make arrangements, negotiations, and contracts for and on account of the bank, to hypothecate,

[10] Messages and Doc. of Arkansas, 1856, pp. 11-19.   [11] *Ibid.*

pledge, and make conditional and positive sale of the state bonds" belonging to the bank and "to use and pledge the name, credit, and assets of the bank, in any way or manner which he may think proper and necessary for the credit and welfare of the institution." In conformity with these instructions the cashier on October 7, 1840 hypothecated $500,000 of the state bonds with the North American Trust and Banking Company, expecting to obtain $250,000 but in reality receiving only $121,336.59. This was a violation of the ninth section of the bank's charter which prohibited all sales below par and conferred no authority upon any agent of the bank to pledge the bonds as collateral.[12]

The North American Trust and Banking Company succeeded in inducing a number of British bankers to take some of the bonds the company held. The transactions of this company with Frederick Huth and Company of London who ultimately agreed to take $660,000 of the Arkansas stock reveals the arguments advanced by their high-pressure salesmen in disposing of the Arkansas securities and the difficulties encountered by English financiers in dealing with unscrupulous American bankers. On March 14, 1839 Huth was requested by an agent of the North American Trust and Banking Company to make an offer for $500,000 of the Arkansas bonds; or for an amount not less than $300,000 with the privilege of selling the remainder on commission. The agent pointed out that the United States government had purchased $500,000 of the bonds at par "as an investment." This was "sufficient evidence" of the estimation in which Arkansas stock was held "by an authority the most competent to judge of its security." Attention was also called to the fact that Florida bonds were then selling in London at 95. "Without wishing in any way to detract from that security," wrote the agent to Huth, "I need hardly remind you that Florida is a territory whereas Arkansas is a state possessing vast resources."[13]

At length on May 24, 1839 Huth signed a contract agreeing to take $500,000 of the State Bank bonds and $100,000 of the Real Estate Bank bonds. In consideration of their being appointed agents for the payments connected with these bonds, Huth purchased on their own account $200,000 of the bonds at 95 with an allowance

[12] Ibid., Arkansas House Journal, 1842, App., pp. 33-35.
[13] Curtis to Huth, March 14, 1839. Huth Mss.

of 3½ percent as commission for their services. The purchase price of £41,175 was to be paid in five monthly installments beginning in July. Messers Palmer, MacKillop, Dent and Company likewise agreed to purchase $100,000 of the bonds on exactly the same terms. The remaining $300,000 were placed in the hands of Huth on consignment to be sold on account of the North American Trust and Banking Company at a price not less than 91½ net. The proceeds of the sales of $100,000 of this stock was to be credited to the company. The remaining $200,000 was pledged as collateral security for a drawing credit of £32,000 on Huth and Company; and this credit was to continue until Huth was able to sell the bonds but on no account beyond twelve months from the date of the agreement. The interest and capital on the bonds were to be in the hands of Huth and Company at least one month before they fell due; and it was understood that as far as circumstances permitted the Arkansas banks were to make their remittances in cotton consigned to the Liverpool house of Huth and Company.[14] This contract clearly reveals that the North American Trust and Banking Company hypothecated Arkansas bonds abroad in direct violation of the state statutes over a year before the Real Estate Bank violated their charter by pledging bonds with the North American Trust and Banking Company.

In order to convince Huth and Company of the undoubted security behind the Arkansas bonds, Murray, the agent of the North American Trust and Banking Company, on June 18, 1839 sent the firm a letter which he had written to a prospective purchaser. Murray sent this inquirer a copy of the charter of the Real Estate Bank "with certificates from the Treasury and War Departments of the United States showing their confidence by actual investments to a very large amount in these bonds." "The nature of these securities," wrote Murray, "is of a very high order, not only having the faith and property of a young, vigorous, and triumphant state pledged for their redemption, but also the effects of the Bank itself." A transcript of this letter was sent to Huth "to make such use as he might think proper." In view of these statements it is not strange that Huth and Company issued a prospectus stressing the great resources of Arkansas. Investors were assured that every dollar

[14] Murray to Huth, May 29, 1839. Huth Mss.

borrowed by the planters of the State Bank would be expended to augment the security of the stock; and that the bank which was also liable for the amount of the bonds, was in successful operation.[15]

By the fall of 1839 Huth was finding it difficult to enforce the provisions of this contract. Kindermann, a partner of the firm then in America, informed the home office that no one in this country could see how the governments of the new states could raise the means of paying the interest on their stocks. "As for laying taxes upon their thin and semi-barbarous population," wrote Kindermann, "it seems quite out of the question and the very idea is treated with ridicule."[16] This evidently alarmed Huth, especially as he was unable to receive any replies from the Arkansas banks respecting the payments of the dividends due January 1, 1840. At length on December 6, 1839 the North American Trust and Banking Company forwarded 30 additional Arkansas bonds of $1,000 each with the request that Huth sell these bonds and apply the proceeds to the payment of the coupons. Huth protested that this was contrary to the terms of the contract. As it was utterly impossible to sell any American securities, Huth advanced the January interest to satisfy their customers and retained the bonds as security.[17] About the same time Kindermann informed the London office that it was understood the Arkansas banks were in good condition; but "the people of Arkansas," wrote this caustic critic, "do not bear the best character. They are considered the scum of the population of the southwestern states in which generally morals stand at a low discount."[18] Huth was soon forced to reprimand the North American Trust and Banking Company a second time for their interpretation of the terms of the agreement. The company overdrew its credit with Huth although the contract specifically limited their drawing account to twelve months after the agreement was signed.[19] Yet on March 16, 1840, Huth received a letter from the State Bank of Arkansas in which the president of that institution claimed that the bank had sent the necessary funds to the North American Trust and Banking Company for the payment of the January dividends and that the company had

[15] Murray to Huth (with enclosure), June 18, 1839; Huth Prospectus. Huth Mss.
[16] Kindermann to Huth, Oct. 31, 1839. Huth Mss.
[17] Huth to Beers, Dec. 6, 1839. Huth Mss.
[18] Kindermann to Huth, Jan. 17, 1840. Huth Mss.
[19] Huth to Beers, Jan. 18, 1840. Huth Mss.

deviated from the instructions given them in sending additional bonds to Huth.[20]

Huth's difficulties with the North American Trust and Banking Company are illuminating of the manner in which this company lived up to the terms of its engagements. In its dealings with James Holford, a private banker of London, the business methods of this company are further revealed. In 1841 the North American Trust and Banking Company pledged the $500,000 of Real Estate Bank bonds which had been hypothecated with them to Holford as security for a loan of $325,000. Holford afterwards claimed that he was totally ignorant of the fact that the company was not in actual possession of these bonds when they were transferred to him; and he confessed "he had never seen nor thought it necessary to see the charter of the Real Estate Bank or the law authorizing the loan" when he accepted these securities. He endeavored to excuse his negligence upon the ground that "it would fetter all trade and commerce in the United States if every individual was chargeable with a knowledge of the statute law of the twenty-six states in the Union and the various and conflicting amendments of that law which are made from year to year." [21] This was a weak argument as Holford must have realized; but it sheds much light upon the lack of precaution exercised by some British bankers in accepting American state securities without carefully investigating the circumstances surrounding the issuance and negotiation of the loans. Shortly after the transfer of these bonds the North American Trust and Banking Company became insolvent.

In the meantime the political and economic situation in Arkansas was growing serious. In 1840 Governor Archibald Yell, the implacable foe of all banks, began his assaults upon the Arkansas banks. An investigation of the banks was ordered by the legislature; but the report submitted by the committee defended their suspension of specie payments and expressed complete confidence in their solvency.[22] It was later claimed "that some of the members of the legislature were so much in debt to the Real Estate Bank that an honest investigation was impossible." The judiciary committee of the House reported that the legislature "had no right to examine the affairs of

[20] Huth to Field, March 16, 1840. Huth Mss.
[21] Arkansas House Journal, 1842, App., pp. 29-35.
[22] Arkansas House and Senate Journal, 1840, 3 Sess., p. 98.

the Real Estate Bank and its branches." [23] Apparently the action of the legislature enraged the governor for he renewed his attacks with increased vigor.

That the banks were not in a sound condition was soon disclosed. In January 1841 the State Bank made its last interest payment; and in July the Real Estate Bank defaulted upon its payments. In September the Real Estate Bank issued a statement warning the public that the bank would not be responsible for the payment of the principal and interest on the bonds held by Holford on the ground that the North American Trust and Banking Company had no authority to assign these bonds to third parties. The company immediately replied through the columns of the *New York Herald* that the Real Estate Bank was fully aware that the bonds had been hypothecated. [24]

In the election of 1842 the anti-bank party was victorious. Only seven of the representatives who had sat in the session of 1840 were reëlected. Fearing the possibilities of an investigation the Real Estate Bank on April 2, 1842 made an assignment of all of its assets to fifteen trustees "all of whom held official positions in the Bank." These fifteen trustees owed the bank $151,425.32 as principal and were sureties of notes of others for $145,227.30, making a total liability of $296,652.52." [25]

Meanwhile Holford and Governor Yell were carrying on an extended correspondence. On October 2, 1841 Holford wrote to the governor inquiring what steps he should take in order to secure payment of the overdue July dividends and also to recover the money he had advanced upon the bonds in his possession. It was quite evident that Holford was seeking to induce the governor to recognize a liability upon the part of the state for the payment of these bonds. In his reply Governor Yell declared that Arkansas was neither legally nor morally bound to pay these bonds since the charter of the bank specifically prohibited their sale below par. "You will find the people of Arkansas as sensitive in their regard for honesty and punctuality as those of any state in the Union," wrote the governor. "But it would be absurd to suppose and you mistake the character of the people, if you flatter yourself that they will calmly submit to be

[23] Herndon, D. T., Centennial History of Arkansas, Vol. I, p. 484.
[24] *Arkansas Gazette*, Oct. 13, 1841.
[25] Herndon, *op. cit.*, Vol. I, p. 484.

taxed to pay the bonds hypothecated to stocks jobbers, to enable the bank to carry on her speculations without the authority of law and in express violation of her charter."

From this strictly legalistic position Governor Yell never deviated. He maintained the contract was null and void since the bank possessed no power to dispose of them below par. On the other hand Holford argued not on the basis of his legal rights but on the ground of justice and equity that the state should recognize his claims. He suggested that the question should be referred to the courts for decision. Governor Yell refused to refer the subject to any other tribunal than the legislature; and declared that "the irritation produced by the insulting tone of a few pensioned papers of the country in regard to the repudiation of the bonds illegally and fraudulently sold or disposed of is not well calculated to place their claims on higher ground. Arkansas is free to act," defiantly announced the governor, "as she shall deem it fit and correct. Her unsullied faith and unaided sense of justice will prompt her to her duty. All menace and abuse will be met and treated as it shall deserve." [26]

At the November session Governor Yell laid before the legislature his correspondence with Holford on the subject of the liability of the state for the payment of the Holford bonds. "However much we may value the applause and good opinions of other nations," stated the governor, "we have a perfect reliance on our wisdom and virtue . . . ; and independence enough to spurn with scorn any who attempt to defraud and swindle her citizens." In the estimation of the governor the Real Estate Bank had violated and forfeited its charter by its actions. In the first place the bank had failed to provide for the payment of the interest on the state bonds. It had also perverted the facts in its report to the last legislature where the bank stated it still had possession of the bonds although they had actually been hypothecated with the North American Trust and Banking Company in express violation of the charter. Furthermore there was a question whether the bank had not forfeited its charter by assigning all of its assets to trustees. By this assignment the whole responsibility for the payment of the bonds had been thrown upon the

[26] The correspondence carried on by Holford and Gov. Yell can be found in Arkansas House Journal, 1842, App., pp. 7, 8, 26-39.

state. To meet these payments the people would have to submit to heavy taxation. "We are left," declared the governor, "either to suffer in credit, or to oppress the citizens to sustain a worthless corporation." [27]

The legislature sustained the governor. The auditor's report clearly showed that Arkansas was in no position to meet these obligations. During the past year the state had collected in revenue $173,769.10; but the total expenditures were $169,822.65, leaving a balance in the treasury on October 1, 1842, of $3,946.45. At that time the Real Estate Bank owed interest on the state bonds to the amount of $91,169.64; of which the sum of $80,601 was payable in New York and $10,568.64 in London. The State Bank owed $58,331.87 of unpaid interest on its bonds, $30,000 of which was payable in London and the remainder in New York. Thus the total amount of interest due and unpaid on the state bonds issued to these banks was $149,501.51. [28]

The economic distress then existing in Arkansas and the popular hatred toward the banks is vividly portrayed in a letter written at this time by the president of the Real Estate Bank to the North American Trust and Banking Company. In this letter, Davies, the bank president, candidly confessed that there was no hope of any payment on the state bonds for some years. Taxation of the people was out of the question. "Ours is a community (at least the mass of it)," wrote Davies, "that knows nothing of monied or commercial transactions; they do not and cannot understand the moral force of sustaining the public faith; and in the legislature there is neither moral courage nor political honesty enough to do it; so far from it, to advocate the reverse position is the demagogic stepping stone to political preferment." During the past six years the population of the state had barely doubled itself while the resources of the state had not been developed even in proportion to the increase in the number of the inhabitants. Consequently it was oppressive to collect even the amount required to meet the contingent expenses of the state government. It was, therefore, impossible to expect anything through legislation. The only hope was that the resources of the banks might prove sufficient; but this depended upon the ability

[27] Arkansas House Journal, 1842, App., pp. 7, 8, 25.
[28] Ibid. pp. 16-20.

and solvency of their debtors. Small debtors, however, were unable to pay, while the larger ones, the stockholders, who could pay something would not do so until they could purchase these bonds or "bank paper for something like twenty-five cents on the dollar." Naturally, the North American Trust and Banking Company would ask: Why not sue them and make them pay? "From such a course," wrote Davies, "we would gain nothing but to entail bankruptcy on every individual whose property was brought under the hammer." There was no money in the country and even though Davies acknowledged that his own county would ship that year 15,000 bales of cotton he felt confident that if the negro or personal property of the planters were put up for sale in the spring after the crops were disposed of, they would not command 25 percent of what they cost two years ago. Real estate was not worth ten percent of its value five years previous. Even after a suit was commenced, two or three years would elapse before the little money the property would sell for could be realized. Under these circumstances all the banks could do was to use all their exertions to keep the debts due them as secure as possible, save what they could, and wait until either time relieved them or buried all under one general wreck. There was no way in which the bankers could exert political pressure to avert these evils, "for nothing but suspicion and prejudice followed the individual whose life, either public or private, has been blended with them however much he may have been impelled to act by the public voice or however honest may have been his motives or intentions. It is enough," concluded Davies, "that he can no longer feed the public man to condemn him. Scarcely an individual of us who was in the legislature of 1837 when the banks in this state were chartered is now permitted to occupy a public station; we are left in fact perfectly powerless." [29]

The courts of Arkansas did not succumb to the anti-bank and repudiation sentiment then sweeping over the state. In April 1842 an application was made by the trustees of the Real Estate Bank requesting the Chancellor of the Chancery Court to issue a writ of mandamus to the Judge of the Fifth Judicial Circuit Court commanding him to grant an injunction restraining certain stockholders from interfering with the trustees in the disposal of property and

[29] Davies to Beers, Dec. 6, 1842. Huth Mss.

assets of the corporation. The Chancellor refused to grant the injunction "for want of jurisdiction." The trustees then presented their petition to the Supreme Court of Arkansas which granted their request. In delivering their opinion the Court said: "The assets of the bank are required to be realized as fast as practicable by the trustees; and forthwith, after the receipt of money arising from any source, the funds are to be applied in the payment of the debts in the following manner and order: (1) paying all balances due the officers of the bank; (2) the deposits; (3) calling in the outstanding circulation; (4) the interest upon all State bonds, except those hypothecated to the North American Trust and Banking Company; (5) bonuses due the State; (6) the principal of all the State bonds, except those hypothecated; (7) whatever is legally due upon the bonds hypothecated. The fourth and sixth clauses are to be paid rateably." In reference to the Holford bonds, the Court stated: "The bank is liable for these as well as the other bonds. Should her assets, however, unfortunately prove insufficient, then the State is responsible for whatever amount is justly and equitably owing by her; and the holders of these bonds as well as those of our public securities need be under no apprehension but that she will faithfully and honorable discharge to the utmost farthing, all her engagements, regardless alike whether they be in the hands of foreign or domestic capitalists. The principles of private virtue, as well as of public justice (which we are confident our citizens and our government will ever respect and obey) utterly forbid the idea that this young, free, and prosperous State, will ever permit one jot or tittle of her plighted faith or recorded honor to fall to the ground."

A motion for reconsideration of this opinion and judgment was refused by the Court. A second motion for re-argument and re-hearing was pressed by the respondents and a letter of Governor Yell's was read in the Court requesting the Court to set aside its judgment on the ground that the judgment would place "the assets and management of the bank beyond the reach of the State" and that the interests of the people of Arkansas were involved in the manner in which the institution was controlled. Upon this the Court became highly indignant and declared: "It is for the Legislature to *declare* the public will, the Judiciary to *interpret* and the Executive to *enforce* it. If the Executive department shall so far lose sight of its boundaries as to *encroach* upon or *usurp* the powers of the Judiciary, or attempt under a pretext of a deep interest in the general welfare, to influence its judgment or control its action, such interference shall be repelled with firmness but with dignity. I have discovered no sufficient cause," stated Judge Dickinson, "to justify me in disturbing the judgment of the Court as heretofore announced; and as I cannot without compromising the independence of the Tribunal, recognize the right of the Executive to interpose his wishes or opinions upon a matter already solemnly adjudicated, the motion must be refused." [30]

To Huth and other holders of Arkansas bonds this decision was satisfactory in so far as it did not make an exception to any of the bonds which they held. [31] But they had received no dividends on their Real Estate bonds since July 1, 1841. In order to bring this to the attention of the legislature a memorial was sent by the foreign bondholders to the governor with a request that he lay it before the General Assembly. In this memorial the bondholders stressed the fact that they had purchased these securities because the faith and credit of the state was pledged and because the United States government had invested a large amount of trust money in the same stock. The memorial also stated that many of the bondholders were dependent upon their subsistence "on the punctual payment of the interest, having few or no other sources of income." [32]

In his message of November 1844, Governor Adams referred to this communication. The governor declared the state was in no condition to pay off the interest which had already accrued on the state bonds; and he refused to recommend an increase in taxation on the ground that the people were already overburdened with taxes. He suggested, however, that the means and assets of the banks be applied to discharge the interest "upon all such bonds as had been sold in good faith and in strict accordance with the bank charters." [33]

This recommendation was endorsed in a report of the Ways and Means Committee to whom the bondholders memorial was referred.

[30] Arkansas Reports, Vol. 4, pp. 302-408; cf. also comments on this decision in *Arkansas Gazette*, Jan. 25, 1843.

[31] Meinertzhagen to Huth, Feb. 14, 1843. Huth Mss.

[32] Arkansas House Journal, 1844-1845, App., pp. 79-81.   [33] *Ibid.*, pp. 54, 55.

The committee declared that "the people nor the legislature which authorized the issuance of the bonds never contemplated a direct tax to pay either principal or interest, until the assets and means of the banks" had first been exhausted. Furthermore the imposition of such a tax at that particular time would be "extremely unjust, onerous, and oppressive"; and would tend to retard the growth of the state, thus making it forever impossible for the state to redeem these bonds. The committee therefore proposed that as both of the banks were then in liquidation, the officers of both of these institutions should be authorized "to take in payment of the debts due the banks, the bonds of the state or to exchange property with holders of the bonds at fair and equitable rates. If it be charged," stated the committee, "that the state is acting in bad faith to the bondholders, we reply that we have tried to preserve inviolate the means and assets of the banks for the purpose of liquidating the claims against them, and the State bonds issued for their benefit; and it was to these means that all parties looked for the payment of the principal at the time the bonds were negotiated." [34] This report was unanimously adopted; and in 1858 was cited by Gouge and Rutherford, state accountants appointed to investigate the Real Estate Bank as evidence of the good intentions of the people of Arkansas "even in the darkest times of their adversity." [35]

Notwithstanding these "good intentions," little progress was made in liquidating the state debt. In 1851 the governor openly acknowledged that the people were unable to pay; and suggested that the solution of this problem be left to future generations. [36]

During the 'fifties, however, Arkansas began to contemplate the building of railroads. This stimulated a renewed interest in the payment of the old debts. Some of the people of Arkansas began to agitate the refunding of the state debt. It was proposed that the legislature issue new bonds for the principal and interest the dividends on those representing the former to begin in five years, and those on the latter in ten years. These new bonds were to be made payable respectively in twenty-five and thirty years. At the same time the legislature should pass a resolution declaring that the

[34] Arkansas Senate Journal, 1846, pp. 268, 269.
[35] Quoted in Worthen, Early Banking in Arkansas, p. 94.
[36] Hunt's Merchants' Magazine, Vol. 24, p. 111.

present rate of taxation would not be reduced until the entire debt was paid. The advocates of this scheme urged its adoption not only from the standpoint of state pride but also because it was to the interest of the people to meet their obligations. In sponsoring this plan the *Arkansas Gazette* pointed out that there were few states in the Union where the taxes were not higher than in Arkansas. In some of the states, the taxes for education alone were more than Arkansas levied for all purposes. In 1854 the people of Arkansas were taxed ¼ of one percent which on 80 acres of land amounted to 60 cents a year. This was less than a farmer in Arkansas spent each week "for tobacco, whiskey, or some other useless luxury or extravagance." The hue and cry against higher taxes did not come, however, from the poorer classes. According to the *Arkansas Gazette*, it was the rich who owned large tracts of land, and the speculators who opposed all attempts to increase the taxes. "There are persons in the State," bluntly declared the *Arkansas Gazette*, "who own and control over 100,000 acres." It was this group who were interested in keeping the taxes low without regard to the effects upon the state. But these forces were too well organized; and all efforts at refunding the old debts or raising the taxes failed.[37]

The advocates of resumption were also handicapped by the difficulties encountered in adjusting the affairs of the banks. The control of the Real Estate Bank was in the hands of the trustees; and all attempts to find out the actual condition of the bank by the state proved fruitless. Naturally this did not make the public more willing to listen to suggestions looking toward the state assuming some of these obligations. In 1856 Governor Conway declared that the mortgaged lands held by the Real Estate Bank were sufficient, owing to their increased value, to pay off the whole debt of the state; and he recommended that steps should be taken to make them available for that purpose. But the legislature declined to follow the governor's suggestions.[38]

Even the increased prosperity of Arkansas did not lessen the public opposition to the payment of the Holford bonds. Holford

[37] *Arkansas Gazette and Democrat*, July 21, 1854.
[38] Hunt's Merchants' Magazine, Vol. 36, p. 541.

tried unsuccessfully in 1850 to induce the legislature to work out a funding scheme; but the representatives were reluctant to listen to any suggestion from a foreign creditor. Upon his death, a few years later, the administrators of the estate determined to employ more aggressive measures. In 1854 Joseph D. Beers and William A. Platenius, the administrator of the Holford estate in America, brought suit in the Pulaski Court. After the suit was brought and while it was pending in the Circuit Court, the legislature passed an act which provided that in every suit brought to enforce the collection of the principal or interest of any bond issued by the state, before judgment could be rendered, the original bonds should be produced and filed in the office of the clerk; and if this was not done, the court should dismiss the case.[39] As the plaintiff refused to file the bond, the Pulaski Court dismissed the case. This judgment was afterward affirmed in the Supreme Court of Arkansas; and on a writ of error was brought before the United States Supreme Court. In delivering the opinion of this tribunal, Chief Justice Taney held "that the sovereign cannot be sued in its own courts without its consent and permission"; but that "it may preserve the terms and conditions upon which it consents to be sued and may withdraw its consent whenever it may suppose that justice to the public requires it." Chief Justice Taney, therefore, dismissed the case on the ground that the Court had no jurisdiction to override the legislative decree of a state.[40]

In 1862 the legality of the issue was brought before the Supreme Court of Arkansas. In rendering his decision, Chief Justice E. H. English pointed out that as the ninth section of the charter of the Real Estate Bank prohibited the sale of the bonds at less than their par value, the pledging of the bonds by the bank to the North American Trust and Banking Company "was a transaction illegal and void." Nevertheless the Court held that "the bank, having thought proper to receive and appropriate to its use the money advanced to the agents of the New York banking company upon a pledge of the bonds, it is just and reasonable to conclude that the bank thereby became bound in equity and good conscience to repay

[39] Arkansas Laws, 1854, p. 17.
[40] Howard, U. S. Supreme Court Reports, Vol. 20, pp. 528-530.

the money so advanced to it." [41] This decision failed to dispose of the troublesome Holford claims; and after the Civil War the people of Arkansas were again to be called upon to determine the liability of the state for these bonds along with numerous other issues of state bonds. The final disposition of the Holford bonds will, therefore, be discussed in the chapter dealing with the financial problems of Arkansas arising out of the Reconstruction era.

[41] Williams, Arkansas Reports, Vol. 24, pp. 22-30.

CHAPTER XIII

THE AFTERMATH OF DEFALCATION AND REPUDIATION
BEFORE THE CIVIL WAR

IN the spring of 1847 Prime, Ward and Company issued a statement based on official documents summarizing the status of the public debts of the various American states on January 1 of that year. Of the twenty-six states and one territory which then composed the Union the following ten had no public debt: Maine, New Hampshire, Vermont, Rhode Island, Connecticut, New Jersey, Delaware, North Carolina, Iowa, and the Territory of Wisconsin. The District of Columbia also was without any public debt while that of Missouri was less than one million dollars, none of which was held in England. The following nine states had regularly paid the interest on their public debt without interruption: Massachusetts, New York, Ohio, Virginia, South Carolina, Georgia, Tennessee, Kentucky, and Alabama. The delinquent states in 1847 were Maryland, Illinois, Indiana, Michigan, Mississippi, Louisana, Arkansas, and Florida. Mississippi, Arkansas, Michigan, and Florida had repudiated either the whole or a portion of their liabilities. Pennsylvania had defaulted in August 1842; but had resumed payment in February 1845. Maryland had failed to pay in January 1842; but was on the verge of resuming payments in 1847. Illinois had ceased payment in January 1842; but in 1845 a number of her creditors had agreed to lend the state additional funds to complete the Illinois and Michigan Canal; and by 1847 Illinois had commenced to pay a part of the interest on her debt. Indiana had defaulted in July 1841; but in 1847 was negotiating with her creditors looking toward the transfer to them of the Wabash and Erie Canal. Louisiana had defaulted in December 1842 on the interest payments on the state bonds issued in favor of the property banks; and the state had made no effort up to 1847 toward the settlement of the claims of her creditors beyond passing a law enabling the debtors to the banks to pay off their indebtedness in state bonds.[1]

In view of this unfortunate state of affairs, it is not strange that foreign creditors were exasperated at the continued delinquency of some of the American states. The holders of the bonds of the defaulting states had suffered severe losses on account of the non-payment for a number of years of the interest due on their bonds; while those who held the bonds of the repudiating states had lost their entire investment. What especially enraged foreign creditors was the apparent indifference on the part of the citizens of those states which regularly met their engagements to the nonpayment of the other states. Foreigners could not understand why the former states did not bring pressure to bear upon the defaulting and repudiating states to meet their obligations. The vitriolic *London Times* indiscriminately denounced all Americans; and prophesied that the American name would not recover for half-a-century the slur which had been cast upon it by the temporary or complete failure of some of the states to pay their debts.[2] Was this actually the case? Did repudiation destroy American credit abroad for fifty years? Did it injure the standing of those states which had regularly met their engagements as well as those which refused to do so? Did foreign investors after their costly experiences with some of the American states exercise more prudence in the future in the purchase of American securities or did they display the same credulity and make the same mistakes within a relatively short space of time? These are interesting questions and can best be answered by reviewing the financial fortunes of the American states in the two decades preceding the Civil War.

When the *London Times* made the above prediction regarding the future effect of defalcation and repudiation upon American credit, there appeared to be good grounds for believing that the prophecy would be fulfilled. In 1842, it will be recalled, the United States government had found it impossible to float a loan in European money markets, notwithstanding the fact that the federal government had a long and honorable record of paying its debts. Edward Everett, United States Minister to England, warned the Secre-

---

[1] Quoted in the *London Times*, May 19, 1847; cf. also another discussion of the debts of American states in the *London Times*, Jan. 2, 1847.
[2] *Ibid.*, Sept. 6, 1847.

tary of State Webster early in May 1842 that attempts were being made beforehand to create a prejudice against the proposed United States loan. According to Everett these efforts were traceable to two causes. One was the political hostility and willingness on all occasions for Europeans to embarrass the American government. The other was the notion among the financial groups in Europe that by withholding the relief sought by the national government, British capitalists could coerce the government of the United States to make some provision for the payment of the state debts. "It is idle to attempt to combat the first," wrote Everett. As for the other idea Everett declared that it was his intention to make clear to British capitalists interested in state securities that the best policy for them to pursue was to uphold and not to destroy the credit of the federal government as nothing could be gained and everything might be lost by involving the United States Treasury in the embarrassments of state credit. Nevertheless American commissioners were unable to convince European capitalists; and the federal government failed to obtain any funds abroad.[3]

Two years later Everett in commenting on the unfriendly tone of the European press toward Americans ascribed it mainly to the efforts of those who had suffered by their investments in American stocks. "Great bitterness of feeling," wrote Everett to Webster, "is very naturally felt by individuals and they are numerous—of this class. Many of them have by their investments lost all the earning of active life and the fund on which they relied for their support in old age. That this feeling should find vent in the public press is natural. In addition to this an opinion has been formed here (London) that nothing is so likely to lead the United States to redeem their credit as strong and unanimous condemnation of default on this side of the water; the more indiscriminate these censures, the more likely are they, in the opinion of their authors, to produce the desired effect." In Everett's estimation the material injury which had thus accrued to the United States was, in all essential respects, that of a general bankruptcy. At a time when capital was so abundant that the 3 percent stocks of Europe were above par, the United States was unable to obtain a loan at any rate of interest. Everett viewed this state of affairs as a "calamity of no ordinary magni-

[3] Everett to Webster, May 6, 1842. State Dept. Mss.

tude"; and an evil so enormous as to call for the best efforts of "patriotic American statesmanship." [4]

The unwillingness of the British to invest their surplus funds in this country was disclosed in various ways. Such was the distrust of the British investors of everything American during these years owing to the delinquency of Pennsylvania and Maryland and the other defaulting states that they sold their interests in the Reading Railroad and the Lehigh Navigation Company as soon as they could and announced they would have nothing more to do with this country. [5] A circular of the Barings issued in 1846 called attention to the small number of sales abroad of American stocks, even at low prices. Furthermore the Barings declared that they anticipated no disposition upon the part of foreign investors "to purchase either old or fresh securities until the differences between the United States and Great Britain were amicably settled, and those states which were still defaulters had shown their willingness and ability to recommence and continue the regular payment of future dividends." [6] As a matter of fact old reliable banking houses in England felt as if they had lost caste with the public in recommending American securities to their clients. [7] Railroad promoters in Florida and Mississippi found it impossible to interest Hope and Company and the Barings in their proposed plans. [8] *De Bow's Review* in 1844 declared that "the suicidal act of Mississippi" had killed the credit of the slave states in Europe. Mississippi's repudiation had dragged down the public funds of Alabama, although that state had ever been true to her faith; and forgetting the delinquencies of Louisiana, the angry author of this article in the *Review* blamed Mississippi for "the lukewarmness of the London market" to the bonds of the City of New Orleans. [9]

To some Americans, this loss of credit in European money markets was not considered a great misfortune. It was claimed that the inability of Americans to borrow in England would free this

[4] Everett to Calhoun, Nov. 14, 1844. State Depart. Mss.
[5] *American Railroad Journal*, Vol. 18, p. 474.
[6] Quoted in *Niles*, Feb. 28, 1846.
[7] American Bankers Journal, Vol. I, p. 269.
[8] Jaudon to Hope, Nov. 17, 1847; Hope to Jaudon, Dec. 14, 1847. Hope Mss. Stites to Baring, Nov. 5, 1849. Baring Mss.
[9] *De Bow's Review*, Vol. 15, p. 413.

country of dependence upon foreign capitalists. For years England had been the banker or money-lender of the world. All countries had contributed to swell the overgrown wealth of England. Now this was all changed; and a significant social revolution was taking place. English investors were returning their state stocks to this country for sale although it was noticeable that they retained those of the insolvent states. The margin for improvement in these depreciated securities was so great that foreign holders evidently preferred to retain them in the hope of securing some future adjustments rather than dispose of them in American markets at reduced quotations. In the meantime the return of American state stocks made it possible for Americans to acquire their securities at reduced prices; and in the future the interest payment on these stocks would be paid to our citizens, instead of foreigners. By means of the bankruptcy law of 1842 several millions of sterling indebtedness held in England had been cancelled. By many of the states ceasing to pay either the principal or the interest on their securities, "millions on millions of English wealth had been added to the real capital of this country." At the same time the demand in England for American foodstuffs was increasing the profits of merchants and farmers and these profits were being scattered broadcast throughout the land. Thus it was said that the wealth of England was being absorbed in this country through individual American bankruptcies, state bankruptcies, and through the unprecedented amounts received from freight and provisions. And the more English newspapers controlled by English capitalists kept harping on repudiation and listed states like Illinois and Indiana among the repudiators without recognizing the efforts made by these defaulting commonwealths to meet their obligations, it was claimed the less likelihood was there that foreign creditors would ever receive any returns upon their holdings. Perhaps when it was too late to remedy the mistakes, foreigners would understand that the people of the western states could not be intimidated by threats or coerced by the sneers of Europeans. Meanwhile Americans would benefit—at least so argued some groups in America.[10]

[10] These arguments were advanced by the *New York Herald* quoted in the *London Times*, Oct. 11, Dec. 1, 1847. The same points are stressed in *Niles*, Jan. 30, 1847. How Americans freed themselves from foreign debts by means of the bankruptcy act,

Gradually, however, the capital of Europe began to flow back to the United States for investment. The first indication of a return of confidence among foreign investors followed the resumption of payments by Pennsylvania and Maryland upon their public debts. This was heralded in Europe as an indication of the good intentions of the American states to meet their engagements; and as the other defaulting states did make arrangements with their creditors to liquidate their indebtedness, even though the terms proposed were not always advantageous to the bondholders, American credit was strengthened. The adoption of free trade measures by England gave a decided impetus to the improvement of economic conditions in this country; and as American farmers benefited from the widening of the markets for their produce, and new supplies of gold were discovered in California, the United States grew prosperous.[11] During these years, the states also passed more stringent banking laws and in their constitutions placed restrictions upon the contraction of state debts without providing the means for their payment.[12] All of these factors helped to increase the faith of European capitalists in the future growth of the United States. By August 1848 United States 6 percent stock was selling higher in London in the open market than the French threes. The fact that the two great houses of Rothschilds and the Barings were interested in pushing the sales of these stocks was indicative of the improved status of federal credit.[13] The following May Pennsylvania 5 percent stock was selling at 80 whereas ten years previous it had sold at $32\frac{1}{2}$. The preceding month the Barings displayed their confidence in American

dishonored state securities, etc., and were growing rich through the export of foodstuffs is discussed in American Bankers Magazine, Vol. *II*, pp. 201-203. It is hardly necessary to remark that these arguments were not accepted by the conservative groups in this country.

[11] London Bankers Magazine, Vol. 5, p. 219; *London Times,* Feb. 23, 1849. The *London Times* raised the interesting question what effect the discovery of gold would have upon the repudiating states toward inducing them to acknowledge their obligations. The difficulty was to get anyone to agitate afresh so disagreeable a subject. As the *Times* said: "Claims that have been dishonored for one-third of a generation may well be left for another week, month, or year, and so the affair goes on." On Aug. 23, 1850 the Barings wrote to Ward inquiring whether it was not an opportune time to bring pressure to bear upon the repudiating states to meet their debts; but they finally agreed with Ward that the only way to do this was to arouse public opinion in favor of payment and "this," wrote the Barings, "will be exerted when enough (of the stock) is held on your side to make it worth while to agitate." Baring to Ward, Aug. 23, 1850; Baring to Ward, Sept. 27, 1850. Baring Mss.

[12] See comments on these changes in *London Times,* Dec. 30, 1852.

[13] Democratic Review, Vol. 23, New series, p. 182.

enterprises by purchasing £200,000 of Baltimore and Ohio Railroad bonds.[14] The revolutions of 1848 and rumors of war in Europe stimulated the migration of foreign capital and French and Germans as well as Englishmen, began to invest in American securities. In February 1849 United States 6 percent stock was selling in London at 106 to 106½; New York 5 percent and Ohio 6 percent at 93 to 95; Massachusetts 5 percent sterling bonds at 100; Virginia 6 percent at 91 to 93; but Mississippi was listed at 50.[15] The *London Times* reported in May of that year that there was a steady demand for American state stocks, chiefly on German account; but the bonds of private companies and those of the repudiating or doubtful states remained unsalable.[16] Three years later the same paper called particular attention to the fact that in the four repudiating states of Mississippi, Michigan, Florida, and Arkansas no new financial measures had been introduced to remedy old abuses nor had any movement been made by them towards a recognition of their obligations.[17]

As the new flood of American stocks and bonds began to appear in the European money markets, there was a noticeable degree of caution exercised by old conservative banking firms in accepting them for sale to their clients. When Georgia in 1851 sought a loan for railroads the Barings informed Ward it was most important that the state should be directly liable for the bonds and in case of default in the payment of the interest or principal the bondholders should have a lien on the railroad and its receipts. The Barings also requested Ward to send them a duly authorized copy of the state law authorizing the issue as well as proof that the parties delivering the bonds were authorized to negotiate a loan. The Barings also expressed a desire to see a statement of the debt, revenue, population, and property valuation of Georgia and its system of taxation.[18]

Ward found it extremely difficult to interest the Barings in any of the American railroad loans. They were afraid the Americans were entering upon another period of speculation, which would end, like that of the 'thirties, in defalcations and repudiations. But, as

[14] *London Times*, May 17, 1849; Ward to Baring, Apr. 10, 1849. Baring Mss.
[15] Democratic Review, Vol. 24, pp. 280, 281.
[16] *London Times*, May 17, 1849.
[17] *Ibid.*, Dec. 30, 1852.
[18] Baring to Ward, Nov. 21, 1851. Baring Mss.

Ward wrote the Barings, it was not in their power to keep entirely aloof from the railroad schemes which were projected in this country during the 'fifties. The high rates of interest carried by the stocks and bonds of American railroads attracted the European investors; and the Barings felt the pressure of their clients for these securities. It was, therefore, wiser, suggested Ward, for the Barings to take the loans of sound railroad corporations and endeavor to guide the investing public and check speculation than to remain entirely out of the market.[19]

The Barings recognized the soundness of this advice; but they were determined, if possible, to safeguard the reputation of their own house as well as the interests of their clients from unnecessary risks. For these reasons the Barings made careful inquiries through Ward and Captain William H. Swift of the engineering corps of the United States Army regarding the need for more railroads in the United States and which roads were likely to prove the safest investment.

Captain Swift assured the Barings there was a real need for railroads in the United States owing to the vast extent of the country and the desire for rapid means of communication. Although some of the American railroads thus far had been unproductive, and some of them would probably remain so, Captain Swift informed the Barings there was a large class which then yielded but a very small return upon the investments made in them but which in the future, as population increased, and the business needs of the communities multiplied, would certainly become desirable property. This was especially true of the New England railroads and those of New York and Pennsylvania. With the exception of the Reading Railroad, Captain Swift pointed out that the railroads in the United States had cost much less per mile than those in Europe; and, therefore, would afford a fair return upon the capital employed. The rate of interest in American railroad bonds varied from 5 to 8 percent per year; and in some instances 10 percent. Some of these securities were convertible into stock, at the option of the holder; and nearly all were secured by mortgages upon the road and its equipment.

The first consideration which in Captain Swift's opinion should govern the Barings in making railway investments should be the

---

[19] Ward to Baring, July 26, 1852. *Ibid.*

location of the road. If the road was in the right location—that is, connected populous districts or was so situated that the districts were likely to become populous with the growth of the country—the road was a good investment whether its present condition was good or bad. For this reason Captain Swift held the great railroads connecting the Atlantic coast with the Mississippi Valley or the Great Lakes with the Mississippi River were deserving of careful investigation. Occasionally a good paying line was injured and sometimes ruined by the construction of competing lines; but as long as the road did not pay more than 6 percent it might be considered tolerably safe from rival projects. When the rate advanced beyond that sum there was always the danger that a new competitive line would be built. In Captain Swift's opinion, railroad companies should not exceed a rate of 8 percent in their dividends. If they did, competition was almost certain to arise; therefore, it was better for the company to put its surplus into a second track, bridges, or other improvements.

Captain Swift also thought it was better to invest in a long line owned and worked by a single company rather than a short one since the work could be done more cheaply per mile.

If the road was well situated and there was a certainty of traffic with little exposure to competition, Captain Swift recommended that the Barings take the bonds rather than the stock of the company, for there was more certainty, in his estimation, of the returns and generally speaking the rate of interest was fully equal to the rate of the dividends. Captain Swift pointed out that in New York and the West the common rate of interest was 7 percent and sometimes 8 percent. If the road possessed a business capable of yielding such a rate of dividend upon its stock, Captain Swift declared it was plain that the bonds of such roads ought to be considered safe investments. In giving the bonds preference over the stocks as a permanent investment, Captain Swift, of course, went on the assumption that the companies were to act in entire good faith and never repudiate nor even approach a repudiation of their securities.[20]

The Barings gave careful consideration to the reports submitted by Captain Swift. For his services he received $1,000 a year; and

[20] Swift to Ward, Feb. 14, 1852. Baring Mss. For a detailed report of Swift on various American railroads consult Swift to Ward, Oct. 29, 1853. *Ibid.* Consult also chapter VI for Captain Swift's investigations in the West.

he was consulted by the Barings about the Eastern, Illinois Central, Michigan Central, Pennsylvania, Toledo, Norwalk and Cleveland railroads and many other roads. Upon the recommendation of Captain Swift and Ward the Barings refused to have anything to do with the Illinois Central.[21] As the *American Railroad Journal* remarked Illinois was "an unfortunate field" in which to invite foreigners "to a feast" after all the losses they had sustained there.[22] It was pointed out to English capitalists that as Congress had granted lands for the construction of the road, the company would be amenable to the jurisdiction of the United States Supreme Court and not the legislative assembly of Illinois. "If the reverse were the fact," declared the *London Times*, "it would be necessary to protest against the introduction of any of the securities of the company on this side." [23] Perhaps this helps to explain why many British investors, including men like Richard Cobden, were willing to invest their funds in the Illinois Central; but such arguments did not weigh against the objections raised by Ward and Captain Swift to the personnel of the management of the road.[24]

But other British capitalists and investors were not so conservative and cautious as the Barings. The *American Railroad Journal* warned the British against purchasing the securities of roads that were not well managed or were not recommended by reputable American houses. There was no justification for the wholesale denunciations of American stocks and bonds by the *London Times* because of previous failures of Americans to meet their obligations. English capitalists needed a channel for the employment of their surplus funds as well as the Americans required foreign capital to carry on their enterprises. But there was a danger, according to the *American Railroad Journal* that John Bull on account of his obstinacy and ignorance of what was taking place in the United States would be "humbugged" in the buying of American securities. Having made some bad bargains in times past, he had adopted a general

[21] Ward to Baring, Sept. 21, Nov. 19, 1852; Baring to Ward, Jan. 21, 1853. *Ibid.*
[22] *American Railroad Journal*, Vol. 24, p. 792.
[23] *London Times*, June 10, 1852.
[24] The story of English investors and the Illinois Central can be traced in *Herapath Railway and Commercial Journal*, Vol. 14, pp. 631, 632; Vol. 15, p. 576; Vol. 20, pp. 751, 775, 776, 1217; Vol. 21, pp. 31, 32, 40, 719; Vol. 22, pp. 288, 445, 478, 558, 744, 794, 1213; the *London Railroad Times*, Vol. 20, p. 1574; Vol. 21, p. 900; and in the columns of the *London Times*.

maxim that the great mass of American securities were good for nothing and would not take the trouble to inquire into their character nor inform himself as to their real merits. The result was that American bond salesmen had changed their technique in dealing with prospective British purchasers of American stocks and bonds, continued this journal. Knowing John Bull's frame of mind, shrewd American salesmen would go to him, humor him in his way of thinking, blow up "in the English papers our whole system of doing things," echo "every sentiment and whim of the old fellow," until he had secured a strong hold on his good graces. John Bull would begin to think his "new acquaintance a mighty fine fellow"; and so much like himself that his opinion could certainly be relied upon. "Having gotten into position, the operator," stated the *American Railroad Journal*, "tells him that his opinion of our securities is correct, quite correct, entirely correct; that too great caution cannot be used in reference to them, and winds up by gently suggesting that there are some few things that are good, one of which he has, out of great regard, brought with him, for Mr. Bull's special use, 'seeing it's him.'" In this manner the English capitalist was induced to buy a security in direct defiance of all properly established business principles; and by violating such rules would very likely make a bad bargain, as he certainly would, if he continued to buy of parties who went to England to peddle American securities for no other reason than that they could not be sold in American markets.

According to the *American Railroad Journal* the safest way for British capitalists to purchase American railroad stocks and bonds was to buy only those recommended by reputable American houses. The reason for this was obvious. Americans were in a better position to know the character of the road offered to the investing public. They were acquainted with the route of the road, its local resources, and the relation it bore to the commerce of the country. They knew, or could easily find out, the persons who had charge of the work, their integrity, and capacity to manage its affairs properly and successfully. "Our transatlantic friends," stated the *American Railroad Journal*, "may rely upon it, that none of our securities are taken abroad by first hands, that can find a market at fair rates here. The only reason why they are taken abroad is that they will not sell at home." In all probability English capitalists would make some unlucky investments for they were just in the frame of mind to be imposed upon and led astray.

The French and German buyers of American stocks and bonds declared the *American Railroad Journal* adopted a more sensible course. They bought through responsible American houses. But their precaution was not confined within this limit. They sent out to the United States competent men who critically examined all the projected public works, and studied their condition and prospects, until they were enabled to form a correct opinion as to their merits and the value of the securities upon which they were based. Their prejudices did not preclude investigation, nor warp their judgment. The consequence was, that knowing what they were purchasing, they took the choicest securities, leaving the others to the less fastidious or less-informed buyers.[25]

This was sound advice which the *American Railroad Journal* gave to the British capitalists; and it was prompted by the eager desire on the part of Americans to warn the British against making unwise investments and then condemning all American companies for the actions of a few unscrupulous promoters. The Americans needed the surplus funds of Europeans to carry out their railroad, mining, and other enterprises.[26] In their eagerness to obtain foreign capital, Americans assured the disappointed holders of unpaid American state bonds that these states would undoubtedly redeem their securities. "We must, we can, and we will pay our debts," wrote the American correspondent of the *London Times*. "Our resources are so enormous, our public and private wealth is so great, that we can neither expect nor desire to escape the indignation of mankind, if we do not redeem honorably and truly every obligation that has been given, whether fraud was used by our local agents or not, since it is perfectly certain that in every instance they gained the faith of foreign capitalists only by showing commissions by our

[25] *American Railroad Journal*, Vol. 25, pp. 185, 417, 418; Vol. 26, p. 744. It will be noticed that the advice given by the *American Railroad Journal* was the same as that advanced by the Barings when state commissioners began to peddle their securities abroad in the 'thirties. As Bates said at that time such a method deprived English capitalists of the advantage of the reactions of their American agents.

[26] On the mining investments of the British consult *Herapath Railway and Commercial Journal*, Vol. 13, pp. 1184, 1199; Vol. 14, pp. 53, 151, 388-390, 1193; Vol. 15, pp. 117, 341, 552, 622; Vol. 16, p. 465; Vol. 17, p. 392; *The Mining Journal, Railway and Commercial Gazette* (London), Vol. 19, p. 63; Vol. 20, p. 238; Vol. 22, pp. 122, 184, 493, 566; Vol. 23, pp. 135, 191; *The Mining Magazine* (London), Vol. I, pp. 67, 164-166, 413, 489; Vol. *II*, pp. 13, 54-55, 304, 305, 422, 636-638; Vol. 4, p. 185.

States to which were affixed the official seals of the commonwealths they represented." [27] Americans would not have to pay such high rates of interest for the sums which they borrowed if it were not that the European capitalists had so little faith in American promises to meet their debts. [28] Southern states urged the people of Mississippi to recognize their outstanding bonds, warning them that they would never be able to escape the rappings of the ghosts of their repudiated bonds. [29] Foreign capitalists were advised by Americans not to purchase the bonds of the Mobile and Ohio Railroad and of the New Orleans, Jackson and Northern Railroad which ran through the counties of Mississippi which had given the heaviest vote against taxation for the state bonds issued to the Planters' Bank until the state had removed the stigma of repudiation. [30]

Nevertheless foreign capital found its way for investment to the United States because in this country it yielded a higher rate of interest than could be realized in Europe. It is extremely difficult to determine the exact amount of foreign capital invested in American stocks and bonds; but several official computations were published during the 'fifties of the approximate aggregate amount of American securities held by foreigners. In March 1854 the Secretary of the Treasury submitted a report to the Senate in which he estimated that as far as could be ascertained the aggregate amount of federal, state, county, railroad, canal and other corporation bonds, stocks, or other evidences of debt held by foreigners was $184,184,-174 out of a total of $1,178,567,882. At the same time Winslow, Lanier and Company of New York estimated the holdings of foreigners at $222,225,315. The difference between these two computations was due to the fact that Winslow, Lanier and Company estimated that foreigners held $110,972,108 of American state stocks; while the Treasury department placed the state stocks held by foreigners at $72,931,507. [31] Since a number of the American states made no returns of the amount of their state stocks held by

[27] *London Times*, Jan. 22 1853.   [28] *Ibid*. March 21, 1851.
[29] American Bankers Magazine, Vol. 8, pp. 99-103.
[30] Hope to Baring (enclosing letter from Jaudon), Feb. 27, 1855. Hope Mss.
[31] Senate Document, No. 42, 33 Cong., 1 Sess., Vol. *VIII, passim*. Ward wrote the Barings that the Treasury report was "wide of the mark and entirely too low" for the amount of American securities held abroad. Ward to Baring, March 8, 1854. Baring Mss. Ward estimated that $35,000,000 of American railroad bonds were held abroad, to which should be added an additional $35,000,000 for iron bonds. Ward to Baring, Nov. 22, 1853. *Ibid*.

foreigners the *London Times* maintained that both sets of figures were too low. According to the *London Times* the total amount of all kinds of United States securities held abroad was a little short of £45,000,000, or almost one-fifth of the total amount of American stocks and bonds.[32] Two years later the Secretary of the Treasury placed the whole debt of the United States at $1,407,518,894 and estimated that of this amount foreigners held $202,902,000.[33] The bulk of the foreign investments were in state stocks and American railroad stocks and bonds. The *New York Herald* claimed that British investors owned most of the western railroads;[34] while the *London Railway Times* maintained that the bulk of English capital invested in American railroads was centered in the Michigan Central, New York and Erie, Illinois Central, New York Central and Philadelphia and Reading railroads.[35] Even though these estimates are based upon insufficient data it is quite evident that a large proportion of foreign capital was invested in the United States on the eve of the Civil War.

To inspire confidence in American securities, many of the devices employed in the 'thirties were again utilized. English firms dealing in American railroad stocks and bonds issued circulars calling the attention of the public to the lucrative returns offered by American investments. It was pointed out that the maximum returns on English investments in 1856 was 5 percent; whereas it was claimed the principal American stocks yielded "a minimum return of 10 percent." The *London Times* was severely criticized for publishing discouraging reports of investments in American railroads. The *London Railway Times* maintained that time would show that the derogatory reports published in the *London Times* prejudicial to the American character were unwarranted. "To those who are conversant with American business," stated the *London Railway Times*, "it is well known that the merchants and bankers of New York and other principal cities of the Union, merit the highest respect for the spirit of integrity and liberality by which they are guided in business, combined with the most enlightened enterprise. Well-selected investments may be made in America with as much confidence as

[32] *London Times*, Apr. 7, 1854.
[33] Quoted in *London Railway Times*, Vol. 20, p. 183.
[34] *New York Herald* quoted in *London Railway Times*, Vol. 20, pp. 1526, 1527.
[35] *Ibid.* Professor Hobson estimates that £80,000,000 of American railroad stock was held in England in 1857. Hobson, C. R., The Export of Capital, pp. 128, 129.

to security, as in any country in the world; and they yield greater returns than can be obtained elsewhere." [36] Extravagant predictions of the future business of American railroads which appeared in American journals were republished in English papers. Thus *Herapath's Railway Journal* of London quoted the following article on the future prospects of the Chicago, St. Paul and Fond du Lac Railroad which originally appeared in the *American Railroad Journal*. "The country through which it passes from Chicago to Janesville," stated the *American Railroad Journal*, "is of the most beautiful and fertile description. Nowhere, in the whole west, is seen a better improved country or a more enterprising and intelligent people. In the future, it is to be like a highly cultivated garden, and so salubrious and beautiful is the climate, that the productions of the soil, abundant as they are, will not keep pace with the increase of population. The time will come when it will appear along the whole of this route, like a continuous village, such as exists in Belgium and other parts of Germany, while the whole country will be studded with farm houses. To predict what the business of a railroad will be through such a country, in all time to come, would be impossible, while a mere approximation would seem so extravagant to persons unacquainted with it, that we will not attempt it in figures." [37]

Ward and the *London Times* did not entertain such optimistic views of the large returns upon investments in all American railroads. Ward wrote to the Barings that the standard of railroad morals in the United States was low and was deteriorating. [38] The *London Times* warned British capitalists to be careful about their investments in the United States as it had cautioned them in the speculative era of the 'thirties. [39] The fears of Ward and the *London*

[36] *London Railway Times*, Vol. 19, pp. 1109, 1110, 1286.

[37] *Herapath Railway and Commercial Journal*, Vol. 19, p. 31. In 1855 Captain Douglas Galton, R. E., made a rapid journey through the United States; and upon his return submitted a very able report to the Board of Trade on American railroads. This report was frequently quoted on the relative returns from American and British railroad investments and other matters pertaining to the need and character of American railroads. Accounts and Papers, Vol. 16, pp. 599-655. It is significant to compare these glowing accounts of the future growth of the United States and the need for railroads with those given out by state commissioners in the 'thirties when attempting to dispose of their bonds in European money markets.

[38] Ward to Baring, July 9, 1853. Baring Mss.

[39] The *London Times* kept constantly referring to the repudiation of the Mississippi bonds and the defalcation and repudiation of other states. Although the *Times* was not always accurate in its statements it would have paid the British investor to have listened more carefully to its warnings. See especially *London Times*, Nov. 27, 1851; Oct. 16, 1852; Jan. 11, 1853; July 7, Sept. 19, Oct. 1, 1857.

Times were verified by the scandalous disclosures of the frauds and forgeries perpetrated by Robert Schuyler, president of the New York and New Haven Railroad, and the financial distress of many of the American railroads following the panic of 1857.[40] As some of the railroads defaulted in their payments on their stocks and bonds, American credit was materially damaged abroad. German as well as English newspapers denounced all Americans. "This principle of violently breaking contracts and making a mockery of the principles which govern all honest people in their business transactions," stated the *Augsburg Allegemeine Zeitung*, "has caused in the interested circles a feeling of hatred and contempt for the American character from which it is plain that for a long time to come, American securities will be under the ban—they certainly will never again attain the position among sound investments which they once occupied in Germany and Switzerland." [41]

In the 'fifties, the *London Times* was not so confident, however, that these predictions would be fulfilled as it had been in the 'forties. As long as British capitalists thought they could gain an extra one or two percent interest upon their investments, the *London Times* cynically remarked that they would never manifest "any want of credulity so long as even credulity could hold on." [42]

Yet the shock administered to American finance and American credit by the repudiation of state bonds in the 'forties was never entirely repaired. The gaunt specter of repudiation dampened the ardor of the English investing public for American securities.[43] As *Herapath's Railway Journal* said in 1859 in commenting on the low price of American railroad securities in comparison with those of England: "The reason is that we do not like American things. We have not that confidence in them which their intrinsic merit warrants. No doubt this is unreasonable; but there is no accounting for

---

[40] On the Schuyler disclosures consult *Herapath Railway and Commercial Journal*, Vol. 16, pp. 800, 837; Hunt's Merchants' Magazine, Vol. 31, p. 207; *London Railway Times*, Vol. 17, p. 773; Vol. 19, p. 1305. According to *Herapath's Railway Journal*, the misdemeanors of Schuyler was another "striking instance of the folly of treating a mortal as more than a mortal. We do not mean that any and every man placed in position of great temptation would be unable to withstand it; but blind and unlimited confidence in any man is a dangerous folly."

[41] Quoted in American Bankers Magazine, Vol. 12, p. 838.

[42] Quoted in American Bankers Magazine, Vol. 14, p. 435.

[43] London Bankers Magazine, Vol. 23, pp. 809-812.

taste. Many years ago we had good reason for dreading American securities. Perhaps it is a never-dying record of that experience which now operates as a bugbear to Englishmen even to this day." **

** *Herapath Railway and Commercial Journal,* Vol. 21, p. 39.

CHAPTER XIV

THE PROBLEM OF AMERICAN STATE DEBTS AFTER THE CIVIL WAR

Durng the late 'seventies and early 'eighties the defalcation of ten American states once more occupied the attention of the people of this country and of Europe. The list of delinquent states included Alabama, Arkansas, Florida, Louisiana, Minnesota, North Carolina, South Carolina, Tennessee and Virginia. With the exception of Minnesota, all of these states were in the south. Some of these southern states had had previous financial difficulties before the Civil War; others in this list had enjoyed an enviable reputation for punctuality in meeting their engagements. In some respects the case of Minnesota was different from that of the other defaulting states. The financial misfortunes of Minnesota were caused by her own representatives. The disputed railroad bonds of Minnesota were issued before the Civil War and were held by Americans. On the other hand, the enormous debts of the southern states were contracted during the period of Reconstruction; and many of the bonds of these states were held by English, French, German, and Dutch investors.

In all of these states, in northern as well as southern, there was deep resentment about paying what they considered were illegal and fraudulent bonds. This opposition was intensified by the impoverished condition of the southland after the Civil War, and in the hard times which prevailed in all sections of the country following the panic of 1873. As in the period of the 'thirties and 'forties, the economic situation made it impossible to levy taxes to pay the debts and created a sentiment in favor of repudiation. In the case of the southern states this feeling was strengthened by the knowledge of the corruption and mismanagement of public funds by state officials during the Reconstruction period, aided and abetted by unscrupulous northern promoters. The sordid state of the Reconstruction era is well known; but it is necessary to recount the misdemeanors of these corrupt and ignorant legislators, not for the purpose of apologizing for or excusing any of the actions taken by southern legislatures in the final settlement of their debts, but in order to understand the political and economic atmosphere in which the repudiation and drastic scaling-down measures were drafted and enacted. By statute, constitution and constitutional amendment, and court decisions, debts were repudiated and scaled down in the southland as soon as the conservative whites regained control. By these actions many foreign bondholders suffered severe losses; but in certain instances foreign investors had been duly warned by southern leaders and by southern newspapers that the people would never recognize the "swindling bonds" issued by carpetbag, scalawag, and negro legislators; and these warnings had been recopied in foreign newspapers.

In the case of every one of these states, as in the 'forties, the settlement of the debts became the football of local politics. Even in some of the southern states there were groups who consistently urged that the state was under a moral and legal obligation to pay the debts irrespective of their origin. Their efforts, however, were thwarted by the general opposition of the great mass of the people to increased taxation, to the unsavory circumstances surrounding the issuing of many of these bonds, and to the stupidity of the bondholders at times to accept compromise terms which would have saved them a part of their investment. In Minnesota far-sighted leaders found it necessary to take the final decision out of the hands of the electorate in order to save the state from repudiation. Foreign bondholders always displayed greater willingness to leave the fate of their bonds to the decision of the courts, especially the higher federal courts, rather than to state legislators; and it is significant the effect the obiter dicta of the courts had upon the political leaders of Minnesota in bringing about a final adjustment of the debt. The same has not been true in the case of references made by the United States Supreme Court to the justice of the claims of some of the foreign bondholders of the repudiated bonds of some of the southern states.

The extent which the debts of all of these states were reduced or repudiated and the motives which impelled such actions to be taken are recounted in the following surveys of the respective debt of each state.

ALABAMA

Before the Civil War Alabama occupied an enviable position in the financial world. The state had a reputation of punctually meeting its obligations even under the most adverse circumstances and never attempting to evade its responsibilities. This was shown by the way in which Alabama handled its public debt in the years preceding and during the Civil War. Between the years 1823 and 1826 Alabama contracted a large public debt through the establishment of banks. These institutions were forced to suspend specie payments in 1837; and five years later went into liquidation. The state was held liable for the debts incurred by the banks; but by resorting to heavy taxation Alabama was able to meet regularly the interest payments and pay off a part of the principal. In 1861 the public debt of Alabama was $3,445,000. Of this amount $2,109,000 was payable in New York; and $1,336,000 in London. Throughout the war Alabama continued to pay the interest on the London portion of the debt.[1]

It is not strange, therefore, that Alabama securities after the war found a ready sale in foreign money markets. Railroad bonds authorized or indorsed by a corrupt legislature aided and abetted by unscrupulous promoters were sent in haste to New York and to European financial centers and were bought in large quantities by English, French, German and Dutch investors. These purchasers were assured by the governor of Alabama in 1869 that the roads were "in the hands of gentlemen of capacity, energy, and responsibility"; that there was "every reason to believe" that they would be completed "at an early day"; and that "the interest on the bonds" would be promptly paid as it fell due. Upon the default of the Alabama and Chattanooga Railroad to meet its interest on state bonds two years later Governor Lindsay wired Henry Clews and Company

---

[1] 10 Census, Vol. 7, p. 592. For the early financial history of Alabama consult Abernethy, T. P., Formative Period in Alabama, pp. 93-101; Moore, A. B., History of Alabama, Vol. I, pp. 283-315.

of New York, one of the financial agents of the state, that he could pledge the governor's word "to creditors of the State of Alabama that she will be true and faithful to all her obligations in the future as she has been in the past and that the Democratic party whose representative I am in the administration of the government will never permit a blot upon her name in the commercial world." [2] But upon the return of the conservative whites to power in 1874 a series of investigations were instituted which resulted in Alabama adjusting her public debt and employing both repudiation and scaling-down methods. How both foreign and domestic creditors and the people of Alabama were made to suffer for the financial excesses of the carpetbag régime can best be explained by reviewing the manner in which the finances of the state were administered between the years 1868 and 1874.

The close of the Civil War found Alabama in a prostrate condition. The treasury was without funds; the people were exhausted and disheartened; the railroads were either worn out or had been destroyed; and the social fabric of the community was rapidly disintegrating. To meet the current expenses of the state government, the governor was authorized in 1865 to issue bonds to the amount of $1,500,000 redeemable in twenty years, and bearing interest at the rate of 8 percent per annum if they were dollar bonds and 6 percent if they were sterling bonds. [3] Since it was impossible to collect taxes in 1865 and 1866 the legislature found it necessary to authorize the issuance of more bonds and certificates of indebtedness with the result that the public debt of Alabama was $6,848,400 when the state came under the control of ignorant negro politicians and carpetbaggers in July 1868. By the end of that year the debt had risen to $7,904,398.92; and "after that date no one knew nor did the officials seem to care exactly how large it was." [4]

The rapid increase of the public debt during the carpetbag régime was due to excessive government expenditures, gross mismanagement of the public funds, and the aid given by the state, counties, and towns to numerous railroad companies. Extravagance and dishonesty were largely responsible for the increased cost of running the state government. New offices were created and higher

[2] *Commercial and Financial Chronicle*, Dec. 4, 1869; *London Times*, Jan. 14, 1871.
[3] Acts Ala., 1865, pp. 40, 41.
[4] Fleming, W. L., Civil War and Reconstruction in Alabama, pp. 580, 581.

salaries were paid to all governmental employees; and even if the public funds had been honestly and carefully administered there would have been a large public debt.[5] But the state officials were not honest as later investigations of the use made of the contingent fund clearly disclosed. For instance, Governor Lewis, the Radical Republican elected governor in 1872, spent $800 on a short trip to New York and Florida, a sum which a later investigating committee maintained he could not have spent if he had chartered a private car and had paid hotel bills at the rate of $10 a day. The private secretary of the governor received $21,000 for his services in distributing "political bacon" in 1874; while the secretary of state was paid $952 for signing bonds which it was his constitutional duty to perform. Numerous purchases of refrigerators, mirrors, clothes brushes and hair brushes were also charged by these petty thieves to the state. Funds appropriated for one purpose were used for other purposes. For instance, Governor Lewis drew $484,346.76 out of the treasury presumably to pay the interest on the public debt but used it for other purposes and a careful investigation failed to account for $75,196.56 of this sum. So incomplete and inaccurate were the records of the state's financial transactions that a debt commission appointed in 1874 to ascertain the amount and character of the indebtedness was forced to advertise for information from the debtors and the creditors of the state.[6]

Bonds were issued by the counties and towns as well as by the state during the carpetbag régime. But the financial transactions of the local communities are shrouded in mystery for no records were kept of the amounts raised by these bond issues. Furthermore it is known that some of the towns and counties issued bonds without legislative authorization; and it is estimated that by 1872 the total liabilities of the state, towns and counties were $52,762,000.[7]

As soon as the state bonds were issued they were sent to the north or to Europe where they were disposed of by numerous financial agents of the state. Some of these agents reported their sales; others rendered no accounts. It is known that one of the agents sold certain bonds in 1870; yet two years later there was no record that the proceeds of the sale had reached the treasury. No records

[5] Herbert, H. A., Why the Solid South, p. 51.
[6] Fleming, op. cit., pp. 571-578.   [7] Ibid., pp. 580-582.

were kept of the direct and indorsed bonds issued by the state, or of the interest paid on these bonds. The financial transactions of the state with Henry Clews and Company of New York, one of the financial agents of the state, is indicative of the loose manner in which the state's finances were managed. The debt commission reported that the state on July 10, 1873, owed Henry Clews and Company $299,660.20. Ten days prior to that date Governor Lewis gave to Clews twelve notes and deposited as collateral security $650,000 of the 8 percent bonds of the state. Clews claimed that he disposed of the bonds at 20 to 21 cents on the dollar; and when he failed he handed over the governor's notes to the Fourth National Bank of New York to which he was indebted. A year later he filed a claim against the state for $235,039.43 as the alleged balance still due him. Thus a debt originally amounting to $299,660.20 had grown out of this remarkable transaction between Governor Lewis and Henry Clews and Company to the sum of $1,184,689.63 besides interest. Naturally the reckless issues of state bonds led to their sharp depreciation in the market. By 1873 they were quoted at 60 and Governor Lewis reported by the fall of that year that the state was unable to sell any of its bonds.[8]

In order to attract capital from the north and from Europe the state indorsed and issued bonds direct to numerous railroad companies. There was an urgent need for improving the transportation facilities; but the frauds perpetrated in the construction of these roads was the basis for many of the subsequent controversies between the state and her creditors. On February 19, 1867, the legislature passed an act which authorized the governor to indorse the first mortgage bonds of all railroad companies as soon as they had constructed twenty miles of road to the extent of $12,000 per mile and to continue the indorsement at that rate until the whole road was built. The first Reconstruction legislature increased the indorsement to $16,000 per mile and authorized its continuance at that rate as each section of five miles instead of twenty miles was built. These changes were made because it was claimed capitalists would not invest their funds unless the state raised the amount of its indorsement. It was assumed the state would be protected from any losses since the first twenty miles of each road would be built by private

[8] Alabama House Journal, 1875-1876, pp. 187-198; Fleming, *op. cit.*, pp. 581, 582.

capital. But Governor Smith at the next session of the legislature pointed out the grave defects in the law as it was passed. The governor favored lending the credit of the state to railroad companies; but he feared these companies would rely entirely upon the state's indorsement for their capital; and that roads would be projected where they were not needed. To meet these objections the legislature enacted a new law which provided that definite proof must be given that the five-mile block had been built and that the roadbed was in good condition before the first issue of bonds was authorized. The state's indorsement was to constitute a first lien on the property of the road and if the road defaulted upon its interest payments the governor was authorized to seize and sell the road if necessary.[9]

The first road to apply for state aid was the Alabama and Chattanooga Railroad. Since the bonds of this company were purchased by many foreigners and there was much discussion at a later date over the state recognizing the legality of their claims it is necessary to relate in detail the sordid history of this road. The Alabama and Chattanooga Railroad Company was formed by J. C. Stanton and D. N. Stanton, Boston financiers, out of two older corporations. The Stantons, aided by agents of the New York banking houses of Henry Clews and Company and Soutter and Company, and the French firm of Erlanger and Company of Paris obtained from Governor Smith the indorsement of $4,720,000 of bonds for the whole 295 miles of the proposed road which was $580,000 in excess of what the law allowed to the completed road. Only 240 miles of road were ever built and of these only 154 miles were within the state. Not satisfied with having received 1300 fraudulently indorsed bonds, members of the legislature were bribed by one of the Stantons to pass a law in 1870 authorizing the issuance of $2,000,000 of state bonds to the Alabama and Chattanooga Railroad. Two years later Governor Lindsay claimed the bill providing for this loan did not pass the legislature by the requisite number of votes required by law. By the terms of the act the state bonds were to be issued from time to time as the road was built. Yet within 30 days of its enactment, the bonds were issued and in haste sent to Europe where they were purchased by English, French, German and Dutch in-

    [9] Acts Ala., 1866-1867, pp. 686-694; Ibid., 1868, pp. 198-203; Ibid., 1869-1870, pp. 149-157.

vestors. It was these bonds which the *London Times* recommended to the public because of the former punctuality of Alabama in meeting her engagements; and it was this road which the governor of Alabama declared was "in the hands of gentlemen of capacity, energy, and responsibility." In 1871 the Alabama and Chattanooga Railroad Company defaulted upon its interest payments and Governor Lindsay was instructed to seize the road and to pay the interest due on the 4,000 of bonds legally issued and in the hands of bona fide purchasers. Soutter and Company informed the governor that they had sold 4,000 first mortgage bonds and 2,000 state bonds, all for more than 90 cents on the dollar. Three thousand of the indorsed bonds had been sold in Europe by this house; but the Alabama loan was largely negotiated abroad through Erlanger and Company and J. H. Schroeder and Company of Paris. It is claimed the proceeds of the sales of the state bonds were used to build a hotel and an opera house in Chattanooga.[10]

The story of the other roads which received state aid is a repetition on a smaller scale of similar corrupt methods employed by railroad promoters. The South and North Alabama Railroad received $691,789.43 from the trust fund and $2,200,000 in bond indorsements though the road when equipped was valued at only $1,625,000. In 1870 it was estimated that the road had obtained from the state $2,000,000 more than it cost to construct the road. The East Alabama and Cincinnati corporation secured $400,000 of indorsed bonds and a direct bond issue of $25,000 from the town of Opelika although the road was mortgaged to Henry Clews and Company and the company had no money of its own. The Selma and Gulf Railroad received $640,000 of indorsed bonds in clear violation of the law. The Montgomery and Eufaula Railroad obtained $1,280,000 of indorsed bonds in addition to $300,000 of state bonds. The Selma, Marion and Memphis Railroad received $765,000 of indorsed bonds; and the Selma and New Orleans Railroad $320,000 of indorsed bonds. The total indorsement of railroad bonds was about $17,000,000.[11]

---

[10] For the history of this road consult Fleming, *op. cit.*, pp. 591-594. For the sale of the bonds abroad consult *Commercial and Financial Chronicle*, Dec. 4, 1869, Dec. 2, 1871, Jan. 7, 1877; *London Times*, Apr. 6, 1870, Jan. 5, 14, Feb. 4, 15, 28, 1871; Acts Ala., 1869-1870, pp. 89-92.

[11] Fleming, *op. cit.*, pp. 587-604.

When the conservative whites came to power in 1874 a debt commission was appointed to investigate the state debt and to propose a plan of settlement. The financial condition of the state was then appalling. Alabama was in the grip of the panic of 1873, the rivers had flooded large areas of crops, some of the towns were stricken with yellow fever, and the state treasury was exhausted. There was a strong sentiment in the state in favor of repudiating all the bonds issued during the carpetbag régime. "We will not pay," stated the *Selma Times*, "a single dollar of the infamous debt, piled upon us by fraud, bribery, and corruption, known as the 'bond swindle' debt. Let the bondholders take the railroads." [12] To protect, if possible, the interests of foreign holders of Alabama bonds, the Council of Foreign Bondholders of London appointed David A. Wells to represent them in Alabama.[13] But the report submitted by the debt commission and approved by the legislature on February 23, 1876, in a funding act provided for both the repudiation and the scaling down of the debts.[14]

According to the debt commission the direct and contingent indebtedness of the state, recognized and unrecognized, including accrued interest, was $30,000,000.[15] Of this amount the following bonds were unrecognized by the state on account of irregularities and alleged frauds.[16]

BONDS UNRECOGNIZED BY THE STATE

State indorsement East Alabama and Cincinnati R. R. bonds	$ 400,000
State indorsement Selma and Gulf R. R. bonds	640,000
State indorsement Montgomery and Eufaula R. R. bonds	1,280,000
State indorsement Selma, Marion, and Memphis R. R. bonds	765,000
State indorsement Selma and New Orleans R. R. bonds	320,000
8 percents issued to Montgomery and Eufaula R. R. bonds	300,000
Unpaid interest on above, about	1,000,000
Total	$4,705,000

For the state's indorsement of the $5,300,000 of Alabama and Chattanooga first mortgage bonds the debt commission proposed and

[12] Acts Ala., 1874, p. 75; Moore, *op. cit.*, Vol. 1, pp. 621-623.

[13] For the negotiations with the foreign creditors consult *London Times*, March 15, Oct. 18, 1873; Jan. 30, 1874; *Commercial and Financial Chronicle*, Sept. 5, 1874; Sept. 25, 1875; July 15, Aug. 5, 1876.

[14] Acts Ala., 1875-1876, pp. 130-149.

[15] The reports of the debt commission can be found in Alabama House Journal, 1875-1876, pp. 187-217; *Ibid.*, 1876-1877, pp. 250-256.

[16] The tables and summary of the debt are from *Commercial and Financial Chronicle*, Jan. 13, 1877.

the legislature authorized the issuance of $1,000,000 new state bonds, bearing 2 percent interest for 5 years beginning January 1, 1876, and 4 percent for the remaining 25 years, and renewable at the pleasure of the state at 5 percent. This portion of the debt was known as "Class C."

For the $2,000,000 of state bonds issued to the Alabama and Chattanooga Railroad the state proposed to turn over to the bondholders lands granted to the railroad variously estimated at from 500,000 to 1,200,000 acres. These terms were accepted by the London bondholders.

For the 7 percent gold bonds issued by the state in 1873 for 25 percent of the state's indorsements of railroad bonds, aggregating $1,192,000, it was proposed to issue new 30-year 5 percent currency bonds to the amount of $596,000. These bonds were called "Class B" bonds.

For the 5, 6 and 8 percent direct state bonds it was proposed to give in exchange new 30-year bonds at par for the face value of the old bonds, without recognizing the past due interest. The new bonds were to have interest from July 1, 1876, at the rate of 2 percent for 5 years, 3 percent for 5 years, 4 percent for 10 years and 5 percent thereafter until maturity. The bonds in this class designated as "Class A" aggregated $7,127,709.

The educational fund indebtedness of $2,810,670 and the outstanding 5 percent state certificates were left unchanged.

By this settlement, as shown below, Alabama reduced her public debt from $25,464,470 to $12,574,379.

	Old Debts	New Authorized
5% state certificates	$ 1,040,000	$ 1,040,000
Educational Fund indebtedness	2,810,670	2,810,670
Total Class A	7,416,800	7,127,709
Total Class B	1,192,000	596,000
Total Class C	5,300,000	1,000,000
Total acknowledged debt	$17,759,470	$12,574,379

Unprovided for except as explained above
Alabama and Chattanooga Railroad .... $ 2,000,000
Other state indorsements given in first table 4,705,000

Total old debt, not including overdue interest $25,464,470

ARKANSAS

If Alabama held a proud position in the financial world, the same could not be said of Arkansas. Arkansas had paid no interest on her acknowledged public debt since July 1841; and none on the disputed Holford bonds since September, 1840. The Holford bonds, it will be recalled, were the $500,000 of Real Estate Bank bonds hypothecated with the North American Trust and Banking Company for a loan of $121,336.59 which the latter company handed over to James Holford of London for a loan of $325,000. The principal and accrued interest on these bonds amounted to $2,335,757.10 by January 1868. In that year Arkansas came under the control of the Republican Party which was composed of carpetbaggers, scalawags and negroes. Powell Clayton, the master mind of this highly centralized organization, was elected governor of the state; and from 1868 to 1874 Arkansas was in the hands of the reconstructionists.[1] During this period the public funds were wasted and a large public debt was created. When the conservative whites came to power in 1874, the adjustment of the state debt demanded their immediate attention. There was already much discussion over the "just" and "unjust" portions of this debt; and in 1884 a constitutional amendment was approved by the people of Arkansas repudiating the Holford bonds along with a large amount of bonds issued to aid railroads and for the purpose of constructing levees.

The first move of the Republican leaders when they gained control of the state government in 1868 was to endeavor to restore the credit of the state. At that time the bonded debt of Arkansas was $3,363,503.19.[2] This debt represented the liability of the state for the bonds issued to the State Bank of Arkansas and to the Real Estate Bank. It will be recalled that some of the bonds issued to these banks were held by the United States Treasury in trust for the Smithsonian Institution and for the Chickasaw Indians and when these banks failed the Treasury retained 5 percent of the proceeds of the land sales due Arkansas and applied it to the payment of the interest.[3]

In order to carry out their contemplated plans of economic development the Republican leaders realized the importance of reha-

[1] Staples, T. S., Reconstruction in Arkansas, pp. 166, 276, 277, 347, 348.
[2] *Ibid.*, p. 347.   [3] 10 Census, Vol. 7, p. 603.

bilitating the credit of the state. The legislature, therefore, passed on April 6, 1869 an act funding the entire bonded indebtedness of Arkansas. By the terms of this act new bonds were to be issued in exchange for those due and their unpaid coupons, one-half to be dated July 1, 1869, and the other half January 1, 1870, payable in thirty years after date with interest at 6 percent.[4] Among the bonds included in this adjustment were those hypothecated by the Real Estate Bank, known as the "Holford bonds." The passage of this act met with considerable opposition in the legislature from the Democrats and the anti-Clayton Republicans because the measure provided for the issue of bonds to the extent of $500,000 to absorb the Holford debt which the public held was only $121,339.56 plus the accrued interest. The followers of Governor Clayton did not claim that more was due the Holford heirs but they hoped by recognizing all of the bonds to impress the investing public with the good intentions of the new government. Nevertheless the act was passed and by 1873, $3,050,000 of funding bonds had been issued. A select committee appointed to investigate the state debt reported in 1883 that all of the Holford bonds, with the exception of two, were turned in and cancelled; and that new bonds amounting to $1,370,000 were issued.[5]

The funding of the public debt failed to produce the anticipated results. By 1871 the new bonds were selling at fifty-five cents on the dollar. Two years later they were selling at a greater discount; and in a little while they had disappeared entirely from the market.[6] In 1874 O. A. Hadley visited London in order to interest English investors in Arkansas securities. In a series of letters to the *London Times* Hadley endeavored to vindicate the past conduct of Arkansas to her creditors; but as the state was then finding it difficult to meet her obligations, his arguments failed to convince the public. None of the Arkansas loans were favorably received in London although some of them were floated in Amsterdam. The *London Times* claimed in 1875 that most of the bonds issued by Arkansas during the Reconstruction period were held by Americans.[7]

[4] Acts Ark., 1868-1869, pp. 115-118. On the passage of this act and the opposition it encountered consult Thomas, D. Y., History of Arkansas, pp. 360-371; Staples, *op. cit.*, pp. 348, 349.

[5] Arkansas Senate Journal, 1883, p. 685.

[6] Staples, *op. cit.*, p. 350.

[7] *London Times*, Apr. 27, 28, 1874; Sept. 14, 1875. See also Report of Council of Foreign Bondholders, 1875, p. 39.

In his first message to the legislature Governor Clayton recommended the granting of state aid to railroad companies. The railroads in the state were in a delapidated condition; and there was urgent need for improving transportation. But the same abuses appeared in loaning the credit of the state to the Arkansas railroad companies as was the case in other southern states under the control of the reconstructionists. The legislature promptly acted upon the governor's recommendation by the passage of a bill which was approved on July 21, 1868. By the terms of this act the governor was authorized to issue 30-year $1,000 bonds, bearing 7 percent interest, to railroad companies to the extent of $15,000 per mile where the road had received no land grant from the federal government and $10,000 per mile where it had, the whole amount not to exceed over 850 miles. Each applicant for aid was to give ample proof that ten consecutive miles of the road had already been constructed and that the company had sufficient capital to build 100 miles of road or one-third of its entire length. To pay the interest on these bonds the legislature was required to levy a tax on the road equivalent to the interest charges and five years after the completion of the road a tax of 2½ percent until the bonds were paid.

In accordance with the provisions of the state constitution, the twelfth section of the act provided for the submission of the proposal to the people at the general election in November in order that they might express their will through the ballot box. The Republicans supported the measure on the ground that it was necessary for the economic development of the state while the Democrats pointed out that the state aid would lead to corruption. On the ballot submitted to the electorate there was no indication that the credit of the state was to be loaned to the railroad companies. The electors were simply asked to vote "For Railroads" or "Against Railroads." The measure was carried at the fall election by more than the usual Republican majority.[8]

The Board of Railroad Commissioners appointed to pass on the application was immediately swamped with requests. Within two years 35 new railroad companies proposing to build a total of 6,000 miles of track were chartered; and by the close of 1871 this number had been increased to 86 companies which were under the

---

[8] Acts Ark., 1868, pp. 148-153; Staples, *op. cit.*, pp. 350-352; Clayton, P., The Aftermath of the Civil War in Arkansas, pp. 237-239.

control of less than 20 men.[9] In 1873 all the railroads aided by the state defaulted upon their interest payments and were temporarily placed in the hands of receivers appointed by the state. The following year Governor Baxter put an end to the orgy of railroad grants on the ground that the proposal had not been submitted in the proper form to the electorate in 1868. The railroads were returned to their private owners; and the state found herself liable for the payment of the principal and interest of $5,350,000 of railroad bonds for which she could show only 271 miles of road.[10]

Another scheme of the reconstructionists was the building and repairing of levees at the expense of the state. On July 27, 1868, a law was approved by the governor providing for the issuance of land warrants by the auditor in payment to contractors for the construction of or repair of levees. These warrants were made receivable for the purchase of swamp or overflowed lands in the district in which the work was done at the rate of $1.25 per acre. The law also provided that any railroad company which should construct a road bed which might serve as a levee should be paid for its services in land warrants. As contractors were unwilling to accept land warrants for swamp or overflowed lands in payment for their work, the levee law was amended on March 27, 1871. By this act the legislature was authorized to issue $3,000,000 of 30-year, 7 percent levee bonds to contractors or to railroad companies for the construction or repair of levees or for draining overflowed lands. Although the law limited the issue to $3,000,000, bonds to the amount of $3,005,846.19 were in circulation by the end of 1874. The Little Rock, Pine Bluffs and New Orleans Railroad received levee bonds to the amount of $369,959.47 and $1,200,000 of railroad aid bonds. Its terminal points were Little Rock and Arkansas City; "and if," reported an investigating committee, "it serves to protect any part of the country as a levee your committee is not aware of the fact." The White River Valley and Texas Railroad received $170,196.36 levee bonds; but no such road was ever built. By the end of 1874 the levee bonds were worthless. English investors refused to take them; and prominent New York lawyers declared that they were unconstitutional and not much better than auditor's

---

[9] Staples, *op. cit.*, pp. 352, 353.
[10] The amount of railroad bonds issued is based on the report of the select committee on Arkansas state indebtedness appointed in 1883, found in Arkansas Senate Journal, 1883, pp. 682-690.

warrants. The levee bonds added more than $3,000,000 to the public debt but the state could show little completed work for it.[11]

When the Democrats returned to power in 1874, the task of settling the public debt confronted them. In the estimation of the public certain portions of the state debt were illegal and unjust. To test the validity of the railroad bonds the case of the State of Arkansas against the Little Rock, Mississippi River, and Texas Railway was brought on appeal before the State Supreme Court in June 1877. The higher court confirmed the decision of the Circuit Court that the bonds were unconstitutional and void. The basis for this judgment was that at the time the people voted on loaning the credit of the state there was no law in force as the question was submitted at the election held in November in 1868 while the act did not go into effect until ninety days after April 10, 1869. Furthermore, the court held that the bonds in the hands of innocent purchasers were void because the authority to contract did not exist at the time the bonds were issued. A suit was then brought upon appeal before the State Supreme Court to test the validity of the levee bonds. These bonds also were held unconstitutional and void on the ground that the state constitution required that every act which created a liability or made an appropriation should be passed by a majority of two-thirds of each house of the legislature and the vote entered with yeas and nays upon the journal. Since this formality had been omitted when the levee bond act was passed the court held that the bonds were void. Both decisions were based upon technicalities; and no consideration was taken of the equities of the bondholders. By these court decisions the state debt was reduced $9,990,787.74. This left the undisputed bonded debt on September 30, 1878, for which the state was directly liable $3,193,500, and with the accumulated interest, $5,457,550.[12]

In 1879 a constitutional amendment repudiating the so-called "Holford bonds" and the railroad aid and levee bonds passed the legislature and was submitted for approval to the electorate at the next general election. There was no difference of opinion among the people of Arkansas concerning the validity of the railroad aid and levee bonds. They had been passed upon by the State Supreme

---

[11] This account is based largely on the report of the investigating committee appointed in 1883, found in Arkansas Senate Journal, 1883, pp. 682-690. Consult also Staples, *op. cit.*, pp. 344-347.
[12] 10 Census, Vol. 7, p. 603; 31 Arkansas, p. 701.

Court and had been adjudged fraudulent, unjust and illegal. The public no longer recognized them as a debt of the state. "But as to the repudiation of the Holford bonds," stated the *Little Rock Gazette*, "there is a wide difference in public sentiment. They have never been adjudged to be illegal or unjust . . . (and) until a court of competent jurisdiction and final resort—such as the Supreme Court of the State—passes upon them, and adjudge them to be fraudulent and illegal, these bonds will stand against us so long as Arkansas is a State or time lasts. We cannot get around them, or dodge them, by any such scheme as a constitutional amendment which is itself unconstitutional, until the Supreme Court of the land determines and declares the bonds, and all portions of them, to be illegal and unjust." [13] The same position was taken by A. H. Garland and U. M. Rose during the campaign. In a speech at Russellville on July 12, 1880 Garland said: "I think it (the amendment) is conceived in a mistaken policy. I think its advocates and friends have gravely erred in propounding it to the people of the State of Arkansas and urging it upon them for adoption. If they were the sworn enemies of the state, armed with a sword in one hand and a torch in the other, determined to do the state the utmost damage they could not in my judgment more completely accomplish their end, than by having this proposed amendment incorporated in the constitution." As Garland said Arkansas might "repudiate, ignore, destroy the bonds" but the debt would still remain "to haunt the courts and the state." [14] Furthermore a statement published by the Finance Board, composed of the governor, auditor, and treasurer of the state showed "beyond a question" that the state still owed "legally, justly, and honestly" the sum of $70,321.32 on the Holford bonds. This estimate was based on the hypothesis that the state should pay the interest on the $121,336.59 since 1840. [15]

The amendment was defeated in 1880; but on September 1, 1884 it was again submitted to the electorate and adopted by a vote of nearly eight to one. The amendment declared that the general

[13] Acts Ark., 1879, pp. 149, 150; *Little Rock* (Arkansas) *Gazette*, July 11, 1880. According to this paper the reason for the proposed amendment was the lack of confidence which the people of the southern states had in the integrity of the public officials on account of the "unbridled corruption that existed in the days of reconstruction." But the *Gazette* pointed out that now the legislators were the choice of the people and there was no cause for such actions. *Ibid.*, June 6, 1880.

[14] Speech of A. H. Garland at Russellville, Ark., July 12, 1880 (pamphlet).

[15] *Little Rock* (Arkansas) *Gazette*, Aug. 6, 1880, quoted in *Commercial and Financial Chronicle*, Vol. 31, p. 204.

assembly should have no power to levy a tax or make an appropriation to pay interest or principal on the bonds or claims upon which they were based, known as the Holford bonds, railroad aid bonds, and levee bonds. The aggregate amount of indebtedness, principal and interest, for which the state declined all responsibility was between twelve and thirteen millions. In his farewell message to the legislature delivered in January 1885 Governor Berry stated the undisputed debt, principal and interest, was $4,869,943, more than one-half of which was interest.[16]

FLORIDA

Upon two separate occasions Florida has repudiated bonds issued by her legislature. In 1842, it will be recalled, Florida disavowed her responsibility for the payment of $3,900,000 of so-called "Faith Bonds" issued to the Union Bank, Bank of Pensacola, and to the Southern Life Insurance and Trust Company on the ground that the Territorial legislature did not possess the authority to pledge the faith of the Territory for the payment of the debts of any corporation chartered by the Territorial legislature. At the close of the Reconstruction period the Supreme Court of Florida declared unconstitutional and void $4,000,000 of state bonds which had been given to the Jacksonville, Pensacola, and Mobile Railroad and to the Florida Central Railroad in exchange for a like amount of railroad bonds on the ground that the state constitution did not authorize the exchange of state bonds for railroad bonds. In both instances, foreign creditors suffered severe losses; but the circumstances surrounding the issuance and sale of the railroad bonds were quite different from those connected with the issuance and sale of the so-called "Faith Bonds."

The discussion over the Territorial bonds subsided after the Convention of 1853 was signed settling the outstanding claims of British and American subjects. But the foreign bondholders never entirely lost hope of ultimately inducing Florida to recognize these obligations; and in the fall of 1869 Hope and Company received information which led them to believe that Florida was about to pay her

[16] Acts Ark., 1883, p. 346; *Commercial and Financial Chronicle*, Sept. 6, 1884; Jan. 24, 1885.

old debts. The Dutch house received a letter from their American representatives, James G. King and Sons, of New York, to the effect that there was a possibility of Florida in the near future making some provision for the redemption of the old Territorial bonds. This change of sentiment in Florida was ascribed to the large immigration from the north since the close of the rebellion. A month later King wrote Hope and Company that he had had an interview with the governor of Florida and had been assured by the latter that Florida would pay her debts. These rumors were followed by requests "from friends in Florida" for the purchase of Florida bonds which by 1870 were selling in the market at 15 cents on the dollar.[1]

There were good reasons for the dissemination of such reports. In 1868 the Republicans gained control of the state government; and a group of notorious railroad promoters who had already fleeced North Carolina were anxious to give the impression that Florida bonds were good in order to carry out their own nefarious plans. In 1855 an act had been passed by the legislature of Florida providing for a liberal system of internal improvements in the state through the issuance of state bonds to the extent of $10,000 per mile to certain railroad companies. The interest on these bonds were guaranteed by the trustees of the internal improvement fund created by the act; and the state was given a first mortgage on the roads, their equipment and their franchises.[2] At the close of the Civil War, the railroads of Florida were bankrupt; their equipment worn out; and their traffic gone. They defaulted on their bonds and were taken over by the trustees of the internal improvement fund who, by the terms of the original act, were the governor and his cabinet. As soon as the Republicans came to power the Central Railroad was sold for $110,000 "to a group of men represented by a Mr. W. E. Jackson." A new charter was obtained by the purchasers and the road was incorporated under the name of the "Florida Central."[3]

The following year two more defaulting railroads, the Pensacola and Georgia Railroad, and the Tallahassee Railroad were sold under execution by the trustees. These roads were presumably sold for $1,415,000 in cash; but "the purchasers were allowed the privilege

[1] King to Hope, Sept. 7, Oct. 15, 1869; Herrick to Hope, Nov. 22, 28, 1870. Hope Mss.
[2] 10 Census, Vol. 7, p. 588.
[3] Davis, W. W., The Civil War and Reconstruction in Florida, p. 657.

of paying the purchase money by delivering the road's bonds at their par value." Many of these railroad bonds had been purchased by the counties in Florida through which the roads passed; but it was not a difficult task to induce the ignorant negro county commissioners to sell these bonds for a mere pittance. More than one million dollars of these bonds were bought up at prices ranging from 30 to 35 cents on the dollar by George W. Swepson of North Carolina who in turn obtained his money "by embezzling the funds of a railroad in North Carolina of which he was president."

When it came time to settle, the purchasers found they still lacked $472,065 in cash or bonds of the purchase price. The trustees were induced, however, to accept a check for the balance which later was found to be worthless. Swepson, Milton S. Littlefield of Maine, and their associates were then given "a deed for and took possession of the property." They were now in possession of three railroads which had cost them "about $2000 of embezzled cash per mile." [4]

The next step was to consolidate these roads into one line and to secure a subsidy from the state. To accomplish this Swepson sent Littlefield to Tallahassee where Governor Reed, presumably at the suggestion of Swepson, had called the legislature in special session. Littlefield was well supplied with money in order to obtain the necessary legislation. Champagne, whiskey, and cigars were supplied by the amiable Littlefield to the statesmen of all shades and color; and when these means proved ineffective there was no hesitancy in handing out bribes ranging from $500 up to $6,000. Under such stimulation a corrupt legislature which did not truly represent the people of Florida passed an act on June 24, 1869 consolidating the Pensacola and Georgia Railroad and the Tallahassee Railroad into a new corporation known as the Jacksonville, Pensacola, and Mobile Railroad. The new company was given state aid in the form of state bonds to the amount of $14,000 per mile of road. The original charter was somewhat amended on January 28, 1870, by authorizing the issuance to this corporation of 8 percent 30-year state bonds to the amount of $16,000 per mile of road. The trustees of the internal improvement fund were to accept the bonds of the railroad company in exchange for those guaranteed by the state. This

[4] *Ibid.*, pp. 658, 659.

subsidy was granted ostensibly for the purpose of enabling the railroad company "to complete, equip, and maintain the road." The same legislature authorized the issuance of state bonds to seven other railroad companies, varying in amount from $10,000 to $16,000 per mile.[5]

Upon the passage of this act, Governor Reed executed and delivered to Littlefield in exchange for a like amount of railroad bonds, $3,000,000 of state bonds issued to the Jacksonville, Pensacola, and Mobile Railroad, and $1,000,000 of state bonds for the Florida Central Railroad. Littlefield proceeded to New York with these bonds where they were placed in the hands of S. W. Hopkins and Company, a New York and London brokerage house, the fiscal agents of Florida, for sale. On November 14, 1870 a contract was signed by Littlefield, as president of the Jacksonville, Pensacola, and Mobile Railroad, and S. W. Hopkins and Company whereby the latter was given the exclusive right to sell the $4,000,000 of bonds already issued, as well as $3,200,000 that were authorized to be issued.[6]

A month later a meeting was called in London by the Council of Foreign bondholders of holders of Florida territorial bonds. Then a proposition was submitted by S. W. Hopkins and Company, as the fiscal agents of Florida. After some discussion it was agreed: (1) that the fiscal agents of Florida should pay holders of Florida territorial bonds 1 percent in cash, being 2 pounds for each $1,000 bond, and a sum of 8 pounds, being 4 percent additional, upon the ratification of the present agreement by the State of Florida; (2) that the State of Florida should give the bondholders in exchange for every $1,000 bond and arrear coupons, land warrants of 500 acres; (3) that the government of Florida should take measures to obtain payment from such Florida banks as were liable for these bonds and all funds realized by these measures were to be employed in repayment of the land warrants at not less than $5 per acre; and (4) that the fiscal agents were to recommend to Florida to accept these land warrants in payment of any public loan that might be issued after 1872.[7]

[5] Wallace, J., Carpet Bag Rule in Florida, pp. 102-105; Brevard, C. M., History of Florida, Vol. II, pp. 153-159; Davis, op. cit., pp. 659-661.
[6] House Reports, No. 22, 42 Cong., 2 Sess., Vol. II, p. 343; U. S. Reports, Vol. 103, pp. 118-145.
[7] Circular of Hope and Company, Hope Mss.; London Times, Dec. 15, 1870.

The reactions of Dutch and English bondholders to these proposals are most interesting in the light of subsequent events. Hope and Company interpreted this offer as an acknowledgment on the part of Florida of "the rights of the bondholders" and her own obligation to satisfy their claims.[8] In England a storm of protest arose from the bondholders many of whom refused to listen to a proposal to accept in exchange for a $1,000 bond worth arrears of interest £500 or £600, a cash payment of £10, not 5 pence in the pound, and the assignment of waste land for the balance. The Council of Foreign Bondholders was severely criticized for entertaining such a proposal and the Stock Exchange was called upon not to sanction "such a whitewashing" nor "again admit the State of Florida to the privileges of honest borrowers." The *London Times* was urged by correspondents "as a guardian of financial faith to make known as widely as possible to the British public the fashion in which this state may be expected to meet its monetary engagements." Under the pressure of public opinion the London Stock Exchange notified the governor of Florida that until the old debt "was in some way adjusted, no bonds of the state would find a market or be suffered on the Exchange."[9]

If the offer of Hopkins and Company was designed to obtain possession of the territorial bonds at a reduced figure in the hope of later inducing the legislature to redeem them at par, it proved a failure. But if the proposal was made in the hope of facilitating the sale of the new bonds it was partially successful. The British, as already shown, were unwilling to trust Florida; but the Dutch evidently thought this was a move toward the ultimate redemption of the territorial bonds and therefore they were more favorably disposed toward the floating of new loans in Holland for Florida. Most or all of the $4,000,000 of railroad bonds were sold to citizens of Holland at about 70 cents on the dollar, netting some $2,800,000; but only $308,938 of the proceeds were applied to the building and equipping of the Florida roads.[10] Even Governor Reed who was accused of working in collusion with the railroad promoters stated

---

[8] Hope to Baring, Dec. 24, 1870. Baring Mss.
[9] *London Times*, Dec. 29, 1870; Jan. 13, 16, 19, 23, 27, 1871.
[10] U. S. Reports, Vol. 103, pp. 127-133; House Report, No. 22, 42 Cong., 2 Sess., Vol. *II*, p. 343.

in his message of 1872 that it appeared that the bonds of the company had been "entrusted to one of the firms of swindlers who abound in New York" and that "much of the proceeds" had been diverted "by fraud and villainy" from the work "for which they were issued." Yet Governor Reed had issued the bonds in direct violation of a pledge he had given that no issue of bonds would be made until the company paid the outstanding first mortgage bonds of the Pensacola and Georgia and Tallahassee railroads which constituted a first lien upon the property and franchise of the Jacksonville, Pensacola, and Mobile Railroad.[11] Furthermore, the *Floridian* published a letter of the Attorney General of Florida in 1873 warning Dutch investors that the state would never recognize the railroad bonds because "of the enormous frauds perpetrated in the issuing and circulation of these bonds and the want of legal authority on the part of the governor then in office to sign the bonds.[12] Unfortunately these statements were made after the railroad bonds had been introduced to Dutch investors; but the reaction of the British to Hopkins' offer regarding the territorial bonds should have made the Dutch more cautious in accepting new Florida loans.

Early in the 'seventies the roads defaulted on their interest payments and the state, as authorized by law, took possession of them. Florida was anxious to sell the roads but for a long time was prevented from doing so because of the opposition of the Western North Carolina Railroad which had acquired a first mortgage lien on the Florida Central. In the course of the litigation the case of Holland versus the State of Florida was brought before the Supreme Court of Florida at the January term, 1876. In rendering the decision the Court declared: "Where in the constitution can authority be found that will authorize the state bonds issued to be exchanged for railroad bonds? This *swapping* of state obligations for railroad paper at the will of the legislature, *ad libitum*, is certainly a new idea begotten by those who believe that the legislature is the dispenser of all power, and that it only requires a sufficient number of legislative votes to do anything. But this court will guard the constitution

[11] Davis, *op. cit.*, p. 663; Brevard, *op. cit.*, pp. 156-158.
[12] *Floridian*, July 15, 1873 quoted in *Commercial and Financial Chronicle*, Sept. 6, 1873.

from such pernicious construction." [13] By this decision the state was relieved of her responsibility for the payment of the railroad aid bonds amounting to $4,000,000 with accrued interest. Three years later the United States Supreme Court granted a lien in favor of the "Dutch" bondholders against the Florida Central for $197,000 and interest for about nine years, and against the Jacksonville, Pensacola, and Mobile Company for about $2,750,000 with like interest. "The bonds were undoubtedly steeped in fraud at their inception," declared Justice Bradley in rendering the decision, "but they were nevertheless apparently state bonds on the market in a foreign country, among a people largely unacquainted with the English language and offering tempting inducements by reason of their liberal interest (8 percent) to those who were seeking investments." In the course of his decision Justice Bradley pointed out that the Supreme Court of Florida on three separate occasions had pronounced the state bonds unconstitutional. Furthermore, in the case of the State of Florida versus Anderson, the United States Supreme Court had declared that this delicate question was "one it was eminently proper the courts of Florida should determine." Therefore, Justice Bradley declared: "while we are not now prepared to say that these decisions are conclusive on us, they certainly are not of such doubtful correctness as to make it proper that they should be disregarded." [14]

GEORGIA

Georgia, unlike Florida, had only one attack of the disease of repudiation. It came at the close of the Reconstruction period in Georgia when the conservative whites gained control of all branches of the government and began to investigate the various bond issues of Governor Bullock's administration. Revelations of fraud and corruption were disclosed in connection with the bonds issued and indorsed by the state for the construction of different railroads and

---

[13] 15 Florida, p. 491.
[14] U. S. Reports, Vol. 103, pp. 118-145. The three cases decided by the Supreme Court of Florida declaring the state bonds unconstitutional were: Holland vs. State of Florida (15 Florida, p. 455); State of Florida vs. Florida Central (*Ibid.*, p. 690); and Trustees of the Internal Improvement Fund vs. Jacksonville, Pensacola and Mobile Railroad Company (16 Florida, p. 708). See also *Commercial and Financial Chronicle*, June 7, 1879.

the currency and gold bonds issued in 1870. Georgia repudiated these bonds first by statute, and then incorporated an article in the state constitution forbidding the legislature from appropriating funds for the payment of the interest or the principal of any of the bonds declared illegal by the legislature.

The financial history of Georgia during the period of Reconstruction is a sordid tale of the looting of the public funds by a gang of thieving politicians. As Godkin stated in the *Nation* the Georgia officials were "probably as bad a lot of political tricksters and adventurers as ever got together in one place." [1] In 1868 Rufus B. Bullock, a native of New York who had gone to Georgia before the war, was elected by the radical Republicans governor of the state. The intimate friend, financial adviser, and mentor of Governor Bullock was Hannibal I. Kimball. Kimball was the directing genius of the gang of marauders who pilfered the state treasury and plunged the state into a morass of debt. No opportunity was lost by this enterprising and resourceful leader in his raids upon the public funds. Kimball was the president of three Georgia railroads which fraudulently obtained state aid. He bought an unfinished opera house in Atlanta for $30,000, remodeled it, and sold it to the state for a capitol for $400,000. He was never able to convince many Georgians that he had not paid for the Kimball House, a hotel which he built in Atlanta, with state bonds. In his capacity of semi-official financial agent of the state, Kimball marketed the state bonds and never rendered an account of his transactions. As a partner of the Tennessee Car Company, he sold the state cars for the Western and Atlanta Railroad, which he never delivered. His extravagant manner of dispensing state funds where it would do him the most good caused the negroes to sing his praises in a popular song with the refrain:

> "H. I. Kimball's on de floor
> 'Taint gwine ter rain no more."

As an investigating committee said, "he was in pretty much everything about that time"; but his specialty was the building of railroads subsidized by the state. The manner in which these railroad and other state bonds were issued and disposed of by Kimball with

[1] Quoted in Fleming, W. L., The Sequel to Appomattox, p. 226.

the connivance and assistance of the governor reveals the corruption and frauds which were perpetrated during the Bullock régime.[2]

The constitution of Georgia adopted in 1868 specifically stated the conditions under which the state could loan its credit to corporations. One of these provisions of the constitution reads as follows: "The general assembly shall pass no law making the state a stockholder in any corporate company; nor shall the credit of the state be granted or loaned to aid any company without a provision that the whole property of the company shall be bound for the security of the state, prior to any other debt or lien, except to laborers; nor to any company in which there is not already an equal amount invested by private persons; nor for any other object than a work of public improvement." [3]

Under this provision of the constitution the state indorsed the bonds of thirty-seven railroads for a total sum of over $30,000,000. Among the railroads which received state aid were the Brunswick and Albany, the Bainbridge, Cuthbert and Columbus, and the Cartersville and Van Wert railroads (later the Cherokee). Kimball was president of each of the railroad companies. The state treasurer, who was a Republican but not in the inner circle, intimated as early as 1869 that Governor Bullock was making corrupt use of the public funds; but it was not until 1872 when the Democrats gained control of all branches of the government, and Governor Bullock had fled from the state, that a Bond Committee was appointed for the purpose of investigating the various bond issues of the Bullock régime.[4] The work of the committee was greatly handicapped by the fact that Kimball had kept no records of his transactions. Furthermore, bonds had been issued without the signature of the state treasurer and without proper registration. The committee proceeded to New York where it is claimed they registered and examined nearly $10,000,000 of Georgia state and railroad bonds held in or near the city; and received the sworn testimony taken before various American consuls in Europe given by foreign holders of about $4,000,000 more of Georgia bonds.[5]

---

[2] Thompson, C. M., Reconstruction in Georgia, pp. 216-219; Coulter, E. M., A Short History of Georgia, p. 353; Oberholtzer, E. P., A History of the U. S., Vol. II, p. 330.
[3] Quoted in Tenth Census, Vol. 7, 582.
[4] Acts Georgia, 1871, p. 14; Thompson, op. cit., pp. 229, 230, 236.
[5] London Times, May 4, 1872.

The report submitted by this committee related the circumstances surrounding the different bond issues and contained specific recommendations for the guidance of the legislature in dealing with the public debt question. The committee recommended: (1) That the indorsed bonds of the Alabama and Chattanooga Railroad, amounting to $164,000, should be recognized as valid since the only informality in these bonds was a failure to attach the seal of the State; (2) in the case of the state indorsement of $600,000 of bonds for the Bainbridge, Cuthbert and Columbus Railroad, the committee recommended that these bonds be declared null and void because the bonds were issued by Governor Bullock before a single mile of the road was completed though the law required the completion of 20-mile sections for indorsement. Furthermore the committee pointed out that the bonds were devoid of the state seal and without the signature of the secretary of state; (3) the committee recommended that the state indorsement of $275,000 of bonds issued by the Cartersville and Van Wert Railroad and of $300,000 bonds of the same road under the name of the Cherokee Railroad also be declared null and void. The report showed that Governor Bullock had indorsed $275,000 of bonds of the Cartersville and Van Wert Railroad when he personally knew that only three miles of track had been laid though the law called for indorsement on the completion of five-mile sections; and also because no private funds had ever been invested in the road. The $300,000 of bonds indorsed for the same road under the name of the Cherokee Railroad were declared illegal because the Cartersville and Van Wert Railroad had already received all of its bonds when the legislature, evidently considering the Cherokee Railroad a new road, granted additional aid; (4) the $2,000,000 of currency bonds issued under the provisions of the Act of August 27, 1870 were declared not binding on the state because they were cancelled by the quarterly gold bonds issued under the provisions of the Act of September 15, 1870; and also "because there was no evidence that the state had received any money on the bonds hypothecated by Kimball as agent for Bullock"; (5) under the provisions of the Act of September 15, 1870, $3,000,000 of 7 percent gold bonds, payable quarterly, were issued for the purpose of redeeming all outstanding bonds and coupons then due or to become due. The committee reported that $250,000 of these bonds had been given to Kimball in payment for the Atlanta Opera House, and $100,000 to James H. James "for the purchase of the executive mansion in Atlanta." The remainder, amounting to $2,650,000 had been placed on the market by Kimball and Henry Clews and Company, the financial representative of Georgia in New York. Of this amount, $2,548,000 were disposed of; the remaining $102,000 were held by Clews. The committee declared that Clews had sold 1650 bonds and had delivered to the state's account $1,432,250; but that he had paid $609,192.12 on drafts drawn by Governor Bullock and the superintendent of the state road, the Western and Atlantic Railroad, in favor of that road. The committee held that this was an illegal transaction as it violated the terms of the law authorizing the issuance of the bonds. The committee reported that Kimball had hypothecated the remainder of the bonds for an amount unknown. They, therefore, recommended that those issued for the purchase of property or sold by Governor Bullock and his agents be recognized as good, those on which money had been borrowed by the state agent be returned and the money, with interest, and covering the cost of returning the bonds, be paid with new currency bonds or in cash; but that the $102,000 of bonds held by Clews and Company without legal right as collateral should not be paid; (6) the committee also held that the state indorsement of $3,300,000 of bonds of the Brunswick and Albany Railroad and of $1,800,000 bonds issued direct to the road were null and void. The committee declared that these bonds were illegal because they were issued to pay damages claimed by the company against the state for iron seized from the road whereas it was the Confederacy and not the state that had seized the iron; and moreover the iron taken had been paid for. As for the claims presented by the road for the transportation of troops during the war, the committee held that these contracts were nonenforceable as the troops had been used to further the cause of the Confederacy. The committee also pointed out that the bonds were issued and indorsed before the completion of twenty-mile sections as the law required; and they intimated in their report that these grants had been obtained from the legislature by the use of corrupt means; (7) the committee recommended the state indorsement of the Macon and Brunswick Railroad bonds be declared legal; also those indorsed for the South Georgia and Florida Railroad and the state road mortgage bonds issued by Governor Jenkins and used by Governor Bullock.[6]

While these investigations were being carried on, the creditors of Georgia were not inactive in their own defense. Henry Clews and Company published a card in the *Atlanta Constitution* in which they related their operations as financial agents for Governor Bullock. They stated that the bonds in question had been passed upon as legally issued and properly signed by their best lawyers. Admitting the proceeds of the bonds were misapplied and that the state had failed to receive value for them, Messrs. Clews counseled the people of Georgia, as they valued their credit, not to repudiate them. The January interest on the gold bonds was paid by Henry Clews and Company in New York and London; and the interest on the bonds issued prior to 1868 was paid by the Fourth National Bank of New York. This probably helps to explain the continued sale of Georgia bonds in New York while the investigation was being carried on and after the report was submitted. Furthermore, the *Commercial and Financial Chronicle* expressed the opinion that the legislature would not adopt the recommendations of the committee because it would seriously impair the credit of Georgia to repudiate bonds on purely technical grounds.[7]

The Georgia bonds were held by foreigners as well as by residents of this country; but it is practically impossible to determine the amount held by foreign bondholders. Henry Clews and Company secured the admittance of George bonds to dealings at the New York Stock Exchange and also introduced them in the London, Berlin, and Frankfort markets. The *London Times* cautioned the British against subscribing for the 7 percent gold bonds. As the paper said it was a very inopportune moment to ask the British to take Georgia bonds just as the public was informed of the default of Alabama. Nevertheless, Clews later maintained that $77,000 of the

---

[6] The work of the Bond Committee and their recommendations is published in *Commercial and Financial Chronicle*, Aug. 3, 1872; see also Thompson, *op. cit.*, pp. 229-233.

[7] *Commercial and Financial Chronicle*, Jan. 6, July 22, 1872; Clews, Henry, *Twenty-eight Years in Wall Street*, pp. 263, 270, 271.

gold bonds were in the hands of European bankers when the Georgia Bond Committee came to New York. As evidence of the excellent sales ability of his firm, Clews declared that the first million dollars of Brunswick and Albany Railroad bonds were offered in the Berlin and Frankfort market at 104; and was so heavily oversubscribed that it was found necessary to distribute them pro rata among the bidders. As additional proof of the confidence of the investing public in Georgia securities Clews later stated that his firm sold the $102,000 of bonds they held before Georgia repudiated them at ninety-seven and one-half; and that the proceeds of the sale were credited to the state's account.[8]

In August 1872 the Georgia legislature repudiated the indorsed railroad bonds and the others designated by the Bond Committee. There was a difference of opinion in Georgia on the advisability of adopting such measures; but under the leadership of Robert Toombs, Benjamin Hill, and W. M. Wadley, the repudiation party won out.[9] Upon receipt of the news in Frankfort, a resolution was passed by the committee of the Stock Exchange excluding every admission of the State of Georgia from future dealings until the claims of the holders of the repudiated bonds were satisfied.[10]

Georgia did not stop with these repudiations. The investigations and repudiations were continued by the legislature of 1875. Although the legislature of 1872 had declared that the state's indorsement of the Brunswick and Macon Railroad bonds was valid, the governor claimed in his message delivered in 1875 that a portion of the bonds indorsed were invalid on the ground that the state had only a second mortgage on the property. The legislature followed the governor's suggestion and bonds whose aggregate face value was $600,000, were repudiated. At the same session state-indorsed bonds of the Alabama and Chattanooga Railroad were repudiated as they were second mortgage bonds and were issued, therefore, in defiance of the prohibition in the state constitution.[11]

In 1876 the lengthening list of repudiations was enlarged by the addition of $375,000 more bonds. In 1854 the legislature authorized the issuance of $375,000 of 6 percent bonds to be ex-

---

[8] *London Times*, Jan. 10, 1871; Clews, *op. cit.*, pp. 274-277.
[9] Acts Georgia, 1872, pp. 5-8; Thompson, *op. cit.*, pp. 234, 235.
[10] *London Times*, Sept. 8, 1872.
[11] Georgia House Journal, 1875, p. 26; Acts of Georgia, 1875, pp. 13, 14.

changed for a similar amount of outstanding bonds of the Central Bank. As the bonds of the Central Bank bore 7 percent, the change to 6 percent led to a disagreement between the governor and the holders of the bonds of the bank. The new bonds were executed but were not issued. In 1864, it was claimed that state bonds were taken from the treasury, by unauthorized persons, and negotiated for this purpose. On February 26, 1876 an act was, therefore, passed declaring these bonds null and void.[12]

The following year all of these repudiations were made binding upon the state. In February 1877 the legislature approved a constitutional amendment confirming the repudiation statutes. This was ratified by the people the following May. In the Constitutional Convention which assembled that year for the purpose of drafting a new constitution a feeble effort was made to secure a provision calling for an investigation and adjudication by the Supreme Court of Georgia of the claims of individuals or corporations against the state. This was defeated by the repudiation party and in the Constitution of 1877 there is a provision which reads: "The general assembly shall have no authority to appropriate money, either directly or indirectly, to pay the whole or any part of the principal or interest of the bonds or other obligations which have been pronounced illegal, null, and void by the general assembly, and the constitutional amendments ratified by a vote of the people on the first day of May, 1877. . . ."[13] The minimum face value of the repudiated bonds of Georgia, exclusive of interest, is estimated at $9,352,000.

LOUISIANA

In March 1861 the finance committee of the House of Representatives of Louisiana submitted a tabular statement of the public debt of the state for the period from 1840 to 1861 inclusive. This report showed that the debt had been reduced from over $23,000,000 in 1840 to $10,099,074 in 1861.[1] An analysis of these liabilities disclosed that the debt consisted of two classes. There was the "debt

---

[12] Acts of Georgia, 1876, pp. 9, 10.
[13] Ibid., 1877, pp. 24, 25; Georgia Constitutional Convention, 1877, pp. 307-309; Tenth Census, Vol. 7, pp. 585, 586.
[1] 10 Census, Vol. 7, pp. 597, 598.

proper" which the state had incurred through the issuance of bonds to railroad companies, trust funds, and various loans to the state. Then there was the debt due for the property banks and the municipalities of New Orleans which had been incurred through the issuance of state bonds in aid of these corporations. In 1861 this portion of the debt amounted to over half of the total indebtedness.

During the Civil War and the Reconstruction era the credit of Louisiana was destroyed. Reconstruction began in Louisiana as early as 1862; and for fourteen long weary years Louisiana suffered from military autocracy and colored and carpetbag despots. No other southern state, with the possible exception of Virginia, felt so severely the ravages of war. New Orleans fell into the hands of the Union forces when the Confederacy was at the zenith of its power; and General Butler ruled the city as only a military tyrant can. The fall of Vicksburg ruined the commerce of New Orleans; and each succeeding year of the war added to her misery, humiliation and poverty. When peace finally came, it brought no relief or hope to the downtrodden people. Their means of livelihood were gone, their wealth was dissipated, and the negroes were unruly and menacing. The State of Louisiana and the City of New Orleans were bankrupt. Interest on the state and city bonds were in default. No taxes were collected between the years 1860 and 1867 and the value of the assessed property within the state dropped from $470,164,963 in 1860 to $250,063,359.63 in 1870. The public roads were mere mud trails; there were only four paved streets in New Orleans; the rest of the streets were at times impassable.[2] The levees were in a deplorable condition; and in order to defray the expenses of repairing and constructing new levees the legislature in 1866 and 1867 authorized the issuance of $5,000,000 of state bonds.[3] But the credit of Louisiana had sunk so low that it was practically impossible to sell these securities. There was a general distrust of all southern bonds and especially those of Louisiana. They were not listed on the New York Stock Exchange; and by October 1868 Louisiana state bonds were selling in the market for 47 cents on the dollar and

---

[2] The description of conditions in Louisiana after the war is based upon the accounts found in Warmoth, H. C., War, Politics and Reconstruction, pp. 79-81; Lonn, E., Reconstruction in Louisiana, pp. 17-18.

[3] Louisiana Acts, 1866, No. 3, p. 6; 1867, No. 115, pp. 213-217.

some of the levee bonds were as low as 25 and 30 cents.[4] Such was the financial condition of the state when in July 1868 the Radical Republicans assumed control.

Of all the reconstructed governments in the south, that of Louisiana was probably the worst. It was saturated with corruption; it represented the lowest and most ignorant groups within the state. Nearly one-half of the members of the House were negroes; in the Senate there were seven negroes; and the lieutenant governor was a negro house painter. The conduct of the legislature was disgusting and vulgar. The Speaker had to forbid the members from bringing liquor into the House. Some of the amendments offered were too obscene to print; while the general disorder which prevailed in the legislative chambers was notorious. There was no law against bribery in Louisiana; and charges of corruption were openly made upon the floor. One member boldly challenged another: "I want to know how much the gentleman gets to support the bill." Another under oath declared that "it was generally understood all round that anyone who wanted to get a bill through had to pay for it." Governor Warmoth publicly declared that he had been offered bribes; but there is no evidence that he ever accepted any although his enemies frequently commented on his capacity to save $100,000 a year on a salary of $8,000 and to accumulate a fortune of a million dollars in four years.[5]

Governor Warmoth was only twenty-six years of age when he assumed the responsibilities of office. He lacked experience and fitness for the position; but for a time at least he ruled with a rod of iron. His native state was Illinois; and before the war he had moved to Missouri to practice law. He enlisted in the Union army; but was dishonorably dismissed from service by General Grant for circulating false reports of the northern losses at Vicksburg. President Lincoln, however, restored him to his command. In November 1864 Warmoth left the army, returned to New Orleans, and opened a law office where he claims he soon had a lucrative practice. In 1865 Warmoth was chosen territorial delegate from Louisiana to Congress. When the Grand Army of the Republic was organized, he was made Grand Commander, and a few months later was elected governor of the state. Such was the political atmosphere

[4] Lonn, *op. cit.*, p. 18. [5] *Ibid.*, pp. 8, 28, 68, 77, 88.

in which the bills granting state aid to numerous enterprises were drafted.[6]

The public debt of Louisiana was contracted through the granting of state aid for the building of railroads, the perfecting of the water communication within the state, and the repair and construction of levees. There was a universal demand for the state to undertake these works; and the Democrats as well as the Republicans were instrumental in securing the introduction and passage of many of these measures. Throughout the entire south there was a conviction that improved transportation facilities were essential for the economic rehabilitation of the section. The lobbyists who urged the enactment of these laws were drawn from both parties in Louisiana. Conservative as well as radical organs of the press sponsored the movement for an extensive system of internal improvements. "It is noteworthy as a sign fraught with good promise," stated the *Commercial Bulletin*, "that the railroad spirit is alive in the northern parishes of the state, and that those whom it inspires are evidently bent on the early accomplishment of substantial results." The press of New Orleans, the Chamber of Commerce, and other commercial bodies clamored for the construction of a railroad connecting New Orleans on the east with Mobile and on the west with Houston, Texas, with a branch to Shreveport. "It is certainly to be hoped," declared the *Crescent*, "that we shall soon have direct railroad communications with Mobile and that all efforts to prevent the consummation of so desirable an object will fail." The *Picayune* alone sounded a note of warning against the prodigal lending of the credit of the state "unless the projects are of certain and undoubted practicability and profitableness and are secured beyond all peril of losses." [7]

Such advice was wasted upon the ignorant and corruptible members of the General Assembly. Each session of the legislature an increasing number of bills were passed lending the credit of the state to numerous enterprises. On February 17, 1869, the New Orleans, Mobile, and Chattanooga Railroad was authorized to issue second mortgage bonds, bearing 8 percent interest, payable in forty

---

[6] See characterization of Warmoth given in Lonn, *op. cit.*, p. 7 and compare with this Warmoth's own account of his career to 1868 in his book, War, Politics, and Reconstruction, pp. 1-80.

[7] *Commercial Bulletin, Crescent,* and *Picayune* quoted in Lonn, p. 36.

or fifty years, guaranteed by the state to the extent of $12,500 for each mile of track built west of New Orleans within the state.[8] The following year the legislature authorized the issuance of $3,000,000 of state bonds to the same company, the bonds to be delivered in installments as the road was constructed.[9] The next year the second mortgage bonds of two other railroad companies were also indorsed by the state to the extent of $12,500 per mile of track.[10] In order to improve the water communications, the governor was authorized in 1869 to issue $600,000 of bonds to aid in the construction of the Mississippi and Mexican Gulf Ship Canal;[11] and the next year the New Orleans and Ship Island Canal Company was granted the funds and assets of the drainage commissioners amounting to nearly $2,000,000, besides a patent for 400,000 acres of land.[12] Numerous small appropriations were made to different companies for the purpose of improving water navigation through the removal of obstructions in various bayous.[13] In 1870 the governor was authorized to issue $3,000,000 of state bonds, payable in five years, bearing 8 percent interest, and the proceeds of their sale was to be applied exclusively to the payment of work done on the levees of the state. For the payment of the principal and interest of these bonds the faith of the state was unconditionally pledged and the act provided for a special tax levy to pay the principal and interest.[14]

The following year the Louisiana Levee Company was chartered and given the exclusive management and control of the levees of the state. In order to aid this company the governor was authorized to issue $1,000,000 of 8 percent state bonds.[15] In addition to these grants in aid the legislature at its regular and special sessions in 1870 and 1871 indorsed the bonds of the Louisiana Warehouse Company;[16] authorized the issuance of $1,500,000 of bonds for the erection of a State house;[17] subscribed for $100,000 of the capital stock of the Mississippi Valley Navigation Company;[18] issued $3,000,000 of state bonds for the payment of the floating debt of

[8] Louisiana Acts, 1869, No. 26, pp. 22-30.   [9] Ibid., 1870, No. 31, p. 60.
[10] Ibid., 1871, No. 28, pp. 66-72; No. 40, pp. 88-97.
[11] Ibid., 1869, No. 116, pp. 166-169.
[12] Ibid., 1870, extra session, No. 4, pp. 5-10.
[13] Ibid., 1870, No. 59, p. 87; 1871, No. 35, 45, 53, 59, 70, pp. 83, 84, 137, 138, 155, 164, 165, 173-174.
[14] Ibid., 1870, No. 32, pp. 63-65.
[15] Ibid., 1871, No. 4, pp. 29-38.   [17] Ibid., 1871, No. 31, pp. 79, 80.
[16] Ibid., 1871, No. 41, pp. 98-103.   [18] Ibid., 1870, No. 84, pp. 116, 117.

the state;[19] authorized the governor to negotiate a loan to supply any deficiency that might exist to meet the payment of interest due on bonds of the state;[20] and issued $134,000 of bonds for the relief of P. J. Kennedy for work done on the construction of certain levees.[21] Some of these laws were passed over Governor Warmoth's veto; but many of them received his approval even though an amendment to the state constitution ratified in 1870 limited the debt of the state prior to 1890 to $25,000,000.[22]

Notwithstanding this constitutional limitation the total bonded debt of the state by March 1, 1871 was $26,280,000. Besides this the state had obligated itself to indorse the bonds of the New Orleans, Mobile and Chattanooga and the New Orleans, Baton Rouge and Vicksburg railroads to the extent of $12,500 for each mile of track built by these respective roads. Furthermore the state might be called upon at any time to pay $4,839,933.33 of bonds issued to the property banks although these institutions claimed they were amply secured by their assets.[23]

At the same time that the public debt mounted there was an appalling increase in the rate of taxation. Before Governor Warmoth's administration the rate of taxation in New Orleans had been 15 mills on the dollar; in 1869 it was 23¾; in 1870 it rose to 26⅓; by 1871 it was 27½; and in 1873 it stood at 30 mills.[24]

The legality of the state debt did not go unquestioned by the citizens of Louisiana. In 1871 a large number of property owners and taxpayers of New Orleans issued a statement in which they declared that the legislature had exceeded the constitutional limitation on the public debt; and bankers, brokers, and dealers in securities, in this country and in Europe, were notified that all loans, indorsements, and pledges made by the legislature would be considered null and void. Furthermore the signers of this notification declared that they would sustain the authorities in resisting their issue, and if issued, they would endeavor, by every legal means, to prevent the payment of any interest or principal or the collection of any tax levied for that purpose. The public was informed that the only debt which the state would recognize as legal obligations were

[19] *Ibid.*, 1870, extra session, No. 69, pp. 153, 154. [20] *Ibid.*, No. 10, p. 52.
[21] *Ibid.*, 1870, No. 105, pp. 174-176.
[22] Poore, B. P., Federal and State Constitution, Pt. *II*, p. 771.
[23] Louisiana Reports, Vol. 23, pp. 402-408. [24] Lonn, *op. cit.*, p. 252.

the state bonds, auditor's warrants, and certificates and miscellaneous debts given in the state auditor's report, amounting to $25,021,-734.40; but the accruing debt, amounting to $15,395,000, was classified as unconstitutional legislation. This included the bonds authorized but not yet issued for the Mississippi and Mexican Gulf Canal; the North Louisiana and Texas Railroad; New Orleans, Mobile and Chattanooga Railroad, and New Orleans, Baton Rouge and Vicksburg Railroad; and the subscriptions to the shares of the Mississippi Valley Navigation Company. This circular was printed in French, German, and English and copies were sent abroad and to New York and distributed in every banking house in this country and in Europe.[25]

At the same time that this circular was published a prospectus was issued in London by Robinson, Fleming and Company inviting the public to subscribe to a $2,000,000 Louisiana state loan for levee purposes. The prospectus called attention to the fact that "for the payment of the principal and accruing interest on these bonds, the special act of the legislature pledges the faith of the State of Louisiana unconditionally, and levies a special tax of one quarter of 1 percent upon the estate, real and personal, throughout the state subject to taxation to continue until the principal and interest of these bonds are fully paid."[26]

Yet a month later the Supreme Court of Louisiana refused to issue a writ of mandamus to compel the auditor to issue a warrant on an appropriation of $50,000 in favor of a Mr. Nixon on the ground that "the state debt exceeded the constitutional limitation and that the revenues of the state were inadequate to meet the current expenditures."[27]

By 1874 the political and economic conditions in Louisiana were becoming unbearable. There was a government in power, the Kellogg administration, which had been foisted upon the people by the Federal authorities. The treasury was empty and the state was no longer able to pay the interest on her bonds. The average price of Louisiana bonds was less than 50 cents on the dollar;[28] yet the cor-

---

[25] *Commercial and Financial Chronicle*, Apr. 1, 1871. Consult Warmoth, *op. cit.*, p. 83, for the alleged reasons for issuing this circular.
[26] *London Times*, Apr. 25, 1871.
[27] Louisiana Reports, Vol. 23, pp. 402-408.
[28] Louisiana Legislative Doc. 1874, pp. 6-20. Governor Kellogg's message of 1874.

rupt legislature continued to encourage the improvement spirit.[29] The propertied class was rapidly becoming impoverished by the heavy taxes and large amounts were in arrears. A committee of citizens appointed by Governor Kellogg to investigate the state debt reported that on December 15, 1870, when the amendment of the constitution limiting the debt to $25,000,000 was promulgated, the obligations of the state, including the contingent liabilities, amounted to upwards of $42,000,000. Consequently the committee held that the liabilities created by acts passed since that date, amounting to $8,087,500, were null and void. They also regarded the other contingent liabilities, amounting to $13,003,000, which were created prior to the amendment null and void because all or nearly all had lapsed or become forfeitable by neglect. The committee reported that there were still outstanding bonds amounting to $4,297,333.33 issued to the Citizens Bank, and $531,447 of bonds of the Consolidated Association of Planters; but the committee did not think the state would be called upon to meet these liabilities because the assets of these banks were thought to be sufficient to secure the payment of the principal and interest of these bonds. But the committee held that $2,500,000 of bonds issued to pay the state's subscription for stock of the New Orleans, Mobile, and Texas Railroad under an act approved May 20, 1871 might be regarded as null and void because it was in violation of the constitutional limitation. The committee estimated that the state debt in 1874 was $53,000,000; and if from this amount there was deducted over $30,000,000 of unwarranted guaranties, there still remained $23,000,000 of outstanding obligations, bearing an annual interest of $1,500,000. But the legality of many of these obligations was denied in the courts. Therefore the committee recommended that all void, lapsed, and forfeited contingent liabilities be declared null; that the courts pass upon the validity of all questionable obligations; and that the state debt be reduced as soon as possible to $12,000,000.[30]

Under these circumstances, Governor Kellogg recommended the passage of a well-digested funding bill accompanied by appropriate constitutional amendments. Accordingly, on January 24, 1874, an act was passed for the purpose of consolidating and reducing the

[29] Louisiana Acts, 1874, No. 145.

[30] For this report consult *Commercial and Financial Chronicle*, Jan. 17, 1874, and Governor Kellogg's message given in Louisiana Legislative Doc., 1874, pp. 6-20.

floating and bonded debt of the state. The governor, lieutenant governor, auditor, treasurer, secretary of state, and speaker of the House of Representatives were created a board of liquidation; and were authorized to issue bonds, known as "consolidated bonds of the state" to the amount of $15,000,000, payable in forty years, bearing 7 percent interest. These new bonds were to be exchanged by the board of liquidation for all valid outstanding bonds and warrants at the rate of 60 cents in consolidated bonds for one dollar in outstanding bonds and all valid warrants. A tax of 5½ mills was levied to pay the interest and principal of the consolidated bonds; and the entire state debt prior to 1914 was never to exceed $15,000,000. At the same time the legislature passed an act proposing amendments to the constitution indorsing the funding bill and the consolidated bonds, reducing the state debt to $15,000,000, and limiting taxation to 12½ mills. These were submitted to the people and ratified by a large vote at the next election.[31]

The passage of the funding bill was denounced by the domestic and foreign holders of Louisiana securities. New York bondholders declared that the funding bill was simply a proposition of a forced purchase from present holders at the rate of 60 cents on the dollar of the outstanding obligations of the commonwealth, which, the governor had frequently shown, was perfectly able to discharge in full. "The guilt of such unnecessary and wanton repudiation would be almost without parallel"; and they could not believe that the citizens of Louisiana would at one blow destroy their well-earned character for scrupulous honesty.[32] London bondholders refused to accept the conversion proferred by Governor Kellogg on the ground that it meant the confiscation of 40 percent of the capital and interest of their bonds.[33] As there were a great number of bona fide holders of Louisiana bonds in the Netherlands, a committee of the Bourse at Amsterdam joined with the Council of Foreign Bondholders in their protest.[34]

The people of Louisiana as well as the creditors were dissatisfied with the funding act. The law provided that the board of liquidation should decide what were the valid outstanding bonds and warrants; but the holder of any bond or valid warrant rejected by a

[31] Louisiana Acts, 1874, No. 3, pp. 39-42; No. 4, pp. 42, 43.
[32] *Commercial and Financial Chronicle*, Feb. 7, 1874.
[33] *Ibid.*, Aug. 15, 1874.   [34] *London Times,* Jan. 31, 1874.

majority of the board might apply to the proper court for relief. As the board was composed of officials of the Kellogg administration it was claimed that in the funding and exchange of old securities for new bonds many frauds and speculations were committed. It was later claimed that the funding board, having discretionary power, "funded some $6,000,000 of bonds alleged to have been fraudulent. . . . It was charged, and generally believed, that some of these chief officers combined with brokers and speculators in buying up fraudulent and dishonest securities, and warrants of doubtful validity, at very low rates, and funding and exchanging them for new bonds." [85]

In order to provide means for testing the validity and legality of the various bond issues, the legislature on May 17, 1875 passed a supplemental act. In this law some $14,000,000 of bonds were designated as "questionable and doubtful obligations of the State"; and the board of liquidation was prohibited from funding any of these bonds until their legality and validity had been passed upon by the Supreme Court of Louisiana. The list of questionable and doubtful bonds and warrants included nine issues to aid various railroad companies, three issues for the construction of levees, those issued for the relief of the state treasury, and the Mississippi and Mexican Gulf Ship Canal, for the relief of P. J. Kennedy, to aid the Boeuf and Crocodile Navigation Company, and the bonds purporting to have been issued for the redemption of certificates of indebtedness. The attorney general was authorized to conduct the suits testing the legality of these issues; and the presidents of the Cotton Exchange and of the Board of Trade of New Orleans were added to the board of liquidation. [86]

As soon as this law was passed the validity of many of the doubtful issues were tested in the courts. Evidently the British bondholders were more willing to trust the decision of the courts than those of the board of liquidation for they promptly decided to present their bonds for conversion under protest against the arbitrary reduction of the principal and interest. [87] They had little cause to regret their decision for the courts pronounced valid most

[85] Herbert, H. A., Why the Solid South, p. 419; McClure, The South, pp. 122-125.
[86] Louisiana Acts, 1875, No. 111, pp. 110-112.
[87] Commercial and Financial Chronicle, June 5, 1875.

of the "questionable and doubtful" obligations. In 1876 the Supreme Court of Louisiana declared nearly $8,000,000 of levee bonds valid as well as $124,000 issued to aid the Mississippi and Mexican Gulf Ship Canal. But $2,500,000 of bonds issued to the New Orleans, Mobile and Chattanooga Railroad were pronounced unconstitutional on the ground that the constitutional limit of the state debt had already been reached before the passage of the act which authorized the issuance of these bonds.[38]

When the constitutional convention of 1879 assembled there was general dissatisfaction throughout the state with the disposition made of the state debt question. The public was convinced that many of the bonds declared valid by the courts were illegal; and the 7 percent interest rate was considered excessive. After considerable debate the convention adopted a "debt ordinance" which was subsequently ratified by the people and became a part of the fundamental law of the state. The "debt ordinance" recognized the consolidated bonds as legal but scaled the interest from 7 to 2 percent for five years from January 1, 1880, 3 percent for fifteen years, and 4 percent thereafter. The holders of consolidated bonds were given the option of exchanging their 7 percent bonds for new bonds representing 75 percent of their face value and bearing interest at 4 percent.[39]

The bondholders showed little disposition to accept the terms of the "debt ordinance." By 1882 only $200,000 of the $12,000,000 consolidated bonds had been presented to the treasury to have the new interest rates stamped on them. By the terms of the debt ordinance no interest was to be paid until the bondholders accepted its provisions; and consequently the interest money collected for this purpose accumulated in the treasury.[40] An attempt was made by some of the bondholders to compel the board of liquidation to apply the funds in the treasury derived from taxes to the payment of their coupons. A suit was instituted in the State Court of Louisiana for a mandamus against the auditor, and treasurer, and other members of the board of liquidation; and another suit was brought in the

---

[38] Louisiana Reports, Vol. 27, pp. 577-585; Vol. 28, pp. 219-227, 393-400.
[39] Journal of the Constitutional Convention of Louisiana, 1879, App., pp. 23, 24, 105, 305.
[40] Commercial and Financial Chronicle, July 8, 1882.

Circuit Court praying for an injunction forbidding them to recognize as valid the debt ordinance. These cases were brought on writ of error before the United States Supreme Court where Justice Waite, in rendering the decision, declared: "Neither was there when the bonds were issued, nor is there now, any statute or judicial decision giving the bondholders a remedy in the state courts, or elsewhere, either by mandamus or injunction against the State in its political capacity, to compel it to do what it has agreed should be done, but it refuses to do." [41] Some of the consolidated bonds were also assigned by their owners to the states of New Hampshire and New York; and these states filed bills of equity in the United States Supreme Court against Louisiana. But the court held that this action was an evasion of the Eleventh Amendment of the federal constitution and dismissed the cases. [42]

When the Louisiana legislature assembled in May 1882 the bondholders in desperation decided to submit a proposition for the settlement of the troublesome debt question. They proposed that the terms of the debt settlement should be so altered as to give the bondholders 2 percent for five years from January 1, 1880 and 4 percent thereafter. This proposition was approved by the legislature and an amendment to the state debt ordinance was submitted to the electors embodying these provisions. This was ratified by the people in May 1884 and was accepted by the bondholders. [43]

MINNESOTA

There has been a great deal written about the defalcation and repudiation of southern state debts. There has been less attention paid to the drastic manner in which certain northern states have dealt with their debts. We have had occasion in another connection to recount the settlement of the public debts of Indiana, Illinois, and Michigan. We have seen how these people in these respective states reacted to the demand that these states acknowledge their legal and moral obligation to pay debts which the public were convinced were

---

[41] 107 U. S. Reports, pp. 711-769.
[42] 108 U. S. Reports, pp. 76-92.
[43] *Commercial and Financial Chronicle,* July 8, 1882; May 17, 1884; Louisiana Acts, 1882, No. 76, pp. 96, 97.

fraudulent and unjust. Without condoning or in any way apologizing for any of the actions taken by any of the southern states either before or after the Civil War in adjusting their debts, it is well to remember the struggle over the settlement of the debts of some of the northern states.

For this reason the inclusion of the history of the adjustment of the railroad debt of Minnesota in this particular chapter has an added significance. The people of Minnesota could not complain as did their southern brethren that this debt had been foisted upon them by a corrupt reconstruction government. Nor were the Minnesota bonds held by "conquerors" or by "foreigners" as southerners pleaded in extenuation for their actions. Nor was Minnesota ravaged during the Civil War as was the case of all the southern states. And yet the electors of Minnesota were as unwilling to recognize the moral and legal obligation of their state to pay for "swindling bonds" as were the citizens of every one of the southern states at the close of Reconstruction. Minnesota actually passed a constitutional amendment on the eve of the Civil War repudiating a debt which her own representatives had voted; and for over twenty years every attempt to adjust this debt was defeated either by her own obdurate electorate or by the unwillingness of the creditors to accept the proffered terms. No progress was made toward a settlement of this debt until the question was taken out of the hands of the electorate and a special tribunal declared the repudiating constitutional amendment of 1860 null and void. It is therefore interesting to recount the reactions of a northern community toward the payment of a debt which the people were convinced was unjust and fraudulent at a time when many of the southern states were wrestling with their own debts which had largely been incurred during the dark days of reconstruction.

By an act approved March 3, 1857 Congress granted to the Territory of Minnesota to aid in the construction of six lines of railroads, on routes designated in the bill, six sections of land per mile, in alternate sections, along the line of the projected roads as they were built. The territorial legislature accepted the land grants in trust and in turn on May 23, 1857 granted them conditionally to the Southern Minnesota Railroad Company, the Transit Railroad Company, the Minneapolis and Cedar Valley Railroad

Company, and the Minnesota and Pacific Railroad Company. By the terms of this act the lands granted to these four companies were exempt from all taxation. As soon as any of these companies had located twenty continuous miles of their road, it was to receive the title of 120 sections of land; and when it had completed twenty continuous miles of road so as to admit of the running of regular trains, it was to receive a further quantity of 120 sections of land and thereafter similar amounts of land until the road was completed. In consideration of the grants, privileges, and franchises conferred on the companies, each one was to pay into the state treasury in lieu of all taxes the sum of 3 percent of the gross earnings of the road.[1]

Before these companies were in a position to take advantage of this aid, the panic of 1857 swept over the country. With business houses in Minnesota failing, banks closing their doors, and the public overwhelmed with debts, it was impossible for the railroad companies to interest anyone in their enterprises. Yet if any one of them could locate and survey 20 miles of road, it would receive 76,800 acres of land. At $5 an acre, these lands would be worth $348,000; and like amounts of land would be given to them from time to time as they built and put into operation additional twenty-mile sections of their roads. In the midst of the business depression, however, no one was willing to buy or loan money on these prospective land grants. The Transit Railroad Company found it impossible to interest purchasers even though it offered 500,000 acres of its land at $1 an acre.[2]

In their desperation it was only natural that the railroad companies should look to the state for financial assistance. Other states had aided in the promotion of internal improvements, why should not Minnesota? But the state constitution prohibited the legislature from contracting public debts in excess of $250,000; and provided that every law authorizing the debts should carry a provision for a tax sufficient to pay the principal within ten years. Moreover section 10 of article 9 of the constitution forbade the state from loaning

---

[1] 11 U. S. Statutes-at-Large, pp. 195-197; Laws Terr. Minn., extra session, 1857, pp. 3-26. The Minnesota debt has been discussed in detail by Folwell, W. W., The History of Minnesota, Vol. *II*, pp. 37-59; Vol. *III*, 418-441; Folwell, W. W., The Five Million Dollar Loan of Minnesota, Minnesota Historical Society Collections, Vol. 15, pp. 189-214. Consult also Saby, R. S., Railroad Legislation in Minnesota, Minnesota Historical Society Collections, Vol. 15, pp. 1-188.

[2] Folwell, History of Minnesota, Vol. *I*, pp. 363, 364; Vol. *II*, p. 43.

her credit to any individual association, or corporation.[8] Yet it was this section which gave the railroad companies hope. By amending this clause of the constitution the state could issue its state bonds and help the railroad companies out of their dilemma.

Undeterred by the evil results which had followed from other states loaning their credit to aid internal improvements, the Five Million Dollar Loan Bill was introduced and passed on March 9, 1858 with little opposition by the Minnesota legislature. The act proposed an amendment to section 10 article 9 of the constitution and provided for its submission to the people for their approval or rejection. Section 10 article 9 was to be amended so as to permit the governor to issue and deliver to each of the four railroad companies special bonds of the state, bearing 7 percent interest, payable semi-annually, as a loan of public credit, to an amount not exceeding $5,000,000. These bonds were to be designated "Minnesota State Railroad Bonds" and the faith and credit of the state was pledged for the payment of the interest and the redemption of the principal. Whenever any of the companies produced satisfactory evidence that it had graded 10 miles of road, the governor was to issue and deliver $100,000 of bonds; and a like amount of bonds for every additional ten miles graded. Another $100,000 of bonds were to be issued and delivered for every 10 miles "actually completed and cars running thereon"; and for every additional 10 miles completed a further like amount of bonds was to be issued and delivered. Each company was to provide for the payment of the interest and redemption of the bonds issued to it. As security for the loan, each company was to pledge its net profits for the payment of the interest; and execute and deliver to the governor a conveyance for the first 240 sections of land. The proceeds of the sale of these lands were to be applied to the payment of the interest accruing upon the bonds in case of default of payment and to form a sinking fund to meet any future defaults in the payment of the interest and principal. As further security each company was required to give first mortgage bonds on its road, lands and franchise equal to the amount of state bonds received. In case any company defaulted upon the payment of the interest or principal, the governor was to sell the lands and foreclose the mortgages. In further consideration of the loan, each company was required to complete 50 miles by

[8] Poore, B. P., Federal and State Constitutions, Pt. *II*, p. 1038.

the close of 1861, 100 miles by the close of 1864, and 4/5 of its road by 1866.[4]

The adoption of this amendment was thoroughly debated by the people of Minnesota. The public was assured by the advocates of the measure that the state would not be called upon to pay the bonds. Sixty-seven members of the legislature issued a statement in which they pledged themselves "individually and collectively to vote against any proposition to levy a tax either for the interest or principal of the proposed loan of state credit. We claim to have removed all probable chance of taxation . . . and we shall resist, as one man, any proposition of the kind." The Democratic party and the leading Democratic newspaper urged the ratification of the proposed amendment. The Republican party tacitly sponsored the bill although the leading Republican newspaper opposed its adoption. At the ensuing election the amendment was ratified by a large majority, the only opposition coming from a few of the rural counties.[5]

As soon as the amendment was adopted, the railroad companies commenced work upon their respective lines. Before the state bonds were issued, however, a dispute arose over the interpretation of the act. The governor insisted that the railroads should give exclusive first mortgage bonds to the state equal to the amount of state bonds they received. The companies objected to this construction of the law and instituted proceedings in the Supreme Court of the state to compel the governor, by writ of mandamus, to deliver the state bonds. A divided court sustained the position taken by the railroad companies; and in accord with this decision Governor Sibley issued and delivered the state bonds. But the publicity given to the disagreement between the executive and the companies weakened the value of the bonds in the money markets. They were regarded with suspicion; and it was with considerable difficulty that they were marketed.[6]

It was not long before the railroad companies were in financial difficulties. By 1859 they were unable to meet the interest payments; and all construction soon ceased. In his message of 1859 to the legislature Governor Sibley recited the history of the bond issue

[4] General Laws Minn., 1858, pp. 9-13.   [5] Folwell, *op. cit.*, Vol. *II*, pp. 47, 48.
[6] Minn. Reports, Vol. *II*, pp. 13-30; House Journal Minn., 1859-1860, pp. 16, 17.

and declared that all the state could show for its generous aid was 240 miles of disjointed, poorly graded road.[7]

Both Governor Sibley and his successor Governor Ramsay urged the legislature to recognize the obligation of the state for the payment of these bonds and immediately settle the debt question. Governor Ramsay warned the legislature that if the question were not then settled it would cause endless discussion and discord among the people. He proposed that the legislature grant new railroad charters providing for a " 'bonus of $10,000 a mile in State bonds bearing a graduated interest of less than 7 percent per annum' for every 20 miles of continuous road completed, on condition that an equal amount of Minnesota State Railroad Bonds be returned to the treasury for cancellation." He believed that the stockholders would accept these liberal terms and resume work. For the remainder of the outstanding bonds, the governor suggested that new ones be issued. Unless the legislature settled the issue at once, the governor prophesied that the bonds would fall into the hands of a few men who would purchase them at greatly reduced prices; and these men would "knock year after year at the door of the legislature for their payment in full," would subsidize the press, and ultimately would "pile up almost fabulous fortunes obtaining a recognition of their disputed paper and its payment at par." [8]

The legislature and the public refused to listen to this sound advice. The majority of the people were convinced that the state was not responsible for the payment of the "swindling bonds," as they were called. Let the speculators who had bought the bonds look to the railroad companies for their payment. Agents of these companies had assured the people that these were debts of the railroads not those of the state. In this frame of mind the legislature on March 6, 1860 passed an act making it the duty of the governor to foreclose the deeds of trust. He was furthermore authorized to purchase at the sale the property, rights, and franchises of the four railroad companies. Pursuant to this act the governor in June bought at public auction all the properties and franchises of these companies for the nominal sum of $1,000 for each company. In

[7] House Journal Minn., 1859-1860, pp. 10-27.
[8] Folwell, op. cit., Vol. II, pp. 53, 54.

1862 and 1864 the state regranted all the properties and franchises of the original companies to new corporations.[9]

The same legislature which authorized the foreclosing of the mortgages and the purchase of the railroads passed a concurrent resolution proposing two amendments to the state constitution. The first provided that no law levying a tax or making other provisions for the payment of interest or principal of the Minnesota State Railroad bonds should take effect until adopted by a majority of the electors of the state; the other expunged the entire amendment to section 10 of article 9 adopted in 1858 which had permitted the credit of the state to be loaned to the land grant railroads. These amendments were submitted to the people on November 6, 1860 and ratified by overwhelming majorities.[10]

During the next two decades various acts were passed by the legislature and submitted to the people providing for an adjustment and payment of the Minnesota State Railroad bonds. Some of these laws were rejected by the people; others by the bondholders. The first of these acts was passed in 1866. It provided for the appointment by the governor of three commissioners to ascertain who were the holders of the railroad bonds, the amount due each holder, and the amount paid by each bona-fide owner.[11]

In the summer of that year it was discovered that Minnesota had a claim to 500,000 acres of public lands for internal improvements under the provisions of an act passed by Congress, September 4, 1841.[12] Immediately there arose a demand from many quarters that these lands be used to pay off the old bonds. It was suggested that either the proceeds of the sales of these lands be set apart as a sinking fund to pay the railroad bonds or that the creditors be given these lands in exchange for their bonds. Governor Marshall in his message to the legislature of 1867 mentioned both of these possible ways of using the lands and urged the assembly to adjust the debt. The legislature carried out his recommendations by passing an act March 5 setting aside the proceeds of the sale of the 500,000 acres as a "State Railroad Bond Sinking Fund." Whenever this fund should have accumulated the sum of $20,000 the

[9] General Laws Minn., 1860, p. 269; Minn. Reports, Vol. 29, pp. 479, 480.
[10] General Laws Minn., 1860, p. 297; Folwell, *op. cit.*, Vol. *II*, p. 56.
[11] General Laws Minn., 1866, pp. 9, 10.
[12] 5 Statutes-at-Large, p. 455; Folwell, *op. cit.*, Vol. *III*, p. 34.

treasurer was to invite the bondholders to bid for this cash and those whose proposals should be most advantageous were to surrender their bonds and receive the money.[13]

Under the terms of the amendment of 1860 this act was submitted to the electors at the next general election. They rejected it by a vote of 49,763 to 1,935. Their decision may have been influenced by the revelations of the commissioners appointed to investigate the extent and character of the railroad bond debt. Their report disclosed that the bonds had been purchased at prices ranging from 17½ cents to par. The largest holder of the bonds was Selah Chamberlain of Ohio, a railroad contractor. He held 967 bonds which he claimed had cost him par in work and materials furnished. The commissioners employed an experienced engineer to examine the work; and he reported the grading had cost Chamberlain $2,803.42 per mile instead of $9,500 as he alleged. According to this estimate the bonds had cost Chamberlain a little over 30 percent of their face value. The report of the committee naturally confirmed the suspicions of the people that the claims of the creditors were unjust.[14]

In 1870 the legislature passed another act to utilize the 500,000 acres of lands "providentially" given to the state to settle the debt. This act provided that these lands should be sold in tracts of 160 acres at $8.70 per acre; and that the railroad bonds should be accepted at par in payment for these lands. At this price the 500,000 acres would yield $4,350,000 which was just about enough to redeem the bonds with accumulated interest. The lands were to be exempt from taxation for ten years. This act was ratified by the people but was never put into operation. The act was not to go into effect unless 2,000 bonds were deposited; only 1,032, including those held by Chamberlain, were turned in. Holders of 1,080 bonds resolved at a meeting in New York to "decline to accept an offer not equal to 25 percent of our just claims against a debtor able to pay in full." [15]

The bondholders were sharply reprimanded for taking this position by Governor Austin in his message of 1870 to the legislature.

[13] General Laws Minn., 1867, pp. 93, 94; Saby, Railroad Legislation in Minn., pp. 38, 39.

[14] Saby, op. cit., p. 40; Folwell, op. cit., Vol. III, pp. 423, 424.

[15] General Laws Minn., 1870, pp. 19-21; Folwell, op. cit., Vol. III, pp. 425, 426.

"The bonds," he said, "are of questionable validity and if not actually fraudulent are so intimately connected with what the great majority of the people believe to have been a fraud upon the state, as to make them odious, while it has been established . . . that a large proportion of the bonds cost their present owners and holders but 17½ to 50 percent of their face (value)." [16]

Nevertheless the legislature of 1871 determined to make another attempt to settle the railroad debt. On March 6 the so-called Chamberlain bill was passed. The preamble of the act stated that as doubts prevailed as to whether the railroad bonds constituted a legal and valid indebtedness against the state, it was the purpose of the act to test their validity and to provide for an equitable adjustment of the claims. The governor was authorized to appoint three commissioners to determine whether the deposited railroad bonds were a "legal and equitable obligation against the state," and if so, to ascertain the amount due each bondholder on the basis of the cost of the bond to him. Should the commissioners decide the bonds constituted a legal obligation against the state, the governor was authorized to issue new 30-year bonds with interest so "funded as a part of the principal" as to make the average interest 7 percent and appropriated all railroad taxes to pay the interest and principal. As might have been expected the electors rejected the act at the special election held in May; and the following year approved the adoption of a constitutional amendment prohibiting the appropriation of the proceeds of the sale of the 500,000 acres of internal improvement lands until voted upon by the people. The ratification of this amendment made impossible the adjustment of the debt in the near future.[17]

Since the bondholders were unable to obtain relief from the legislature, Chamberlain determined to refer his case to the courts. In 1873 he brought suit against the St. Paul and Sioux City and Southern Minnesota railroads seeking to charge with the payment of his bonds the 240 sections of land mortgaged by the original railroad companies under the amendment of 1858 and purchased by the state under the foreclosure of this mortgage and now held by the defendant railroad companies. He contended that the position of

---

[16] Folwell, *op. cit.*, Vol. *III*, p. 426.

[17] General Laws Minn., 1871, pp. 52-55; *ibid.*, 1872, pp. 62-64; Folwell, *op. cit.*, Vol. *III*, p. 428.

the state in relation to the bonds was simply a surety. The original Southern Minnesota Railroad Company which indorsed the bond was the principal debtor. Hence, "upon the doctrine of subrogation, the conveyance by that company of any property to the state to indemnify her" created "a trust in favor of the holder of the bonds." The court refused to grant his claims but in an obiter dictum Justice Dillon said: "That the bonds held by the plaintiff are the legal obligations of the state, and binding upon it in law, honor, and justice, I have no doubt. . . . In the amendment to the constitution the faith and credit of the state are pledged for the payment of the interest and the redemption of the principal of the bonds. . . . Under these circumstances, if the state were suable in the courts, there can be no doubt that the bonds would be legally enforcible against it. Justice and honor alike require the state to recognize these bonds as binding upon it, and, in the end, the court cannot doubt that the people of the state will so ordain. A state with such a future before it as the State of Minnesota, cannot afford to bear the odium of repudiation." Chamberlain appealed his suit to the United States Supreme Court where the decision of the lower court was affirmed. But in rendering the decision Justice Field said: "The bonds issued are legal obligations. The state is bound by every consideration of honor and good faith to pay them. Were she amenable to the tribunals of the country as private individuals are, no court of justice would withhold its judgment against her in an action for their enforcement." [18]

In these casual statements of the United States Supreme Court the State of Minnesota was branded as a defaulter and a repudiator. The great mass of the people were apparently unmoved by these obiter dicta; but those in authority realized their full significance and redoubled their efforts to induce the state to pay the railroad bonds. Governor Davis and his successor Governor Pillsbury urged the legislature to take some definite action; but the assembly remained obdurate. Committees in both houses of the legislature submitted reports in which a labored attempt was made to show that the state was under no moral or legal obligation to pay the bonds. But public opinion was beginning to change. The State Baptist Convention of 1876 passed resolutions calling upon every Christian

[18] 92 U. S. Reports, pp. 299-307; Folwell, *op. cit.*, Vol. *III*, p. 429.

"to arouse the public mind and conscience to the legal and moral obligations of the State." Similar resolutions were passed by the Congregational and Presbyterian churches.[19]

In the hope of taking advantage of these symptoms of an aroused public opinion on the subject of adjusting the debt, Chamberlain came forward with a proposition to scale the debt. He offered to exchange his 7 percent bonds of the nominal value of $1,750 for new 6 percent coupon bonds equal in amount of $1,550. The legislature accepted his proposal and passed an act embodying these terms; but the act provided that no new bonds were to be issued until a majority of the electors at a special election held on June 12, 1877 should ratify a constitutional amendment authorizing the appropriation of the proceeds of the sale of the 500,000 acres of internal improvement lands to the payment of the principal and interest of the new bonds. As usual the electors rejected the proposed amendment and so killed the chance to settle the debt.[20]

The following year the legislature made another attempt to settle the question. An act was passed which provided that the 500,000 acres of internal improvement lands should be exchanged for bonds at a rate which should make the whole amount of the lands cancel the whole amount of outstanding bonds, unpaid coupons, and other claims. Each bondholder was to have a preferred choice of lands in the order in which his bonds were deposited. At the November election of 1878 this act was rejected by the electors.[21]

Undaunted by these several rebuffs, Governor Pillsbury made a final effort in 1881 to arouse the public consciousness to the obligation of the state to pay the railroad bonds. At his urgent request the legislature passed an act which provided for the submission to the people of the question of paying the debt only in the event that the tribunal of five judges of the Minnesota Supreme Court to which the question was submitted should decide that the repudiatory constitutional amendment of 1860 was valid. If this tribunal decided against the validity of the constitutional amendment or that the legislature had the power to provide for the settlement of the bonds without submission to the people, the governor was authorized to

[19] Appleton's Annual Cyclopædia, 1876, p. 558; Folwell, op. cit., Vol. III, p. 427.
[20] General Laws Minn., 1877, pp. 25, 26, 183-186; Appleton's Annual Cyclopædia, 1877, pp. 522, 523.
[21] General Laws Minn., 1878, pp. 143-145; Appleton's Annual Cyclopædia, 1878, p. 564; ibid., 1881, pp. 590, 591.

issue new bonds styled Minnesota State Railroad Adjustment Bonds, bearing 5 percent interest; and the state auditor was to deliver to holders of the old bonds these new ones equal to 50 percent of the original bonds. In case the tribunal decided in favor of the validity of the constitutional amendment of 1860 the act was to be submitted to the electors at the next general election; and if any of the judges of the Supreme Court declined to serve the governor was to appoint district judges.[22]

The validity of this act was tested in the Minnesota Supreme Court. The court decided that the act was void on the ground that it delegated legislative power to the tribunal created by it; but at the same time the court held that the constitutional amendment of 1860 was invalid for the reason that it impaired the obligation of the bonds which was repugnant to the clause of the federal constitution prohibiting any state from passing any act impairing the obligation of contracts.[23]

This decision left the legislature free to settle the question of the bonds without submitting its acts to the people. The governor accordingly called the legislature in extra session; and on November 4, 1881 the preceding act was substantially reënacted with the omission of the provisions for submission to a tribunal or to the people. Before the new bonds were issued, however, a suit was instituted to restrain the governor from signing or issuing the bonds and on November 16, 1881 "a writ of injunction was allowed by a court commissioner and served upon the governor, who, nevertheless, proceeded to sign the new bonds." Action was then brought against the state treasurer to restrain him from paying the interest on the bonds on the ground "that the constitutional amendment of 1858 was void; that the act of the extra session under which the new bonds were issued was void; and that the new bonds were signed and issued in violation of the injunction." The Supreme Court denied the injunction on the ground that "whatever irregularities, if any, existed in the mode of submitting the constitutional amendment of 1858 to the people, or of them adopting it, must be deemed cured by the subsequent admission of Minnesota as a state in the Union, and by the action of the State subsequent to its admission in recognizing

[22] General Laws Minn., 1881, pp. 117-123. All of the judges of the Supreme Court declined to serve on this tribunal; five district judges were appointed by the governor.
[23] 29 Minn. Reports, pp. 474-554.

this amendment as valid, and ratifying it." This decision disposed of all obstacles toward the settlement of the debt; and within a year almost all of the old bonds had been surrendered.[24]

NORTH CAROLINA

The adjustment of the public debt of North Carolina has attracted considerable attention. In 1879 the legislature passed an act to settle the portion of the debt which the state recognized as valid. The outstanding bonds were divided into three classes and new bonds were issued and exchanged for the old ones after drastically scaling down their principal. Other acts were passed to adjust certain other portions of the recognized debt; but no provision was made for the payment of the bonds issued by the carpetbag régime in the years 1868 and 1869. In order to make this settlement final a constitutional amendment was ratified prohibiting the payment of these bonds. Most of these securities were held by Americans residing in the north.

The public debt of North Carolina was largely contracted in aid of internal improvements. When North Carolina issued her ordinance of secession, May 20, 1861, the total bonded indebtedness of the state was over eleven millions of dollars.[1] This debt was contracted between 1848 and 1858 by the state loaning her credit to numerous railroad, canal and plank road companies.[2] As security for the bonds issued, the state received stock in these corporations. During the war additional bonds were issued for the building of railroads under the authority of acts passed before the outbreak of the conflict. Although these bonds were not issued for war purposes, they had no market value because they were payable in Confederate money. At the close of the war the state continued the policy of granting aid for internal improvements; and by January 1, 1868 the public debt of North Carolina amounted to $13,724,000.[3] Thirteen days later a convention assembled in Raleigh to draft a constitution for the state.

The new constitution contained important provisions relating to

[24] General Laws Minn., 1881, extra session, pp. 13-17; 29 Minn. Reports, pp. 555-561; Appleton's Annual Cyclopædia, 1881, pp. 591, 592.
[1] Hamilton, J. G. de R., Reconstruction in North Carolina, p. 68.
[2] 10 Census, Vol. 7, p. 567.   [3] Hamilton, op. cit., p. 428.

the public debt and the granting of state aid to corporations. The public debt contracted before and after the war was declared valid; but the war debt was repudiated. Provision was made for the payment of the interest on the debt and after 1880 a specific annual tax upon real and personal property was to be set apart as a sinking fund for the payment of the principal. The General Assembly was prohibited from contracting any new debt until the bonds of the state should be at par, except to supply a casual deficit for suppressing an invasion or insurrection, unless there was a provision in the bill for the levying of a special tax to pay the interest annually. The General Assembly was also prohibited from granting or loaning the credit of the state to any person, association, or corporation, except to aid in the completion of such railroads as were unfinished at the time of the adoption of the constitution, or in which the state had a direct pecuniary interest, unless the question was submitted to a direct vote of the people and was approved by a majority of them. There was also a provision that every act levying a tax should state the special object to which it was to be applied and the proceeds were to be used for no other purpose.[4]

If these constitutional restrictions had been observed, the state in all probability would have suffered no severe losses. Unfortunately they were flagrantly disregarded during the carpetbag régime. Bonds were recklessly issued with little regard to the law by the convention of 1868 and by the legislature at its special session in 1868 and its regular session of 1868-1869. The governor, W. W. Holden, was personally honest but unfitted for the position he occupied. He was under the domination of the masterful United States senator, John Pool; while the legislature was controlled by a gang of railroad lobbyists under the leadership of Milton S. Littlefield and George W. Swepson. The methods which these plunderers later used in Florida were first employed in North Carolina. Most of the negro members of the legislature and some of the white were illiterate; and all too many of them were susceptible to bribery and corruption. In order to facilitate the passage of railroad legislation, Littlefield installed a bar in the west wing of the capitol where the pliable legislators were abundantly supplied with wines, liquors, and cigars. Swepson was the paymaster of the Ring and it is claimed

[4] Poore, G. P., *Federal and State Constitutions*, Pt. *II*, pp. 1420, 1429, 1430.

that he paid out over $133,000 to different members of the legislature and to other influential persons in the state in order to obtain the legislation desired. On one occasion two members were each given $20,000 to withdraw their opposition to certain laws. Swepson claimed that Littlefield exacted from all the presidents of the railroad companies a flat rate of 10 percent of the bonds received for the services he rendered. By employing such methods the Ring was able to induce the convention and the legislature by the end of 1869 to authorize the issuance of state bonds amounting to $27,850,000 to various railroad companies in exchange for their stocks and bonds. Of this amount $17,640,000 were actually issued; and as many of the bonds carried, as required by the constitution, provision for the levying of taxes to pay the interest, they were popularly known as special tax bonds. These bonds were largely marketed in the north by Henry Clews and Company and Soutter and Company of New York. The proceeds of the sales were squandered and it is estimated that less than $2,000,000 of the $4,000,000 received by the presidents of the railroad companies was spent on the roads.[5]

These acts were not passed by the legislature without a protest from the conservative groups in North Carolina or without an intimation that the bonds issued would not be recognized as valid obligations of the state. "The impression prevails among the people," stated one newspaper, "that a considerable amount of the appropriations are going unfairly into the pockets of a set of speculators and sharpers whose influence induces the legislature to make them; therefore no one need be surprised if a disposition to favor repudiation is engendered by extravagance and burdensome taxation. The time may come when the people of the state will not be willing to be taxed to pay $100 in gold to the man who holds a bond that cost him only $50 or $70 in paper money, or that cost him nothing at all, except a little scheming about Raleigh and the Halls of Legislation." There were substantial grounds for making such charges as later investigations revealed. It was disclosed that bonds had been issued to the Chatham and Williamston and Tarboro railroads without proper registration. Both roads were required by law

---

[5] The Republican Régime and the railroad legislation in North Carolina is described in detail in Hamilton, *op. cit.*, Chs. 9-11. The workings of the Ring are clearly revealed in Report of the Commission to Investigate Charges of Fraud and Corruption, session 1871-1872, W. M. Shipp, chairman, *passim*. This paragraph is based upon these two works.

to give mortgages on their property; but the Chatham mortgage included lands which the company did not then possess. The western and eastern divisions of the Western North Carolina Railroad received bonds before the required amount of stock was subscribed. Chief Justice Pearson of the Supreme Court of North Carolina was of the opinion that all the special tax bonds were unconstitutional; and the court did declare some of these bonds null and void.[6]

When the legislature assembled in the fall of 1869 measures were taken to check the exorbitant growth of the state debt. An act was passed repealing all appropriations to the railroad companies; and the presidents of these companies were instructed to return all bonds in their possession to the state treasurer. Furthermore all the funds in the state treasury which had been levied and collected for the payment of the interest on the special tax bonds were appropriated for the use of the state government. A resolution was also passed instructing the treasurer not to pay any more interest on the special tax bonds; and at the same time a commission was appointed to investigate all bonds issued to the railroad companies since 1865.[7] This move evidently frightened Littlefield. He invited a large number of the Republican members to an oyster supper where wine flowed freely. Speeches were made denouncing the investigation as a "stab at the Republican party"; and the next day the fraud commission was abolished.[8]

But the rule of the carpetbaggers was about over. In the election of 1870 the conservatives acquired a majority in the legislature and promptly proceeded to impeach and convict Governor Holden. Two years later another fraud commission was appointed; and this time was more successful in ferreting out the frauds. In 1874 the legislature was entirely freed of carpetbaggers; and two years later Z. B. Vance was elected governor.

The problem of settling the state debt confronted the conservatives on their return to power. No interest had been paid on the special tax bonds for a number of years; and all attempts to force the state through the courts to use the funds in the treasury for such purpose was unsuccessful. There was a general conviction among the people that the state was unable to meet all of its obligations;

[6] Hamilton, *op. cit.*, pp. 433, 434, 436, 437, 441.
[7] North Carolina Laws, 1869-1870, pp. 119, 120, 337, 338.
[8] Hamilton, *op. cit.*, p. 404.

and also a belief that the state was not obligated to pay certain portions of it. The treasurer's report for 1873 placed the state debt at $28,419,045 and distributed the debt as follows. In the first class the treasurer placed the old or ante-war bonds, dated prior to the war, which principal and accrued interest then amounted to $10,-891,660. These, according to the treasurer, had been sold by the state or by its agents on an average at par for gold. There was no charge that their proceeds had not been honestly expended, although in many instances the investments had been unfortunate. The second class of bonds, amounting to $2,728,000, consisted of those issued since the war but under acts passed before the war. These bonds had been sold for not more than 60 cents on the dollar in currency when gold was at a large premium. The third class of bonds were those issued during the war for the building of railroads. Although these bonds were not used for war purposes, they had no market value because they were payable in Confederate money. The total amount of these bonds was $913,000. The fourth class comprised those issued under the funding acts of 1866 and 1868 to take up past-due interest. The total principal of these bonds was $4,128,000. The fifth class consisted of those issued under ordinances or acts passed since the war, aggregating $1,350,000. These bonds had been issued to the Chatham and Williamston and Tarboro railroads. The Chatham Railroad bonds had been disposed of, according to the treasurer, at about 60 cents in currency. He was unable to tell what amount the $150,000 to the Williamston and Tarboro Railroad had brought; but the investment had been disastrous to the state. In the last class were the special tax bonds, aggregating $11,407,000 in 1873. "Omitting the special tax bonds altogether," stated the treasurer, "the interest on the rest of our debt, supposing our accrued interest to be funded, would be $1,406,663.99 per annum. To this add the expense of supporting the state government, and it will be necessary to raise $1,900,000 per annum, or 1 and 3/5 percent of the real and personal property. Add an amount for county taxation equal to that for state government expenses, and we have, outside the towns and cities, 2 and 1/10 percent of our property. And in many of the cities and towns the levies for municipal purposes are as large, if not larger. Now add, as the holders of special tax bonds propose, a tax of $855,090, or ¾ of 1 percent on the property and we have a grand total of 2 and 8/10 percent. It is manifest that our people cannot and will not pay such enormous levies. Any attempt to enforce it would result in total repudiation. Even if the General Assembly should vote a levy at present, even omitting special tax bonds, the people would reverse their action at the next election." [9]

This was the sentiment of the majority of the people of North Carolina. They were convinced that the "honest" debt must be scaled down; and the remainder repudiated. A few extremists, represented by the *Raleigh Daily Observer*, were for the complete repudiation of the whole debt. They defended their position on the grounds that the impoverished condition of the state was due primarily to the northerners who now held the bonds and that the state should not enrich these bondholders when at the same time it made no provision to help its own citizens who had loaned their money to the state during the war.[10]

In his message to the legislature in 1876 Governor Vance endorsed the view that the special tax bonds should be repudiated and the remainder of the debt scaled down. "In regard to much the greater part of these claims," declared the governor, "there is not the slightest moral obligation resting upon the conscience of any honest citizen of North Carolina. The story of the iniquities practiced upon us is an ample justification of our delay. The most that I can say to you on this weighty matter is to recommend the appointment of a commission to negotiate with our creditors and see what terms can be obtained." [11]

The governor erred, however, in stating that there was no moral obligation on the part of North Carolina in regard to the payment of a large part of these claims. The recognized debt then amounted to $25,542,160; while the special tax bonds, principal and accrued interest, amounted only to $16,246,550. Yet the governor's opinions in regard to the special tax bonds were held by the general public.

[9] Treasurer's Report 1873 quoted in *Commercial and Financial Chronicle*, Feb. 14, 1874. In the third class the Treasurer might have added $215,000 of bonds issued for the building of the Chatham Railroad under an ordinance of Jan. 10, 1862. These bonds had been included in this group in the Treasurer's report for 1871 found in *Commercial and Financial Chronicle*, March 4, 1871.

[10] The views of the *Raleigh Daily Observer* are summarized in Ratchford, B. U., North Carolina Debt, 1870-1878, North Carolina Historical Review, Vol. 10, p. 15.

[11] Governor's message quoted in *Commercial and Financial Chronicle*, Jan. 20, 1877.

Various suggestions had already been made to adjust the debt; and an act had been passed in 1875 providing for the settlement of the debt. But its terms were so harsh that no bonds had been returned; and all efforts of the bondholders to point out to the state the need of increased taxation in view of the light taxes which were levied in North Carolina in comparison to those in other states had been rejected.[12] Nevertheless there was a growing feeling that the debt problem should be settled since it weakened the credit of North Carolina in the money markets. A commission was therefore appointed in 1877 to study the question; and as a result of their efforts the legislature in 1879 passed a series of laws to settle the state debt.

The principal act was passed on March 4, 1879. This act divided the bonds which the state recognized into three classes. Those in the first class were the old or ante-war bonds. For these the state agreed to give in exchange new 4 percent thirty-year bonds at the rate of 40 percent of the principal of those outstanding. The second class, consisting of bonds issued for certain railroads since the war were to be exchanged for new ones at the rate of 25 percent of the principal. In the third class were the bonds issued under the funding acts of 1866 and 1868. These were to be exchanged for new securities after scaling down the principal 15 percent. No provision was made for the accrued interest on any of the outstanding bonds. By this act North Carolina authorized the exchange of bonds to the amount of $12,727,045 classified as follows:

Class	I	$ 5,577,400 at 40% in new bonds	$2,230,960
Class	II	3,261,045 at 25% in new bonds	815,261
Class	III	3,888,600 at 15% in new bonds	583,290
		$12,727,045 bonds to be exchanged for	$3,629,511

The act also provided that "all state taxes levied or collected from professions, trades, incomes, merchants, dealers in cigars and ¾ of all the taxes collected from wholesale and retail dealers in spirituous, vinous, and malt liquors should be held and applied to payment of interest on these bonds." In case there was an insufficiency of funds accruing from these taxes and a deficit in the treasury, contingent bonds were to be issued for the payment of the interest.[13]

---

[12] This paragraph is based upon Ratchford, op. cit., pp. 12-14.

[13] North Carolina Laws, 1879, Ch. 98, pp. 183-188. The above table is taken from 10 Census, Vol. 7, p. 567. Compare with these figures the estimates of Ratchford, op. cit., pp. 159-162.

A week later an act was passed to settle the portion of the state debt known as the Williamston and Tarboro Railroad. By the provisions of this law the treasurer was authorized to exchange for the $150,000 of state bonds issued to this company, which with unpaid interest amounted to $226,000, new bonds at the rate of 1/3 of the principal of the old bonds. Before these bonds were issued, the company was to execute a first mortgage on its property.[14]

On March 14 one more act was passed to adjust the portion of the state debt incurred to aid in the construction of the North Carolina Railroad. These construction bonds had been issued to pay for stock in this company and were secured by a lien on that stock. A receiver had been appointed by the courts to administer the stocks owned by the state. By this act the governor was authorized to appoint three commissioners for the purpose of negotiating with the bondholders. The commissioners were empowered to contract for a renewal of the old bonds, to issue certificates to those surrendering their securities, and to sell new bonds and invest the proceeds in the purchase of the outstanding bonds. In 1882 an agreement was reached with the bondholders which compromised the debt at about 80 percent with interest.[15]

None of these acts, however, provided for certain outstanding bonds of the state. These bonds, mostly special tax bonds, amounted to $12,655,000.[16] In order to prevent any further recognition of these obligations, the legislature passed an act on March 14, 1879 to alter the constitution of the state. Section 6 of Article I was amended to read: "Nor shall the General Assembly assume or pay, or authorize the collection of any tax to pay, either directly or indirectly, expressed or implied, any debt or bond incurred, or issued, by authority of the Convention of 1868 nor shall any debt or bond incurred or issued by the legislature of 1868 either at its special session or at its regular session of the years 1868-1869 and 1869 and 1870, except the bonds issued to fund the interest on the old debts of the state, unless the proposing to pay the same shall have first been submitted to the people, and by them ratified by a vote of a

---

[14] North Carolina Laws, 1879, Ch. 180, pp. 336-338.

[15] Ibid., Ch. 138, pp. 261-264. There is a good discussion of the construction bonds in Ratchford, op. cit., pp. 162-165, 251-253.

[16] These figures are based on the 10 Census, Vol. 7, p. 568, as corrected by the North Carolina laws. The census figures are $12,805,000; but from this figure should be deducted $150,000 of bonds issued to the Williamston and Tarboro Railroad which were adjusted as shown above.

majority of all the qualified voters." [17] At the next general election this amendment was ratified by the voters.

The adjustment of the state debt did not end North Carolina's troubles. The settlement was approved by the people of the state and was generally accepted by the holders of the recognized portion of the debt. But there has been much litigation and controversy over the repudiated bonds. After the incorporation of the amendment prohibiting the payment of these bonds, one of the holders of certain of these securities commenced action in the Supreme Court of North Carolina for the recovery of overdue interest on his coupons. The plaintiff contended that the constitutional amendment impaired the obligation of a contract and therefore was contrary to the provisions of the federal constitution. The court dismissed the suit on the ground that "the power of the court to recommend claims to the favorable consideration of the legislature" had been repealed by the constitutional amendment and "that the court was without jurisdiction to render judgment of recommendation on a claim against the state when its validity was denied by the state constitution." On a writ of error the case was brought before the United States Supreme Court in 1896 where the decision of the state court was affirmed. In rendering the decision Justice White held that as the authority given by North Carolina to its courts before the adoption of the constitutional amendment was only recommendatory, and was in no way a remedy, its repeal did not impair the obligation of a contract.[18] Three years later Congress passed an act to reimburse the states and territories for the expenses incurred by them in equipping soldiers for the Spanish American War. In this act there was a clause which directed the Secretary of the Treasury to institute proceedings against any state or its representatives to secure the payment of the principal and interest on defaulted bonds or stocks of the state which were held by the United States.[19] The next year, however, this section was repealed;[20] but the following year (1901) Schafer Brothers of New York gave 10 bonds of the North Carolina Railroad which had not been exchanged to the State of South Dakota. The latter state commenced action in the United

---

[17] North Carolina Laws, 1879, Ch. 268, pp. 436, 437.
[18] Baltzer vs. North Carolina, U. S. Reports, Vol. 161, pp. 240-246.
[19] Statutes-at-Large, Vol. 30, p. 1358.
[20] *Ibid.*, Vol. 31, p. 612.

States Supreme Court for the recovery of the amount due on these bonds. The court held that the bonds were valid and that South Dakota had a clear title to them; and decreed that North Carolina should pay South Dakota $27,400, the amount of principal and unpaid coupons due on the ten bonds; and that in default of payment an order of sale was to be issued to the marshal of the court directing him to sell at public auction 100 shares of state stock in the North Carolina Railroad at the east front door of the Capitol building in Washington. The governor laid the matter before the legislature; and an agreement was reached with the bondholders that the state should pay 25 percent of the principal and interest on the securities held by Schafer Brothers.[21] In 1910 North Carolina offered new bonds for sale in order to meet the payment of the funding bonds which made up the recognized debt maturing in that year. Strenuous efforts were made by holders of North Carolina special tax bonds to prevent the sale of these securities; but the loan was oversubscribed by the bankers and business men of the state. The American Tobacco Company, then under indictment, subscribed $1,000,000; a fact which called forth much bitter comment from the Council of Foreign Bondholders.[22] In 1916 Cuba came into possession of some of the repudiated bonds of North Carolina through the Council of Foreign Bondholders and instituted proceedings against the state in the United States Supreme Court; but on January 4, 1917 withdrew the motion to sue before

[21] South Dakota vs. North Carolina, U. S. Reports, Vol. 192, pp. 286-354. The political background of this case is fully discussed in Ratchford, op. cit., pp. 258-263.

[22] On this subject Ratchford says: "The governor acknowledged the aid of the bankers and business men; and the Treasurer remarked that considering the circumstances . . . it is wonderful that our credit was so that we could not only sell our bonds at par but get a small premium of $2,732.27." Another view of the same transaction was set forth in the Council of Foreign Bondholders Report 1910, p. 33, which said: " . . . Investors outside the boundaries of the state left the new issue severely alone. The government, however, by means of the pressure it was able to exert over a large industrial company, which was a defendant in certain suits brought by the state, and by granting other corporate bodies extraordinary exemptions from taxation, eventually succeeded in getting the bonds taken up within its own borders . . . but the methods adopted to obtain subscriptions . . . would appear to be more in keeping with the Middle Ages than the present century."

"The references here were, apparently, to the suit of the United States Government against the American Tobacco Company under the Anti-Trust Law and to a case which was decided by the North Carolina Supreme Court May 11, 1910. In this case the court held that, in the assessment of bank stocks for taxation, that part of the bank's surplus which was invested in tax-exempt state bonds should be deducted from the total surplus (Pullen vs. Corporation Commission, 52 N. C. 548). The latter fact may have given some appearance of justifying the charge made, but the facts fail to support such an accusation." Ratchford, Conversion of the North Carolina Debt after 1879, North Carolina Historical Review, Vol. 10, p. 267.

the case came up in the court.[23] Some of the repudiated bonds have been offered to New York, Michigan, Rhode Island, Nevada, Missouri, Connecticut, and Colorado; but every attempt to bring the state before the United States Supreme Court has failed.[24]

SOUTH CAROLINA

Previous to the Civil War, South Carolina had an excellent reputation in the financial world. Her legislature was careful to make no unnecessary addition to her debt and jealously guarded the credit of the state. At the outbreak of the war the state debt was only about $4,000,000. During the war the state issued bonds for military defense and for other purposes. The war debt, amounting to $3,000,000 was later repudiated; and by January 1, 1868 the state had reduced its indebtedness to $5,407,306.27. Within the next four years there was a rapid increase in the public debt due to mismanagement and frauds; and the credit of the state was wiped out. These were terrible days for the native whites of South Carolina. The government was in the hands of the carpetbaggers. The negroes far outnumbered the whites in the legislature. The economic and social conditions of South Carolina during these years beggar description; but they help to explain the resentment of the whites to the payment of the entire state debt contracted at this time.[1]

In January 1868 a convention assembled in Charleston to frame a new constitutional and civil government for the state. Like many of the other southern constitutional conventions it was dominated by the radicals; but with the possible exception of that of Louisiana, none contained so large a proportion of black members. Seventy-four of the one hundred and twenty-four delegates were negroes. Many of them were ex-slaves and the majority were illiterate. But the convention was not controlled by the black delegates. It was dominated by a "group of non-southern adventurers of both races."[2]

---

[23] This is discussed by Ratchford, *op. cit.*, p. 327.
[24] *Ibid.*
[1] *Commercial and Financial Chronicle*, March 11, 1871; Simkins, F. B., and Woody, R. H., South Carolina during Reconstruction, p. 148. For a vivid description of the South Carolina legislature consult Pike, J. S., The Prostrate State, pp. 10, 11, 15, 21.
[2] Simkins and Woody, *op. cit.*, pp. 89-93.

Some of these men were highly educated; and under their direction a constitution was drafted which embodied some of the most advanced legal principles of the age. Section 7 of article 9 of the constitution dealt with the subject of the public debt. It stated that "for the purpose of defraying extraordinary expenditures, the state may contract public debts; but such debts shall be authorized by law for some single object, to be distinctly specified therein; and no such law shall take effect until it shall have been passed by the vote of two-thirds of the members of each branch of the General Assembly, to be recorded by yeas and nays on the journals of each house respectively; and every such law shall levy a tax annually sufficient to pay the annual interest of such debt." [3] The convention also passed an ordinance that the faith and credit of the state was pledged for the redemption of the bills receivable of South Carolina. These bills receivable were issued under the authority of an act of December 21, 1865 and were receivable for all taxes due to the state. [4]

In July 1868 the radical government was inaugurated. Within a month the legislature began to pass laws which rapidly increased the public indebtedness. On August 8 an act was passed authorizing the governor to negotiate a loan of $125,000 and to use as collateral security bills receivable, bonds, stocks, "or other securities owned by the state." [5] This was followed on August 26 by an act authorizing the governor to borrow, on the credit of the state, on coupon bonds, within twelve months, a sum not exceeding $500,000 to redeem the bills receivable of the state. The faith, credit, and funds of the state were solemnly pledged for the punctual payment of the interest and the redemption of the principal of the loan. The bonds were to bear 6 percent interest and were redeemable in twenty years. They were to be sold by the financial agent of the state at a price fixed by the governor, attorney general, and treasurer; and an annual tax was to be levied to pay the interest on the loan. This act was passed in both houses, by a two-thirds vote of the members present, a quorum voting, but not by a two-thirds vote of the entire number of members qualified. [6]

On the same day another act was passed authorizing the governor

[3] Poore, B. P., Federal and State Constitutions, Pt. II, p. 1659.
[4] S. C. Statutes, Vol. 14, pp. 27, 28.
[5] Ibid., p. 2. [6] Ibid., p. 17; 12 S. C. Reports, p. 205.

to borrow, on the credit of the state, on coupon bonds, within twelve months, a sum not exceeding $1,000,000. This act also contained the same provisions regarding the annual tax levy, the pledging of the faith and credit of the state, and the price at which the bonds should be sold; but the act did not specify the amount of bonds which were to be issued. At a later date some of the state officials claimed that the law called for the issuance of a sufficient amount of bonds to realize $1,000,000; while others maintained only $1,000,000 of bonds could be issued.[7]

The next act which was passed authorized the governor to close the operations of the Bank of the State of South Carolina; and provided for the issuance of bonds in payment and redemption of the bills of the bank. The credit and faith of the state was pledged for the punctual payment of the principal and interest of the bonds; but the act made no provision for an annual tax levy.[8]

Next followed an act approved February 17, 1869 authorizing the governor to borrow, within twelve months, on the credit of the state, on coupon bonds, a sum not exceeding $1,000,000 for the relief of the treasury of the state. The loan was to be effected by a deposit of the bonds as collateral security for loans by the financial agent of the state in accordance with the directions of the governor, attorney general, comptroller-general, and treasurer or by the sale of the bonds at a price fixed by these officials. An annual tax was to be levied sufficient to pay the interest.[9]

This was followed by an act providing for the appointment of a land commissioner. It was the duty of the land commissioner to purchase lands in any portion of the state, improved or unimproved, at a price fixed by an advisory board composed of the governor, comptroller-general, state treasurer, secretary of state, and attorney general. One of the sections of this act provided that the treasurer was authorized to issue to the land commissioner bonds of the state in the sum of $200,000, bearing 6 percent interest, the principal payable in twenty years. The faith and credit of the state was pledged for the payment of the principal and interest of the bonds; and sufficient taxes were to be levied to pay the interest accruing on the bonds annually. All the lands purchased by the land commis-

[7] S. C. Statutes, Vol. 14, pp. 18, 19.
[8] *Ibid.*, pp. 21, 22; 12 S. C. Reports, pp. 205, 206.
[9] S. C. Statutes, Vol. 14, pp. 182, 183.

sioner were to be subdivided into sections of 25 to 100 acres and sold to actual settlers on easy terms. A further issue of $500,000 in bonds was authorized under an amendatory act of March 1, 1870.[10]

On March 23, 1869 an act was passed "to provide for the conversion of state securities." By the terms of this law the treasurer was authorized to issue, on the application of any person holding stock of the state, coupon bonds, bearing 6 percent interest, payable in twenty years, in exchange for the state stock. In like manner state stock was to be exchanged for outstanding coupon bonds. But the conversion act did not comply with any of the special provisions required by the constitution in cases of the creation of a public debt.[11]

Three days later an act was passed authorizing the financial agent of the state to pledge bonds of the state then and hereafter in the possession of the state as collateral security for state loans; and the time within which the loans authorized under the act to redeem bills receivable and under the act to pay interest on the public debt might be negotiated was extended twenty-four months from the passage of those acts.[12]

The last of the acts passed by the radical government to increase the public debt was approved March 7, 1871. This act created what was known as the sterling fund debt. By the provisions of this law the governor was authorized to borrow on coupon bonds of the state, bearing 6 percent interest in gold, the principal and interest payable in London, a sum not exceeding 1,200,000 pounds sterling. The proceeds of the sale of these bonds were to be used exclusively in exchange for or in payment of the existing public debt. An annual tax levy was to provide a sinking fund to redeem the bonds; the faith, credit, and funds of the state were pledged for the payment of the principal and interest; and no new debt was to be created by the state until this was paid.[13]

The opposition press of South Carolina denounced the passage of these acts and questioned the validity of the bonds authorized by the various laws. Investors in America and in Europe were cautioned not to purchase them. Capitalists in New York were warned that the state would never pay "the bayonet bonds issued

[10] Ibid., pp. 275-277, 385.
[11] Ibid., p. 241; 12 S. C. Reports, p. 206.
[12] S. C. Statutes, Vol. 14, pp. 258, 259.   [13] Ibid., pp. 616-618.

by a bogus legislature." The whole scheme was stigmatized "a job and a swindle." The public was informed by the newspapers of South Carolina that the state would never recognize these bonds when "the property holders and honest men" gained control of the government.[14] "Would New York or Boston touch these bonds," declared the *Charleston Daily News,* July 17, 1868, "issued by authority of a horde of negroes and in the face of the protest of the white people of the state." "No bonds issued by this so-called legislature will ever be paid," stated this paper on August 17, "no loans . . . recognized. . . . No bills receivable, issued by the so-called governor of the state, with the sanction of the pretended legislature, to carry on an illegal government will be permitted to be received in payment of the taxes of the state."[15] Yet in the face of these warnings nearly all of the conversion bonds were disposed of in New York and a considerable amount was held by savings banks whose officers carefully concealed the fact that they had invested "the funds in their charge in securities of such doubtful character."[16] The English, however, were not so willing to accept South Carolina securities. When it was announced abroad that a large amount of sterling bonds were to be issued, the *London Times* remarked: "It is difficult to imagine any Englishman of sense investing in them, even if they were issued."[17]

The attacks of the press, the rumors of fraudulent issues, and the mismanagement of the public funds destroyed the credit of the state. In order to market the bonds, Governor Scott appointed H. H. Kimpton, financial agent of the state in New York City. Kimpton was a former class mate of Attorney General Chamberlain at Yale and had less than two years of banking experience when he was appointed agent. Kimpton sold some of the bonds in the market; others were hypothecated or deposited as collateral for loans. The rapid increase in the amount of bonds issued and the alleged irregularities, illegalities, and frauds connected with their issuance forced the price of the bonds down. As the bonds declined in value, more collateral was required for the loans. When Kimpton was

---

[14] These statements are based on Governor Scott's message to the legislature in 1871, summarized in 12 S. C. Reports, pp. 223, 224.
[15] *Charleston Daily News* quoted in Simkins and Woody, *op. cit.,* p. 164.
[16] *Commercial and Financial Chronicle,* Nov. 23, 1872.
[17] *London Times,* Nov. 20, 1871.

unable to furnish this, holders of collateral securities offered their bonds in the market at reduced prices. By the close of 1871 South Carolina bonds issued before 1868 were selling at 75 while the new bonds were at 50. Within a short time it was impossible to sell any of the state bonds even at a forced sale.[18]

Because of the grave charges of illegality in the issuing of the bonds under the various acts of the legislature and the threatened issue of the sterling loan bonds in 1871, two investigations were made in that year of the financial condition of the state. At the suggestion of the Charleston Chamber of Commerce a taxpayers' convention assembled in May in Columbia for the purpose of investigating the accounts of the comptroller and the financial agent and of determining the actual amount of the public debt. No one knew the number and amount of bonds that had been issued because the state treasurer kept no correct registration. "The only registration made was that the financial agent in New York had so many bonds, numbers of which, in the gross, were accurately kept." [19]

The taxpayers' convention was representative of the intelligence and property of the state; but the results of its efforts were disappointing. The convention recorded its opposition to all bonds issued by the radical government and advised the people of the state "to resist the payment" or "the enforcement of any tax" to pay these obligations "by all legitimate means in their power." The public was likewise warned not to purchase or loan any money on any bond or obligation issued "by the present State Government, or by any subsequent government, in which the property holders of the State are not represented." But the committee appointed to investigate the accounts of the comptroller and the treasurer made only a superficial examination and reported that they were satisfied "the records there were correct." According to the comptroller the "total funded debt" was $7,665,908.98. To this amount the committee "added $800,000 in cash advanced by the financial agent and for which he had hypothecated $1,800,000 in bonds, and the further sum of $400,000 for bonds sold by Kimpton." The total debt as reported by the committee was $8,865,908.98 "to which should be added the $1,800,000 hypothecated bonds, making a grand total of $10,665,908.98." In their estimation "the several issues and sums of

[18] Simkins and Woody, *op. cit.*, pp. 152, 154.   [19] 12 S. C. Reports, p. 207.

bonds" described in the comptroller's statement were "of unquestionable legality and force as obligations of the State." After the convention was over the governor, attorney general and the financial agent "laughed at the manner in which they had succeeded in deceiving the members." [20]

Meanwhile the legislature had instituted an investigation of the financial affairs of the state. A committee was appointed by the House "to inquire into the matter of the over issue of state bonds"; and a joint committee of the House and Senate was appointed "to examine the accounts of the state treasurer, comptroller-general, and financial agent." The elaborate reports of these committees were full and unsparing and evinced "a spirit of candor somewhat surprising, considering the active complicity of its authors in the profligate financial legislation of the period." [21] The joint committee placed the aggregate old and new bonded debt of the state at $22,371,306.27. To this add the contingent debt of $6,787,608.20 and the entire indebtedness of the state in 1871 was $29,158,914.47. The committee appointed to investigate the matter of the over issue of state bonds reported the fraudulent issues amounted to $6,314,-000. They found that the American Bank Note Company had printed bonds and certificates to the amount of $22,500,000. This was far in excess of the amounts authorized in the various acts and the state officials were unable to explain satisfactorily the reason for printing such a large amount of bonds and certificates. According to the sworn statement of the state treasurer there were then signed and outstanding $9,514,000 of new bonds. The committee pointed out that making all allowances for the state treasurer's report, the entire bonded debt, actual and contingent, was $21,708,-914.47. From this deduct contingent railroad bonds amounting to $6,787,608.20 and it would leave the real bonded debt $14,921,-306.37. From this debt also deduct the old bonded debt $5,407,-306.27 and there remained "the extravagant and unwarranted issues of stocks and bonds" of not less than $9,514,000, which was just the amount represented to have been delivered to the financial agent. By deducting the legally authorized bonds amounting to $3,200,000 which were outstanding on October 31, 1870 from the $9,514,000 of

    [20] Simkins and Woody, *op. cit.*, pp. 156-159. Extracts of the results of Tax-payer Convention Investigation as given in Pike, The Prostrate State, pp. 137-139.
    [21] 12 S. C. Reports, p. 238.

bonds placed in the hands of the financial agent, there remained outstanding $6,314,000 of bonds which had been illegally issued.[22]

Notwithstanding these disclosures, the legislature, a little more than two months after these reports were submitted, passed on March 13, 1872 an act declaring that all the bonds named in the treasurer's report, October 31, 1871, amounting to $11,793,000, were legal and valid bonds of South Carolina. The faith, credit, and funds of the state were pledged for the payment of these obligations; and an annual tax sufficient to pay the interest was levied.[23]

The year following the passage of the validating act, Morton Bliss and Company who held a large amount of the state stocks applied for a writ of mandamus to compel the comptroller-general to levy a tax to pay the interest on the bonds. In rendering the judgment, the Supreme Court of South Carolina declared that the "bills receivable," "the interest on the public debt bonds," "the relief of the Treasury bonds," and the "land commission bonds" were valid obligations of the state; and a peremptory mandamus was issued requiring the comptroller-general to levy a tax sufficient to pay the interest. But to defeat the practical operation of this judgment the legislature on December 22, 1873 repealed the provision of the law which required the comptroller to levy taxes. The operation of the writ of mandamus was thus avoided and the bondholders were left without means of redress. They were also in doubt as to what amount of the debt the state was liable for and what remedies were available to them to enforce their demands.[24]

In order to effect a settlement of the bonded debt of the state the legislature passed on December 22, 1873 an act "to reduce the volume of the public debt," commonly known as the consolidation act. By the provisions of this act the state repudiated $5,965,000 of the conversion bonds and provided for the funding at 50 cents on the dollar of the entire remainder of the outstanding bonds and certificates of stock and all the outstanding coupons maturing and to mature on January 1, 1874. To prevent any misunderstanding of the amounts of the outstanding bonds and certificates of stock issued under each act the law carefully enumerated the figures as

[22] The report of the legislative investigation is quoted in Pike, *op. cit.*, pp. 129-137. Consult also *Commercial and Financial Chronicle*, Dec. 23, 1871.

[23] S. C. Statutes, Vol. 14, pp. 278-281.

[24] 12 S. C. Reports, p. 239.

given in the report of the treasurer, October 13, 1873. According to this statement the debt of the state evidenced by bonds and certificates of stock was $15,851,627.35. The act declared null and void $5,965,000 of the conversion bonds, leaving a balance of $9,886,627.35 which funded at 50 percent gave $4,943,313.67 as the ultimate consolidated debt of the state. This was less than one-third of the original indebtedness.[25]

But the passage of the consolidated act did not remove the uncertainty in the minds of the taxpayers as to the real amount of the valid indebtedness of the state. To remedy this situation the General Assembly on June 8, 1877 adopted a general resolution providing for the appointment of a bond commission consisting of three members from the Senate and four from the House. This commission was instructed to investigate and report to the legislature the exact amount of the valid indebtedness of the state. Upon the submission of their report the General Assembly on March 22, 1878 passed a joint resolution providing for the establishment of a Court of Claims. This court, consisting of three of the circuit judges, selected by joint vote of the General Assembly were to hear and determine all cases "brought up to test the validity of any of the consolidated bonds, coupons, and certificates of stock." The act permitted the right of appeal to the Supreme Court of the state.[26]

In 1879 a number of these cases were brought upon appeal before the Supreme Court of South Carolina. In rendering its decision the court declared that all the bonds issued under an act entitled "an act to reduce the volume of the public debt and to provide for the payment of the same" were valid obligations of the state except as follows: (1) Such as were issued in exchange for bonds issued under an act entitled "an act to authorize a loan for the relief of the Treasury, or for the coupons of such bonds. (2) Such as were issued in exchange for the second issue of bonds under an act entitled "an act to authorize a State Loan to pay the interest on the public debt" or the coupons of such bonds. (3) Such as were issued in exchange for those conversion bonds which were issued in exchange for either of the two classes of bonds last mentioned, viz.

[25] S. C. Statutes, Vol. 15, pp. 518-523; 12 S. C. Reports, pp. 239-240.
[26] S. C. Statutes, Vol. 16, pp. 318, 669-673.

bonds for relief of the Treasury and the second issue of bonds to pay the interest on the public debt, or "in exchange for the coupons of *such* conversion bonds."

In regard to the legality of the bonds issued for the relief of the Treasury, February 17, 1869, the court said: "This act we regard as liable to two constitutional objections: (1) It purports to create a debt which was not 'for the purpose of defraying extraordinary expenditures'; (2) the debt therein sought to be created is not 'for some *single* object' and such object is 'not distinctly specified therein'; and it is, therefore, in violation of two of the clauses of Section 7 Article 9 of the constitution. . . . The debt which this act purports to authorize cannot be said to be 'for some *single* object' nor is such object '*distinctly* specified therein.' Money borrowed 'for the relief of the Treasury' might and would be applied to as many different objects as there were demands upon the Treasury. We think, therefore, that this act clearly violates both clauses of the constitution above referred to, and upon the principles heretofore announced in that opinion, every bond, together with its coupons, issued under the authority of this act is absolutely void even in the hands of a bona fide holder because issued without any authority whatever, and hence every consolidation bond resting upon such bonds or coupons is, to the extent that it does rest upon such bonds or coupons, not a valid debt of the State of South Carolina."

With regard to the validity of the second issue of bonds under the act "to authorize a state loan to pay interest on the public debt" the court decided: "In the case of the second issue . . . there does not seem to have been the shadow of authority of any kind, and which (bonds) therefore, are absolutely void, no matter in whose hands they may be."

The court also declared: "If any consolidation bond rests wholly upon any of the three objectionable classes of bonds or coupons just mentioned, then it is wholly void; but if it rests only in part upon such objectionable bonds or coupons, then it is only void to the extent which it does rest upon such objectionable bonds or coupons, and for the balance it is a valid obligation of the state." [27]

At the next session of the legislature an act was passed creating the office of special commissioner whose duty it was to ascertain and

[27] 12 S. C. Reports, pp. 293, 294.

establish the validity, or the percentage and amount of invalidity, of each and every consolidated bond and stock certificate under the decision of the Supreme Court. On November 26, 1880 the commissioner submitted a report which placed the total invalidity in bonds and stocks outstanding February 12, 1880 at $1,126,762.99; the total valid consolidated debt at the same time was $4,479,048.05.[28] Accordingly on December 23, 1879 an act was approved, later amended February 19, 1880, which provided for the final adjustment of the consolidated debt of the state. By the provisions of the act as amended every holder of any bond or certificate of stock, or of the unpaid interest thereon to July 1, 1878, reported by the special commissioner as wholly valid, or as partially invalid, had the right to surrender the same for cancellation and to receive from the state treasurer a new bond or certificate of stock, bearing 6 percent interest, for the exact amount of the valid portion of the bond, or certificate, or coupon, or interest. The same privilege of exchanging or refunding was extended to embrace detached coupons and interest orders due on or before July 1, 1878. The interest due and unpaid to July 1, 1878 on the valid portion of the bonds reported by the commissioner partially invalid and on the bonds reported wholly valid was funded in new bonds bearing interest from July 1, 1878.[29]

An act of March 22, 1878 approved and amended December 24, 1878, provided for the settlement of the unfunded debt of the state incurred before November 1, 1876. A court of claims was established which had jurisdiction to adjudicate all claims in existence on November 1, 1876 which had not been funded in bonds or stocks. These claims included bills of the Bank of the State, so much of the funded debt as was known as the "Little Bonanza," the warrants drawn by the comptroller in pursuance of an act of December 24, 1875 providing for the settlement and payment of "certain claims against the state," and the liability of the state by guarantee of the Spartanburg and Union Railroad bonds. "Deficiency" bonds and certificates were issued in settlement of such claims. On October 1, 1881 the amount of "deficiency" bonds and stock outstanding was $562,577.50.[30]

[28] 10 Census, Vol. 7, p. 578.
[29] *Ibid.*, p. 579; S. C. Statutes, Vol. 17, pp. 104-107.
[30] S. C. Statutes, Vol. 16, pp. 555-558; 10 Census, Vol. 7, p. 579.

TENNESSEE

In many respects conditions in Tennessee during the Civil War and the Reconstruction period were unique. Tennessee contained many loyal supporters of the Union cause throughout the war. She was the last state to leave the Union and the first Confederate state occupied by the Federal armies. Within six months after it came into power the Confederate government in Tennessee collapsed under the sledge-hammer blows of General Grant. This prepared the way for the appointment of the indomitable Andrew Johnson as military governor of Tennessee. For three years Governor Johnson strove to bring Tennessee back into the Union. In 1865 the eccentric and violent "Parson" Brownlow was inaugurated governor and military rule was supplanted by civil government. The following year Tennessee was readmitted to the Union and adopted negro suffrage. As a consequence she was the only seceding state which escaped military reconstruction and carpetbag government. But the disfranchisement of former Confederates during the Brownlow régime created internal strife between her own people; while the increase in her state debt was typical of the reconstruction governments. Governor Brownlow and his Radical Republican followers maintained their harsh and unscrupulous rule until 1869 when the Republican party divided into two factions, one wing advocating further proscription of ex-Confederates, the other a milder course. In the ensuing gubernatorial campaign each faction nominated a candidate for governor. The Democrats supported the conservative Republican who was elected and at the same time a Democratic legislature was chosen. The new legislature inherited a legacy of debt which for thirteen years was to worry the people and succeeding legislatures of Tennessee before it was finally settled on a permanent basis.[1]

The foundations of the public indebtedness of Tennessee were laid before the Civil War. In 1833 the state issued $500,000 of bonds for stock in the Union Bank. Five years later the Bank of

---

[1] The political aspects of Tennessee during the Civil War and Reconstruction periods are described by Fertig, J. W., The Secession and Reconstruction of Tennessee; Patton, J. W., Unionism and Reconstruction in Tennessee, 1860-1869; Winston, Andrew Johnson.

Tennessee was chartered and under a provision of that charter $2,500,000 of state bonds were issued to form part of the capital stock of the bank. Subsequently the legislature authorized the issuance of $48,000 of bonds for the purchase of the Hermitage property, the estate of Andrew Jackson, $30,000 for the Agricultural Bureau, and $866,000 for the building of the Capitol. In the financial reports of Tennessee these items of indebtedness were known as the "state debt proper." [2]

In addition to this the state incurred a contingent indebtedness through the loaning of its credit to various railroad companies. By an act passed February 11, 1852 the state provided for the establishment of a system of internal improvements. By the terms of this act the governor was authorized to issue to the railroad companies 6 percent coupon bonds to the amount of $8,000 for the purpose of ironing and equipping their roads as soon as the company had assured the governor it had obtained private subscriptions sufficient to grade, bridge, and prepare for the iron rails the whole extent of the main trunk line and had actually constructed a section of thirty miles at either terminus. For each additional 20-mile section the same amount of bonds were to be issued; and when the road was completed the state was to be invested with a prior lien or mortgage on its property and franchise. The companies receiving these bonds were required to deposit with the Bank of Tennessee at least fifteen days before the interest became due an amount sufficient to pay the same. They were also required, five years after the road was completed, to pay into the state treasury 1 percent upon the amount of bonds issued for their benefit as a sinking fund for the payment of the bonds at maturity. In case any of the companies failed to provide for the interest, the governor was authorized to take possession of the defaulting roads and to run them until the net earnings were sufficient to meet the unpaid interest. The state also reserved the right to enact such legislation as it might deem necessary to protect its interest and to secure the state against any loss; "but in such manner as not to impair the vested rights of the stockholders of the companies." By subsequent amendatory acts the amount set apart by the companies as a sinking fund for the ulti-

[2] 10 Census, Vol. 7, p. 604; Tennessee House and Senate Journal, 1881, App. pp. 14-21.

mate redemption of the bonds was raised first to 2 percent and then to 4 percent on the amount of their indebtedness; and the state secured the right to sell the roads in case they defaulted in the payment of interest or sinking fund. Under the authority of these acts bonds to the amount of $13,909,000 were issued to aid various railroad companies before Tennessee seceded; and up to that time but few of the companies had failed to provide promptly for the interest accruing upon the bonds loaned them.[3]

As in the case of the other seceding states, the economic and social life of Tennessee was thoroughly disorganized at the close of the war. Her trade and industry were paralyzed; her people were impoverished; her transportation system was in ruins; and the revenues of the state were insufficient to pay current expenses and the interest on the debt. On January 1, 1866 the total liabilities of the state, actual and contingent, were $25,277,347.[4]

During the next two years the state debt was greatly increased. This was largely due to the funding bills that were passed and the bills authorizing the issuance of more bonds to aid the railroad companies. In November 1865 the legislature passed the first funding act. This authorized the governor to issue 6 percent coupon bonds to an amount sufficient to pay off all the bonds and interest past due as well as that to fall due during the next two years. Under the provision of this act $4,941,000 of bonds were issued. Three years later another funding act was passed which provided for the funding of all bonds maturing between 1868 and 1870; and under the authority of this act $2,200,000 of 6 percent bonds were issued. At the same time the railroad companies were soliciting the financial assistance of the government. Under the pressure of powerful railroad lobbies bills were passed providing for the issuance of $14,393,000 of bonds to railroads, and $113,000 to turnpike companies.[5] The scandals which attended the passage of the so-called Omnibus Bill of 1866 granting aid to the railroads were later revealed in a report of a legislative investigating committee appointed in 1879. The committee reported that "many corporate presidents, agents, and

---

[3] Acts Tenn., 1851-1852, pp. 204-215; *ibid.*, 1855-1856, p. 144; *ibid.*, 1865-1866, pp. 10-12; Tennessee House and Senate Journal, 1881, App., pp. 14-21.
[4] Appleton's Annual Cyclopædia, 1866, p. 732.
[5] Acts Tenn., 1865-1866, pp. 10-12; *ibid.*, extra session, 1868, pp. 15-17; Phelan, J., Tennessee, pp. 290-292.

representatives came to Nashville to attend the sittings of the legislature. All known influences were used upon the supposed representatives of the people. From the pulpit to the bagnio, recruits were gathered for the assault upon the treasury of the state. Fine brandy by the barrel was on hand to fire thirst and muddle the brain, and first-class suits of clothing to capture the vanity or avarice of the gay and needy. Money, and proceeds of the bonds issued by the state, for specific purposes to these men, were here in abundance, and it was used." By the passage of these various bills the legislature added $21,647,000 to the state debt within two years at a time when the assessed value of the taxable property in the state had declined from $388,936,794 in 1860 to $225,393,410 in 1867. This period of reckless financing has been aptly described as "a carnival of revelry and corruption." [6]

To make matters worse, the taxation system was defective. The rate of taxation up to 1871 was only twenty cents on the $100, a figure much too low to provide for the ordinary expenses and to make provision for the interest on the debt. Furthermore the assessments of property in different counties were unequal and in numerous instances far below value. The obligation of the state to accept the defunct Bank of Tennessee notes in payment of taxes further reduced the available resources. The lack of adequate penalties for the nonpayment of taxes led to their evasion; while the collectors were irresponsible men who defrauded the state of large amounts. By September 30, 1871 the delinquent tax list amounted to the enormous sum of $1,283,115. [7]

Other actions of the Brownlow administration contributed to the financial troubles of the state. The members of the Funding Board did not work harmoniously and soon after the Board was organized two resigned. They immediately began to attack the policy adopted by the Board. This injured the credit of the state and as a consequence the Board was unable to raise the necessary funds to meet the interest due in July 1869. An act passed February 25, 1869, primarily in the interest of the railroads, did tend to afford the state some relief. By the terms of this act the railroads were permitted

---

[6] Tenn. Senate Journal, 1879, App. pp. 3-43; Phelan, *op. cit.*, p. 293.
[7] *Commercial and Financial Chronicle*, March 18, 1871.

to pay their debt to the state in any of the state bonds. As some of the state bonds were then quoted as low as 40½, the solvent railroads quickly bought up the worthless bonds floating on the market and liquidated their accounts. But the law acted as a restraint upon the railroads because it required them to liquidate their indebtedness in bonds of the same series as those issued. To remedy this a new act was lobbied through the legislature on January 20, 1870 which allowed any railroad company to pay into the state, in liquidation of the principal of the debt, any of the legally issued 6 percent bonds of the state; and the railroad companies were allowed to fix the rate of interest of their bonds.[8]

When the Democratic legislature assembled in the fall of 1869 the state debt demanded their immediate attention. In order to restore full confidence in the credit of the state, the Senate passed a resolution denouncing all intention of repudiating any portion of the debt. This was followed by the passage of two acts to facilitate the sale of the state's interest in delinquent railroads. By means of these acts and those allowing the railroads to retire their indebtedness to the state on liberal terms, the state debt was gradually reduced from $43,052,625.25 in 1870 to $30,632,200.76 in 1873.[9]

Meanwhile three distinct factions developed in Tennessee entertaining opposing views on the subject of the settlement of the debt. One group, including some of the most prominent leaders of the state, held that all the outstanding bonds should be paid in full. A large number of the citizens believed that the state could not meet its obligations in full on account of the demoralized business conditions and, therefore, favored an agreement with the creditors to scale the debt. A third faction favored open repudiation of the railroad bonds on the ground that they had been illegally issued because the conditions laid down in the Act of 1852 and its amendments had not been complied with.

In his message to the legislature, January 9, 1873, Governor Brown devoted much space to the consideration of the financial condition of the state. Although the bonded debt had been greatly

[8] Appleton's Annual Cyclopædia, 1868, p. 725; Acts Tenn., 1868-1869, pp. 50-53; ibid., 1869-1870, pp. 61, 62.
[9] Appleton's Annual Cyclopædia, 1869, p. 664; Acts Tenn., 1869-1870, pp. 126-128; ibid., 1870-1871, p. 25; Commercial and Financial Chronicle, Aug. 15, 1874.

reduced during the past three years and there was a perceptible improvement in the value of Tennessee securities, the governor declared that the debt was too large. No interest had been paid on the public debt for more than three years. The governor, therefore, recommended the funding of the entire bonded debt, including the past-due coupons, in a new series of bonds to mature in forty years, bearing interest at the rate of 6 percent. Accordingly an act was passed on March 15, 1873 providing for the funding of "all the outstanding legally issued bonds of the State," as well as all past-due coupons, due on and before January 1, 1874 into new bonds bearing 6 percent, redeemable after July 1, 1884 and payable July 1, 1914. The faith, honor, and credit of the state was pledged for the payment of these bonds at maturity; and provision was made for the creation of a sinking fund. But the legislature adjourned without increasing the tax rate so as to ensure the successful operation of the act.[10]

The funding act of 1873 did not dispose of the debt question. Although the law provided for the funding of "all bonds legally issued," the state officials funded all bonds presented.[11] The state found it extremely difficult to meet the interest payments since the annual interest charges were increased by funding the past-due interest. At the same time the panic of 1873 and a succession of bad crop years made it more difficult to collect the taxes. By 1877 the taxes due and uncollected amounted to $1,570,659. In view of this situation the creditors deemed it advisable to suggest a compromise of the debt in order to forestall any movement in form of repudiation. In 1876 Governor Porter received a communication from several of the largest creditors of the state proposing a conference for the purpose of reaching a permanent and equitable adjustment of the debt. The governor transmitted this request to the legislature and in 1877 a committee was appointed to confer with the creditors. After prolonged negotiations, the creditors agreed to compromise the whole debt at the rate of 60 cents on the dollar at 6 percent interest. The legislature, however, not only rejected this proposal, as well as a second one offered by the creditors to settle the debt on the basis of

[10] Appleton's Annual Cyclopædia, 1872, p. 755; Acts Tenn., 1873, pp. 34-38; *Commercial and Financial Chronicle*, Apr. 5, 1873.

[11] The only bonds registered were the bonds of the Mineral Home Railroad, Insurance Company of the Valley of Virginia, and Tennessee Confederate war bonds. *Commercial and Financial Chronicle*, May 10, 1873.

50 cents on the dollar, but even went so far as to reduce the rate of taxation from 40 cents to 10 cents, making it absolutely impossible to pay the interest.[12]

The question of the adjustment of the state debt now became a political issue. Party lines were not strictly drawn, although the Republicans generally favored a compromise on either the 60 cent or 50 cent basis. When the legislature assembled in January 1879 it was agreed that the state debt should be settled; but there was a division of sentiment regarding the basis on which it should be adjusted. A committee was appointed to investigate the extent and character of the debt. This committee reported that there was then outstanding 20,219 bonds, amounting to $20,221,300. During the past ten years the state had paid only three installments of interest; seven were past due, making the arrears of interest $4,052,717. The total of the debt, principal and interest, in 1879 was, therefore, $24,274,017. The majority of the committee recommended the funding, with accrued interest, of the Capitol, Hermitage, and Agricultural bonds, and the bonds held by the widow of James K. Polk, at 60 cents with 4 percent interest; the funding of the Union Bank, Bank of Tennessee, Turnpike, Hiawassee, East Tennessee, Virginia and Georgia, and the La Grange and Memphis Railroad bonds at 50 cents with 4 percent interest; and the bonds funded under the acts of 1868 and 1873 at 33 cents with 4 percent interest. They also recommended the rejection of the Mineral Home Railroad, and some other bonds, and the payment of the railroad bonds issued since the war in non-interest bearing warrants at 33 cents, receivable for taxes and other dues to the state. The minority of the committee denied the charges preferred against the railroads that they had evaded the provisions of the internal improvement acts; declared that the stories of corruption were based largely upon rumors; and recommended the payment of all outstanding bonds on the ground that they were "evidence of indebtedness containing a solemn promise to pay." The majority report of the committee was rejected and a joint committee of both houses and the bondholders drafted a bill. This bill proposed the funding of the greater part of the debt at the rate of 50 cents on the dollar with 4 percent interest. This settlement was to be subject to

[12] Appleton's Annual Cyclopædia, 1876, p. 742; ibid., 1877, pp. 709, 710; Acts Tenn., 1877, p. 239; Commercial and Financial Chronicle, Jan. 13, March 17, 31, Dec. 15, 1877.

the acceptance of at least two-thirds of the bondholders and the approval of the people. The bill was passed on March 31 by a close vote. Before the governor signed the bill he transmitted a message to the legislature announcing that the managers of the different railroads had agreed to waive the immunity from taxation extended to the railroads in their charters and that the railroads would pay an annual tax of $100,000 for the extinction of the principal and interest of the state debt. The governor appointed a committee to confer with the bondholders who accepted the proposed settlement. On August 7, 1879 the proposed settlement was presented to the people for their approval; and to the chagrin of those who had sponsored the scheme, it was rejected by a large majority.[13]

The debt question became the paramount issue in the gubernatorial campaign of 1880. The Republican platform denounced the Democratic party for refusing to accept the 60 and 6 proposition. According to the Republicans as soon as the repudiating element of the Democratic party of Tennessee, and of the other southern states had succeeded in wiping out the debts of their respective states, they would advocate the repudiation of the entire Civil War debt. The Greenback-Labor party declared that neither the state nor its citizens were legally or morally bound to pay the railroad bonds. They opposed the scaling of the railroad debt or the passage of any act to recognize it; but they were in favor of paying the state debt proper. The Democrats favored the adjustment and speedy payment of the state debt proper; but they denied the validity of the railroad bonds and the bonds issued for the war interest. In no event should any settlement make the coupons receivable for taxes. Due to a split in the Democratic party, the Republican candidate, Alvin Hawkins was elected by a large majority.[14]

Governor Hawkins and the newly elected legislature were both favorably disposed toward the bondholders. The creditors immediately submitted another compromise scheme. They proposed that the entire debt should be funded at 100 cents on the dollar in bonds bearing 3 percent, payable in ninety-nine years, but redeemable at

[13] Appleton's Annual Cyclopædia, 1878, p. 780; ibid., 1879, p. 827; Acts Tenn., 1879, pp. 247-249; Tenn. Senate Journal, 1879, App., p. 3-43; Commercial and Financial Chronicle, March 15, Apr. 26, 1879. E. D. Morgan and Company, who represented about $200,000 of the Tenn. bonds held in Europe declined to accept the proposal, Commercial and Financial Chronicle, Apr. 26, 1879.
[14] Appleton's Annual Cyclopædia, 1880, pp. 677-681.

any time after five years at the pleasure of the state; and that the interest coupons of the new bonds, at and after maturity, be receivable for all taxes and debts due to the state. A bill incorporating these provisions passed the Senate by a majority of the vote. The *Commercial and Financial Chronicle* congratulated the people of Tennessee upon the successful adjustment of their debt; but upon a test question the State Supreme Court by a three to two decision declared the act was unconstitutional and void. The court held that the 3 percent adjustment was legal but the part of the act making the coupons receivable for taxes was declared unconstitutional on the ground that the legislature had no power to contract away the state revenues for such a time, or to make any contract which a subsequent legislature could not modify or repeal.[15]

As a consequence of this decision the governor called the legislature in extraordinary session for the purpose of once more adjusting the debt. The bondholders submitted a new proposition and, after modifying some of its terms, the legislature passed a new funding act on May 20, 1882. This act authorized the funding of the debt by issuing new bonds for 60 cents on the dollar, bearing 3 percent for the first two years, 4 percent for the next two, 5 percent for the next two, and 6 percent thereafter. This act was put into operation but before the funding had proceeded very far difficulties arose. All of the bondholders failed to avail themselves of the terms of the act within the specified time; the treasurer announced that he would not pay the coupons falling due in January 1883; and "the legislature adopted a resolution directing the comptroller and the treasurer to pay no more interest on the state bonds, except on those held by charitable institutions, Mrs. Polk, and the United States government."[16]

The debt question became a leading issue in the fall elections. The Democrats were still divided into two factions, the "State-Credit" and the "Low-Tax" wings. The Republicans hoped by an alliance with the "State Credit" wing of the Democratic party to carry the election; but warned by the defeat administered to them in 1880 due to their internal dissensions, both wings of the Demo-

---

[15] *Ibid.*, 1881, pp. 830, 831; *ibid.*, 1882, pp. 782, 786, 787; Acts Tenn., 1881, pp. 279-282; *Commercial and Financial Chronicle*, Apr. 9, 1881, Feb. 11, 18, 1882.

[16] Acts Tenn., 1882-1883, 3rd extraordinary session, pp. 6-10; *Commercial and Financial Chronicle*, Jan. 6, 1883.

cratic party met in convention and nominated General W. B. Bates. A group of the "State-Credit" Democrats left the convention, organized a separate party and nominated their own candidate. Nevertheless General Bates was elected governor.

In his message to the legislature Governor Bates declared the payment of the interest on the bonds funded under the Act of 1882, together with a recent defalcation, had left the treasury practically empty. He maintained that none of the five funding acts had actually expressed the will of the people. At the recent election, however, he declared that the people had taken the matter in their own hands and had shown themselves in favor of a new adjustment. The governor then outlined his ideas of a settlement which were incorporated in the Act of May 20, 1883.[17]

This act settled the long controversy over the state debt. By the terms of this act the state debt proper was funded in full with the contract rate of interest, four years interest being deducted. Bonds held by educational institutions in the state and by Mrs. James K. Polk were funded in full, and the balance was funded at 50 cents on the dollar with 3 percent interest. By the passage of this act Tennessee reduced her total indebtedness from $28,786,066.39 to $15,784,608.19.[18]

VIRGINIA

Prior to the Civil War the financial record of Virginia was unblemished. Until the outbreak of hostilities the state paid regularly and promptly the interest upon her public debt which on January 1, 1861 amounted to $33,897,073.22.[1] This debt was contracted largely for the purpose of aiding internal improvements; and many of the projects were undertaken at the insistence of the western counties. Virginia had been one of the pioneer states in encouraging the construction of such works at public expense; and George Washington was one of the earliest advocates for developing the means of communication between the eastern and western sections of the

[17] Appleton's Annual Cyclopædia, 1882, p. 787; Acts Tenn., 1883, pp. 76-84; *Commercial and Financial Chronicle*, Feb. 10, March 3, 1883.
[18] Tenn. Senate Journal, 1885, p. 91. [1] 220 U. S. Reports, p. 27.

state. In 1816 the legislature gave its sanction to such undertakings by passing a law which provided for the organization of a Board of Public Works and for the creation of an internal improvement fund. This fund consisted of the shares held by the commonwealth in the stock of various turnpike and canal companies and banks and was administered by the Board of Public Works. In response to the popular enthusiasm for internal improvements in the 'thirties the legislature in 1838 authorized the Board to negotiate loans by the sale of state bonds to aid such enterprises. The passage of this act marks the beginning of the state debt. Twelve years later a decided impetus was given to the system of internal improvements by the passage of a law, which was still in force at the outbreak of the war, authorizing the Board "to borrow from time to time, on the credit of the State of Virginia, such sums of money as may be needed to redeem the engagements of the state." [2] The punctuality with which Virginia met her obligations, together with the known wealth of the state, made it comparatively easy to dispose of the state bonds at high figures. Only a month before the firing on Fort Sumter, Virginia bonds were selling at 81; and at that time a large portion of the debt was held in England. [3]

The war wrought profound economic and social changes in life of the Old Dominion. During the conflict Virginia lost nearly one-third of her territory and her people by the formation and admittance to the Union of the State of West Virginia. This was a serious loss for it reduced the taxpaying capacity of Virginia. The accumulated wealth of the state was further reduced by the abolition of slavery upon which the agriculture of Virginia depended; while the drop in value of the state bonds and the ruination of the public works seriously affected these investments. Meanwhile the state debt had risen to $38,000,000 by the nonpayment of the interest. [4] During the war Virginia had been unable to pay the interest on its public debt beyond the remittance in coin of a few small sums to

---

[2] Revised Code of Virginia, Vol. *II*, p. 20; Code of Virginia 1849, pp. 342-344; *ibid.*, 1860, p. 386. On the early history of the Virginia debt consult Morton, R. L., The Virginia State Debt and Internal Improvements, 1820-1838, Journal of Political Economy, Vol. 25, pp. 339-373.

[3] American Law Review, Vol. 23, p. 924; Royall, W. L., Some Reminiscences, pp. 100-154.

[4] Pearson, C. C., The Readjuster Movement in Virginia, p. 8.

foreign bondholders in London or the payment in Virginia of small amounts in Confederate money.[5]

The legislature which assembled in December 1865 was the last that was representative of the old régime. For that reason its actions in regard to the payment of the public debt are significant of the attitude of Virginia before new political forces began to exert an influence. The state was bankrupt and her people impoverished. The legislature should have frankly recognized this fact and proposed certain compromises to her creditors which it was later claimed would have been accepted. Instead the General Assembly passed an act, March 2, 1866 which not only acknowledged the state's liability for the payment of the principal of the ante-bellum debt but also provided for the funding of the war-time interest in bonds bearing the same rate of interest as the principal, the payment of the interest on the whole debt to begin the following July. Furthermore, in order to remove any apprehensions on the part of the creditors that Virginia might not meet her engagements, a joint resolution was passed announcing that the state had no intention of repudiating its debt. Such legislation, declared the General Assembly, was prohibited by both the state and federal constitutions and would be no less destructive of the future prosperity of the state than of its credit, integrity, and honor. Old Virginia in sackcloth and ashes was too proud to contemplate such drastic measures.[6]

Another resolution passed by the legislature is indicative of the lack of understanding of its members of the economic and social revolution that had taken place as a result of the war. On February 28, 1866 a resolution was passed stating "that the people of Virginia deeply lament the dismemberment of the 'Old State' and are sincerely desirous to establish and perpetuate the reunion of the states of Virginia and West Virginia." To effect this, commissioners were appointed to proceed to West Virginia to treat on this subject; and these commissioners were also empowered "to treat with West Virginia upon the subject of a proper adjustment of the public debt of the State of Virginia due or incurred previous to the dismemberment of the state and of a fair distribution of the public property."

[5] This is based upon a statement of Justice Field found in 102 U. S. Reports, p. 676.
[6] Virginia Acts, 1865-1866, pp. 79, 80; *ibid.*, 1866-1867, pp. 499, 500; Pearson, *op. cit.*, pp. 9, 10.

Since the whole state had created the indebtedness and had partici-pated in the benefits, Virginia maintained that it was only just that West Virginia should assume her share of the debt. But as Virginia and West Virginia were unable to reach a peaceful settlement of their respective proportions of the debt and as Virginia was unable to pay the full interest due to her immense loss of property, the legislature was compelled the following March to pass an act reduc-ing the interest on the public debt from 6 percent to 4 percent, "that being the interest which this state feels obliged to pay until there is a settlement of accounts between Virginia and West Vir-ginia." [7]

At the close of this session of the legislature, Virginia passed into the hands of the radicals. Negroes, scalawags, and carpetbag-gers dominated the constitutional convention of 1867-1869. There was more discussion of the need of scaling or repudiating private obligations; but the conservative elements were still strong enough to obtain a recognition of the public debt in the constitution. [8]

Notwithstanding the constitutions of both Virginia and West Virginia recognized the respective liability of each state for an equitable proportion of the old debt of Virginia, all attempts to reach a satisfactory agreement proved futile. Under these circum-stances, Virginia determined to propose to her creditors a separate adjustment of what she deemed her own share of the debt which she estimated to be two-thirds of the whole amount. Accordingly an act was passed on March 30, 1871 known as the "Funding Act" of the state. By the provisions of this act Virginia offered to issue to her creditors new 6 percent bonds for two-thirds of the entire debt, prin-cipal and accrued interest to July 1, 1871, payable in thirty-four years. These bonds were to be coupon or registered, at the option of the creditor, and were to be convertible the one into the other at like option. In order to secure "the prompt and certain payment of the interest" and to give the coupons greater value the act made them "receivable at and after maturity for all taxes, debts, dues and demands due the state." This declaration was to be on the face of the bonds. For the remaining one-third of the amount due upon the old bonds, certificates were to be issued setting forth the amount

---

[7] Virginia Acts, 1865-1866, pp. 453, 454; *ibid.*, 1866-1867, p. 805.
[8] Pearson, *op. cit.*, pp. 17-19.

of the bond that was not funded, with interest thereon, and that their payment would be provided for in accordance with such settlement as might be subsequently made by Virginia and West Virginia in regard to the public debt; and that Virginia would hold the bonds surrendered, so far as they were not funded, in trust for the holder or his assignees. At that time the bonded debt of Virginia, principal and accumulated interest, was about $45,000,000.[9]

The Funding Act was no sooner passed than the legislature of Virginia began to enact new measures to embarrass the holders of the coupons from using them freely in the payment of taxes. The creditors realized that if the coupons were receivable as money in payment of taxes, they would be worth, whether redeemed or unredeemed, almost their face value. This induced a large number of creditors holding bonds amounting with unpaid interest to over $30,000,000 to surrender their bonds and to take in exchange new ones with interest coupons annexed for two-thirds of their amount and certificates for the balance. By the terms of the Funding Act the state had agreed to pay the interest semi-annually or accept the coupons in payment of taxes. The coupons, therefore, constituted a first lien on the state's revenue; they must be paid before any money could be raised for the public schools or for the current expenses of the government.[10]

The Funding Act became one of the issues in the fall elections of 1871. Opponents of the measure declared that it had been passed "by the corrupt influence of brokers and speculators"; that Virginia should not have assumed these obligations until a settlement had been made with West Virginia; that the Funding Act made "the taxes of the rich payable in coupons at far less than par value, while the poor . . . (would) be compelled to pay . . . dollar for dollar." Undoubtedly these arguments had their effect upon the masses for only 26 of the 132 members of the previous House were reëlected.[11]

As soon as the newly elected legislature assembled, the attacks on the Funding Act began. An act was promptly passed suspending its operation. When the governor vetoed this measure the legis-

---

[9] Virginia Acts, 1870-1871, pp. 378-381; 102 U. S. Reports, pp. 676-683; Royall, op. cit., pp. 100-154.

[10] American Law Review, Vol. 23, p. 925; 102 U. S. Reports, pp. 676-683.

[11] Pearson, op. cit., pp. 41, 42.

lature on March 7, 1872 passed an act prohibiting collectors of taxes from receiving in payment "anything else than gold, or silver coin, United States Treasury notes or notes of the national banks of the United States." By this act the state not only refused to accept the coupons in payment of taxes from those creditors who had already exchanged their bonds in accordance with the provisions of the Funding Act; but it also indirectly refused to exchange old bonds in the future for new ones with coupons attached receivable in payment of taxes. Those creditors in the future who surrendered their bonds subject to the amendatory act of March 7, 1872 received what were known as "peeler bonds." [12]

As might be expected, the validity of this act was tested in the courts. In the case of Antoni vs. Wright the Court of Appeals of Virginia pronounced the act unconstitutional on the ground that it impaired the obligations of a contract. In rendering the decision Justice Bouldin declared: "We think . . . that temporary relief from pecuniary pressure is too dearly bought at the price of the violated faith of Virginia. She has just emerged from a terrible trial —an ordeal of fire—without a stain on her escutcheon. Impoverished, crushed, and dismembered but not dishonored, she is now taking a new departure, and we would hope to see it in the right direction. In the language of a vigorous writer: 'Now is the seed time of faith and honor. The least fracture *now* will be like a name engraved with the point of a pin on the tender rind of a young beech, the wound will enlarge with the tree, and posterity will read it in full grown characters.' " [13]

For a few months subsequent to this decision collectors of taxes accepted the coupons at their face value. But on March 25, 1873 the legislature passed an act taxing the coupons. By this act a tax equal in amount to 50 cents on the $100 market value of the bonds was to be deducted from the matured coupons paid by the state or received by it in payment of taxes. This was partial repudiation; and the United States Supreme Court subsequently declared this law unconstitutional on the ground that it impaired the obligation of a contract and because "the act was not a legal exercise of the taxing power since it compelled one set of men to pay the taxes of

[12] Virginia Acts, 1871-1872, p. 141; American Law Review, Vol. 23, pp. 926, 927; Pearson, *op. cit.*, p. 42.
[13] 22 Grattan, pp. 833-887.

another set." [14] As a result of these court decisions and the legislation on the public debt there were created three classes of obligations against the state: (1) the bonds with tax-receivable coupons issued under the funding act of March 30, 1871 before the repealing act of March 7, 1872; (2) the bonds issued under the funding act subsequent to March 7, 1872 and subject to the provisions of that act whose coupons were not tax-receivable; and (3) the original unfunded bonds of the state. These classes became popularly known as consols, peelers, and unfunded. [15]

Meanwhile the dissatisfaction over the debt settlement continued to grow. The panic of 1873 added to the financial troubles of Virginia; while the influx of coupons increased the deficit in the treasury. Schools were closed and teachers went unpaid as funds were diverted to the payment of the debt. This led to more criticism of the debt settlement; while the uncompromising attitude of the foreign bondholders increased the tension. In 1874 the British holders of consol bonds declined to exchange their tax-receivable coupons for 4 percent in cash and 2 percent in deferred interest certificates unless they were guaranteed the punctual payment of their interest. But the interest could be paid only by raising the taxes; and the burden of the new taxes would fall primarily upon the farmers already suffering from the decline in agricultural prices. [16]

It was at this opportune moment that William Mahone came forward with a proposition to "readjust" the state debt. "Readjustment" was merely a euphemism for a plan to repudiate a large portion of the debt; but it appealed to all those who were disgruntled with the old conservative leaders who kept insisting upon the scrupulous payment of the public debt without regard to its possible effects upon the public school system and to all those who were convinced that the government was controlled by "money rings" and "brokers." [17]

The threat of "readjustment" caused the creditors to assume a more conciliatory attitude. As a result of negotiations with the

[14] Virginia Acts, 1872-1873, p. 207; 102 U. S. Reports, pp. 673-675; American Law Review, Vol. 23, p. 929.
[15] Journal Senate Virginia, 1891, Doc. 6, pp. 15-28.
[16] Pearson, *op. cit.*, pp. 52, 53.
[17] On the origin of the Readjuster movement consult Pearson, *op. cit.*, pp. 46-73; Royall, *op. cit.*, pp. 100-154.

American bondholders, represented by the Funding Association of New York, and the Council of Foreign Bondholders, of London, a new scheme of funding was adopted in the Act of March 28, 1879. For purposes of designation the outstanding indebtedness of the state was divided into two classes. Class I embraced all bonds issued under the funding bill of March 30, 1871 prior to the repealing act of March 7, 1872. Class II included all bonds issued under the funding bill as amended by the Act of March 7, 1872, and also two-thirds of all bonds and accrued interest which had never been funded. In exchange for these outstanding bonds, new ones, with tax-receivable coupons attached, were to be issued, payable in forty years, with interest at 3 percent for ten years, 4 percent for twenty years, and 5 percent for five years. The act provided that the proportion of Class II refunded should never exceed in amount one-third of the whole amount refunded until $18,000,000 of Class I should be retired. The Funding Association of New York, and the Council of Foreign Bondholders, of London, were given the exclusive privilege of funding the debt providing they accepted the terms of this act by May 1, 1879, and funded at least $8,000,000 by 1880 and at least $5,000,000 every six months thereafter. Besides these bonds, certificates for West Virginia's third of the original debt were also issued; and their acceptance was to be taken as "the full and absolute release of Virginia from all liability" for this part of the debt. This measure was always referred to as the "McCulloch bill" by its advocates and as the "brokers bill" by its opponents.[18]

The McCulloch bill was the principal issue in the fall elections of 1879. The readjusters carried on an aggressive, well-organized campaign. They denounced the act as an attempt to perpetuate the worst features of the funding bill; they opposed any increase in taxes, sponsored public education, proposed partial repudiation, and demanded a popular referendum on the debt question. Their arguments appealed strongly to the masses who were convinced the debt burden imposed upon them was too great. Yet it is estimated that the successful operation of the McCulloch Act would have meant ultimately a saving of at least $26,000,000 in interest to Virginia;[19] and the census of 1880 showed that the ratio of taxation to true

[18] Virginia Acts, 1878-1879, pp. 264-268. There is a good account of the events leading to the passage of this act in Senate Journal Virginia, 1891, Doc. 6, pp. 15-28.
[19] Pearson, op. cit., pp. 88, 95-102.

valuation in Virginia was .67 as compared with .70 for the whole United States and .62 for all the southern states.[20] In the ensuing election the readjusters gained control of both branches of the legislature; and that body promptly elected Mahone to the United States Senate. For two years, however, the readjusters were held in check by the debt-paying Governor Holliday. But in the elections of 1881 they secured control of all departments of the state government.[21]

Early in 1882 the legislature adopted a policy of forcible readjustment of the public debt. On February 14 the historic Riddleberger Act was passed which was the heart of the readjustment legislation. In the preamble of this act the legislature restated the account between the state and its creditors. On July 1, 1863 the act declared the principal of the debt was $33,141,212.92 and the unpaid interest amounted to $5,954,716.08. The act stated that Virginia assumed two-thirds of this debt, principal and interest, as her equitable portion; but the corrected principal and interest was then reduced to the sum of $21,035,377.15, including interest in arrears to July 1, 1882. On this debt the act declared that the state was not able to pay more than 3 percent interest for the future. The indebtedness of the state was then reclassified and bonds were authorized to be issued, bearing 3 percent interest, in exchange for outstanding bonds of the different classes scaled at rates ranging from 53 percent to 69 percent, and in one class, as high as 80 percent, which were to be retired and cancelled. The coupons of the new bonds were not made receivable in payment of taxes.[22]

It was obvious that holders of bonds issued under the acts of 1871 and 1879, with tax-receivable coupons attached, would be unwilling to surrender them for new ones issued under the Riddleberger Act. In order to coerce the creditors to make the exchange, several supplementary acts were therefore passed by the legislature for the purpose of discouraging and hampering the use of the tax-receivable coupons of 1871 and 1879. One of these bills, popularly called "Coupon Killer No. 1" was approved January 14. The alleged reason for this act, as recited in the preamble, was that many spurious, stolen and forged bonds were in circulation, which made

[20] 10 Census, Vol. 7, p. 20.
[21] Royall, *op. cit.*, pp. 116-120.
[22] Virginia Acts, 1881-1882, pp. 88-98; 114 U. S. Reports, p. 305.

it imprudent to accept coupons in payment of taxes without first investigating their genuineness and validity. The act, therefore, provided that whenever a taxpayer tendered to a tax collector "any papers purporting to be coupons," he should receive them only "for verification." The collector was then required to demand and force the taxpayer to pay his taxes "in coin, legal tender notes, or national bills." The coupons were to be delivered by the collector to the county court and the taxpayer was then authorized to institute proceedings in the court to have the genuineness of his coupons passed on by a jury. If they were found genuine, the treasurer was required to receive them and to refund to the taxpayer the money previously paid by him. By a subsequent act the taxpayers remedy by mandamus to compel the acceptance of his coupons was abolished.[23]

On January 26, 1882, another act, commonly called "Coupon Killer No. 2" was approved. This provided that tax collectors should receive nothing but money in payment of taxes; that should a collector "take any steps" for the collection of the taxes, the taxpayer might pay his taxes in money under protest, and within thirty days, and not after, sue the officer. If it should be determined that the taxes were wrongfully collected, the amount should be refunded to the taxpayer; and finally that no other remedy or recourse except by such suit was allowed the taxpayer.[24]

Naturally the validity of the readjustment legislation was tested in the courts. In March 1882 Andrew Antoni tendered a coupon in payment of taxes to Richard C. Greenhow, treasurer of the City of Richmond. The tender was refused whereupon Antoni applied to the Supreme Court of Appeals of Virginia for a *mandamus* to compel its acceptance. The judges of the state court divided equally upon the constitutionality of the Act of January 14, 1882, "Coupon Killer No. 1." The writ was accordingly denied and an appeal was taken to the United States Supreme Court.

The opinion of that tribunal upholding the constitutionality of the act, was delivered by Chief Justice Waite. Justice Mathews concurred in the judgment of the court but dissented from the

[23] Virginia Acts, 1881-1882, pp. 10-12; Senate Journal Virginia, 1891, Doc. 6, pp. 15-28.
[24] Virginia Acts, 1881-1882, pp. 37-39; Senate Journal Virginia, 1891, Doc. 6, pp. 15-28.

grounds on which it was based; Justices Field and Harlan rendered elaborate dissenting opinions. The Chief Justice pointed out that the State of Virginia, by the Act of 1871, had entered into a valid contract with the holders of its bonds to receive their coupons in payment of taxes. Therefore the question before the court was whether the Act of 1882 was a breach of this contract. In discussing this question the court reached the conclusion that the remedy given in the Act of 1882 was not such, as in its opinion, was sufficient to impair the obligation of the contract.[25]

This decision was received with astonishment and dismay by the creditors; but notwithstanding the obstacles with which they had to contend, the bondholders still found a way to utilize their tax-receivable coupons. They could still refuse to pay taxes, after tendering their coupons, and when the collector levied upon their property either apply for an injunction or institute a suit for the recovery of their property. The legislature soon realized that more stringent legislation was needed in order to prevent the use of the tax-receivable coupons altogether.

In the session of 1883-1884 the General Assembly proceeded to pass several acts with this purpose in view. By an act of March 12 it was made the duty of the attorneys of the commonwealth to defend all suits brought by taxpayers; and in case they were decided against the state to carry the case to higher state courts and in the federal courts to the United States Supreme Court. The following day another act was approved which declared that no action of trespass should be brought or maintained against any collecting officer for levying upon the property of a taxpayer who had tendered any coupons or who refused to pay his taxes in currency. Two days later, March 15, another act was approved which required all tax-receivable coupon brokers to take out a special license of $1,000 for each office of business and in addition pay a tax of 20 percent upon the face value of all tax-receivable coupons sold by him. Still another act, approved March 19, required that "all coupons received for taxes, beyond what they would have been exchanged for under the Riddleberger Act, should be charged to the bond from which they were clipped, as a payment on the principal of the bond."[26]

[25] 106 U. S. Reports, 769.   [26] Virginia Acts, 1883-1884, pp. 504, 527, 590, 721.

In April 1885, after the passage of these various acts, the United States Supreme Court delivered an important opinion in a series of Virginia bond cases. There were eight of these cases. All related to the Act of March 30, 1871 authorizing the tax-receivable coupons and to the subsequent legislation forbidding their acceptance in payment of taxes. The leading opinion of the Court was given in the case of Poindexter vs. Greenhow. Greenhow was the treasurer of the City of Richmond. He refused to receive from Poindexter coupons of 1871 in payment of taxes, and seized the personal property of the latter. Poindexter brought suit for the recovery of his property and the case was taken on appeal before the United States Supreme Court. In rendering the decision, Justice Stanley Matthews declared that from the time of the passage of the Act of March 30, 1871 "it became the legal duty of every tax collector to receive coupons from these bonds, offered for that purpose by tax-payers in payment of taxes, upon an equal footing, at an equal value, and with equal effect, as though they were gold, or silver, or legal-tender treasury notes." But the defendant claimed that the Act of January 26, 1882 forbade him to receive coupons in lieu of money. "That, it is true," declared Justice Matthews, "is a legislative act of the Government of Virginia, but it is not a law of the State of Virginia. The state has passed no such law, for it cannot; and what it cannot do, it certainly, in contemplation of law, has not done. The Constitution of the United States, and its own contract, both unrepealable by any act on its part, are true laws of Virginia; and that law made it the duty of the defendant to receive the coupons tendered in payment of taxes, and declares every step to enforce the tax, thereafter taken, to be without warrant of law, and therefore a wrong. He stands, then stripped of his official character; and, confessing a personal violation of the plaintiff's rights for which he must personally answer, he is without defense. . . . When, therefore, by the Act of March 30, 1871 the contract was made, by which it was agreed that the coupons issued under that act should thereafter be receivable in payment of taxes, it was the contract of the State of Virginia . . . and inasmuch as, by the Constitution of the United States, which is also the supreme law of Virginia, that contract, when made, became thereby unchangeable and irrepealable by the state, the subsequent Act of January 26, 1882 and all other like acts, which deny the obligation of that contract and forbid its performance, are not the acts of the State of Virginia. . . . The whole legislation, in all its parts, as to creditors affected by it, and not consenting to it, must be pronounced null and void." [27]

This decision was a victory for the bondholders; but the resourcefulness of the legislature was not exhausted. Since the fall of 1883 the Democratic party had been in control of the state government; and they were apparently as determined as their former opponents, the readjusters, that the creditors should accept the Riddleberger debt settlement. In fact upon their advent to power, debt-paying Democrats and readjuster Democrats had united in sponsoring the passage of a joint resolution by the legislature stating that "any expectation that any settlement of the debt, upon any other basis, will ever be made or tolerated by the people of Virginia, is absolutely illusory and hopeless." [28]

The legislature, therefore, was not long in drafting new legislation, designed to embarrass the creditors. The coupons were simply engraved, not signed; their genuineness could be proved only by expert evidence. On January 21, 1886 the legislature passed an act which declared that expert evidence should not be received in these trials. In order to further hamper the creditors another act was passed five days later which required the production of the bond from which the coupons were actually cut in order to prove their genuineness. On the same day still another act was passed declaring that any person who solicited or induced any suit or action against the state was subject to fine and imprisonment. A month later, another act was passed which provided that no petition should be filed or other proceeding instituted to test the genuineness of coupons within a year after the coupons fell due. The next month two more acts were passed. One declared that any lawyer who should solicit or induce any suit or action to be brought against the state should be forever disbarred from practicing in the commonwealth. The other required all license fees to be paid in currency; and if coupons should be tendered in payment, no license was to be issued until they were verified in the manner prescribed by the Act of 1882.

[27] 114 U. S. Reports, pp. 269-338.
[28] Virginia Acts, 1883-1884, p. 7; Pearson, *op. cit.*, pp. 165, 166.

Finally as the decisions in the Virginia Coupon Cases made tax collectors liable to action for proceeding against the property of taxpayers who had tendered coupons in payment of their taxes, an act was passed on May 12, 1887 authorizing suits to be brought against such taxpayers for taxes due from them.[29]

These acts were reviewed by the United States Supreme Court in October 1889. The court once more declared that the Act of 1871 constituted a contract between the state and the holders of the bonds and coupons issued under that statute. With regard to the subsequent legislation the court said: "The various acts of the Assembly of Virginia passed for the purpose of restraining the use of the said coupons for the payment of taxes and other dues to the state, and imposing impediments and obstructions to that use, and to the proceedings instituted for establishing their genuineness, do in many respects materially impair the obligation of that contract, and cannot be held to be valid or binding in so far as they have that effect." Nevertheless the court held "that no proceedings can be instituted by any holder of said bonds or coupons against the Commonwealth of Virginia, either directly by suit against the Commonwealth by name, or indirectly against her executive officers to control them in the exercise of their official functions as agents of the State." [30]

The lawyers representing the bondholders made a gallant fight in behalf of their clients; but it was a losing battle. The maximum amount of coupons received at the treasury between 1883 and 1890 was $258,938, the minimum $40,450.[31] It was apparent that the bondholders must ultimately submit to the principles embodied in the Riddleberger Act. Early in 1887 the governor called the legislature in extra session to receive and consider a proposition from the bondholders for a settlement of the debt. A legislative committee was appointed to negotiate with a bondholders' committee; but the negotiations failed largely due to the fact that the amount of outstanding obligations actually represented by the bondholders' committee was very small and because they could give no satisfactory assurances "of being able to bring in enough securities to consum-

[29] Virginia Acts, 1885-1886, pp. 37, 40, 312, 384; ibid., 1887, pp. 257-260.
[30] 135 U. S. Reports, pp. 665-684.   [31] Pearson, op. cit., pp. 172, 173.

mate a settlement." The following year another legislative committee was appointed to receive a proposition for funding the debt from
duly authorized representatives of the creditors; and after lengthy
negotiations the long standing controversy between the state and its
bondholders was finally terminated in 1892.[32]

In that year an act was passed which was described as a "final
and satisfactory" settlement of the debt. This bill provided for the
issue of $19,000,000 of new bonds to be exchanged for $28,000,000
outstanding obligations, not funded, the new ones to bear interest
at the rate of 2 percent for the first ten years and 3 percent for
ninety years; and certificates similar in form to those provided by
the Riddleberger Act. The coupons and other interest obligations
were not to be receivable for taxes. In agreeing to the provisions of
this act, the creditors accepted the "essential principles of the Riddleberger Act."[33]

There still remained the task of compelling West Virginia to
assume her share of the original debt. Both Virginia and West Virginia in their constitutions recognized their respective liability for
an equitable proportion of the public debt of the undivided state.
Between 1865 and 1871 both states at different times made an
attempt to ascertain their contributive proportions; but all such attempts proved ineffectual. A peaceable settlement became even
more remote after Virginia passed her different funding acts. By
these acts Virginia obtained a reduction of the principal of the debt,
a lower rate of interest, and other advantages. Furthermore in the
acts subsequent to the funding act of 1871 Virginia endeavored to
free herself of all liability for the portion of the debt which she had
assigned, without consulting West Virginia, as that state's share of
the original debt. At length Virginia, unable to reach an agreement
with West Virginia, invoked the power of the United States Supreme
Court to procure a decree for an accounting between the two states
and the adjustment and determination of the amount due by West
Virginia.[34]

[32] Senate Journal Virginia, 1891, Doc. 91, pp. 22-28.
[33] Virginia Acts., 1891-1892, pp. 533-542; Pearson, *op. cit.*, p. 173.
[34] There is an excellent discussion of this subject by Randall, James G., entitled,
"The Virginia Debt Controversy," Political Science Quarterly, Vol. 30, pp. 553-557.
The early stages of the history of this controversy can be found in 206 U. S. Reports,
p. 290.

The case came before the United States Supreme Court in 1906. West Virginia presented a demurrer and vigorously objected to the Supreme Court's jurisdiction in the case. The court overruled the demurrer "without prejudice to any question"; and by decree the cause was referred to a master "to ascertain the facts for the basis of apportionment." [85]

Upon the completion of the master's report, a hearing was held before the Supreme Court in 1911. The court held that the public debt of Virginia, as of January 1, 1861, amounted to $33,897,073.82; but in view of the reduction secured by Virginia in her funding acts with the consent of the creditors, the sum of $3,333,212.26 was deducted from this amount, leaving $30,563,861.56 as the sum to be apportioned between the two states. The court declared that the apportionment should be made according to the master's estimated valuation of the real and personal property of the two states, exclusive of slaves, in June 1863; and that upon that basis the proportion of Virginia was 76.5 percent, of West Virginia, 23.5 percent. This made West Virginia's share of the principal of the debt $7,182,507.46. [86]

This disposed of the fundamental issues; but there still remained the question of interest. In discussing this matter the court came to the conclusion that, in view of the character of the litigants and the fact that the cause was "a quasi-international difference referred to this court in reliance upon the honor and constitutional obligations of the States concerned," it was best at that stage to go no farther but to afford the states an opportunity to settle their difficulty by conference. Should the states be unable to reach a settlement it was understood that the Supreme Court would impose a final decree based upon a master's estimation. [87]

During the next three years little progress was made toward a final settlement. West Virginia refused to appoint a debt commission to confer with one appointed by Virginia on the ground that the legislature alone had the power to deal with such matters, and that the special session of May 1911, which had been called for another

[85] 206 U. S. Reports, 290; 209 U. S. Reports, pp. 514, 534.
[86] 220 U. S., pp. 1, 35, 36. This decision is summarized in 238 U. S. Reports, p. 204.
[87] This statement is based on a summary of the decision found in 238 U. S. Reports, pp. 204, 205.

purpose, could not legally consider the debt. At the fall term of the Supreme Court in that year Virginia petitioned the court to proceed at once to a final hearing, claiming that there was no reasonable hope of an amicable settlement. The court denied the motion on the ground that "a State cannot be expected to move with the celerity of a private business man." Another petition was presented by Virginia in November 1913 and was again refused; and the case was set for a final hearing in 1914.[38]

When the case came before the Supreme Court in 1914 West Virginia asked permission "to file a supplemental answer" claiming she had "discovered" the existence of credits which would materially reduce her obligations. The court granted the application "to the end that this public controversy should be determined only after the amplest opportunity for hearing and with full recognition of every equity that might be found to exist."[39] The subject matter of the supplemental answer was referred to the master with directions to hear the arguments of both Virginia and West Virginia and to report his conclusions to the court.

Finally in June 1915 the case came before the Supreme Court for final decree. In rendering the decision Justice Hughes allowed West Virginia's claim for the credits submitted in the supplemental answer but sustained Virginia's contention that West Virginia should assume her share of the interest. "Using, in the main, the master's valuation of these assets as of January 1, 1861, the court found the total amount of the credits to be $14,929,161.44. West Virginia was credited with 23.5 percent of this amount, but at the same time charged with $541,467.76 received, in money and securities, from the 'restored government' of Virginia. This would give West Virginia a credit of $2,966,855.18 which, deducted from the $7,182,507.46 of the 1911 decision, would leave as her equitable proportion of the principal debt the sum of $4,215,622.28. . . . The court came to the conclusion that the equitable rights of both states would be substantially respected by figuring the interest from January 1, 1861, to July 1, 1891, at 4 percent, and from July 1, 1891, to July 1, 1915, at 3 percent. The interest thus amounted to $8,178,-

[38] 222 U. S. Reports, p. 17; 231 U. S. Reports, p. 89.
[39] 234 U. S. Reports, p. 117.

307.22, and West Virginia's total obligation, principal and interest, was set at $12,393,929.50." [40] West Virginia accepted the judgment of the court and in 1919 passed an act providing for the payment of her part of the debt. [41]

[40] Randall, *op. cit.*, pp. 575, 576. The decision can be found in 238 U. S. Reports, p. 204.
[41] West Virginia Acts, 1919, pp. 19-29.

CHAPTER XV

REFLECTIONS ON AMERICAN STATE DEBTS

To many Americans the defalcation and repudiation by some of the American states of their debts is a forgotten episode in the annals of the United States. The average American vaguely associates the repudiated bonds with the events of the Civil War. He is under the impression that the debts were contracted by the Confederate states during the war; and these, he recalls, were repudiated by the adoption of the Fourteenth Amendment to the Constitution.

Within recent years, however, there has been a revival of interest in these unpaid American state debts. The controversy between the United States and the Allied Powers over the collections of the war debts has led to many references in the American and European press to the nonpayment by some of the American states of their obligations. The attempt of the Principality of Monaco to bring suit against the State of Mississippi for the payment of bonds issued by the state over ninety years ago has also attracted some attention. The result has been a greater curiosity upon the part of the American public with regard to the origin of these debts and the alleged reasons for their repudiation.

As one reflects upon the history of the American state debts and recalls how some of the states found it possible to adjust their financial difficulties without resorting to repudiation, while others adopted such a policy to relieve themselves of their liabilities, certain aspects of the study stand out in bold relief. It is apparent that both debtor and creditor were responsible for their respective misfortunes. In the years preceding the panic of 1837 the American states rushed blindly into debt in order to carry out their internal improvement and banking projects. It is evident that the agents of the states violated state statutes in negotiating the loans and that American bankers aided and abetted them. These acts were unknown to foreign investors when they purchased the bonds. It was the guaranty of the states, the high rate of interest which American securities carried, the high standing of the national credit, the apparent prosperity of the United States, and the confidence of foreign bankers in the United States Bank which induced European capitalists to introduce American securities to their clients. The panic of 1837 in England and the United States temporarily checked the flood of American stocks and bonds to European money markets; but the revival of business, the cotton transactions of the United States Bank, and the resumption of specie payments by American banks led to a new orgy of borrowing upon the part of the American states. The prestige of the United States Bank, the high-pressure salesmanship of American agents, and the knowledge that the federal government was investing its funds in the securities again led to a lack of caution and prudence upon the part of the bankers. At first signs of a collapse of the American financial structure, European bankers tactlessly suggested that the federal government assume the state debts. Whatever merits the scheme might have possessed was lost by the hostility created by its supposedly foreign origin and the scramble for votes in the Presidential election of 1840. The sneers and jeers of the foreign press at American integrity fanned the flames of national prejudices; while the universal indebtedness gave an impetus to the movement in favor of repudiation. In those states where the population and resources permitted of increased taxation, there was courageous and forceful executives who inspired confidence by their candid exposition of the state's finances, and the creditors showed some patience and willingness to help the debtors out of their dilemma, the debts were ultimately settled. In other states repudiation resulted from a series or combination of forces— speculative mania, ignorance of sound banking, a ruinous depression, blatantly demagogic leadership, and the stupidity of the bondholders in refusing to consider propositions that might have resulted in partial payment of their holdings. The lack of concentrated effort upon the part of the creditors and the fact that public opinion had already been mobilized against their claims largely account for the unsuccessful efforts of the bondholders in Mississippi and Florida. While it is true that the meagre resources of the American people in the eighteen thirties and 'forties made it impossible for them to meet their obligations when they fell due, an inability to pay was no justification for refusal to pay.

When one turns to review the history of the circumstances leading to the repudiation of the bonds of the reconstructed governments of the southern states, new factors are encountered. These bonds were issued by governments that were not representative of the southern people. Foreign investors were warned not to purchase them. The forced repudiation of the Confederate war debts strengthened the southerners' opposition to the payment of the "bayonet bonds," especially since a large proportion of these securities were held by the "conquerors of the north" who had foisted and maintained the hated reconstruction governments in the south. The ravages of the Civil War, the misrule of the reconstruction period, and the hard times following the panic of 1873 increased the heavy burdens of the southern people; but in no case were the debts scaled or repudiated until it was apparently impossible to discharge them.

Notwithstanding the fact that some of these bonds were repudiated almost a century ago, the controversy over their payment continues to attract attention. Creditors in Europe are no more willing to give up all hope of receiving payment than the government and people of the United States are of collecting the war debts. Each stage in the acrimonious discussion over the collection of the war debts has brought sharp reminders from the foreign holders of repudiated bonds of the past offences of American states in meeting their engagements. On April 1, 1925 the Chancellor of the Exchequer of England, Austen Chamberlain, was asked in the House of Commons if he was aware that the States of Alabama, Arkansas, Florida, Georgia, Louisiana, Mississippi, North Carolina and South Carolina were still in default in the payment of their state debts; and if any representations had been made by His Majesty's Government to the Government of the United States at Washington with a view toward obtaining repayment of their state debts. The Chancellor replied that His Majesty's Government had never made any representations on the subject to Washington. "I hope," he said, "that my noble friend (Lady Astor) will apply her persuasive eloquence to the legislatures and governments of those states." A few days later in reply to another question concerning the total amount owing by the states, Chamberlain declared that numerous attempts had been made in the past to gather accurate figures but that it had been found impossible to secure complete or accurate information. "As far as can be ascertained," stated Chamberlain, "the approximate amount in default with compound interest accrued at 5 percent would be about £180,000,000 but it has not been possible to ascertain what part of this sum is owing to British subjects." Practically the same reply had been given on previous occasions by Stanley Baldwin and Ramsay MacDonald to questions concerning these debts.[1]

On March 12, 1930 there was a debate on the subject in the House of Lords. Lord Redesdale raised the question whether "His Majesty's Government would consider the advisability of representing this matter to the United States Government with a view to its early adjustment." Lord Redesdale declared the total amount owing by the eight defaulting southern states of the Union was £78,000,000 which was about 1/12 of the sum owed by Great Britain to the United States. The Earl of Limerick pointed out that with compound interest, these repudiated debts must now amount to $1,000,000,000, not all of which, however, was owing to British subjects. "A settlement of this question," remarked Lord Redesdale, "would raise the defaulting states from the level of Russia, which was the only other State at the present time which was a defaulter by repudiation and which was regarded by the United States as a sort of financial leper." It would also give the United States an opportunity of erasing from its history "a painful and shameful page." "Those were strong words," stated Lord Redesdale, "but they were not his own; they were the words of the late President Roosevelt and expressed a view shared at various times by many eminent statesmen of both parties in the United States."

In reply Lord Ponsonby, Parliamentary Secretary, stated that "the question had been considered at different times since 1843, but it had never been found possible to take it up with the United States Government, and no representations on the subject had ever been made to Washington. In arriving at that decision His Majesty's

[1] Parliamentary Debates: House of Commons, Vol. 161, p. 1775; Vol. 172, p. 964; Vol. 182, pp. 1286, 2414.

Government had been influenced by the knowledge that the United States Government had no concern with the financial obligations assumed by the individual states forming the American Union, whose independence in such matter was safeguarded by the Constitution. The money advanced to the defaulting states by the British subjects concerned was freely offered by the latter, and His Majesty's Government were in no way responsible for their action, particularly as the Eleventh Amendment to the United States Constitution was approved long before the debts were contracted. It had never been possible to compile an accurate list of the holders of the stock or to ascertain with accuracy the amount of the sums owing. In 1911-1912 these debts came under discussion in this country when negotiations were taking place between the British Government and the United States Government in regard to the Pecuniary Claims Convention, and efforts were made to obtain particulars of the claims; but owing to the lapse of time since the debts were contracted, and the impossibility of tracing the holders of the securities, the Council of Foreign Bondholders were unable to furnish the Foreign Office with any list of holders which could be regarded as in any way complete or accurate. His Majesty's Government considered that even if representations were addressed to the Government of the United States the latter would have no power to compel the defaulting states to pay, and there was no reason to suppose that the Federal Government would be disposed to assume any liability in the matter, particularly when it was not possible to furnish them with any definite or reliable information. His Majesty's Government were unable to see any connexion between the repudiation of debts by certain southern states of the American Union and the British war debt to the United States. The former debts were in respect of loans made by foreign individuals to the State Governments with which the Federal Government were in no way concerned, while the latter was money lent by the United States Government to the British Government for certain specific purposes." [2]
Again in 1931 and 1932 the same questions were raised in the House of Commons and similar replies were given by representatives of the Government. Upon his return to England, Ramsay MacDonald stated in the House of Commons that the question of the debts

[2] Parliamentary Debates: House of Lords, Vol. 76, pp. 862-886.

owing by American States had not been raised during his recent visit to the United States.[3]

Besides these discussions in the British Parliament, there have been other repercussions of the nonpayment of these debts. On May 13, 1931 the Amsterdam Stock Exchange issued a communication to its members on the old debts of Mississippi. After reciting the history of the Mississippi loans, and the large interest held by the Dutch public in these loans, the circular called attention to the "injustice on the one hand that belligerent countries in Europe have to pay to the United States, amongst other things, for supplies of cotton during the world war, which were sold by the State of Mississippi, for high prices," while, on the other hand, the Government of the United States had not been able "to force the State of Mississippi to fulfill as yet its obligations of ninety years ago."[4]

In view of the recent decision of the United States Supreme Court in the case of the Principality of Monaco versus the State of Mississippi, it is interesting to quote the views of William Howard Taft on the subject of the indebtedness of American states. In discussing the reservations of the Senate to the Knox Arbitration treaties Taft mentioned the exclusion by the Senate of all questions "of the alleged indebtedness or moneyed obligation of any State of the United States. I agree," stated Taft in the course of his lecture on Arbitration Treaties, "that a sovereign State is not obliged to allow a suit against herself by any citizen or any individual, and that immunity from such a suit is one of the attributes of sovereignty. But the very object of international arbitrations and of general treaties to provide them is to do away with such immunity as between the parties. The commonest form of litigated questions in an international arbitration is a question of liability of a debt of one of the parties to the other.

"Why should the indebtedness of the separate States be excluded in an arbitration by the United States with foreign countries? The United States is the representative of the States. Under the Constitution the United States acts for and represents the whole country, States and all. The Federal Government is the only one

---

[3] Parliamentary Debates: House of Commons, Vol. 256, p. 1045; Vol. 261, pp. 1020, 1026; Vol. 278, p. 30.

[4] Vereeniging voor den Effectenhandel: Mededeelingen van het Bestuur ann de Leden. Translated for author by Hope and Company.

the other nations know. That was what our Constitution was intended to effect. If we are in favor of settling controversies between sovereignties by arbitration, in order to avoid war, the only way we can make our States parties to such arbitrations is through the National Government. It is said that the United States is not liable internationally for the debts of the States. That may or may not be true, but if it is not liable, then the arbitral tribunal may say so. If it is liable in international law then it should pay the debts of the States and it would have a right of action against the States, which it might enforce because it has the right to sue a State. Why should the sovereign States of our nation be represented as complainants by our central government in arbitration and not be made defendants through the same representation? Even the Senate did not attempt to exclude debts of the United States from such arbitration. Why should the debts of the States be excluded? Of course, the treaties only affected controversies thereafter arising, so that past indebtedness was not included within their first clause. I am not at all sure that it would not be a very wholesome arrangement to fix some responsibility upon the States and to give them more motive than they have had in the past to avoid repudiation of their just obligations. The necessary exclusion of such indebtedness from questions that might be arbitrated seem to me both unnecessary and improper." On numerous occasions, however, the Senate has amended arbitration treaties so as to exclude questions of alleged claims against any State of the United States from becoming the subject of arbitration.[5]

In 1928 Charles P. Howland proposed an interesting plan for the settlement of these disputed debts. He suggested that the United States offer to Great Britain to accept, at their face value and accrued interest, such of the bonds of the eight defaulting states held by British subjects as "might be found valid" on account of the principal of its war debt due to the United States. This would open the way for the British Government to acquire them from its own citizens; and an impartial tribunal should be created to consider the cases and make the fund awards. According to Howland "if the

---

[5] Taft, W. H., The United States and Peace, pp. 120-123. The U. S. Senate's fear of submitting these debts to any type of international tribunal is discussed in Randolph, B. C., Foreign Bondholders and the Repudiated Debts of the Southern States, American Journal of International Law, Vol. 25, p. 76.

amounts allowed British holders on these bond issues should be credited against the last payments (discounted) on the British debt schedule, no American taxpayer living would know any difference"; while in view of the irremediable damage done the southern states by the emancipation of the slaves, the campaigns of the federal armies, and the "carpetbag" governments, he was of the opinion that it would be just and proper for the federal government to forego bringing suit against the individual states and allow the debts "to be absorbed by the whole body of the American people." [6] While it is conceded by some southerners that such an arrangement would promote international good will there is a fear that if the plan were adopted it would lead to endless litigation through the efforts of American bondholders to institute suits against the States. [7]

The present generation might learn much from the perusal of the history of the American state debts. In essence, it is the story of borrowers and lenders and the difficulty each had in understanding the other in periods of enthusiastic optimism and pessimistic depression. But how often does one generation give careful consideration to the historian's portrayal of the experiences of past generations?

[6] Foreign Affairs, Vol. 6, pp. 395-407.
[7] Ratchford, B. U., The Conversion of the North Carolina Public Debt after 1879, North Carolina Historical Review, Vol. 10, No. 4, pp. 270-273.

BIBLIOGRAPHY

MANUSCRIPTS

The Baring Papers.

These papers are deposited in the Archives Building, Ottawa, Canada. They include Official Correspondence, 1832-1871; Printed Material, 1781-1874; Miscellaneous Correspondence, 1819-1871; Maps, 1827-1873.

Frederick Huth and Company Correspondence.

This is the collection of the private correspondence of Frederick Huth and Company of London to which the writer was given access.

Hope and Company Correspondence.

The writer was given access to the private correspondence and records of Hope and Company of Amsterdam.

Manuscripts in the Public Record Office London, England.

1. Records of the Foreign Office of Great Britain; United States of America, Series II, F. O. 5, 115, 116, 281, 282.
2. Records of the Board of Trade, B. T., 1, 2, 3, 4.

Manuscripts in the State Department, Washington, D. C.

1. Edward Everett Correspondence, Vol. 49.

Manuscripts in the Library of Congress, Washington, D. C.

1. Daniel Webster Correspondence, 1836-1845.
2. Duff Green Correspondence, 1830-1844.

BRITISH DOCUMENTS

Annual Register, 1830-1860.

Parliamentary Debates: House of Commons, Vol. 261, 273, 278.

——: House of Lords, Vol. 76.

Parliamentary Papers:

Accounts and Papers:

1. Report to Board of Trade by Captain Douglas Galton, Vol. 16, pp. 599-655.
2. Report from the Select Committee appointed to inquire into the operation of the Acts of the 7 George 4, C. 46 permitting the establishment of Joint Stock Banks. 1836 (591) *IX,* 411.

3. Report from the Select Committee appointed to inquire into the operation of the acts permitting the establishment of Joint Stock Banks in England, Ireland, and whether it is expedient to make any amendment in those acts. 1837 (531) *XIV*, 1.

4. Report from the Select Committee appointed in the following session to consider the same subject. 1837-1838 (626) *VII*, 1.

5. Report from the Select Committee appointed to inquire into the expediency of renewing the charter of the Bank of England and into the System on which Banks of Issue in England and Wales are conducted. 1831-1832 (722) *VI*, 1.

6. Report from the Select Committee appointed to inquire into the effects produced on the circulation of the country by various banking establishments issuing notes payable on demand. 1840 (602) *IV*, 1.

7. First Report from the Select Committee of Secrecy in the following session to consider the same subject. 1841 (366), Vol. *I*.

8. Second Report from the Select Committee of Secrecy. 1841 (410), Vol. *V*.

9. Report from the Select Committee on Investments for the Savings of the Middle and Working Classes. 1850 (508) *XIX*, 169.

10. Report on the present state of manufacturers, commerce, and shipping. 1833 (690) *VI*, 1.

11. Reports of Committee on Agricultural Distress: 1820 (255) *II*, 101; 1821 (668) *IX*, 1; 1822 (165) *I*, 1; 1836 (79) *VIII*, Pt. *I*, 1; 1836 (189) *VIII*, Pt. *I*, 225.

12. Report of House of Lords' Select Committee on Agricultural Distress. 1837 (464) *I*, 1.

FEDERAL DOCUMENTS

United States Census, 1880, Vol. 7.

Cases Argued and Adjudged in the Supreme Court of the United States, Vols. 102, 107, 114, 135.

The Congressional Globe, 1840-1844.

Statement relative to the public debt. Sen. Doc., No. 24, 20 Cong., 2 Sess., Vol. 1.

Letter of Sec. Woodbury relative to state banks. Sen. Doc., No. 471, 25 Cong., 2 Sess., Vol. 6.

Power of the Union to assume debts of states. Sen. Doc., No. 45, 26 Cong., 1 Sess., Vol. 2.

Message of President Van Buren concerning Florida bonds. Sen. Doc., No. 43, 26 Cong., 2 Sess., Vol. 2.

Power of the Union to assume state debts. Sen. Doc., No. 18, 26 Cong., 1 Sess., Vol. 2.

Report on assumption of state debts. Sen. Doc., No. 197, 26 Cong., 1 Sess., Vol. 5.

Report on resolutions as to assuming state debts. Sen. Doc., No. 153, 26 Cong., 1 Sess., Vol. 4.

Message of President Van Buren relating to Florida bonds. Sen. Doc., No. 447, 26 Cong., 1 Sess., Vol. 7.

Resolution on repudiation of state debts. Sen. Doc., No. 69, 27 Cong., 2 Sess., Vol. 2.

Report relating to investment of Indian moneys. Sen. Doc., No. 116, 27 Cong., 1 Sess., Sept. 8, 1841.

President Tyler on assumption of state debts. Sen. Doc., No. 15, 27 Cong., 3 Sess., Vol. 2.

Resolution on debts of states. Sen. Doc., No. 130, Pt. 5, 27 Cong., 3 Sess., Vol. 3.

Resolution relating to debts of states. Sen. Doc., No. 181, Pt. 3, 27 Cong., 3 Sess., Vol. 3.

Report on claim of E. J. Forstall. Sen. Doc., No. 163, 29 Cong., 2 Sess., Vol. 3.

Resolution on national bank, state debts. Sen. Doc., No. 150, 29 Cong., 1 Sess., Vol. 4.

Proceedings for adjustment of claims under convention with Great Britain. Sen. Doc., No. 15, 34 Cong., 1 Sess.

Statement on condition of state banks. Exec. Doc., No. 172, 26 Cong., 1 Sess., Vol. 5.

Report on issue of $200,000,000 of stock to states and territories. House Reports, No. 296, 27 Cong., 3 Sess., Vol. 4; ibid., No. 120, 27 Cong., 3 Sess., Vol. 1.

Letter of Sec. Woodbury relative to state banks. House Doc., No. 227, 25 Cong., 3 Sess., Vol. 5; ibid., No. 179, 25 Cong., 2 Sess., Vol. 4.

Letter of Sec. Woodbury regarding investment of state stocks. House Doc., No. 145, 26 Cong., 1 Sess., Vol. 3.

Condition of state banks. House Doc., No. 111, 26 Cong., 2 Sess., Vol. 4.

Report on negotiation of loan in Europe. House Doc., No. 197, 27 Cong., 3 Sess., Vol. 5.

Assumption of state debts. House Doc., No. 40, 27 Cong., 3 Sess., Vol. 3.

Debts of the several states. House Doc., No. 254, 27 Cong., 2 Sess., Vol. 5.

Resolutions against repudiation. House Doc., No. 136, 28 Cong., 2 Sess., Vol. 3.

Report on banks and banking. House Doc., No. 226, 29 Cong., 1 Sess., Vol. 8.

Report on railroad statistics. House Exec. Doc., No. 2, 34 Cong., 3 Sess., Vol. 2.

STATE DOCUMENTS

Alabama

Acts of the General Assembly of Alabama, 1865-1876.

Journal of the House and Senate of Alabama, 1873-1876.

Arkansas

Acts of the General Assembly of the State of Arkansas, 1868-1883.

Acts relative to the Real Estate Bank of the State of Arkansas, 1836-1855.

Journals of the General Assembly of the State of Arkansas, 1836-1846, 1854-1856.

Debates and Proceedings on bill entitled, "An Act to Provide for the Funding of the Public Debt of Arkansas." 1869.

Florida

An act to incorporate the subscribers to the Union Bank of Florida. 1837.

An act to suspend the exercise of the banking power by the Union Bank of Florida. 1843.

Journal of the Proceedings of the House and Senate of the Territory of Florida, 1840-1845.

Journal of the Proceedings of the General Assembly of the State of Florida, 1845-1848.

Cases Argued and Adjudged in the Supreme Court of Florida, Vols. 15, 16.

Georgia

Acts and Resolutions of the General Assembly of the State of Georgia, 1869-1877.

Proceedings of the Constitutional Convention of Georgia, 1877.

Journal of the House of Representatives of the State of Georgia, 1875.

Illinois

Acts of the State of Illinois, 1836-1847.

Journal of the House and Senate of Illinois, 1839.

Reports of the Senate and House of Representatives of Illinois, 1840, 1842.

Indiana

Journal of the House of Representatives of the State of Indiana, 1842-1843.
Journal of the Senate of the State of Indiana, 1841-1848.
House and Senate Doc. of Indiana, 1840-1845.
Report of the Investigating Committee appointed by the Senate to investigate the transactions of the different agents of the state, 1842.
Report of the Debates and Proceedings of the Convention for Revision of the Constitution of the State of Indiana, 1850.

Louisiana

Acts passed by the General Assembly of the State of Louisiana, 1824-1852, 1874-1884.
House and Senate Journal of Louisiana, 1835-1846.
Debates of the Louisiana Constitutional Convention, 1844-1845.
Journal of the Louisiana Constitutional Convention, 1852.
Louisiana Legislative Documents, 1874.
Report of the Cases Argued and Determined in the Supreme Court of Louisiana, Vols. 23, 27.

Maryland

Maryland Documents, 1840-1848.
Journal of the Senate and House of Delegates of the State of Maryland, 1840-1848.

Michigan

Acts of the Legislature of the State of Michigan, 1837-1848.
Journal of the House of Representatives of Michigan, 1839-1843.
House and Senate Documents, 1840-1849.
Report of the Board of Fund Commissioners of the State of Michigan, 1878.

Minnesota

General and Special Laws of Minnesota, 1858-1881.
Session Laws of the Territory of Minnesota, 1855-1857.
Journal of the Senate of Minnesota, 1858.
Journal of the House of Representatives of Minnesota, 1859-1860, 1871.
Minnesota Executive Documents, 1869, 1875.
Reports of Cases Argued and Determined in the Supreme Court of Minnesota, Vols. 2, 4, 29.

Mississippi

Laws of State of Mississippi, 1830-1880.
Journal of the House and Senate of State of Mississippi, 1831-1843.

North Carolina

Public Documents of the General Assembly of North Carolina, 1879.
North Carolina Executive and Legislative Documents, 1881.
Report of the Commission to investigate charges of fraud and corruption, 1872.

Pennsylvania

Journal of the Senate and House of State of Pennsylvania, 1840-1845.

South Carolina

South Carolina Statutes, 1865-1880.
Journal of the Senate of State of South Carolina, 1873.

Tennessee

Acts of the General Assembly of State of Tennessee, 1865-1885.
Journal of the Senate of Tennessee, 1879, 1885.
House and Senate Journal of Tennessee, 1881.
Journal of the House of Representatives of Tennessee, 1883.

Virginia

Code of State of Virginia, 1849, 1860.
Revised Code of the Laws of State of Virginia, Vols. *I, II*.
Acts and Joint Resolutions of the General Assembly of State of Virginia, 1819, 1848-1850, 1859-1860, 1865-1867, 1871-1892.
Journal of the Senate of the Commonwealth of Virginia, 1874, 1878, 1887, 1891.
Reports of Cases of the Supreme Court of Appeals of Virginia, Vol. 22.

West Virginia

Acts of the General Assembly of State of West Virginia, 1919.

NEWSPAPERS

American Sentinel (Phila.), 1832-1838.
Arkansas Advocate, 1830-1837.
Arkansas Democratic Banner, 1843-1845, 1847-1848.
Arkansas Gazette (weekly), 1840-1846.
Baltimore American, 1841-1844.
Baltimore Sun, 1842, 1843, 1847-1851.

Boston Daily Advertiser and Patriot, 1832-1843.

Circular to Bankers (London), 1828-1853.

Columbus (Miss.) Democrat, 1837, 1839-1841, 1843-1844, 1853-1854.

Commercial and Financial Chronicle, 1865-1885.

Courier (Natchez, Miss.), 1841, 1853.

Economist (London), 1843-1877.

Flag of the Union (Jackson, Miss.), 1850-1853.

Floridian (weekly), 1840-1842.

Florida Sentinel, 1841-1843.

Hazard United States Commercial and Statistical Register, 1839-1842.

Herapaths Railway and Commercial Journal and Scientific Review, 1840-1860.

Indiana State Journal (weekly), 1841, 1842.

Kendall's Expositor, 1841-1843.

Little Rock Daily Republican, 1867-1877.

Mining Journal, Railway and Commercial Gazette (London), 1839-1845, 1849-1860.

Mississippian, 1835-1838, 1841, 1843-1850.

Morning Chronicle (London), 1839-1860.

National Intelligencer, 1837-1844.

New York American, 1835-1845.

New York Evening Post, 1841, 1842.

New York Express, 1836-1839, 1841-1843.

New York Herald, 1835-1836, 1843-1850.

New York Journal of Commerce, 1839-1842.

New York Shipping and Commercial List and Price Current, 1837, 1838.

New York Tribune, 1841-1844.

The News (St. Augustine, Florida), 1842-1843.

Niles Register, 1838-1849.

North American and Daily Advertiser (Phila.), 1840-1845.

Palladium (Richmond, Ind.), 1841, 1842.

Pennsylvanian, 1833-1844.

Picayune (New Orleans), 1853.

Public Ledger, 1842-1846.

Railway Times (London), 1850-1860.

Railway Gazette (London), 1850-1860.

Southern Argus (Columbus, Miss.), 1841.

Spectator (London), 1844.

Star of Florida, 1841-1843.

Times (London), 1837-1860.

United States Gazette, 1842-1844.

Vicksburg Weekly Sentinel, 1839, 1844-1848, 1853-1855.
Wabash Express (Terre Haute, Ind.), 1842.
Washington Globe, 1840-1843.

MAGAZINES

American Railroad Journal and Advocate of Internal Improvement, 1832-1838.
American Railroad Journal and Mechanics Magazine, 1838-1842.
American Railroad Journal and General Advertiser, 1845-1847.
Bankers Magazine and State Financial Register, 1847-1849.
Bankers Magazine and Statistical Register, 1849-1877.
Bankers Magazine and Journal of the Money Market (London), 1844-1845.
Bankers Magazine, Journal of the Money Market, and Railway Digest, 1846-1860.
De Bow's Commercial Review of the South and West, 1846-1860.
Edinburgh Review, 1832-1844.
Hunt's Merchant's Magazine, 1839-1860.
Railway Magazine (London), 1835, 1836.
Railway Magazine and Annals of Science (London), 1836-1839.
United States Magazine and Democratic Review, 1838-1851.

SPECIAL WORKS AND MONOGRAPHS

ABERNETHY, T. P., The Formative Period in Alabama, 1815-1828 (Montgomery, Ala., 1922).
ACKERMAN, W. K., Early Illinois Railroads, Fergus Historical Series, No. 23 (Chicago, 1884).
ADAMS, H. C., Public Debts (N. Y., 1890).
ANDREADES, A., History of the Bank of England, 1640-1903 (London, 1924).
BAGEHOT, W., Lombard Street (London, 1873).
BELL, G. M., Guide to the Investment of Capital (London, 1845)
——, The Merchant's and Banker's Commercial Pocket Guide (Glasgow, 1856).
BENTON, E. J., The Wabash Trade Route in the Development of the Old Northwest, Johns Hopkins Studies, Vol. 21, pp. 1-113 (Balt., 1903).
Bishop, A. L., The State Works of Pennsylvania, Trans. Conn. Acad. Arts and Sciences, Vol. 13, pp. 149-297.
BISSCHOP, W. R., The Rise of the London Money Market, 1640-1826 (London, 1910).

BLOCHER, W., Arkansas Finances (Little Rock, 1876).

BOGART, E. L., Internal Improvements and State Debt in Ohio (N. Y., 1924).

BREVARD, C. M., A History of Florida, 2 vol., 1763-1860 (Deland, Fla., 1924).

BROUGH, C. H., History of Banking in Mississippi, Miss. Hist. Soc. Publ., Vol. *III*, pp. 317-341.

BROWNING, GEORGE, The Domestic and Financial Condition of England (London, 1834).

BRYAN, A. C., History of State Banking in Maryland, Johns Hopkins Studies, Vol. 17, pp. 1-145 (Balt., 1899).

BUCK, N. S., The Development of the Organization of Anglo-American Trade, 1800-1850 (New Haven, 1925).

CHAPMAN, S. J., The History of Trade between the United Kingdom and the United States (London, 1899).

CLAPHAM, J. H., An Economic History of Modern England (Cambridge, 1930).

CLAYTON, P., The Aftermath of the Civil War in Arkansas (N. Y., 1915).

CLEWS, H., Twenty-eight Years in Wall Street (N. Y., 1887).

COULTER, E. M., A Short History of Georgia (Chapel Hill, 1933).

DAVIS, R., Recollections of Mississippi and Mississippians (Boston, 1889).

DAVIS, W. W., The Civil War and Reconstruction in Florida, Columbia Univ. Studies, Vol. 53 (N. Y., 1913).

DEWEY, D. R., Financial History of the U. S. (N. Y., 1922).

——, State Banking before the Civil War, Senate Doc., No. 581, 61 Cong., 2 Sess., Vol. 34.

DOWRIE, G. W., The Development of Banking in Illinois, 1817-1863, Univ. Illinois Studies, Vol. 2, No. 4 (Urbana, 1913).

DUDEN, M., Internal Improvements in Indiana, 1818-1846, Indiana Quarterly Magazine of History, Vol. *V*, pp. 160-171.

ESAREY, L., A History of Indiana, 2 Vol. (Indianapolis, 1918).

——, Internal Improvements in Early Indiana, Indiana Hist. Soc. Publ., Vol. *V*, No. 2, pp. 47-158 (Indianapolis, 1912).

——, State Banking in Indiana, 1814-1873, Indiana Univ. Studies, Vol. *I*, pp. 219-330 (Bloomington, 1913).

ESCOTT, T. H. S., City Characters (London, 1922).

EVANS, D. M., Fortune's Epitome of the Stocks and Public Funds (London, 1851).

FICKLEN, J. R., History of Reconstruction in Louisiana, Johns Hopkins Studies, Vol. 28 (Baltimore, 1910).

FLEMING, F. P., Memoirs of Florida, 2 Vol. (Atlanta, 1902).

FLEMING, W. L., Civil War and Reconstruction in Alabama (N. Y., 1905).

FORD, T., History of Illinois (Chicago, 1854).

FORTIER, A., History of Louisiana (N. Y., 1904).

FULLER, G. N., Messages of the governors of Michigan, 2 Vol. (Lansing, 1925).

FOLWELL, W. W., A History of Minnesota, 4 Vol. (St. Paul, 1924-1930).

FRANCIS, J., Chronicles and Characters of the Stock Exchange (London, 1849).

——, History of the Bank of England, 2 Vol. (London, 1848).

GAYARRE, C., History of Louisiana, 4 Vol. (New Orleans, 1903).

GIFFEN, R., The Growth of Capital (London, 1889).

GILBART, J. W., The History of Banking in America (London, 1837).

——, A Practical Treatise on Banking (Phila., 1860).

——, The History, Principles and Practice of Banking, 2 Vol. (London, 1882).

GREENE, E. B., and THOMPSON, C. M., ed., Governor's Letter Books, Coll. Ill. State Hist. Library, Vol. 7, Exec. Series, Vol. 2 (Springfield, 1911).

HALE, W. T., and MERRITT, D. L., A History of Tennessee and Tennesseans, 8 Vol. (Chicago, 1913).

HAMILTON, J. G. DE R., Reconstruction in North Carolina, Col. Univ. Studies, Vol. 58, No. 141 (N. Y., 1914).

HANNA, H. S., A Financial History of Maryland, 1789-1848, Johns Hopkins Studies, Vol. 25, pp. 349-483.

HEMPSTEAD, F., Historical Review of Arkansas, 2 Vol. (Chicago, 1911).

HERBERT, H. A., Why the Solid South (Balt., 1890).

HIBBARD, B. H., A History of the Public Land Policies (N. Y., 1924).

HOBSON, C. K., The Export of Capital (London, 1914).

——, An Economic Interpretation of Investment (London, 1911).

HOLLAND, LADY, A Memoir of the Reverend Sydney Smith (London, 1855).

JENKS, L. H., The Migration of British Capital to 1875 (N. Y., 1927).

KNOX, J. J., A History of Banking in the United States (N. Y., 1900).

LAVINGTON, F., The English Capital Market (London, 1921).

LAWSON, W. J., The History of Banking (London, 1855).

LEVI, L., The History of British Commerce, 1763-1878 (London, 1880).

LONG, E. C., Florida Breezes (Jacksonville, 1883).

LONN, E., Reconstruction in Louisiana after 1868 (N. Y., 1918).

LOWRY, R., and McCARDLE, W. H., A History of Mississippi (Jackson, 1891).

McCulloch, J. R., A Statistical Account of the British Empire, 2 Vol. (London, 1837, 1847).

——, A Dictionary, Practical, Theoretical and Historical of Commerce and Commercial Navigation (London, 1840).

McCulloch, H., Men and Measures (N. Y., 1888).

McClure, A. K., The South: its Industrial, Financial and Political Condition (Phila., 1886).

MacLeod, H. D., A Dictionary of Political Economy (London, 1863).

——, The Theory and Practice of Banking, 2 Vol. (London, 1856).

McGrane, R. C., The Correspondence of Nicholas Biddle (Boston, 1919).

——, The Panic of 1837 (Chicago, 1924).

Marshall, J., A Statistical Display of the Finances, Navigation, and Commerce of the United Kingdom (London, 1838).

Moore, A. B., History of Alabama and Her People, 3 Vol. (Chicago, 1927).

Moore, J. B., History and Digest of the International Arbitrations to which the United States Has Been a Party, 6 Vol. (Wash., 1898).

Myers, M. G., The New York Money Market (N. Y., 1931).

Nolte, V., Fifty Years in Both Hemispheres, or Reminiscences of a Merchant's Life (London, 1854).

Patton, J. W., Unionism and Reconstruction in Tennessee, 1860-1869 (Chapel Hill, 1934).

Pearson, C. C., The Readjuster Movement in Virginia (New Haven, 1917).

Pease, T. C., The Frontier State, 1818-1848 (Springfield, 1918).

Phelan, J., History of Tennessee (Boston, 1889).

Philippovich, E., History of the Bank of England in National Monetary Commission Reports, Sen. Doc., 591, 61 Cong., 2 Sess., Vol. 41.

Poore, B. R., The Federal and State Constitutions (Wash., 1878).

Poor, H. V., Sketch of the Rise and Progress of Internal Improvements and of the Internal Commerce of the United States (N. Y., 1881).

——, History of the Railroads and Canals of the U. S. of America, 3 Vol. (N. Y., 1860).

Porter, G. R., The Progress of the Nation (London, 1851).

Prentiss, G. L., The Union Theological Seminary (Asbury Park, N. J., 1899).

Price, F. G. H., A Handbook of London Bankers (London, 1876).

Powell, E. T., The Evolution of the Money Market, 1385-1915 (London, 1915).

Putnam, J. W., The Illinois and Michigan Canal (Chicago, 1918).

RAYMOND, W. L., American and Foreign Investment Bonds (Boston, 1916).

REID, S. J., A Sketch of the Life and Times of the Rev. Sydney Smith (London, 1884).

REIZENSTEIN, M., The Economic History of the Baltimore and Ohio Railroad, Johns Hopkins Studies, Vol. 15, pp. 281-371.

RICHARDSON, J. D., A Compilation of the Messages and Papers of the Presidents (Wash., 1905).

ROWLAND, D., ed., Encyclopedia of Mississippi History, 2 Vol. (Madison, 1907).

——, Jefferson Davis, Constitutionalist, 10 Vol. (Jackson, 1923).

——, History of Mississippi, 2 Vol. (Chicago, 1925).

ROYALL, W. L., History of the Virginia Debt Controversy (Richmond, 1897).

——, Some Reminiscences (N. Y., 1909).

SCOTT, W. A., The Repudiation of State Debts (N. Y., 1893).

SEMMES, J. E., John H. B. Latrobe and his Times (Balt., 1917).

SIMKINS, F. B., and WOODY, R. H., South Carolina during Reconstruction (Chapel Hill, 1932).

SINGEWALD, K., The Doctrine of Non-suability of the State in the U. S., Johns Hopkins Studies, Vol. 28, No. 3 (Balt., 1910).

SMART, W., Economic Annals of the Nineteenth Century, 2 Vol. (N. Y., 1917).

STAPLES, T. S., Reconstruction in Arkansas, Columbia Univ. Studies, No. 245 (N. Y., 1923).

STEPHENSON, G. M., The Political History of the Public Lands, 1840-1862 (Boston, 1917).

STODDARD, F. H., The Life and Letters of Charles Butler (N. Y., 1903).

TAFT, W. H., The United States and Peace (N. Y., 1914).

THOMAS, D. Y., Arkansas and its People, 4 Vol. (N. Y., 1930).

THOMPSON, C. M., Reconstruction in Georgia, Columbia Univ. Studies, Vol. 64.

TOOKE, T., and NEWMARCH, W., History of Prices, 6 Vol. (London, 1857).

TROTTER, A., Observations on the Financial Position and Credit of such of the States of the North American Union as Have Contracted Public Debts (London, 1839).

VAN TYNE, C. H., ed., The Letters of Daniel Webster (N. Y., 1902).

WALLACE, J., Carpetbag Rule in Florida (Jacksonville, 1888).

WARD, G. W., Early Development of the Chesapeake and Ohio Canal Project, Johns Hopkins Studies, Vol. 17, pp. 425-539.

WEBSTER, F., ed., The Private Correspondence of Daniel Webster, 2 Vol. (Boston, 1857).

WELLINGTON, R. G., The Political and Sectional Influence of the Public Lands, 1828-1842 (Cambridge, 1914).

WORTHEN, W. B., Early Banking in Arkansas (Little Rock, 1906).

WORTHINGTON, T. K., Historical Sketch of the Finances of Pennsylvania, Publ. of the American Econ. Assoc., Vol. 2, No. 2, pp. 1-102.

SPECIAL ARTICLES AND PAMPHLETS

BRAXTON, A. C., The Eleventh Amendment, the Report of the XIX Annual Meeting of Virginia State Bar Assoc., Vol. 20, pp. 172-193.

CALLENDER, G. S., The Early Transportation and Banking Enterprises of the States in Relation to the Growth of Corporations, Quart. Journal Econ., Vol. 17, pp. 111-162.

CAMPBELL, J. A. P., Union and Planter's Bank Bonds. Miss. Hist. Soc. Publ., Vol. 4, pp. 493-499.

COLE, A. H., Cyclical and Sectional Variations in the Sale of Public Lands, 1816-1860, Review of Economic Statistics, 1927, pp. 41-53.

——, Statistical Background of the Crisis, 1837-1842, Review of Economic Statistics, 1928, pp. 182-195.

——, Evolution of the Foreign Exchange Market of the United States. Journal of Economic and Business History, Vol. I, pp. 384-421.

——, and FRICKEY, E., The Course of Stock Prices, 1825-1866, Review of Economic Statistics, 1928, pp. 117-139.

Council of Foreign Bondholders: Annual Reports, 1874-1933.

CURTIS, B. R., Debts of the States. North American Review, Vol. 58, pp. 109-154.

EVERETT, A., State Debts. Democratic Review, Vol. 14, new series, pp. 3-15.

FOLWELL, W. W., The Five Million Dollar Loan, Minn. Hist. Soc. Coll., Vol. 15, pp. 189-214.

GRAY, M., The Coupon Legislation of Virginia. American Law Review, Vol. 23, pp. 924-945.

GILBART, J. W., An Inquiry into the Causes of the Pressure on the Money Market (London, 1840).

GILPIN, H. D., A Statement of the Case of the Bonds and Guarantees Issued by the Territory of Florida (Phila., 1847).

GREEN, G. W., Repudiation, Economic Tracts *XI* (N. Y., 1883).

GUTHRIE, W. D., The Eleventh Amendment of the Constitution of the United States, Columbia Law Review, Vol. 8, pp. 182-207.

HAMILTON, J. G. DE R., Those Southern Repudiated Bonds, Virginia Quarterly Review, Vol. 3, pp. 490-506.

HOWLAND, C. P., Our Repudiated State Debts, Foreign Affairs, Vol. 6, pp. 395-407.

JENKS, W. L., Michigan's Five Million Dollar Loan, Michigan History Magazine, Vol. 15, pp. 575-634.

JUNIUS: Reply to Webster: a letter to Daniel Webster in reply to his legal opinion to the Baring Brothers and Company (N. Y., 1840).

McGRANE, R. C., Some Aspects of American State Debts in the 'Forties, American Historical Review, Vol. 38, pp. 673-686.

MORTON, R. L., The Virginia State Debt and Internal Improvements, 1820-1838, Journal Political Economy, Vol. 25, pp. 339-373.

RANDALL, J. G., The Virginia Debt Controversy, Pol. Sc. Quart., Vol. 30, pp. 533-577.

RATCHFORD, B. U., The North Carolina Public Debt, 1870-1878, North Carolina Hist. Review, Vol. 10, pp. 1-21.

——, The Adjustment of the North Carolina Public Debt, 1879-1883, North Carolina Hist. Review, Vol. 10, pp. 157-168.

——, The Conversion of the North Carolina Public Debt after 1879, North Carolina Hist. Review, Vol. 10, pp. 251-273.

RANDOLPH, B. C., Foreign Bondholders and the Repudiated Debts of the Southern States, American Journal International Law, Vol. 25, pp. 63-82.

ROBINS, T. E., and SMEDES, W. C., An Inquiry into the Validity of the Bonds of Mississippi (N. Y., 1847).

SABY, R. S., Railroad Legislation in Minnesota, 1849-1875, Minn. Hist. Soc. Coll., Vol. 15, pp. 1-188.

VAN HORNE, J. D., Jefferson Davis and Repudiation in Mississippi (Glyndon, Md., 1915).

WALKER, R. J., Jefferson Davis and Repudiation (London, 1864).

ANONYMOUS, Nine years of Democratic Rule in Mississippi (Jackson, 1847).

——, Articles on State Debts, Hunt's Merchants' Magazine, Vol. 17, pp. 466-480, 577-587; Vol. 18, pp. 243-255; Vol. 20, pp. 256-269, 481-493; Vol. 21, pp. 148-163, 389-410; Vol. 22, pp. 131-145; Vol. 27, 659-671.

——, A Vindication of the Public Faith of New York and Pennsylvania in Reply to the Calumnies of the London Times (London, 1840).

——, The State Debts, Christian Review, Vol. 9, pp. 93-114.

——, The Crisis in the American Trade, Edinburgh Review, Vol. 65, pp. 221-238.

A Citizen of Maryland, A Short History of the Public Debt of Maryland (Balt., 1845).

INDEX